Peter Gzowski's Book About This Country in the Morning

Hurtig Publishers
Edmonton

Peter Gzowski's Book About This Country in the Morning

Hurtig Publishers
Edmonton

Grateful acknowledgement
is made to the Macmillan
Company of Canada Limited
for permission to reprint
an excerpt from
Who Has Seen the Wind
by W.O. Mitchell,
and five essays by
Andrew Allan from
Andrew Allan: A Self-Portrait.

Hurtig Publishers
10560 105 Street
Edmonton, Alberta

ISBN 0-88830-081-6

Printed and bound
in Canada

Conversations

Musings

by Peter Gzowski

by Andrew Allan

by Harry Bruce

by Vic Dardick

by Paul Hiebert

by Listeners and Contributors

This is not a dedication. You don't dedicate something to the people who created it. And while all the flaws in this book are mine, its strengths are the result of three years of passionately hard work by a number of people, among them Dave Amer, Hilary Armstrong, Bonnie Bisnett, Judy Brake, Nancy Button, Bill Casselman, Alex Frame, Ron Grant, Herb Johnson, Gary Katz, Krista Maeots, Marilyn Meenan, Betty McAfee, Ellen Nygaard, Bob Rhodes, Harriet Weideman and Sheilah White.

The other people who made this book are those who listened to our program and who participated in it; their contributions appear throughout.

To both groups, to those behind the microphone and in front of the radio, I owe debts I can never repay for the most rewarding years of my life. I hope this book will serve as a down payment.

Introduction

When I grow up I want to be Paul Hiebert. Paul Hiebert, of course, is the creator and biographer of Sarah Binks, the Sweet Songstress of Saskatchewan, and the winner of the first Stephen Leacock Award. I say "of course" because that's all I knew about him before I got to meet him through the CBC radio progam I worked on for three years, "This Country in the Morning." One day a bunch of us from the program were talking about how much we enjoyed the deliberately bad poetry Professor Hiebert had written years before, and wondering what had become of him. We found him in Carman, Manitoba, where he has retired after a long career of teaching chemistry at the University of Manitoba. We called him and I talked to him on the air, about Sarah and other things. He told me that he'd started to write bad poetry because, as a young academic, he'd found that he didn't have the right kind of small talk for faculty parties. So he created Sarah, and started quoting her— deadpan— to his colleagues. Sarah grew on him, and eventually he put together a "critical" book about her and her works. The manuscript made the rounds of a few publishers (being rejected by, among other people, a New York editor who wasn't quite sure whether Sarah— this mythical writer of hilariously lousy poetry of the Canadian prairies— was quite "major" enough to be the subject of a full-length book), until Oxford University Press finally saw the point and brought out his small Canadian masterpiece.

I kind of fell in love with Professor Hiebert in my first conversation with him, but it wasn't until later that someone told me he had written another book as well. That book is called *Tower in Siloam*, and it is a religious work. It is the study of a man in search of God, and— I don't know why, on reflection, this should have come as a surprise— in reading it I found that the man I had known as a satirist, whom his students had known as a chemist, was also one of the wisest and most gentle-minded men I have ever read. I talked to him about that too, on the radio, and later, when we were winding up our second season, we asked Professor Hiebert to fly to Toronto and to sit in a studio with three other people who had become important to the program, as we, I hope, had become important to them: Bob Ruzicka, an Edmonton dentist who is, I think, the best song writer in Canada today; Sneezy Waters, an Ottawa street-singer who is just fun to have around, and Edith Butler, a tall, shy, graceful Acadian who may have the most beautiful eyes in Canada— she certainly writes and sings some of the most beautiful songs. The

singers sang and Dr. Hiebert read bad poetry, and we all glowed. The party carried on after the program ended, and Professor Hiebert, the satirist, scientist and philosopher, who is, I'd guess, about sixty years her senior, made twinkly-eyed, flirtatious remarks to Edith. Actually, I had to remind him of this fact and threaten to blackmail him before he would agree to type up the bad Christmas poetry he'd written for us in our third year and allow me to put it in this book. He signed his letter of concession to me in purple ink. His wife, he said, had given him a box of different-coloured felt pens for Christmas, and he was trying them out.

On my way to becoming Paul Hiebert, I'd like to be W.O. Mitchell. Bill Mitchell is— and this really is an "of course"— the creator of Jake and the Kid, the author of, most recently, *The Vanishing Point*, and before that the book that I think is the best ever written about the Canadian prairies, *Who Has Seen the Wind?* But he chews cigarettes. Well, he used to chew them. Now he sniffs snuff. He also chews up phonies. I remember one morning when he came in to visit the program; he'd seen something on CBC television the night before that had annoyed him, and he used a phrase that has stuck permanently in my mind. The program he'd seen had been one of those CBC attempts to describe things Cultural. It had been, said Bill Mitchell, "rarefied nightingale piss." There is no RNP about Bill Mitchell. Bill Mitchell, like Paul Hiebert who was Bill Mitchell's chemistry teacher at the University of Manitoba, knows who he is. That's why they're heroes of mine, and that's why one of them appears very near the beginning of this book, and the other very near the end.

In between, there are a lot of other people I got to know because of "This Country in the Morning." There is no way, in these pages, that I can capture everything that program meant to me or to the people who made it, who included not only its staff and its contributors but its listeners, too. There is no way, for example, I can transcribe Jean-Claude Germain's belly laugh from Montreal, or Adrian Hope's five dialects of Cree from Edmonton, or the nervousness of the young girl bagpiper who was to open our program from Sydney, and who could show that nervousness only by wailing away on her pipes for fifteen minutes before the show while Kenzie McNeill, the gentle young genius who wrote "Johnstown Boogie," and some fiddlers and other musicians with whom we'd partied the night before tried to tune up their own instruments for the music we wanted to broadcast live. Nor can I properly convey such moments as the time I was talking to two

is for Avro
and Arrow and air,
But too much was hot
and it never got there.

*Peter Gower
Maxwell, Ontario*

nice old men in Fredericton about the lore of the fiddlehead fern and I asked them how high a fiddlehead could grow. The man to whom I'd directed the question said . . . well, he didn't say anything. He looked me straight in the eye and he held his hand about a foot above the studio table. *He* knew how high they grew, but did the listener? I loved it.

I think, now, if I were asked why "This Country" worked, my answer would be about as eloquent as the man who knew the height of fiddleheads. It worked because a lot of people, some of whom hated each other and some of whom loved each other (and the permutations were not always constant), cared about it. People in other units around the CBC used to call us "the family" and, although the nickname was not born in a flattering way – it originated, I think, about the time of the Manson murders – it was a hard one to dispute. What drew us together was the program. In contrast to some other places I've worked with a tight sense of common purpose, we spent virtually no time together away from the office. I think, actually, that the fact that a lot of us got on each other's nerves created some of the energy that made the program what it was. I guess I haven't even got the right to say "a lot of us." All I know is that a lot of the people who inspired me, drove me, supported me and teased me sometimes got on *my* nerves.

I know too that we had no model. I think that was one of the reasons for our success. We weren't the Canadian *Esquire*, or the Canadian Merv Griffin Show. We weren't the Canadian Goon Show or the Canadian *Pravda*. We were "This Country in the Morning" – a radio program of conversation, puzzles, games, essays, recipes, advice, music, nostalgia, contests, skits, arguments and emotions. Were we trying to keep the country together? People kept asking me that. The best answer I could think of was no. But Alex Frame, the executive producer, once said that if you wanted to do that, a rope would be better than a radio program. We were, I think, a daily *event*. Our mood could be changed by anything from an inter-office argument to the weather, or by the fact that someone on the program was feeling horny – which is how, incidentally, we decided one morning in late February to start collecting signs of spring. Furthermore, we were live – or at least what broadcasters call "live on tape." Wherever we were coming from – and in three years we originated from nearly three dozen places from St. John's to Tuktoyaktuk – we had to be on the network at 9:13 Atlantic time – or 9:43 in Newfoundland, which is an exception to everything. (The world will end at midnight tonight; 12:30 in Newfoundland.) What I said

live to the Maritimes was recorded in Toronto and rebroadcast an hour later, then recorded in Winnipeg and so on, so that everyone, so to speak, heard the same thing at the same hour.

On one of the few occasions we took advantage of the fact that we could, in fact, edit what went live to the Maritimes and change it for the rest of the country, we weren't too happy we'd done so. There is, in what I am about to tell you, the revelation of hypocrisy. There was, I confess, a difference between the way all of us talked away from the microphone and the way I talked on it. I swear. In private, in fact, I talk more like a third baseman than a literary critic (although in my baseball career lately I have been playing third base more like a literary critic than a third baseman). About as naughty as I got on the air was to talk about "doggy do," and at that I was reading a letter. There was one occasion, though, when things got out of control.

Three artists were on the show. We'd asked them to come on – this was one of our more profound ideas – and talk about how they'd paint the federal election. One of them – and if bad words offend you, close your eyes for a minute – one of them used the phrase: "the whole fucking thing." That phrase went live to the whole fucking Maritimes. We thought we might edit it out for the rest of the country. So someone made a note of the precise second at which the phrase had occurred, and someone else, while we were doing our second hour live, went down to what the CBC calls, with Big Brotherish overtones, "Master Control," and tried to bleep it. Bleeping, live, involves riding a key called a "tone key." "Tone" is the horrible noise you hear, for example, giving the time signal. (When I took recorder lessons on the air, incidentally, one person wrote to ask me to stop playing because he thought *it* was the time signal.) But one of the things you learn if you work in radio is that tape stretches. Forty-seven minutes broadcast to the Maritimes may be nearly forty-eight when it reaches B.C. In any case, whether it was reflexes, tape-stretch or an error in marking the time, the producer in Master Control was just a pulse-beat too late. So what the rest of the country heard was not what the artist had said but this: "the whole fucking *bleeeeeeeeeeeeeep* . . . " And I couldn't help wondering about the people who must have said to themselves: "Holy Nelly, if they left 'fucking' in, what on earth did they bleep?"

One of the things that has always surprised me about, for example, men who have been to war, is the way their good memories are able to blot out the bad ones, and in thinking back over the three years I spent on "This Country," I am almost overwhelmed by a sense of . . . I don't

What is the difference between unlawful and illegal?
Unlawful is against the law, and illegal is a sick bird.

May Curtis
St. John's, Newfoundland

know, pleasure, adventure, joy. During the strike of early 1972 that kept us off the air for fourteen weeks, a few of us went to Vancouver Island, to record some leisurely interviews and have a look around. Vicki Meacham, whose son had won one of our earliest contests, along with her husband John – you'll meet them all later on – drove us from downtown Victoria to their home in Milne's Landing, and on the way we stopped to pick up some fresh oysters. Vicki cooked them up for us, and we washed them down with a bottle of their homemade pear wine. On the way back to the city we stopped and turned the car lights out, and the radio off, and it was as dark as it has ever been, and as beautiful.

On Cape Breton, Kenzie McNeill and a friend of his drove us down to Fortress Louisbourg; Kenzie had been smoking some dope on the way and was singing "The Rocky Road to Dublin," and my heart was with him, and then we threw stones into the Atlantic and Kenzie told us that the sound they made was called "cutting the devil's throat." I tried the same thing later, on the shore of Hudson's Bay, but I got too close to the water and I had to rush to the Churchill airport with my pants wet. In Montreal one time, Pauline Julien, trying to explain her feelings about going to jail for what she had sung about, reached across the studio table and clutched both my hands; her English was almost indecipherable, but what she was saying, I'm sure, came over on the air. After I got home from the Arctic trip, about which I've written later on, the phone rang late one Sunday night and Denis Ryan of Ryan's Fancy said the sun was going down in St. John's, as it had never gone down in the Mackenzie Delta, and he wanted to sing me a song. After we taped our Christmas show in Happy Valley, Labrador, the manager of the CBC station there wanted me to go to the Goose Bay officers' mess, but I was tired and not in the mood for officers, and all of us who had made the program went back to our hotel and drank drinks and sang songs . . . just as we had done in Montreal after our last hour there once, when Michel Garneau, a poet, had sung a raunchy drinking song called "Prends un verre de bière, mon Minou" as if it were a love ballad, and all of us realized once and for all that Quebec had what Canada was only beginning to have – a sense of itself – or as we'd done in Thunder Bay where, instead of partying to wind ourselves down, a bunch of us went for one of the world's great saunas.

This sounds sloppy, doesn't it? Parties, new friends, meeting some of the famous people of the country (some of whom, confidentially, are dorks), roaming around the landscape and generally having a good time. The trouble is, it *was* a good time, the best and most exhilarating time I've ever had in my life. But it had its terrible moments too. I imagine most of the people who listened to the program know about Andrew Allan. He was a pioneer of the great days of CBC radio, a writer, actor and director of drama, and a gentleman. Over the years he'd had problems with booze and with women, but when I met him, when he was in his sixties, he was totally dry and, as I have seen few men, totally in control of himself. Each Friday morning, "This Country" used to begin with an essay by Andrew, some of which I've included in this book. I find it odd, incidentally, referring to him as Andrew, which is what I called him. Only after his death did I learn that when he was directing the "Stage" programs that I'd listened to as a young man, he'd been, to everyone, Mr. Allan. Once, as Bernie Braden said on our program after Andrew died, he'd been rehearsing a play with Lorne Greene, and Greene had felt uncomfortable about not only the way Andrew had asked him to do a particular scene, but about the "Mr." form. He'd stopped the rehearsal and asked if he "couldn't talk it over with Andrew." "Tell Mr. Greene," Andrew had said over the talkback, "that Mr. Allan would like Mr. Greene to do the scene the way Mr. Allan wants, but after the rehearsal Andrew will buy Lorne a drink."

Because he had led such a full life, I think all of us at "This Country" were able to cope with Andrew's death, of a stroke, early in 1974. What we were not able to cope with – what I am still barely able to cope with – was the death of Sheilah White. Sheilah had been one of the first people Alex Frame hired when he was putting 'This Country" together. I used to call her "Perfect Sheilah" because she was, as well as being remarkably physically attractive, calm, and funny and lacking in any pretense. *She* got on no one's nerves. During the middle of our second season she went into hospital for major surgery, from which she apparently recovered. I remember that I called her on a Sunday morning, the weekend I had been given an award by ACTRA. I called her because I knew that she had nominated me for that award. She sounded terrific; she'd soon be back at work. When we finished doing the Monday show, Alex told us that Sheilah had died. We didn't know how to honour her. Someone mentioned how much she had loved the song "Amazing Grace." I wrote something that afternoon, a dedication of the hymn. I can remember how we recorded it, because I know I could not have done it live on the air. To read it, I had to turn my back to the control room. There was no producer there, only Ron Grant, the technician who worked with us the whole three years. Ron is a tough, squat guy

13

who used to be a wrestler and a truck driver. Our office name for him was "Archie Bunker." To do Sheilah's obituary, we had to have our backs turned to one another, because when I finished trying to say what all of us felt, I broke down completely. Ron did too. Sheilah was twenty-six when she died. We never played "Amazing Grace" on the radio again.

I don't think I'll ever be Paul Hiebert or W.O. Mitchell. I've started too late. But I do know that the time I spent on "This Country in the Morning" changed me. I don't mean in the magazine-article sense of "How Pot Saved My Marriage" or "How I Found God by Growing Tomatoes," but both publicly and privately I am not the same person Alex Frame hired to host the CBC's new three-hour morning radio show in 1971. I have certainly changed in my attitudes towards my profession, my country, and myself.

In three years, quite a bit was written about me, in everything from the Dartmouth *Free Press* to *Homemakers' Digest*. A lot of that writing was nice, and some of it was flattering, but a lot of it I found superficial. I wish I could be annoyed by that. I'm not. I know what newspaper and magazine writers have to concentrate on. As a writer, in fact, I have dashed off some of the most superficial balderdash that ever saw print. *Maclean's* once asked me to write a profile of Geneviève Bujold. I'd hardly heard of her, let alone seen a movie she'd made. I took her to lunch. We talked. I drove her home. I wrote about her. *Maclean's* gave me six hundred dollars. The next time I saw her she was rude to me. She was right. No one should write publicly about anyone until he or she has been written about publicly first. So I bear no ill will to the persons who characterized me as everything from a jock to a sex symbol. I am aware that the ideal magazine or newspaper article has to have an "angle," and that the best way to write about anyone is to zoom in on one characteristic ("competitiveness," Harry Bruce in *Weekend*; or "shagginess," Bob Blackburn in the Toronto *Sun*) and make that the dominant one. I *am* competitive. I'm almost as competitive as Marci McDonald makes me out to be in *Homemakers' Digest*. I see no point in playing any game, from chess to hockey, if you're not trying to win. I'm also shaggy, one of the least careful dressers since Attila the Hun. But I hope I'm other things too, things that can't be captured in three thousand words. And I hope you won't think, in the glimpses I've tried to give you of a lot of people in this book, that I've tried to define them. All that is here is what they wrote for, or said on, the radio. Here are some of the things that I, except perhaps in passing, never said about myself.

I was born in Toronto on July 13, 1934. I don't know if my father was there or not. It was Depression time and my parents, having been married in one of those run-away deals in Jamestown, N.Y., had decided to split. My father was working in northern Ontario. My mother, whose name was Margaret McGregor Young, was the second of three children of a very successful lawyer, who came from the same UEL stock that had spawned Sir John A. Macdonald. My father was the first of three children of the grandson of Sir Casimir Stanislaus Gzowski, an engineer who came to Canada from Poland in the nineteenth century and got rich. None of those riches were passed on to my generation, nor did any of the money Greg Young earned by being a good lawyer, a good Tory and a good friend of Stephen Leacock. My mother's mother, a proud lady who had taken her daughter on a grand tour of Europe in 1929, once asked me if I'd like to have had any of the first-edition Leacocks ("to Greg from Stephen") that she'd just donated to Upper Canada College. I said I would have. She laughed. I liked her a lot.

I liked my Gzowski grandparents a lot too. My grandfather used to stand as straight as a spear, and when he couldn't do that any more he died. In his eighties. My grandmother outlived him, but after his death she was not the same person she had been. In life, she'd taken my mother and me in. We lived with the Gzowskis for a while and then my mother, divorced, married a nice guy named Reg Brown, who lived in Galt, Ontario. Because my mother, whom I loved very deeply, thought it would be difficult for me to have a different name than my parents, I was Peter Brown from the time I was about six until I was fifteen. At fifteen I was doing badly at high school and at life. I had bad acne, bad habits and a good overhead set-shot at basketball. I ran away to Toronto. My father arranged for me to go to his old school, Ridley, in St. Catharines. I did well there, and got a couple of scholarships to university. Actually, two scholarships. In the meantime, my mother died. If I had one wish now it would be to have lunch with her. She was tall and smart and funny—I think she was the youngest person to get an M.A. from St. Andrew's University in Scotland (too young for a Canadian school)—and I'd like to have known her better.

I didn't do well at university and dropped out; I worked in a number of places and then I went back. One of the places I'd worked was the Timmins *Daily Press*. When I went back to university I was elected editor of the *Varsity*. In the spring of the year I should have graduated, I went instead to be city editor of the Moose Jaw *Times-Herald*. When I was in Moose Jaw I met a woman I wanted to spend the rest of my life with. She agreed that that would be a good idea. I came east to run the Chatham (Ont.) *Daily News*, and while I was running it, Jenny Lissaman, the woman I had met out west, and I got married. On our honeymoon night, we conceived the first of our five children. Before he was born I accepted an offer at *Maclean's* magazine. In the next six years I learned a lot from the editors I worked for. Ken Lefolii was and is as good a friend as I will ever have. Blair Fraser taught me what the word gentleman meant. But before them, Ralph Allen showed me what it meant to be a journalist. He was simply a great writer, a great editor, a great poker player and a great guy. He was fifty-three years old when he died in 1968, and he left an indelible impression on all of us who knew him.

I had a number of jobs after I left *Maclean's* in 1964. I freelanced a lot, and in between I was entertainment editor of the Toronto *Star*, editor of the *Star Weekly*, co-author of a book of sports stories, host of a weekly program called "Radio Free Friday," co-writer of a song, author of an unproduced film script, host of a virtually still-born TV talk show and, despite a lot of other people's better judgement, editor of *Maclean's*. I was pretty good at most of those things — outstanding at some; terrible at others. On looking back I wish I could try some of them again. But on looking back over looking back, I'm glad I had coffee with Alex Frame in the summer of '71.

Frame was then, as he is now, about as different from me as it is possible to be. He is a Baha'i, which means that he doesn't drink and he is very straight with people, which may be the greatest oversimplification ever of the strength of that complex and beautiful faith, but it is an emphasis of how different he and I were and are. I drink. I drink a lot. I also tend to move around people's edges until I can see an opening, and then pounce, both off the air and on. Alex goes straight for the centre. I was down when we met, having been trounced at a couple of things, and I almost mumbled my way out of Alex's offer to host a new CBC radio show. In the years before 1971 I'd sat in for Bruno Gerussi a couple of times and done "Radio Free Friday," both of which Alex had heard. Quite a few people — I've only learned this since — thought that he should have found someone entirely new to radio to host his new show, but he thought that some experience of the kind I'd garnered over the past fifteen years would make it easier to build a crew of other kinds of people. He won his arguments — he wins most of his arguments — and the CBC agreed to take me. Quite a lot has been written since about the way Frame, who is ten years younger than I am, and

I — except for the facts that he too is almost a compulsive smoker and a terrible dresser — are totally dissimilar. What we do share is a driving desire to be the best we can be at our jobs. But there is little else. Alex hired people over my objections for the program we decided to call "This Country in the Morning." People I would have bet a great deal on he didn't hire. For all his generosity of spirit, he showed, as he hired Bill Casselman, Krista Maeots, Nancy Button, Sheilah White, Judy Brake, Hilary Armstrong, and others about whom more later, an incredible sense of what could help his program.

The same people also helped to change me. When Alex finally agreed to hire me, I had to figure out for myself that it was not so much because of my past successes, but because of my failures. If I had blamed, in the past, incompetent management, sluggardly colleagues, a misunderstanding of my aptitudes, I would no longer have a chance to do so. And in thinking about that I realized that my failures had been not so much due to my co-workers or my bosses but myself. Sure, I had been able to inspire some good work; but I had passed some bad work on as well. In the three years I spent working on "This Country" I met more people who are better and smarter than I am than I ever dreamed existed. Some part of their work is represented in this book. As a consequence I have learned about my profession that it is not "them" against "us." It's not a group of people who have "paid their dues" writing to and for a group of people who haven't. It's everyone trying to communicate with everyone else. I wouldn't have known that without "This Country." So that one of the things I learned about myself and my profession was that in no way was I one of the élite. There are, and I think this book proves it, more literate, wise, even brilliant Canadians who have never been paid a cent for what they've written than there are copies of books sold by some people I once considered in a class by themselves.

About my country, I don't know how to express what I've learned. Awe? Incredulity? I don't know. I can't express it. I guess between October 5, 1971, and June 28, 1974, I learned how little I understood of everything. I hope that in these pages you'll be able to share some of the experiences, places, events and people I did grow to know, and perhaps realize why I like them so much.

So many times for her we'd wait,
Unpunctual was she for every date.
But now with irony sublime,
Her funeral was right on time.
Now here she lies, she met her fate,
Leona Smith is really "late."

Leona M. Smith
Kitchener, Ontario

PETER GZOWSKI

Toronto
June 1974

15

A word about how this book was put together

First of all, there is no logical sequence. Hallowe'en sometimes follows Christmas, and some of the things we did first often follow some of the things we did last. Scattered throughout are little things — contest entries, bits of nonsense, exchanges of correspondence, poems, even recipes, that have no relationship whatever to what they're near.

Then again, "This Country in the Morning" often had no logical sequence either. We just tried to do what seemed to come naturally after what we'd done before. And in shaping this book I have tried as best I can to recreate the spirit of the program for those people who knew it, and to parallel it for those who didn't. If I've succeeded, this should be a good book to keep in your bathroom. If I haven't, perhaps it is anyway — for different purposes.

As usual, I'm talking in the first person singular, when so much of the work was done by other people. Betty McAfee spent a major portion of her life combing files of letters, ordering transcripts, nagging me to get down to work, and writing to people to ask if it would be okay to reproduce in print what they'd written for the air. Nancy Button, already overworked at "This Country," sat up late many nights editing transcripts of interviews she'd helped to arrange in the first place. Susan Kent, on whom I called in desperation when I didn't think I could meet a deadline for this work, helped immeasurably, not only in her editing work, but in bringing the view of someone who had not been on the inside of the program to the preparation of its print descendant. My family was more tolerant than even I had any right to expect, and my wife, Jenny, was as always my best editor. I can still remember one evening when a magazine editor, with devastating senti-mentality, asked Jenny if she would be glad I was leaving the program in the summer of 1974, because, of course, then she'd be able to see more of me. "I don't think so," said Jenny. "I liked the program." It's nice to have a fan who is also a friend and someone you love.

Many of the people I have mentioned earlier played a part as well, reading and criticizing — invariably helpfully — episodes in which they'd been involved. But the traditional disclaimer holds true. The choice and the editing of what's in here is mine.

Clove Wine

      Translate words
   into bottles.

       (Scene I)
Find a metal container(s) to
       contain
       One (hundred and sixty ounces)
       Imperial
       Gallon
Fill with water
Turn on
    the heat (fifth button from the right)
"A watched pot . . . etc." so you are free for 25 minutes to
    answer the phone
    read rapidly seven poems
    or slowly one line of L. Cohen
    find your old Brubeck records
    make not-quite-leisurely love
If your water boils away
you must start again at line seven

      Time for the second-best part of the recipe.
Make a little cotton sack with a string tie.
    Introduce one ounce
    (a handfulfull)
    of whole cloves
    a thumb of ginger
    (bruised by dropping complete clothbound works of
    geoffrey chaucer, who would approve, from five feet)
      Now smell it
Hold a lemon in each hand
Are they like duckeggs?
Stretched oranges?
  If the former, you will need three
  If the latter, two.
    Peel them to the quick slowly
    Save the peelings
    Don't cut yourself till you get to the oranges

Find a Seville (or Madrid or Tel Aviv but not Florida and
         especially not California) orange
Peel to quick too quick
and add 4 tsp. thumbblood to the rindpile
    Sack the rindpile
    with gingerthumb and cloves
Tie
  up
    t i g h t
    Simmer spice sack sixty-seven
        minutes

(Scene II) Third-Best Part
Think
    Once the water boils it takes no longer to make a room
    full than a gallon
Think
    Of a room full of clove wine
Think
    What your landlord would say
Think
    Of the parties
Think
    Of making love again
Invite a friend in to feel
    The smell of simmering spice sacks
Slice up oranges and lemons
    Pip them   Pip them   Pip   Pip

Into plastic garbage (!) pail:
        three libs Demerara sugar
        sliced citruses
    (Simmeringhour up yet?
            good)

Pour waterspice over garbage pail mess
    Stir with old wooden spoon
        until all but the slices are dissolved
    Throw away spicesack and cover the pail

            End of Third-Best Part

(Scene III. Much later — eight hours maybe)

Pail of stuff is warm as Luke.

    FIRST-BEST PART (fanfare)
        Make three pieces of toast
        Butter two of 'em
        Jelly one of them
        Salami one of them
        Ignore one of them
                    Dissolve 1/2 oz yeast in
                    third cup warm water
                    spread yeastpaste on
                    ignored toast eat other
                    two pieces (best part
                    coming NOW:)
Float yeastedtoast (yeast up) in the lukewarm garbagepail!
                Watch it swell
                Bread into wine!
Manhandle pail into the furnace
        room
If you spill you are disqualified. Time is no object
        Time is no object
        Time is no object
        A chair is an object
        Is wine an object?
Let it dream for two weeks
    You are permitted seven weeks per week
    Don't touch
Have you ever seen a drunken piece of toast?
Have you ever seen a sober piece of toast?

(Scene IV. Soliloquy in the eighteenth century manner)
    The same, two weeks later.

Invert a chair atop a groaning board.
A flannel square to chair legs should be moored.
Beneath the sheet and 'tween the legs a pot
To catch the strained liquid, spilling naught.

With fondest care now fill a gallon jar
(From A & W, purchased as you are).
A fermentation lock atop apply
Which Earl the friendly druggist will supply.

Ignore the lot completely for one moon,
Nor sample aught for still it is too soon.
Now siphon ('rack,' they say in winesman's phrase)
And leave for yet another ninety days.

Within the brew now magic doth unfold;
Wine groweth strong e'en while it doth grow old.
Unlike poor man, whose pow'rs do surely wane
As years add up; he walketh, but with pain.

Unless, of course, he learneth from this rhyme
And tastes new youth from Bacchus, God of Wine.
Undream't of beauty slumbers in the clove,
Whose secret, tapp'd, ignites the fires of love.

Ron Marken
Saskatoon, Saskatchewan

17

One Hour in High River, Alberta

One winter day in 1972 a bunch of us drove from Calgary some thirty-five miles south to the small cattle town of High River, nestled in the foothills country. It was the first show we attempted to originate from outside a CBC studio. Our technicians had rigged up the High River Centennial Library as a set. Our honoured guest was to be W.O. Mitchell, my scraggly hero. As far as Mitchell knew, the hour he would spend talking to me would simply be a personal chat about his own life in that town. What he did not know was that Nancy Button, who had arranged the program, had been scheming furiously for weeks. Throughout the library, from the mystery section to the basement, we had hidden surprises for him. What follows is a record of those surprises. First, though, here is our cast:

WO: Bill Mitchell
MM: Myrna Mitchell
HM: Hugh Mitchell
PG: Pat Gibson
SG: Stan Gibson
DD: Dave Diebold
ML: Mark Langfeldt
CC: Charles Clarke
GC: Grace Clarke
LL: Lois Laycraft
P: Peter

P: How long did you live in High River?
WO: Twenty-four or twenty-five years, with some time out when we were in Toronto and while I was commuting from High River to Montreal. But we always came back, we always had a home here; it was our point of reference. Before we moved here we had lived in teacherages, pogies and scratch houses and boarding houses, so this was our first real home. We bought a house in Longview and added to it. Over the years our family grew up here with the foothills and the Little Bow. The streets softened with trees just became home in an extension of self. The people were another attraction of High River. This was, though it isn't now, one of those areas in which individuality counted, particularly among ranching people. There was an unconformity, a uniqueness of a human being, people like Jack Kelly, Clem Hanson and Jack Brown. There were so many people like that who became casualties of a more sophisticated, crowded way of life. The ranch country was sort of a last frontier; I found this charming and I loved it. As a writer, it was terribly, terribly important to meet salty individuals and in twenty-four years or so, I found the supply of salty individuals slowly but inexorably dying out.
P: How much of High River was in *Jake and the Kid*?
WO: That's hard to say, but a lion's share of it, because the dramas were built on short stories I had done earlier and so many of those were from incidents, from the things that happened in High River.
P: Then you would admit that you owe a great deal to the people of High River?

WO: Oh my, yes.

P: Now, we're going to do something to you this morning.

WO: Yeah? All right, I can hardly wait. What?

P: You've been telling stories about the people of High River for a long time, so this morning we're going to turn things around and have them tell stories about Bill Mitchell . . . W.O. Mitchell, this is your life in High River, Alberta!

WO: Now, wait a minute! I'm not hedging about but you know, you're a writer, that life and art are not the same thing and that *every single bit*, *every single bit* . . . .

P: Don't get mad at me!

WO: I'm not mad, I'm just passionate!

P: Well, don't kiss me either!

WO: No, no, every single bit is the truth. You can say that about a character and every single bit of that character mosaic is the truth but the whole character, the whole theme, the whole narrative is a more meaningful lie, right? I just want to qualify those stories, okay?

P: Okay. Bill, would you introduce all these people who just walked in?

WO: There's Charles and Grace Clarke, friends and neighbours of ours for all the time we were here; Davie Diebold, the wisest guy I know, who ranches near here, with whom I've hunted — as a matter of fact, Dave and I want to do a novel involving a grizzly hunt in Three Springs with me rolling on my belly and Dave scared shitless — and Mark Langfeldt, a boy from Calgary who looks after my wife while I'm up in Edmonton; Pat and Stan Gibson, friends from down this way, now in Calgary; and over there is my favourite dirty mind, Lois Laycraft — my wife and I went on our honeymoon with Lois and her husband.

P: Okay. Now I want to ask Grace Clarke if she has a favourite W.O. Mitchell story.

GC: Bill, do you remember when you moved that house in from Longview and held a housewarming? The basement was full of water and you and the rest of the guys were fishing in it. . . .

WO: And we had the crap game going in what later became the bedroom. . . .

P: What, you mean you were fishing in the basement?

GC: Well, you see, when Bill decided to build the foundation for his house he brought in all his brothers, swarms of them, to dig the basement. They didn't know just how deep a basement should be, there weren't any regulations then, so they dug and they dug and they dug until it was a pretty deep basement. It was so deep it was below the water line and it flooded, so that's how they were able to fish at his housewarming.

WO: Grace, it was just a wet spring.

GC: Well then, do you remember when you shingled your roof and stranded Myrna on top?

P: What? What happened?

GC: He and Myrna went up to shingle the roof one hot day and I guess Bill decided to go down and have a sip of lemonade or just sit in the shade. For some reason he took the ladder down and forgot all about Myrna up on the roof in the heat.

WO: I was over having lemonade with Mrs. Nightingale and Mrs. McCorquodale across the street.

GC: I'd just like to tell you that we miss you here. . . .

WO: I miss you guys too.

GC: . . . and hope that you come back.

P: Hughie, what's your favourite Bill Mitchell story?

HM: I've been trying to think of one I can repeat on the radio. . . . The one thing

I do remember was the traumatic childhood I had with him as my father because he alienated every friend I had in High River. He scared them; he used to yell at them. They would come over to visit at four-thirty in the afternoon and he would give them hell for interrupting us during lunch. The kids were absolutely petrified of him. That stands out in my mind, but there were other things. I remember hunting with him once and the dog wasn't obeying him very well. . . .

WO: Oh, no!

HM: Father got mad and laid some shot over him. Unfortunately, there were a few more hunters down past the dog. They came barrelling out of the bush and had a few words with us.

P: Dave, is Bill a good hunter?

DD: He was a good goose hunter. We went goose hunting one time; Bill had made all the arrangements to go up to the dam at Bassano with the trailer. Bill said that was the place to get geese, so off we went. The first thing I remember seeing was a bunch of geese sitting in a little slough and by the time we got over to the dam, well, I never, the geese were there till hell was in heaven. So we waited down in a coulee till about four o'clock and, sure enough, they started flying around. Myrna was there with my wife, laying down, and the first bunch went over, Myrna rolled over on her back, braced the shotgun on her stomach and pulled the trigger — that was a pretty novel and painful way to shoot. But the only one who had any luck was our son, who knocked down a big goose that sailed way out over the water before it came down. Well, he was having a fit because his goose was gone, but Bill, being a good swimmer, strips off and dives in after that goose. You could see him chasing around out there, getting close to dark. . . .

WO: And fairly close to Christmas, too!

DD: . . . but he got the goose. He came dragging the thing out, trying to swim, the goose flapping, Bill trying to wring its neck, but eventually getting out with it. Getting out he had to cross a big mudbar and his feet were full of mud so he couldn't put his clothes on. Just behind him there was a steep bank about three feet high so I said, "Bill, jump up and wipe your feet on the grass." Bill bounced up there, let out a holler and bounced right back down. It wasn't grass up there, it was cactus! Finally, to get his feet clean, my wife took off her underskirt to use for a towel and Bill finally got his clothes back on.

So we all went back to town and here was young Peter dragging this big old honker around by the head, the goose being nearly as big as he was. Eventually someone asked him where he got it and Peter said out at the dam. The man said, "Didn't you know that's a sanctuary? Some fellows lost their guns for shooting out there the other day." So we went straight to the trailer and decided we should get out of there very early the next morning.

But in all the rush we'd forgotten to brace up the trailer, and that evening the wind came up, making the trailer rock back and forth all night. Bill's feet were giving him some trouble so here he was with his feet sticking up over the back of a chair, and Myrna with tweezers trying to pick the cactus spines out of his feet, all swaying back and forth. Young Peter watched all this and said it sure was a good thing Bill hadn't sat down! Anyway, the next morning we're set to leave and guess who hadn't gassed up their car? But we got away; the cops never caught us.

P: That's the absolute truth?

WO: Yeah, he's told you the truth. It's probably the only truthful thing you'll hear this morning.

P: We'll see about that. I want to ask the Gibsons if they have a favourite story.

SG: I have a theory about Bill that I think covers all the stories about him, and that

What's dark, hairy, has four legs and drives very fast? Stirling Moose.

Don Edwards
Thunder Bay, Ontario

is that he's a natural magnet for disaster. My phrase is that he generates confusion. Bill prefers to call it a Gestalt, but it's the unfolding of an unexpected series of things that starts very innocently but strays into the greatest and most confused outcome you can imagine. Pat has a good story about Bill.

PG: My favourite story is arriving up at the lake with Bill and Myrna, the children, dogs and a lot of supplies, all of which we loaded into the boat. Bill went to start the motor and hit the power, but he forgot he hadn't connected the steering gear. So the boat took off making figure eights all over the river.

P: Did you make a small error there?

WO: Not really. Hughie and I had always built boats together over Myrna's dead body because of the shouts and cursing it caused. This boat was moulded fiberglass with a great big red hundred-horsepower motor and Myrna was scared to death of it and always expected the worst of me. Ordinarily, I would have just eased it in, but we were at the mouth of the river with a tremendous current and, knowing Myrna expected the worst of me, I said, "Grab your seats, kids, and hit it!" And of course, not having attached the steering cables and with a hundred-horsepower motor, we just went flipping every which way, pretzeling back and forth. So it really wasn't deliberate . . . well, it was, not the cables, but hitting it. . . .

P: Sure it was. Lois, I want to hear about your honeymoon adventures.

LL: It was their second honeymoon, our first. We were together in a small trailer but Bill couldn't understand blocking up trailers . . . I don't think I should go into this.

P: I think you already have.

LL: Anyway, what finally happened was that they would go out one night and we would go out the next, but what I really remember about our honeymoon. . . .

WO: I didn't really notice that. I just suggested that it was time you and Wendell took in a picture show or something.

LL: Well, yes, you did sort of put it that way, but I wanted to tell about the one and only outfit you had to wear on our honeymoon. You have to understand that Bill bought a whole houseful of goose down from the Hutterites and that Myrna spent a whole year sewing: she stuffed a chesterfield with goose down, she sewed sleeping bags with goose down, but with the last bit of goose down she made this parka, a great ungodly red parka for Bill, which is all he brought with him to wear in California. At the time he had a full beard and wore this parka over white swim trunks. From a distance it didn't look as though he had much on except for this great big red thing on top, which he claimed kept the heat out. When we went down to Mexico we were followed everywhere by about a hundred little Mexican children shouting, "Hey, Meester Santa Claus." Then when we were in Tijuana we got separated from Bill when he got into a conversation with a little Mexican across the street. Bill started gesturing towards us and the Mexican took off. Bill eventually caught up with us and we asked what was going on. Apparently this guy came up to Bill and said, "Hey, Meester, you wanta come koochee, koochee, only ten cents," and Bill was haggling about the price.

WO: I was not. What I said was, "Can I bring my wife along," and that's when he put his hands in his pockets and took off.

LL: I should tell you how Wendell first met Bill. When Bill came to High River hardly anyone would speak to him because he was sort of the original hippie, except that you didn't call them hippies then. He went around with his pants tied up with a rope and that sort of thing. Anyway, Wendell was the very friendly type and thought he'd go over and meet this character. Bill was digging a septic tank for his new house and somehow he persuaded Wendell that he should get down in there

Here lie I and my three daughters,
Killed from drinking Sydney water.
If we'd have stuck to epsom salts,
We wouldn't lie in these here vaults.

Mona K. MacDonald
Sydney, Nova Scotia

and help dig, but just by way of being friendly Bill dropped a few rocks on his head. So Wendell got a little hostile and decided to climb out of the hole, at which point Bill accidentally kicked a hammer in on his head. It affected their friendship for a while but not long. We named one of our sons after Bill; we love him anyway.

P: Charles Clarke, have you got a story?

CC: Well, Bill's the only man I ever knew in my life who built a house with a pair of pliers.

LL: Your pliers, I'll bet!

CC: I don't think so — he did borrow the shovel from me . . . Bill was a great guy for borrowing tools. It didn't take very long before all the neighbours around the district were locking up their tool chests. He finally did get the house built except for the bathroom that had only the outside wall up; the rest was open on three sides to public view from the rest of the house. But when Bill finally did get that bathroom completed, it was probably the finest place in the entire house. I remember when the assessor came and Bill didn't want him to assess the pleasure . . . ah . . . bathroom, so he sent Myrna in there to stay until the assessor left.

P: Is that true?

WO: Yes, yes . . . ah . . . well, no . . . well, yes, I guess it is. My mother-in-law was an English war bride from the First Great War with a great sense of style and propriety. She was worried about her little daughter living in the rough foothills without toilet facilities. When we eventually got it hooked up, like Charles said, surrounded just by two-by-fours, I got one of those marvelous insights that you get just like a flash. We phoned Myrna's mother out in Victoria and I just said, "Hi, Ma, your daughter doesn't have to go outside anymore; listen to this." And I stretched the phone over a two-by-four and flushed the toilet for her. That was the longest flush anybody ever heard, clear to Vancouver Island, and the most expensive.

P: Mark Langfeldt, how about you?

ML: Well, it's a death experience to go driving with him. If you're driving, and you want to, he's one of the best back-seat drivers you can find anywhere. But it's worse if he's driving; he thinks he owns the road. For instance, he's always complaining about guys speeding, all they do is go faster to get caught at the next light. But when he gets to a light he says he's going to show those guys and boots it, just floors it right across the intersection up to the speed limit and then slows down. The guy behind catches up and Bill will just sit there, saying watch him try to pass me. And if we're off hunting, he doesn't have much of a sense of direction on back roads.

P: Do you think he's a good hunter?

ML: Not this year. There've been times out on big stubble hunts when there were so many ducks we should have had our limit in half an hour, but we get two. I can say this cause I'm a worse shot than he is. But he says the reason is that he's been hunting pheasant the last four years and he just can't get used to switching back to ducks. If a lot of ducks come we won't hit them, we know that, but he says maybe they'll die of a heart attack from pointing our guns at them. He didn't do too well this season.

P: Hugh, did he teach you to drive and hunt?

HM: I learned to drive from my older brother but he taught me to hunt. He was a pretty good hunter, but he's getting older and his eyesight isn't as good as it used to be.

CC: Hughie, I remember when he drove you to Weyburn in that old station wagon he couldn't trade off to anybody. . . .

LL: That's because it was held together with binder twine!

22

CC: . . . so he figured he couldn't get his money out of it, but on the way back from Weyburn the car suddenly caught fire. Bill very happily drove it into a ditch, piled out all your belongings and sat on the edge of the ditch gleefully watching it burn up.

WO: But then all of a sudden a big semi-trailer truck came along and the damned fool had a fire extinguisher. . . .

P: Just for the heck of it, I'd like each of you to throw out an adjective or two that you think best describes W.O. Mitchell.

PG: Warm, wonderful. . . .

SG: He's the most self-reliant and truly artistic person I've ever come across.

CC: I think that in human living, people find far more of interest in Bill as a personality than they will ever be able to find in his books.

LL: I'd like to say forgetful, because he still can't find the goose decoys of ours he lost five years ago and I won't say another one because Bill says I have a dirty mind and I don't want to spoil my image.

GC: He is one of the most enthusiastic people I've ever met and I think that explains a lot of the things we've been saying about him.

ML: He cares more about other people than himself; he would put himself out for anybody.

HM: I can say one thing: he's introspective, which is part of his problem because he gets so involved in what he considers important that he just forgets less important things. That's how he just about dropped a mast on my wife's head this summer; he was holding on to the cable when he suddenly realized he'd left the pliers on the wharf and started walking back with the cable still in his hand. Down went the mast. . . .

P: Were those the original pliers?

WO: No, they were my own pliers.

HM: But he's also very sensitive because he was really concerned that the mast almost hit her.

WO: It was the mast I was worried about!

LL: We know that. . . .

P: Bill, do you want a last word about your friends — or your former friends?

WO: Not really, except I love them and they are my friends and they've been surprisingly good reporters this morning. They may have made it a little florid, but otherwise. . . .

P: There's one more person here we've not heard from yet, even though that person was talked about all the time. Would you introduce that person, Bill?

WO: Yeah, it's my dearest friend, my wife Myrna.

P: Myrna, you heard those stories; is every one of them true?

MM: Oh, yes.

WO: You think they were true? Really?

MM: Ah. . . .

WO: I mean, I know you were on top of that roof.

MM: Well, you know what Bill was saying: the whole thing is the truth and every bit of it is a lie; there was a lot of creativity involved.

WO: Nobody brought up the seersucker incident in New York. . . .

MM: Stan just told me to but you tell it; you're better at it.

WO: You tell it. Darling.

MM: I'll start it. . . .

WO: And I'll help you if you don't get it right.

MM: . . . because you'll interrupt, you know you will. . . .

WO: Yeah.

MM: Anyway, Bill has some far-out ideas on clothes and he had always wanted a seersucker suit. So he bought two – one wasn't enough. He took a trip down to California where he was able to wear the suits.

WO: That's where I bought them, in San Francisco. . . .

MM: That's right. . . .

WO: Get it right. . . .

MM: Well, on your way back to Toronto you had a stopover in New York and you went into the men's room to wash. . . .

WO: Yeah. . . .

MM: As he turned the water on, it came out with such force that it splashed all over the crotch of this beautiful seersucker suit. . . .

WO: . . . and I was faced with walking out with this great big, dark, self-indulgent stain all down my leg. There were no paper towels to mop it off but there were these blowers right above the pedestal sink. So I got up on the sink on one knee, lifted one leg and turned the blower on to dry it out. But just then two guys smelling strongly of Brute and carrying attaché cases came in – what do you say? I just looked over my shoulder and said "I'll be through in a minute" – and it worked, you know, it dried it right up. The only problem was, those two guys were on the plane to Toronto and on to Calgary, too. And they had just been to Weyburn where I was born and lived till I was twelve, which reminds me of that letter Myrna received last fall from the mayor. . . .

MM: It was a letter I just didn't quite understand at first. It said they were contemplating having statues made of Jake and the Kid to be placed at the entrance of the town – all life-size or bigger, I can't quite remember. But they decided they couldn't afford both so they're just going. . . .

WO: . . . to have Jake. . . .

MM: . . . Jake to start with. . . .

WO: . . . to start. . . .

WO and MM: . . . but Stan Gibson. . . .

MM: . . . feels that. . . .

WO: . . . has a real good suggestion. . . .

MM: . . . it should be just W.O. drying his seersucker suit. . . .

MM: . . . with one knee up on the pedestal.

P: Bill, I've asked you to read a bit from *Who Has Seen the Wind*, the best book, I think, ever written about the prairies. We have a first-edition copy from the library here that the librarian says is still very much in demand. I thought *everyone* in High River would own a copy.

WO: Well, I wrote part of *Who Has Seen the Wind* in High River, the latter parts, when we first arrived here with our infant son. Though it's prairie, a great deal of it depends on the mosaic of life that was High River in those days.

P: Would you read just the ending of it for me, please?

WO: The day grays, its light withdrawing from the winter sky till just the prairie's edge is luminous. At one side of the night a farm dog barks; another answers him. A coyote lifts his howl, his throat-line long to the dog-nose pointing out the moon. A train whoops to the night, the sound dissolving slowly.

High above the prairie, platter-flat, the wind wings on, bereft and wild its lonely song. It ridges drifts and licks their ripples off; it smoothens crests, piles snow against the fences. The tinting green of Northern Lights slowly shades and fades against the prairie nights, dying here, imperceptibly reborn over there. Light glows each evening where the town lies; a hiving sound is there, with now and then some sound distinct and separate in the night: a shout, a woman's laugh. Clear – truant sounds.

As clouds' slow shadows melt across the prairie's face, more nights slip darkness over. Light then dark, then light again. Day then night, then day again. A meadow lark sings and it is spring. And summer comes.

A year is done.

Another comes and it is done.

Where spindling poplars lift their dusty leaves and wild sunflowers stare, the gravestones stand among the prairie grasses. Over them a rapt and endless silence lies. This soil is rich.

Here to the West a small dog's skeleton lies, its rib bones clutching emptiness. Crawling in and out of the teeth an ant casts about; it disappears into an eyesocket, reappears to begin a long pilgrimmage down the backbone spools.

The wind turns in silent frenzy upon itself, whirling into a smoking funnel, breathing up topsoil and tumbleweed skeletons to carry them on its spinning way over the prairie, out and out to the far line of the sky.

is for **Barrett**,
Dave's givin' 'em hell,
First auto insurance,
sweet dreams, B.C. Tel.

Arthur Hister
Vancouver, British Columbia

Harry Bruce: On things he never got to do

I remember I was going to be a bartender in southern California. There was an ad for a bartenders' school in the Los Angeles *Times* and, for a long time, I carried it around in my wallet, next to my heart. When I was very young I had religion, and I loved ships, and therefore I knew I was destined to be a chaplain aboard a Corvette. I remember that my wife and I loved the Arctic, without ever having seen it, and we were going to settle in the Northwest Territories and live happily ever after. I remember we were in England before we were old enough to vote and the Australian government would pay our fares all the way to Sydney or Melbourne, if only we'd agree to settle there, and for a while we were going to do that. I remember that, at that time, we were also going to join the students' crusade to bring blankets and comfort to the Hungarian freedom-fighters. Somehow, we didn't get around to it.

I remember that, when I was eighteen, one of my classmates at a university in Sackville, New Brunswick, was a beautiful waif of a girl from Trinidad. She had an elusive soul, and one day, she said, "Why don't you come down to Port-au-Prince with me this summer and stay with me and my family?" But I didn't go. Once, I was in Antigua for eight days, and for months after that, I knew I could never be happy till my wife and I had a life of our own down among the trade winds. Once, we were going to sail the inland waterway till it ejected us among the islands of the Caribbean. Once, we were just going to move to the west coast of Canada, and sail boats in February.

Sailing. I remember that one night in 1967 I was drinking with a magazine editor, and he said, "This may sound like a funny question, Harry, but what do you really want to *do* in life?"

I said, "I'll tell you what I want to do. I want to take my kids out of school for a year. I want us all to get aboard a good forty-foot ketch, and I want to start sailing, maybe around the whole bloody world. If you guys at the magazine will buy the boat, I'll give you a great article every week and, when it's all over, you can sell the boat and get your money back. I could write that sort of stuff better than anyone else in the country."

He said, "Great. Terrific family appeal. Done. You've got yourself a deal." But the magazine was not profitable. In the hard morning, the editor blushed, and we agreed to forget about what I *really* wanted to do in life.

I remember I was going to write great short stories, rather like Guy de Maupassant's, and they would all spring to life among the old candlestick telephones in the newsroom of the Ottawa *Journal*. I remember I was going to take a job as information officer for Mount Allison University in Sackville and that, during my endless spare time in that sleepy, inspiring town, I would write a great novel. I remember that, the year I graduated, an English professor offered to arrange for me a teaching fellowship in Fredericton. I remember that, in England, I was going to let Lord Beaverbrook discover me; I would become that young Canadian whiz on the *Daily Express*. I remember I was going to join External Affairs in Ottawa, become a diplomat, and we would spend the rest of our years seeing the world in style.

I joined the University Naval Training Division because, some day, I was going to command my own ship. Much later, I had a terrific idea. I was going to talk the railroads into lending my family an entire car, one of those gorgeously ornate old carriages they use to house touring governors general, and I'd get them to haul the car over all the abandoned passenger lines in North America, and I'd write

a fantastic book about ghost towns, and lost ways of life among the beloved boondocks. I wrote to CN about it, but they did not reply.

I remember I was going to get one of those house-trucks, a lavish ship's cabin on wheels, and we'd discover backwoods Canada, the Canada the cities think has died. *I'd* be Pierre Berton, John Steinbeck, and a Jack Kerouac of the middle-class family, all in one, and better than any of them; and, after that, publishers would offer extraordinary advances just to keep the Bruce family rolling endlessly around the world.

I remember, too, that I was going to be a freelance writer who lived by the sea in Nova Scotia, and that's what I am now, and it's not bad at all; and, next summer, I think we'll go up the coast of Labrador, and I'll discover strange things that no writer has ever known.

Fighting the Funk

January 28, 1973

Dear Peter Gzowski:
Here is a list of ideas for combatting the February Funk. If other listeners wrote in ideas, you could make a book like the pickle book. You could call it *Save the Sanity of the Nation's Housewives.*

1. Rummage around in your camping box and find a pot that's still black on the outside from a campfire. Put it on the stove with a little water in it and smell it as it warms up. It'll take you right back to mid-August. If you're so well organized that you don't have a black pot in your camping box, then you probably don't have any trouble with February either.

2. Make a list of twenty-five things you can do in February that an Eskimo housewife can't do. For example:

a) Dump the kids at the library story hour.
b) Pack everybody in the car and go to the A & W.
c) Go and hear the Stuttgart Chamber Orchestra.

3. Get on the bus nearest your house and ride it to the end of the line and back. Sit on the back seat. Take along a sandwich.

4. Put something exciting in your bath water. Bubbles, or an essence, or blue food colouring.

5. Make a list of all the people you had crushes on in high school.

6. Start looking at doorknobs. Remember all the doorknobs in all the places you've ever lived in. Check the doorknob on every door you go through. Make a chart of them. Try to discover which style of doorknob is the most popular.

7. Buy a new tablecloth, and a bunch of flowers.

8. Look in the paper and find a function you'd never attend in a million years. Go to it. If you like chamber music, go to a roller derby. If you're a junior hockey freak, try a meeting of the local historical society.

9. Go to the public library, and ask to look at the *Life* magazines for 1953.

10. Buy an old table lamp from the Salvation Army. Glue macaroni, old buttons and beer-bottle caps all over it. Paint it. Take its picture. Take it back to the Salvation Army. Put the picture you took of it in a frame, and give it to your husband for Valentine's Day.

Signs of Spring

There are dirty wet marks on
   the floor
From puddles that form by the
   door,
The socks smell so bad
As they dry on the rad,
And school is becoming a bore!

Mrs. Marian Read
Govan Elementary School
Govan, Saskatchewan

Come to think of it, it wouldn't have to be just housewives. I could think of some great ones for businessmen.
Sincerely

Jean McKay
London, Ontario

Of course, we asked her to. And here they are:

1. Make a list of all the Musak tunes you hear in one day.

2. Remember what you did on winter Saturday afternoons when you were nine years old. Do the same thing this Saturday afternoon.

3. Buy a table-hockey game for your office. Draw up a coffee-break playing schedule, involving as many people as you can con into joining.*

4. Get one of those clickers that museum guards use to record attendance. Keep it in your pocket, and count the number of times you hear someone say "at this point in time."

5. On your lunch hour, go as high as you can get in the building you work in; then, go as low as you can. Have you ever *seen* the heating plant?

6. Get a picture you like, and tape it on the wall in the men's washroom. When someone tears it down, put up another one. See if you can keep a picture on the wall for all of February without anyone finding out that you are the one doing it.

7. Think about the first car you ever owned. Try to answer the following questions:

   a) How much did it cost?
   b) Were you ever stopped by the police in it?
   c) What colour was the gear-shift handle?
   d) Did you ever kiss a girl in it?

8. Take your camera to work. Take a picture of the view out of your window *every* afternoon at three o'clock for three weeks. When they're developed, put them in a large frame and hang them beside the window.

9. Send absurd unsigned memos. Example:
   To all employees:
   Tomatoes left in the foyer will not be watered for more than fifteen days.

10. Start saving scraps, like bent paper clips, empty scotch tape reels, and old ballpoint pens.

---

*You can get a good one for about ten bucks. **Don't fool** around with the magnetized kind.

Glue them all on to a large piece of cardboard, and give them to your wife for Chinook Day. Don't cheat, and accept scraps from anyone else. She'll appreciate them more if they're all your own.

Plus! Bonus! Extra!

11. Pick three people you see every day, and write down the colour of socks they wear. You'll soon be as familiar with their socks as you are with your own.

12. In case someone *else* is doing number 11, try to throw them off. Take an extra pair of socks to work and change in your lunch hour. Or, wear dark socks *every* day, and on Chinook Day wear hot pink ones.

The Pioneer Life

A chance remark by Helen Hutchinson one day early in the life of "This Country" sparked the first discussion of a topic that was to occupy many hours over the three years: the city *vs.* the country. It also introduced us to two people who were to become occasional and always fascinating guests on the show, Elizabeth Webster and Vicki Meacham, each of whom, along with their families, had fled the comforts of the city for the challenges of the frontier. In Elizabeth's case the "frontier" was a piece of land within easy driving distance of Toronto; in Vicki's, it was the gentle rainforest of Vancouver Island. Reproduced here are the first letters received from each; between them a letter that illustrates the contrasting views of those who chose to go back to the land, and those who had no choice.

December 8, 1971
Dear Peter:
Listening to "This Country . . ." some days ago, I was tickled to hear Helen Hutchinson remark on her difficulties in finding old-fashioned bath oil recipes. As she came on the air I was in the process of emptying our tiny galvanized frog-pond of the family's bathwater from the night before, and the thought of having the additional chore of scouring an unnecessary oil ring off the tub after twelve hours' congealing was too much for me!
  We are, in effect, living in a one-room cabin,

27

without hydro, running water or indoor plumbing, as we are housed in a CP Railway caboose on fifty acres of our own land, and these various services have yet to be extended to us. We are in a farming area with adequate private transportation, and a telephone so we can cut ourselves off as much or as little as we wish. And we are discovering so many of the whys and wherefores of pioneer living that I sometimes feel like one of the Strickland sisters in reverse as I rediscover the flora and fauna, or how to "make do" in a given situation; it is daily a funny, frustrating and challenging affair.

I had thought, when we moved out of our ten-room rented farmhouse, that the thing I would notice most would be the extra time gained from household chores given a much smaller area – but this is an illusion! I hadn't taken into account the daily maintenance chores required of a pioneer wife. First, there is water-carrying: our family of five needs a minimum of five gallons a day – for hair-washing, add an extra two buckets for every female head in the line-up.

Second, firewood: we have a coal- and wood-burning stove with an oven, which both cooks and heats for us very adequately when it's well fed, and on baking days the fire has to be maintained at a fairly high heat for several hours, which makes quite a hole in the woodpile. Here we copped out and bought a load of hardwood, as Hugh is away for most of the winter, and adding wood-cutting to my daily list of "musts" is impossible without a twenty-eight-hour day!

Third, lamps: we operate five oil lamps every winter, morning and evening. These need filling daily, and their chimneys need to be washed. This means separate hot water for dishwashing, or one ends up with sooty dishes, too. Wicks have to be trimmed at least once a week in summer, twice in winter, with additional use.

Fourth, plumbing: as we have small children, we have an indoor chemical toilet whose container needs emptying daily, and the trip is generally combined with one to empty the ash bucket from the stove, or the used water from the dishes, etc. This emptying business is one of the constants one never thinks of in the romance of the pioneer – every bucketful *in* means one to go *out*, and with the bare requirements, the count of buckets per day may well be upwards of thirty – no wonder one is ready to sleep by day's end!

Fifth, barn: we have a milking cow and hens which are producing, plus a young heifer and a pony eating their lives away at our expense, and drinking inordinately! There's always the usual heavy stuff with barns – feeding, minor repairs,

transferring of hay and straw bales from storage areas, weekly decanting of bags of feed into open bins for daily convenience. . . .

All these one expects if one commits oneself to a barn. More often the jarring things are those which come up out of context – like being in nightwear all ready for bed, only to find that the big log that smoulders all night to keep things warm is half an inch too big in every direction! No alternative but to strike out with the big four-foot axe kept handy behind the rocking chair (!) and slice off the extra on each of two sides at least. Generally I break up over the incongruity of the situation (which doesn't help my arm any), and with chips flying in all directions, I eventually chew it to size. By this time I'm hot and sticky and sooty again so I have to start over, wash and get ready for bed. The clock is set for 3:00 A.M. so that the fire can be stoked, and I crawl foggily back to bed – thankful that the two areas are so close.

Kids waking in the night is a panic without lamps – one can never find matches or the flashlight one put handy, and invariably there are several obstacles in the path of mercy. Fortunately, our two little ones sleep soundly most nights, so I can sink deep again till 6:30 A.M., when the alarm goes off a second time for the fire to be speeded up and the kettle put on. Back to bed then till 7:00 A.M., by which time the kettle is boiling and I can make a big pot of tea to carry me through the normal family breakfast rush – with the added urgency of an 8:15 school bus on an exact schedule to be boarded at the crossroads nearly a quarter-mile away. If the fire is temperamental or one oversleeps even five minutes there are no shortcuts, as with electrical equipment, and one just goes without some part of breakfast.

But really, this is a fascinating life, full of glimpses into the past. I'd like to share this with other city people who may never have the chance to find out. In almost every area of daily living, my pattern has had to be changed, and now, though I long for a chance to use my blender and electric sewing machine again, I know that I will be missing a tremendous amount when we are "modernized."

Elizabeth and Hugh Webster
Elmwood, Ontario

January 28, 1972

Dear Peter:
Mrs. Webster is a remarkable adaptable and interesting person. But to those of us who as children lived through the homesteading days in western Canada, the experiences she relates

were the stuff of everyday life. Indeed, with only some modifications, they continue to be so for many farm wives, as you yourself might deduce from a look at the DBS on farm income – income frequently so insufficient that it *must* be supplemented with off-farm earnings, leaving lots of Mrs. Websters to milk the cows, feed the pigs, act as livestock midwives, dung the barns and generally manage the one hundred and one other interminable chores. I suspect there are few who, after years of winters, find it very glamorous or self-fulfilling.

I am one of the fortunate ones who doesn't have to undergo this trial by drudgery. I love living on our farm, even while I thank God that I don't have to live on the income that the farm brings in. For children the farm can be very heaven, even though it is also a place wherein the lessons of reliability, adaptability, self-reliance and cooperation are learned, not always without pain. But I think that the stars shine no less brightly because the barn is lit with an electric bulb instead of a smoking lantern; that the setting sun turns ultra-green the pasture's grass whether the cows are milked by hand or with a milking machine; and the song of the birds is better heard when the burden of work leaves time to stand and stare and listen.

I'm strongly inclined to believe that there is a *plastic romanticism* implicit in the repudiation of the creature comforts of life. Of themselves these are not alien to meaningful, productive and self-fulfilling labour, though man may be alienated by the conditions of their attainment. Strangely enough – or is it so strange? – the city dweller wouldn't think himself particularly blessed if his toilet facilities consisted of an outdoor privy and a bucket of ice water – coated in the winter and brackish in the summer; nor would milady welcome as a means to her self-fulfillment the disappearance of her refrigerator, automatic dryer and washer, her vacuum cleaner, her electric toaster, fry pan, mixmaster, irons, air conditioner, not to mention the countless gadgets ranging from electric can openers to toothbrushes! I left out the tap-drawn bath and this, you must admit, she needs somewhat less than does one who milks the cows and dungs out the barn.

No, dear Peter! A glorification of inadequate housing (so long as it is farm housing!) and a roseate glow around the coal-oil lamp and the old wood-burning stove and tin bathtub, and the haloing of long hours of labour, seven days a week, 365 days a year, smacks of maudlin Uncle Tomism – and this no matter how well-intentioned or how interestingly presented. If you think I'm jaundiced, try it out on the forty-hour-a-week folk, or even the unfortunates who are on welfare.

Farmers, not unlike women's lib proponents, are beginning to demand equal pay for equal work – though they'll be much slower in getting it. Like union workers, they want leisure time for the ingestion of something for the mind; and, if the sons and daughters of farmers aren't to add to the numbers of unemployed roaming city streets, then farming must become something more than a subsistence way of life.

Mrs. N. Peterson
Mayerthorpe, Alberta

January 25, 1972
Dear Peter:
Your recent glimpse into the deliberate pioneer life through the eyes of Elizabeth Webster greatly stirred my emotions and also gave me courage to tell you about the path we have recently chosen.

After ten highly successful years in business on the prairies, my husband and I one day shook friends and family alike by announcing our rejection of our safe, suburban, luxurious lifestyle (in an area where one compensates for the dull, cold climate and surroundings by spending far too much on material comforts), and proclaiming an exodus to seek a new, less pressured, more soul-rewarding life.

Within six months we had completely converted an old prairie school bus into a well-equipped motor home, a conversion we worked on tirelessly every night and weekends – and we enjoyed every minute of it. We prepared ourselves to live for an indefinite period of time in Mexico where, we were convinced, the warmth would cure somewhat the chronic allergies our two boys had suffered during their prairie lives. We left in an absolute whirl (to beat a snowstorm), November 1, 1969, with everyone still unbelieving, and convinced that we were "riding to our doom, and utterly mad."

For six blissful, sun and leisure-filled, *timeless* months, we travelled extensively around Mexico. Without a single clue as to what was going on in any world but ours, we ceased to worry or even need to; the children relaxed with us at last, and their health improved terrifically. Shopping at local markets, living amongst the villagers, we learned the secret of the Mexicans' easy laughter and willing smiles, overriding all the problems of food and ill health they experience daily. Colin (our eldest and yes, the same who won your parents and school contest) picked up the language quickly; he was taught by a Mexican child how to dive and swim underwater (he still can't swim on top of the water!); he hacked his way through jungles fearlessly, collecting creatures everywhere, and

September 29, 1972
Dear Peter Gzowski:
You have a lot of very interesting and entertaining things going on, but please stop taking recorder lessons. I keep thinking it is the time signal, and moving my clocks up to one P.M.

Yours sincerely
Robert Weight
Welland, Ontario

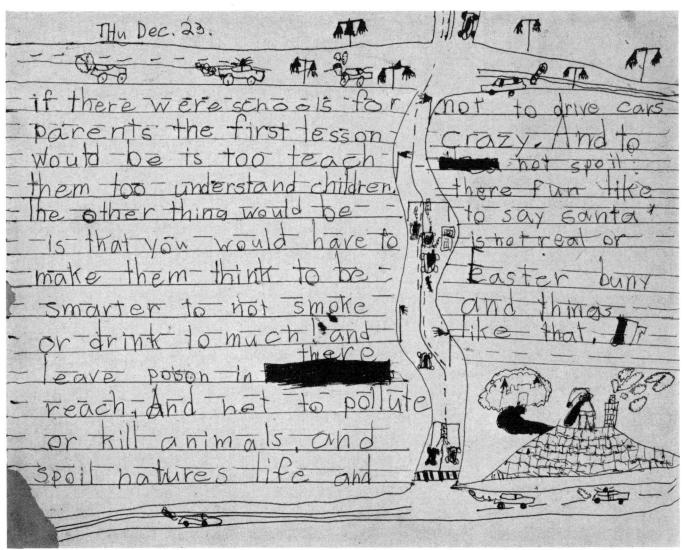

THu Dec. 23.

if there were schools for parents the first lesson would be is too teach them too understand children. The other thing would be is that you would have to make them think to be smarter to not smoke or drink to much! and leave poson in ▇▇▇▇ there reach, And het to pollute or kill animals, and spoil natures life and not to drive cars crazy. And to ▇▇▇ not spoil there fun like to say santa is not real or Easter buny and things like that. Ir

Colin Meacham/Milne's Landing, B.C.

QUIZ

1. After a ragoût de boulettes at La Grange à Seraphin in Montreal with René Lévesque's in-laws, you wish to tell the company that you're full. You should say:
   a) Je suis rassasiée
   b) Je suis pleine
   c) Je suis folle
   d) Je suis remplie

2. Name the family in Hamilton, Ontario, that has used the same snow shovel every winter since 1908.

3. What was being referred to and who wrote this critical remark? "The show's atmosphere is at times aggressively Canadian."

4. List four ways to protect yourself against attack by vampires.

5. Mao is a Chinese word for cat — true or false?

6. Define the following mad words:
   a) madeleine
   b) madrilene
   c) madrigal
   d) madrepore

7. Identify the following phobias, or fears:
   a) ailurophobia
   b) bathophobia
   c) lalophobia
   d) triskaidekaphobia

8. What are the correct nouns of assembly — like a school of fish, a pride of lions, a gaggle of geese — relating to these beasts:
   a) larks
   b) caterpillars
   c) swine
   d) ravens
   e) bass
   f) herons

9. Can you name the following pop singing groups from the synonymous description?
   a) the amorous tidbits
   b the Rorschach blots
   c) two apostles plus one
   d) the serving trays
   e) the fuddle duddle
   f) the coleoptera

10. Instead of straining their imaginations to find more exotic names for their colours, cosmetic manufacturers might try re-cycling a few suggestive, familiar titles. To start with, a home-grown and easy one: Anne of Gables Green. Try these:
   a: How Was My Valley
   b) O'Hara
   c) Blues House
   d) Sidney Street
   e) Ella
   f) Illanimous
   g) Medi
   h) Out dey come

See page 217 for answers

both boys accompanied John fishing for our nightly suppers, or clamming or crabbing. We felt like kings, living off the land.

We continued the school curriculum and struggled to teach the children daily, but with such an engrossing world around us, Dick and Jane seemed pretty distant. As it turned out, Colin's travels were termed his "lapse" when we returned to civilization. . . .

We formed a plan of action at last wherein John, who had been making rings and jewelry to pay for our gas, could perhaps work at what had until then been just a hobby he loved dearly, and we could exist in Canada on lesser means. May I add at this point that, after eleven years of living in Canada, it had all fallen into perspective; we were proud of Canada, homesick for Canadians, and saw it at last as a very admirable land with a fantastic potential, something we could not see when we lived there. At that point we truly became Canadians, returning excitedly to *our* homeland.

The Island was instantly "home" – we bought a house in Victoria and we threw ourselves into our new life with all our healthy strength. John set to work instantly making sterling and gold handcrafted jewelry. It was (and is) hard, precise work, but he loves it. Two months ago we retreated further – we purchased three acres of isolated forest and riverfront with a teeny three-room cottage – our future retirement home.

During our first month we rode crisis after crisis, and even now each day seems to bring some surprising event. We faced bad weather, constant power failures, falling trees (a terrifying experience), an injured and then sick new puppy dog, traumas with the children as they tried to adjust to their new school, plumbing and well-pump problems, river flooding, poachers on the land – just a few of our incredible escapades, which we laugh through and conquer smiling, as they are so constant and unusual and really pretty unimportant.

We have a foot in both worlds. It has become harder and harder to commute to town daily – we take turns, but we now aim eventually to withdraw completely. John can wholesale his crafts at the many outlets on the Island; gradually we hope to be free even of the Hydro and have our own power generator, which John is dying to build. Like a farmer's wife, I now delight in baking for hours, and planning a huge, self-sustaining vegetable garden. The emphasis is now on my home and family, and by home I mean a totally cosy place, with friendly, unmatched accessories and appliances, simpler food – and one day, perhaps, chickens, goats and a pet pig – I hope!

Every day we walk through this ancient forest to the river, ever-changing and full of fish. It is breathtaking, overwhelming. Suddenly we have a challenging goal – it *was* plastic romanticism, I suspect, in our dreams, before we had moved here. Now it's all very real. There is tons of work ahead and we're dying to start the minute the snow retreats. In the meantime, the children help, by carrying logs, clearing and doing odd chores.

If we question our apparent regression (in the eyes of old friends), we find it hard to explain how, in close quarters in the bus and in this house, we became a close-knit family, sharing all our problems and pleasures, hobbies, interests, baking, reading, unhindered by company or outside diversions. I can now face any feminist and say: "I have *done* all that; I *was* free, and exciting, too – to outsiders – I nearly sacrificed my family in that pursuit." Now I find it delightful to be a fellow mate to my husband, both of us sharing and overcoming all the obstacles, to concentrate on existence and survival and not the trivia of the outside world, which can play havoc with marriages when too many people are around and too many things seem to crush in on you daily.

If we can preserve this peace and warmth, the laughter, the crystal-clear air and water, and now and then don our best clothes and have a night on the town, surely we will have found the answer many of the middle-aged thirty-year-olds are seeking. We may have floundered or suffered, but I think we found the answer in travel, observing other lifestyles, other cities, other lands. And two and a half years after our exodus, I believe we've found exactly what we sought.

Thank you for the chance to finally "tell."

Victoria Meacham
Milne's Landing, B.C.

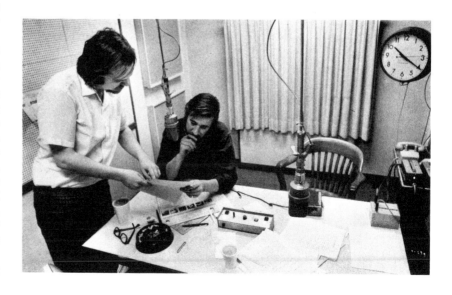

31

Me Tarzan, You Bob

Peter Gzowski . . . Narrator
Danny Finkleman . . . Tarzan
Robert Fulford . . . Jane

is for Canadiana,
Does anyone need
an old player piana?

Marie Greeniaus
Beaconsfield, Quebec

Finkleman: "I am still a wild beast at heart,"
Gzowski: he said, in a low voice, as though to himself. Again they were silent for a time.
Finkleman: "Jane,"
Gzowski: said the man, at length,
Finkleman: "if you were free, would you marry me?"
Gzowski: She did not reply at once, but he waited patiently. The girl was trying to collect her thoughts. What did she know of this strange creature at her side? What did he know of himself? Who was he? Who his parents?

Why, his very name echoed his mysterious origin and his savage life.

He had no name. Could she be happy with this jungle waif?

Could she find anything in common with a husband whose life had been spent in the tree tops of an African wilderness, frolicking and fighting with fierce anthropoids; tearing his food from the quivering flank of fresh-killed prey, sinking his strong teeth into raw flesh, and tearing away his portion while his mates growled and fought about him for their share?

Could he ever rise to her social sphere? Could she bear to think of sinking into his? Would either be happy in such a horrible misalliance?
Finkleman: "You do not answer,"

Gzowski: he said.
Finkleman: "Do you shrink from wounding me?"
Fulford: "I do not know what answer to make,"
Gzowski: said Jane sadly.
Fulford: "I do not know my own mind."
Finkleman: "You do not love me, then?"
Gzowski: he asked, in a level tone.
Fulford: "Do not ask me. You will be happier without me. You were never meant for the formal restrictions and conventionalities of society—civilization would become irksome to you, and in a little while you would long for the freedom of your old life—a life to which I am as totally unfitted as you to mine."
Finkleman: "I think I understand you,"
Gzowski: he replied quietly.
Finkleman: "I shall not urge you, for I would rather see you happy than be happy myself. I see now that you could not be happy with—an ape."
Gzowski: There was just the faintest tinge of bitterness in his voice.
Fulford: "Don't,"
Gzowski: she remonstrated.
Fulford: "Don't say that. You do not understand."

(end)

October, 1970

A year after it all happened, I am surprised at what has stuck in my mind and what has not. I do not, for example, remember exactly how it all began. A British diplomat, a trade commissioner whose name I had not heard before but now, of course, will never forget, had been kidnapped. In a curious way, that seemed more comic than tragic. A diplomat kidnapped in *Canada*? That's kind of nice, isn't it? It was as if we could take pride in having enough conflict in our normally dull country to inspire a real live drama. But surely it would all be over soon. After all, hadn't there been rumours about a plot to kidnap an Israeli diplomat in Montreal just a couple of weeks before? And there, surely, someone was kidding.

No, as it turned out, no one was kidding. Gradually, into our comprehension of the fact that one man — by now, a man with a name, James Cross — had been taken from his family, was being held somewhere, was, perhaps, injured or even dead — into that comprehension seeped also the knowledge that these people, these separatists, these *terrorists*, *had* set off bombs, *had* held up banks, *had* tried, however incredible it might seem to the rest of us, to ally themselves with a world-wide movement of violent revolution. And the joke remained a joke no longer.

That understanding, as I say, dawned slowly, and it is impossible, looking back now, to remember precisely when any of us understood precisely what. In any person's life, only a few moments of *public* history implant themselves in such a way that we carry forever the memory of just how we heard about them. For myself, I can remember riding my bicycle home from school on V-E Day as clearly as if it were last week. I can tell you the name of the boy who not long before that day had told me that Roosevelt was dead, and how he told me, and when. I remember the evening my oldest son came in from the television room to say that Martin Luther King had been killed — and I doubt if there is anyone who cannot recount in perfect detail the way he or she first heard that Jack Kennedy had been shot. It is, I'd suggest, no coincidence that nearly all those events of modern history are in fact events in the modern history of the United States. The U.S., we had been led to believe, was the place where such wrenches of political sanity took place. In Canada, we were spectators, moved, perhaps, and shaken, but spectators all the same. Even the Second World War, which we'd been fighting for more than two years before the U.S. was

drawn in, had somehow, for those of us not *directly* involved, become Americanized. The movies, the songs, the propaganda — American. V-E Day? In public terms — and I thank God I am not among those for whom that war involved personal loss — in public terms, there was nothing especially Canadian about it; we simply happened to be part of the Allies.

And then, there it was, a year ago this month, a public event that would become an indelible and terrible Canadian memory. Tomorrow, October 16, is the anniversary of the implementation of the War Measures Act. That day was surely one of the most significant political occasions of our time, and yet I wonder if, even now, all of us realize precisely what it meant. In practice, the action taken that day may well have been effective; there is some reason to believe that separatism, revolutionary separatism, is weaker in French Canada now than it was a year ago; that a repressive act, in other words, repressed. And if Gallup polls are really any guide to what all Canadians thought, then eighty-three percent of us — French *and* English — thought the War Measures Act was a good idea.

But if it is possible to talk about "some evidence" of a weakening movement, it is also possible to speculate that many people who had preached moderation were driven to consider immoderate means. Whatever it *seemed* to accomplish, the War Measures Act is still an awesome piece of legislation. Our government, acting in our name, arrested and incarcerated people not for what they had done and been convicted of, but for what the government thought they *might intend* to do. Before the events of last October had worked themselves out, more than four hundred people had been taken from their homes and put into jail, with no right to a trial, no right, for the moment at least, even to see a lawyer.

So the other side of a complex argument is simply that the law, as we understand it, is intended to be above men's judgement of what is wrong and what is right, and one interpretation of legislation such as the War Measures Act is that it says, "Okay, government, whatever you say — the usual rule of law is suspended." Can you imagine, for instance, what the editorials in the press of Canada — again, in French as well as English — would be like if the government of the United States were to give J. Edgar Hoover untrammelled rights to jail people he thought *might* do something dangerous in the future? Oh, how holy we can get about other people's transgressions. But when we move from the third row in the spectators' stand to centre ice, oh, how our attitudes change.

On that Friday evening a year ago, of

course, none of those theories were clear to me. Then, I was still trying to cope with the knowledge that eleven days previously it would have been difficult, if not impossible, to consider that people would actually kidnap a total stranger for what they took to be political ends. So that while I was able to deplore the implementation of the act — to me it seemed a monumental overreaction — I was still willing to grant the government the benefit of my doubts. Pierre Trudeau might just know something I didn't know.

In the aftermath, of course, the implementation of the act has been proven unwarranted. There was, it is clear now, no state of "apprehended insurrection" in Quebec; a sad, sorry group of misguided, frustrated, disturbed people had committed a crime of cruelty and stupidity. That much, I think, is clear from the evidence. On October 16, 1970, we did not have that evidence; we were a confused and shaken nation, and we needed shoring up. But a year later, even such tough guys of the time as Jerome Choquette, Quebec's minister of Justice, have questioned the wisdom of implementing that act, and now, on its anniversary, I find it sad that our Parliament has not yet examined the idea of taking it off the books, and replacing it with something that would still protect the rights of individuals in times of national crisis. Still, as deeply as I feel about that act, the memory of last October that has stuck with me most strongly is more personal.

We were playing bridge. My wife and I and two cherished friends. It was late on Saturday evening of that weekend, and the radio was playing softly in the background. The announcements came in bursts, at first confused, rumours, hints, confirmed, contradicted, reaffirmed . . . and finally, correct and indisputable. Pierre Laporte, a man I had met but once and really wouldn't recognize on sight, but a man . . . had been murdered. However one might sympathize with the cause of Quebec independence, whatever one might think of its ultimate goals, nothing, nothing could justify that. We stopped playing bridge. Our world, our country had changed. What had begun as a joke had become an obscenity. I thought that evening of Pierre Trudeau, a man so easy to condemn for those of us who thought that act was wrong, and yet alone that ugly night with his own thoughts. He had behaved as he believed right, and how easy it was then, and how much easier now, for those of us who believed him wrong to criticize him. But Pierre Laporte was a friend of his.

I have said before that if you had to boil down my love of this country to one word, that word would be "hope" — hope for the future, hope that we can work things out here. Neither the murder of Pierre Laporte nor the fact that we lived through a time in our lives when four out of every five Canadians thought civil liberties should be suspended — neither of those things can blunt that hope. But it is tempered, tempered by the fire of last October. This week we have been and this weekend we will be again, inundated with media re-hashes of all those events. Through it all I, as one Canadian, will remember the moment I heard Pierre Laporte was dead.

October 15, 1971

I Resign

One of the most successful contests we ever ran was called "Letters of Resignation." People were simply asked to resign from whatever they wanted. And they did. From their jobs (hypothetically — I hope), their spouses, their kids, their houses, moustaches, pipes, lawns, putters, weight, diets . . . anything they wanted to. A lot of their entries are scattered through these pages. Some of them are silly, some of them quite sharp. But there were other kinds of entries, too. Like this one:

Dear God:
I herewith respectfully submit my resignation. From what, you may ask? From all political systems which make persons into numbers. From all ideologies which make persons cannon fodder. From all churches and religious organizations which think they have a corner on the market in truth. From all committees which purport to do good but exist only to keep on existing. From all competition whatsoever in any field.

Therefore, Lord, I resign from all political systems, all social systems, all ideologies, all churches and religious organizations, all committees, and all competition. I resign from all relationships which make people less than you made them.

This will leave me with most of my time empty. So what will I resign into? What will I sign up for? I will support with my whole being all relationships which make persons more personal, humans more human, love more loving, cooperation more cooperative, joy more joyful, hope more hopeful, and people more divine. I will do this with more "being" and less "doing," more presence and less pretence, more harmony and no discord.

In short, Lord, I resign from death and opt for life.

Wish me luck, Lord. I'll need it.

Father Douglas Skoyles
Calgary, Alberta

A Butterfly Kite

supplies
3 sticks the same length (two sticks that bend easily; the third can be rigid)
a large sheet of paper suitable for covering your kite
string
glue
pencil
scissors

1. Make two bows with the sticks that bend, and string. Overlap the two bows to make a butterfly shape that is wider at the top than at the bottom. Bind the sticks with string where they touch.

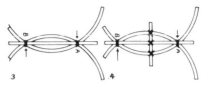

4. Push the shorter piece of stick between the centre stick and the bows.

5. Cover the framework with a large sheet of paper. Put glue along the length of both bows. Lay your sheet of paper flat on a surface. Turn the kite frame sticky side down on to the paper. Cut away all of the excess paper around the frame leaving an inch of border. Now fold the border over to the back of the kite frame and glue it down.

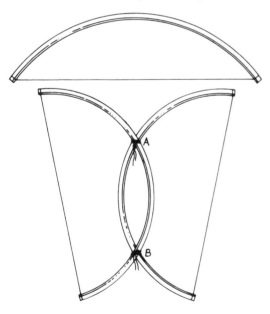

2. Divide the third stick into 3 equal sections. Break off one section.

3. Now the longer piece of stick that is left over is laid up the centre of the butterfly shape. Bind the sticks together where they touch.

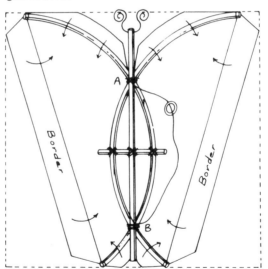

Bridle. The bridle is a piece of string slightly longer than the stick up the centre. Tie the string to points A and B. Let a curtain ring slide freely along the string as in the diagram. Your kite line will be attached to this ring.

Tail. A tail for this kite can be made with 3 lengths of party streamers 3 times the length of the centre stick. Attach the tail to the bottom end of the kite with string. A tail made of the same material as the covering gives best results. A tail is used to stabilize the kite in the air.

Decoration. Make an antenna for the butterfly with a length of copper wire.

Dumb Political Statements

The contest we ran to find the dumbest — real — political statement a Canadian politician had ever made, was a difficult one. I think it was hard for a couple of reasons: first, because there was such an overwhelming wealth of material that people just couldn't choose; and second, because I asked that entrants document their submissions, which meant doing a lot of homework. Our entrants ranged geographically from the west coast to Newfoundland, and our entries ranged in history from Jacques Cartier — he was a Canadian politician? — to some things said the previous week in provincial campaigns in Ontario and Quebec. Some people slightly missed the point by sending in things that made them angry — statements about old-age pensions, for example, which I took to be more cruel than dumb, or about issues with which they simply disagreed. It would do a great many politicians good, however — in particular, eastern politicians — to look over the volume of entries that centred around the sale of wheat. I think they're all summed up by this letter from Paddy Ryan, who lives on Osler Street in Regina:

"Dear Mr. O'Zosky," writes Paddy, "I would like to enter your contest and submit some of the statements I have collected in the last couple of weeks, but unfortunately my finances do not permit it. Unless, or until, we get our wheat-storage payments from the federal government, I simply cannot afford to pay the freight from Regina to Toronto on two box-cars filled with single-spaced, type-written pages."

The single statement that drew the largest amount of obviously very seriously intended mail was General de Gaulle's cry of "Vive le Québec libre." Again, of course, these submissions were disqualified on the ground of the late general's citizenship. But I think it was significant how many people singled him out, people from all over the country. Although, as I said, some entrants dug into history. Mrs. Alice M. Grant of Moncton, N.B., looked up the April 1872 issue of the *Canadian Monthly* and found this from Goldwyn Smith: "But in this country what is there for the conservatives to conserve or for reformers to reform . . . ?" Politicians of today, from Trudeau to Benson to Real Caouette, got shafted most frequently. Phil Gaglardi was a common goat, too. Doug Wilson of Ottawa submitted this Gaglardi-ism, for instance, quoted in his local paper on August 4: "People shouldn't get excited about reports of pollution of the oceans. Everybody knows that oil and water don't mix."

I think this statement, submitted by William Lee, *would* have been the winner, but Mr. Lee didn't document it well enough. He simply quoted an unnamed politician, in a dialogue on CBC radio, as saying during a debate over Pollution Probe: "There are more important things than survival." I *believe* you, Bill, but I'd at least have to have that politician's name, if not his head.

A lot of entries dealt with local issues, one of which I thought showed up a certain kind of civil servant's, if not a politician's attitude of mind. This letter was from Peter J. McAteer, of Toronto:

The dumbest political statement that I can remember was made a few years ago at a time when there had been several accidents on the Don Valley Parkway. Cars were slamming directly into the cement lamp standards, as there were no guardrails protecting the motorist from the cement poles.

Al Boliska had a local television program at that time and he was interviewing the Metro roads commissioner at the scene of such an accident, where one of the cement poles had crushed and killed a motorist. Morton Shulman had suggested that aluminum poles be used in lieu of cement standards, and Al Boliska asked the roads commissioner the question, "Why

Drunk says to bartender: "Do lemons have legs?"
Bartender: "Certainly not!"
Drunk: "Well, then, I think I just squeezed your canary into my drink."

George Burt
Mississauga, Ontario

couldn't aluminum poles be used so that, when a car collides with a pole, the aluminum would bounce instead of crushing the roof and killing the occupants?" The roads commissioner's answer was, "If we used aluminum poles and the accident rate remained constant, we would have aluminum poles lying all over the parkway."

Although a lot of famous politicians got multiple entries, there were three separate and different statements submitted on behalf of one Ottawa alderman, who was a candidate in the 1971 Ontario provincial election. The alderman's name is Rudy Capogreco, and he was running as a Liberal in Ottawa Centre. Chris Scott of that city sent in two of them. In response to a question quite early in his campaign, Mr. Capogreco said: "Yes, we do have a committee room somewhere but they haven't told me where it is." Later, at an all-candidates' meeting in a school, he said he wasn't sure what his party's platform was. "I'm sure there's something for everyone," he said, "though I haven't read all the books they've sent me yet. I've only read the titles." Mr. C.J. McKerral of Henderson was at another all-candidates' meeting where Mr. Capogreco was asked about abortion. "Well," he said, "if you need it, that's okay. If you don't need it, that's okay, too." I'll declare

Chris Scott and Mr. McKerral runners up. Mr. Capogreco, incidentally, ran third in a three-man race, but he got 6381 votes – with 177 of 185 polls heard from – to the winning Conservative's 7704.

All right, now for the winner. There were several in this category – triumphs of style over content – but I just thought this was the best, and I am sending a copy of *The Revolution Script*, by Brian Moore, the current novel that I think has the most things to say about our country, to Colin W. Griffiths, who is administrator and secretary-treasurer of the Metropolitan General Hospital in Windsor, Ontario. His politician is the Honourable Paul Martin, and Martin's statement, which was made when he was a candidate for the Liberal leadership, is adequately documented. It reads as follows:

> I wouldn't be seeking the leadership of the Liberal party if I didn't feel strongly that I could not in all conscience not feel that I was taking objection to the meaning of my public life if I didn't feel that in view of the emphasis I place on what is the important question that I have the right, that I would have the right, not to meet it.

There's something especially Canadian about that.

Donny Osmond's Birthday

I have a note here from my daughter. We don't usually communicate by notes in our family, but last night my wife and I were out and Alison, who is twelve, left me this urgent message:

> Dear Dad: Since today is Donny Osmond's birthday and CHUM [a Top 40 station in Toronto] won't mention it . . . could you mention it on the air? Love, etc.

Well, no honey, I won't. For one thing, you're in school now, and so, I hope, is Donny Osmond, who has a lot to learn, too. And I won't play any of his music – not today, anyway – because I happen to think he is an atrocious musician, and an objectionably bad performer. And . . . well, good for me, right? That's setting the old standards.

And then I began to think, no . . . wrong. What I'm saying about Donny Osmond is

exactly what my parents were saying twenty-five years ago – to me – about Johnny Rae and Frankie Lane and Elvis Presley. And the fact that I happen to be right – Elvis Presley *was* great – and Alison and her friends happen to be wrong – Donny Osmond *is* lousy – is probably no more of a fact than the one *my* parents were trying to implant in me: that Cab Calloway was a musical genius and the Four Lads were over their heads in the St. Michaels' school choir. I mean, look at the way so many people responded when we had those musical recollections of the 1950s last week. However good (or rotten) that music was, it was *ours*, and in many ways it still is; it's still a part of us – either that or there are an awful lot of lying letter-writers out there.

So, gritting my teeth, I'll say it: Happy Birthday, Donny Osmond, wherever you are. May you bring as much pleasure to others with your crumby new bubblegum music as the music of my early teens brought to me and my gang.
                    Begrudgingly, Peter Gzowski.

December 9, 1972

Grandparents

Grandparents smell – usually nicely of lavender or violets, but occasionally just of age. They remind people of smells, too, of the smell of fudge bubbling, of cakes baking, of old English rose gardens, or the woods of the northern fall. Of pipe tobacco and rainy Sunday afternoons.

That was one of the things – or at least the recollection of it and the strength of that recollection – that surprised me about the entries in this contest, the winner and runners-up of which I am about to announce. The contest, you will remember, was simply to define the word grandparent. Not everybody followed my stricture about writing in dictionary-ese, but what the hell, as my own grandfather used to say. These contests are, after all, an attempt to have fun and to find out something, not necessarily to obey a set of formal rules.

One of the things we found out, and, as I said, it surprised me, was the *sensuality* of people's perceptions of grandparents. Smell was far from the only sense that dominated definitions. People remembered the shapes of rooms, the colours of quilts, the feel of velvet, the clatter of tea-cups, the tickle of moustaches or the taste of cookies. It was as if all the memories were felt instead of thought out, sensed more strongly than anyone could analyze. When there was anguish over, for example, separation by geography, that anguish almost seemed to be felt more strongly than separation by death. And when there was love, it was poured out in a way I have very seldom read. A lot of people wrote about spoiling. Grandparents wrote about the delights of spoiling; parents wrote about the threats of having their parents getting all the pleasures of even very young babies – as Trisha Koff wrote from Salt Spring Island, B.C.: grandparents are special creatures with small wrinkles, silvered hair, big hearts, wide-open arms; they have patience, wisdom, laughter, innocence and lots of kisses and love, but they don't like changing dirty diapers – and children wrote about how much they liked being spoiled. Almost everybody who addressed this theme revelled in it, the great North American generational double standard: you can do unto your children's children everything you were afraid to do unto your own. As Quita Walters of Victoria put it: a grandparent is one who is a sucker for the angelic children of one's own brats.

Not everyone, however, was corny. Roughly one out of every ten entries, as nearly as I can figure, was either bitter or sardonic. Under sardonic, for example, this entry from a small town near Brampton, Ontario:

Grandparents: Noun, plural. A married couple who, having worked and worried for a quarter-century, are expected to exist in a state of suspended animation, with no life of their own, ready to welcome their descendants at short notice, or none at all, to their comfortable "crash pad."

Or this, from Mrs. H.E. Rogers, of Erin, Ontario:

Grandparent: (n.) a term used by the advertising industry to persuade mature persons that they are now two generations removed from childhood. Having created feelings of distance and separation in the grandparent, advertisements then encourage him to bridge the generation gap by buying (for example) complicated toys, long-distance phone calls and Coke.

And under bitter, this, unsigned and with no return address:

Definition of Grandparent: That lonely old soul that sits on the park bench day after day with that nostalgic look in his eyes. The decrepit old wino you passed on Yonge Street – looking wretched and lonely. The elderly couple living in that dilapidated old rooming house, trying to pay rent, keep warm and eat on their meager pensions. That huddled, dirty-looking body sleeping on the street with only newspapers for his blanket. Do you think he has no family? That little old lady at the old people's home who sits in her room day after day, waiting for that newsy letter from home, that visit from her friends, that invitation to visit her relatives; none of which comes.

Now, for some winners, all of whom will get a handful of McClelland and Stewart books. The first prize of the morning goes to Patricia Murphy of Halifax for having a grandparent I would like to have known. Patricia wrote:

What is a Grandmother?
A grandmother is someone with white hair and dainty, wrinkled hands, who smells of lavender – only my Granny rinsed her hair with henna, had talon-like fingernails painted blood-red, and smelled of strong tobacco.
A grandmother is someone who dresses all in black or in pale Liberty prints – only my Granny alternated between blue jeans and bold-patterned dresses topped with chunky plastic jewelry in fluorescent colours.
A grandmother is someone who spends her time knitting sweaters and making soup – only my Granny spent her time building her own house and going fishing.

A grandmother is someone who takes children for special outings to the zoo or the museum – only my Granny took us to drive-in movies to see *Diabolique* and to the penny arcade to play the pinball machines.

A grandmother is someone who loves to tell stories, filled with fairy princesses and wicked ogres – only my Granny's stories came from her favourite magazines, *True Crime* and *Real Detective*.

A grandmother is someone who likes to remember how different things were when she was young, with horses instead of cars and long skirts for even little girls – only my Granny remembered how they used to make bathtub gin and go dancing in the speakeasies.

A grandmother is someone who has firm ideas on how young ladies should behave, like crossing legs at the ankles, never shouting, and always wearing a hat to go downtown – only my Granny insisted that girls should be as good as boys at everything, even if it meant beating up my boy cousin.

A grandmother is someone who teaches children how to make cookies and play Old Maid – only my Granny taught us how to roll cigarettes and play Black Jack and Twenty-one.

A grandmother is someone with old-fashioned views on raising children, like eating oatmeal and bread pudding and going to bed early – only my Granny fed us on fried chicken and Coke, and encouraged us to stay up watching horror movies with her until three in the morning (so we'd *all* sleep late in the morning).

No, Granny wouldn't fit most people's definition of a grandmother, unless the definer were a social scientist – for she was a perfect example of the elder partner in an "alternate-generation affinity relationship."

Naughtiness, incidentally, was something a lot of people enjoyed about their own grandparents. Take our next winner, Doreen Wilson, from Burlington, Ontario:

Grandparents stuff you with cake and pop.

They buy you a red balloon and if it breaks they buy you another. They argue over whose nose you've got, his or hers.

They like your pet snake and don't scream at it like your mother does. But they still won't let it sleep in your bed. But they think it might be fun to put it in your parents' bed.

They can lie even better than you can. They buy you a chocolate milkshake before dinner and then say they didn't and the reason you aren't eating dinner is because you're likely "coming down with that bug that's going round."

They tell everyone that you sing better than Anne Murray or Gordie Lightfoot.

You learn some things from grandfathers and other things from grandmothers.

Grandfathers light matches on the seat of their pants. They keep *Playboy* under the bed and say "don't tell the old lady." They teach you new swear words when they're looking for their glasses. They say man's greatest achievement is the miniskirt. They tell stories about the time they worked in the mines and helped lay track for the CPR and made gin in the bathtub. They call your father "a damn fool" when you let slip that he lost fifty bucks at the races and you and him go to the track and he loses *one hundred dollars* and he nicks your thumb and his a bit with an old jack-knife, and you let the blood mingle and you *swear* that you'll never breathe a word of it to a living soul or God will strike you dead and boy, you *believe it*.

Grandmothers teach you other things. They *never* make you eat burnt cookies like your mother does or tell you that the burnt bit puts hair on your chest. Grandmothers win lots of bingo prizes. They tell you you're the spittin' image of a favourite brother who was drowned fishing and then get real mad at grandfather who said "he drowned cause he was too drunk to swim and even if he'd made it to shore the RCMP were waitin' to pick him up." Grandmothers put their arms around people and hug them. *Even cats.* They are the only ones I ever saw kiss an old cat. Grandmothers believe that storks bring babies. That's because in the olden days they didn't get sex education at school. If you even *say* the word sex their faces turn purple as a plum. When you try to tell them about eggs and sperms they run into the kitchen and start banging the pots and pans around and say they have to bake a pie and what's the world coming to and you wonder why they believe that old stork story when it doesn't make half as much sense as eggs and sperms.

Grandmothers tell you stories about your mother when she was little. Like the time she poured a bottle of wine down the sink at Christmas time and the time she gave Uncle John the measles and the time she painted one of the ducks with green house paint and after a while your mother begins to seem almost like a real human being.

Both grandparents and kids are always

"getting the heck" from parents so they learn to stick together. No one in the whole world keeps secrets better than grandparents.

Mrs. Ralph Beadle of Thunder Bay is a grandmother of seven children and of an independent turn of mind. Hers may have been the most liberated — if that word is not being overworked these days — entry we got:

I am a completely selfish grandmother. I believe grandchildren were made to be enjoyed. Any notion of being a power of inspiration in their lives is Rubbish. I don't want to be remembered for a bulging cookie jar. Let them make their own cookies. I don't like the ideas that any grandmother with a grandchild boy or girl over six years old whose cooky jar is not filled with lumpy hand-made cookies in summer holidays is a rotten failure. I expect on the other hand to be remembered long for the time I put the ladders up to the house and took four grandchildren up to the peak where we nested around the chimney exploring the great advantage of observing from a distance at a height.

My own grandmother projected a picture of great confidence; in her presence I felt myself a person of great worth. Not because she did things for me but because she so obviously thought no one had to do things for me. In her independent and sometimes salty way she let us know that although she loved us dearly her world would turn quite nicely in our absence. I hope to pass on to my grandchildren the great freedom this knowledge gave me.

As we approached retirement we bought a piece of wilderness property to bring us full circle back to our beginnings. Between the ages of five and fifteen we expect to see a great deal of them from time to time. We hope and indeed have begun to create an oasis of non-pressure where it is fully recognized that a full fridge and a hollow kid have a beautiful relationship which rules on eating between meals can destroy and where almost anything but persistent bad manners earns less than a lifted eyebrow. My grandchildren are enchanting. Our conversations are filled with chatty wisdom. That they delight me is quite apparent to them; that I delight them makes us equal.

I have not made my grandchildren of prime importance in my life. I love music, poetry, gardening, bird-watching; they are part of the delight of living. I have said to them what my grandmother said to me: "I

don't intend to worry about you. You will do what you have to. If you don't do it *till* you have to, it will slow you up but not destroy you."

I am going to give a prize as well to Mary Maika of Hillsboro, New Brunswick; I think this letter speaks for itself:

I was about eighteen when I became a grandmother. It happened in a boarding school in Poland and after thirty years the girls who gave me that affectionate nickname still call me that and so do their children. Obviously to be a grandma there is a quality that has nothing to do with age. Why did I get that nickname?

It was a sad time of the war. A small private boarding school for girls was trying to instill some education into minds shocked by the experiences, not always understanding the good of education any longer.

Most of us had lost homes, loved ones. During the day the activities of the school kept us busy. But ten o'clock was lights out and the darkness brought back the fears, the memories. It was during these dark hours that I could spin my stories of beauty and enchantment of faraway imaginary places. Fairy tales of lands that never knew poverty and misery and everybody was kind and loving. Stories shared soon crossed from bed to bed like a warm blanket that enfolded us like a peaceful sleep.

Today my own teenage boys have stopped thinking of me as their mother. To them I am a friend, a special person to have fun with and to do a thousand crazy, nutty things.

Maybe I never matured the proper way. Someday I might become a real grandmother and discover what it's all about.

As well as to this entry from Patricia Ferman, of North Vancouver:

Grandparent: verb (from the old Russian, Yiddish, Hungarian, *et al.*). To communicate in quiet desperation by means of soft murmurings, gentle kisses, stroking of cheeks, etc., with children who understand not a word of your language and who could not conceive of your previous life if they did.

And as I thank everyone who entered, and as usual express my wish that everyone who did so could have won, I think I will move that last entry into a tie for first place, and large handfuls of paperbacks will go to Patricia Ferman and to our other grand-prize winner, who is Susan MacLean of Annapolis Royal, Nova Scotia, and who wrote this simple paragraph that perhaps tells it all:

Grandmother. She lies in the old brass bed day after day with her large old quilt pulled up around her. There's a pee-pot on the hardwood floor beside her bed. Grandmother smiles as she tells you stories of her childhood days and the fun she had.

Like the dying fire in her old stone fireplace that was once roaring and flashing with colour, Grandmother will go.

Karen's Diary 1

My first visit to the doctor. . . . We talked about a lot of things. I'm due the eighteenth of November. Nothing seems any different inside.

My husband has gotten very conscious of driving me over bumpy things or not letting me do any heavy work, even yard work that I'm used to doing. He got upset when he caught me using the lawnmower, which is very easy. It's pretty funny.

A woman at work has started calling me fatso. I guess I'm beginning to look a little chubby, although the baby doesn't show yet. I can laugh about it now.

If one more person starts in on the glory of being pregnant, I think I'll scream! Maybe it was the best time in their lives, maybe those nine months were so wonderful, so marvelous, but I don't want to hear about it any more.

I think of the abortion I had a long time ago. . . . I'm thankful that I was cared for and everything was fine afterwards. Being pregnant this time is so different, but I think about that abortion. . . .

I'm going to send home for the English edition of *Mother Goose* that my grandfather read to me when I was little. I'd really like the baby to have it.

My husband is so lovely to me, just so good. He's agreed to go to natural-childbirth classes with me. I didn't talk him into it or anything. He hasn't decided whether or not he wants to go into the delivery room, but I think I'd really like him to be in the labour room. I think it will help me to have him there, even just to talk to me.

I'm Scandinavian and people keep telling me that I must teach the child my own language as well as English. I hadn't thought about it much but it seems to me that it might be awfully confusing to a young child . . . I suppose not. It would be good to know both.

We haven't had many big arguments about naming the child. If it's a girl, and I really hope it is, she's going to be called Birgitta, which is one of my names, and probably Gitta for short. If it's a boy he's going to be called either Christian Charles or Charles Christian, both family names.

We went out and had a lovely dinner tonight, but on our way out of the restaurant my back was so sore and suddenly I felt so sick! Nothing happened but I felt awful. I think that I'm getting nauseated more and more lately. . . . I guess it's just normal. I seem to get evening sickness; I'm just fine in the mornings.

I seem to be getting cravings for some kinds of food, mostly anything spicy, and that's not too good. But most of all I crave a dish we had at home — buttermilk, lemon and eggs with black bread crumbled into it. I make huge bowlsful and finish it off in no time.

For the first time in my life I have a temper . . . and I seem to lose it a lot. I catch myself giving people hell over absolutely nothing. It's not like me.

I've been looking through the chapter on giving birth in my little book on pregnancy. I've already been through it twice and I guess I'll probably go through it at least another fifty times before I give birth myself. It seems like a miracle, and it's so far away.

The Great Canadian Novel #1

After Lister Sinclair and Robert Fulford talked on the air one morning about whether there already was, or whether there ever would be, or whether it even mattered to anyone if there was such a thing as "The Great Canadian Novel," I challenged our listeners to write plot outlines for what they thought such a work might contain. As with the letters of resignation, several of their entries appear elsewhere in this book, and as with most of our contests, I had the devil's own time choosing one single winner. In the end, though, I could not resist this:

A utopian, bilingual, journal of 2072 A.D.
Cast of characters:
Laura Secord "Candy" Trudeau, daughter of Harry S. Trudeau, president of the independent republic of Ontario.
Harry S. Trudeau, originator of one-party, one-level government run by an enormous computer which takes up all of the Experimental Farm in Ottawa; famous for the immortal slogans, "The Buck Starts Here," and "If you can't stand the heat, go out and buy an air conditioner."
Hippolyte Xavier Rabinovitch, a ski instructor and Gaspésian of mixed ancestry, who falls in love with "Candy" Trudeau, and is seduced by
Leonora MacDougall McTavish, a graduate of Miss Edgar and Miss Cramp's School for Young Ladies and a resident of Citadel Westmount.
Jesus Maria Petitbois, chief mogul of Newfoundland, who conspires with the Confederacy of the Maritimes to convert Newfoundland "screech" into rocket fuel at an abandoned Nova Scotia heavy-water plant using Russian capital and technical advisers, thus provoking an invasion by U.S. Marines.
Stompin' Tom Susuki, ardent fiddler and leader of an underground movement dedicated to the secession of Bennettania (formerly British Columbia) from the American union which it joined in 1984.
John George Schleswig-Holstein, leader of the Federated Prairies and chief architect of the Great West Wall erected along the 49th parallel between the eastern border of Bennettania and the western border of Ontario. This wall is permeable by money, gas, oil, water, but not people. His support of the Saskatchewan farmers' right to grow wheat causes the final rupture with Ontario and the creation of the new prairie republic in 1995.
Melody "Mel" Watkins, first female Finance minister in the western hemisphere, who nationalizes poverty in the prairies, making it a criminal offence to own more than $50,000 in any form or to earn less than $15,000. Since this puts the vast majority of citizens behind bars, her tenure is lamentably short-lived.
Mary Juanita LeDain, known as "Potty" because she directs the production and distribution of free pot on demand from Temporary Building #9999 in Ottawa. The grass, widely advertised as LeDain's Finest, keeps the citizenry in a euphoric state of political apathy.
Smiling Jack Armstrong, the all-Ontario boy; chief promoter of The Final Solution, a code-named secret project to cover up Lake Erie, now merely a large cesspool, with high-density polythene. This provides thousands of jobs as maintenance men for unemployed Ontario municipal and provincial politicans (all replaced by Trudeau's computer) but the contract (and profits thereof) goes to an American chemical company and the giant manhole cover is eventually sold to General Motors who use it as a test track for new vehicles.
Archbishop Pierre Vallières, dictator of Laurentia (formerly Quebec), one-time revolutionary socialist and atheist, who runs a police state second to none with American foreign aid and French cultural supervision.
Minor characters, unnamed:
The Drapeau Militia, only hereditary police force in the world; largely employed in enforcing the 8:00 P.M. curfew and checking identity cards.
The Gophers, members of the prairie underground.
Sundry border guards of the balkanized states.
The affluent poor, nominally living well but actually owning nothing.
The dirt poor, especially prominent in the Maritime Confederacy and Laurentia.
Assorted wheelers and dealers.
Various disaffected students.
Former employees of the now-defunct CBC.

Candy meets Hippolyte on a Bennettania ski slope and they decide to flee from North America on a freighter out of Vancouver but are foiled by a biweekly dock strike. Since the U.S., now ruled dictatorially by Bullwhip Wallace and his Sacred Heritage Party, is still fighting a civil war and since using public transport would lead to recognition and detection, they resolve to slog their way across what used to be Canada and hope to smuggle themselves aboard ship in Halifax. Their many adventures along the way are recorded in journal form, bilingually, and involve directly (or indirectly, by hearsay) all of the aforementioned characters. They cross the Rockies on skis, Alberta on horseback, Saskatchewan on snowshoes. They build a Red River cart in Manitoba and steal a canoe from an

Indian in northern Ontario. Disguised and equipped with false identification cards provided by the Ontario underground, they travel by superturbo train through the Toronto suburbs (which now take up most of the southern half of Ontario). Arriving at the border of Laurentia, which is mined and barbwired, they sneak across at night, guided by a Farley Mowat waterdog, specially trained for subversive activities, and manage to penetrate the outer defences of Citadel Westmount. Here Hippy gets involved with the high-class crumpet Leonora and by a series of misadventures ends up in Bordeaux jail, from which he escapes by offering to flood a skating rink (in mid-June). Candy is deported as an undesirable alien and promptly picked up by the Ontario secret police (a sinister remnant of the RCMP) and sent home to her outraged father. As usual, he has the last word about this ill-fated romance: "The bedroom has no place in the affairs of the nation." (Hippy's fate is obscure, but it is rumoured that he went back to the Gaspé and took up woodcarving.)

Critical comments:
"Typically Canadian in that it virtually ignores the Maritimes and Newfoundland, except for the brief appearance of that outrageously unCanadian figure, J.M. Petitbois, and an irrelevant subplot centred in Nova Scotia which does not impinge directly on the central characters. A publisher's nightmare."
– Otis Carp, Halifax *Chronicle-Herald*

"The panoramic sweep of this major novel cannot be grasped by the dilettante reader any more readily than *War and Peace* can be assimilated at the first attempt."
– E. Lusive, Ottawa *Journal*

"The subtle symbolism which tells us so much about ourselves has not been surpassed since the heyday of Al Capp."
– Rosalinda Whiteoaks, Hamilton *Spectator*

"C'est dommage que le grand roman Canadien se présent seulement après le déluge."
– C.R., *Le Devoir*

"A prophetic work." – S. Lewis, *New Democrat*

"A monstrous slur on the moral character of our people."
– W.A.C. Bennett, Vancouver *Sun*

"I don't have time to read novels."
– P.E. Trudeau, Ottawa *Citizen*

Mrs. W.B. Muir
Westmount, Quebec

The Woodchuck

It is late afternoon and I am walking in the pasture along the edge of the woods, ankle-deep in fallen leaves. A dying time of year, a dying time of day, I am thinking — a sad time really.

The sky promises snow. A calf has strayed from its mother so we must find it. My husband takes one end of the pasture; I go in the opposite direction.

Gray and black tree trunks stand naked, their modesty only slightly preserved by the green of a spruce or the bronze feathers of a tamarack. The calf shouldn't be hard to find. I stop and listen. Is that him? No, it is not the calf. It is only the dried brown leaves clinging to a sugar maple, rustling in the wind, trying to attract my attention.

"Look at us," they seem to say. "We are still here, remember how glad you were to see our tiny green buds last April?" Yes, I remember. It had been a long winter. You are still beautiful.

A new sound interrupts the silence of our dialogue. It fades, then comes again. Unfamiliar, but still a sound that I have heard before. I look up and far above me the sun, which by now has disappeared below the horizon, reflects its goldness on a flock of wild geese, waving slightly out of line, then with fluidity back again to a perfect V. Talking, talking as they move southward. How do they know? How *do* they know? Yes, it will snow tonight.

It is almost dark when my husband calls that he has found the calf. I turn, climb a fence and head for home, taking a short cut across the hayfield. Sam, our black Labrador, runs from side to side ahead of me, sniffing out imaginary enemies.

Suddenly he begins barking furiously. I stop short; directly in front of me stands a woodchuck. Late-summer carelessness has left him stranded several feet from his hole. Sam circles around him, waiting for my decision. Chuck doesn't move; he knows there is no escape. I pick up a stick nearby. Thoughts race through my head.

How much of our clover did he consume this summer? It doesn't matter, really. But how many holes did he dig in our fields? Two years ago my husband was badly injured when he fell from a load of hay. The hay wagon had dropped into a woodchuck hole.

The woodchuck stands motionless on his hind legs, back straight as a ramrod, and stares at me. His teeth are chattering but he defies me with an attempt to whistle. Does he have a family, I wonder? Maybe it's a mother and her

's for the Dief,
a right jolly old elf,
And I laugh when I see him
in spite of myself.

Mrs. H.E. Rogers
Erin, Ontario

children are waiting for her at home? No, the young would be grown and on their own now. His eyes blink in the dusk. Is he pleading with me? Is he thinking I don't look like a killer? You are right, Chuck, I have never killed anything in my life.

I think of that man in Alberta who condemned someone for shooting a wild horse to protect his "precious" crops. Would he feel the same way about a precious hayfield, a precious piece of machinery or even a precious husband?

I look at the woodchuck. Do I have to make a choice?

No, there is no choice.

I lift the stick and with one quick, hard blow, the woodchuck lies dead in the darkness. I shove my cold hands into the pockets of my old coat and walk quickly towards home.

The lights are on in the barn and I go in. The hungry calf nuzzles its mother urging her to let down her milk more quickly. We watch in silence. I do not say anything about the woodchuck.

I go to the house. The light from the fire in the old wood stove flickers on the ceiling of the dark, warm kitchen. The aroma of the soup simmering at the back of the stove fills the room. I lean against the door and close my eyes.

Oh God, why did I have to make a choice?

Later my husband comes in from the barn stamping the snow from his boots. "It's really coming down," he says. "I guess it's the end of summer."

We eat supper.

The snow will cover the woodchuck.

Myrtle M. Gallup
Danville, Quebec

Kicking the Habit

February 2, 1972

Dear Mr. Gzowski:

Though there isn't much time, I'm taking it to put heart into Helen Hutchinson for giving up the smoking habit. It may take years and years but I'm sure she'll pull it off in the end. The point is, she's starting to give it up.

My father started my mother off in 1945 and finally accomplished his aim in 1965. I'll admit that having someone else making the commitment for you is not quite the same as doing it for yourself. But their concern is gratifying. In fact, not content with taking mother on, father also tried coercing her maiden sister Flo. He began by telling Flo that all the coughing and wheezing were doing nothing for her sex appeal (it was very dishonest of him to imply that it had ever been there at all). She had returned home from the First World War empty-handed, after the entire expeditionary force had managed to resist her, and at the time, their resistance to nurses was never lower. Anyway, this is how the giving up came about, and how Flo kicked the habit at eighty, and mother did it at seventy.

We lived in a cavernous terrace house and father practised dentistry on the premises. For twenty years a cat-and-mouse game was carried on, which got quite exciting at times, and went something like this. Right after breakfast mother would go into the bathroom, lock the door, throw open the window and then run hot water to get up a beautiful steam. Since work and smoking went together in her mind, instead of washing once a week, she saved little bits and pieces, a sock here, a pair of knickers there, and laundered daily – all the while smoking like mad and, if she was lucky, getting through as many as seven cigarettes on that job alone. The idea of the steam was to conceal smoke. Cooking and smoking were also closely linked, and we ate a lot of ash in our family because once a cigarette was lit it rarely left mother's mouth – it got sucked away. Flo was a master of the art; in fact, her cigarettes usually collapsed. She used to lay them out along the fender to dry before gluing them together again. We called it Flo's washing. She had a permanently nicotine-stained chin and upper lip, which as father pointed out did nothing to enhance her. But she didn't care; if no one else enjoyed her, she might as well enjoy herself.

So the days went by, broken up into a patchwork of little orgies. The years rolled on and, in spite of medical evidence to the contrary, mother and Flo remained physiologically far younger than their years, while quite a few of their non-smoking friends perished. Eventually, a nasty attack of 'flu made mother lose the taste for it, though she said cigarettes really gave her up.

For Flo, it happened in another way. She is accident prone, was always half catching buses or crashing to the floor with television sets; so it followed that, given time, she'd set fire to her bed. She liked that; it brought the fire brigade to her village for the first time in fifteen years. It also gave her the chance to emerge from the cottage dramatically, while the brigade rushed in imprudently and ruined everything in five minutes flat. Her evacuation to mother's house was the end, the very end, father said.

Looking back, I never remember mother in a sitting position with a cigarette, except in the bath. And when you consider the psychological connection of smoking and certain pursuits, it says a lot for mother that she didn't give up cooking, washing and her nightly bath when she finally stopped smoking.

This gets us to the point of this letter, and to the present, and what, exactly, is involved when I give up cigarettes. Please refer to lists below — especially H.H.

Things associated with smoking (and therefore out):

    coffee
    alcohol
    sitting
    reading
  "This Country in the Morning"
    writing
    parties of all kinds
    conversations (inside)
    making love (afterwards) — so there's hope — no there is not — husband is father of all smokers
    Canada — where I carry it on
    England — where it all started

Things not associated with smoking (and therefore in):

    people I have never met
    conversations (outside)
    sports
    farming
    tobacco picking
    oven cleaning
    non-smoking tobacco-growing provinces
    goat's milk

The evidence is inescapable. Forthwith, I'm setting out for the village of Tamish in Abkhasia (USSR), where I shall have no difficulty meeting non-smoking, total strangers. Once there, and if I'm lucky and not too repulsive, an Abkhasian octogenarian with a life expectancy of one hundred and thirty — in other words, a physiologically very okay person and therefore a good influence — will chum up with me. Platonically, that is. This jewel will set me up as a tobacco-picker and local oven-cleaner, allowing for the weakness of stand-up breaks for the intake of goat's milk.

That's all, except to say that I'm absolutely certain there was not the trace of a wheeze when Helen Hutchinson breathed.

Sheila Phillips
Toronto, Ontario

Danny

Two people who played a vital role in "This Country" do not appear very often in this book. One is Helen Hutchinson, who was almost a co-host when the program began. Later there is a glimpse of Helen at her best, talking about something very personal to her, and breaking through a kind of formality that stops her from being as good as she could be, which is the very best. The other is Danny Finkleman, who, along with his anonymous buddy Joe Fann, was part of the show from beginning to end.

There is nothing artificial about Danny. Both on the air and off he is funny, warm, outrageous, self-mocking, silly, kind, outspoken and a good guy to play shuffleboard or anything else with. On the air he talked about his hair problems (he had none), his love life (the only secret he ever kept was the fact that he was to be married about a month before the program ended), his running, his weight, his cooking, his friends, his unique way of life (TV sports and gambling, take-out foods and an addiction to the telephone) and his apparent inability to do things well. There is something he does very well, which is to be Danny Finkleman. He thinks, for example, that he should be a great TV producer. The trouble is, he doesn't know that people who are professionally funny — guys who do schticks — are less funny than he is off the cuff. I have not tried to reproduce any of his greatest moments on the radio in this book because they are unreproduceable. How could I capture his

terror of the iguana we gave him as a pet? Or his stunned silence when, on the day after his marriage — to a terrific woman — he came on and made a formal announcement, and then had it pointed out to him that, even though it was just the day after the event, he had got the date wrong? His disparagement of the Stratford Festival — "There's nothing to *do* there" — lay as much in the quality of his voice as in his comments. Similarly his determination to run in the Boston Marathon, or lose weight, or push the cause of movies that died at the box office but were great, he argued, on late-night TV. Both on and off the air, I have spent a great many happy hours in the company of Danny Finkleman. I'd just like to say how much I like him.

Danny's Recipes for One

Rainbow Trout Dinner

Package of frozen rainbow trout (2 fish in a package)
1 lemon
1 bunch of parsley
1 large tomato
1 baking potato
1 package of frozen green beans (French style)
butter

One hour before you want to eat:

Turn on oven to 425 degrees.
Wash potato, tomato and parsley.
Remove trout from package.
Make 4 or 5 small cuts through the skin of the potato (so it won't explode while cooking).
Put potato in oven: if large it will take one hour, if medium or small, 45 minutes.

12 minutes before potato will be done, turn on your broiler.
Smear fish with butter on both sides.
Smear broiler rack with butter (or oil) so fish skin won't stick.
Put fish under broiler and broil for 4 minutes.
While fish is broiling, prepare beans according to instructions on package (should take 8 minutes to cook).

Cut tomato into thick slices. Dip in salad dressing if you have it and sprinkle with salt and pepper.
3 minutes before eating, place slices on broiler grill alongside the fish. Cook for 3 minutes.

While tomato cooks, melt 2 or 3 tablespoons of butter in a small pan on top of the stove. Let it get to the boiling point but don't let it brown.

Snip 2 tablespoons parsley.
Squeeze in one or two teaspoons of lemon juice, depending on your taste.

Now everything should be done. Take fish, potato and tomato out of oven and put on plate. Drain beans, put on plate, pour lemon butter over fish and *enjoy*!

Clam Chowder and Liver and Onion Dinner

1 Spanish onion
scallions and parsley (should have some left over from previous recipe)
celery
1 can small, whole or minced clams (7 oz. size)
½ pound of liver (pork, beef or calf)
1 very small eggplant
1 large tomato
1 8 oz. container of milk
1 8 oz. container of cream
1 individual-size container of sherbet — lemon or lime

Clam Chowder

Heat electric frying pan to 300 degrees.
Finely chop 2 scallions, ½ stalk celery with leaves, 2 tablespoons parsley.
Melt 2 tablespoons butter in pan.
Add vegetables and cook for 4 minutes, stirring constantly.
Add 1 tablespoon of flour to vegetables. Stir for one minute.
Add salt and pepper to taste.
Add ½ cup of milk, ½ cup cream and ½ cup water.
Turn heat to 250 (or to where mixture just bubbles).
Simmer 5 or 6 minutes. (Don't boil, or cream will curdle.)
Add can of clams, plus liquid.
Stir and cook until very hot. Serve.

Liver and Onions

Turn frying pan to 350 degrees.
Add 2 tablespoons butter.
Put in liver.
Brown on both sides. (About 4 minutes on each side. Liver will be rare. If you like it well done, cook for 3 or 4 minutes more.)
Remove liver from pan, put on plate and keep warm in oven.
Slice onion thinly.
Chop eggplant into small cubes.
Cut tomato into eighths.
Slice 1 stalk of celery thinly (on the diagonal, Chinese style).
Heat frying pan to 325 degrees. (If you have only 1 pan, cook liver first, keep it warm in the oven. Rinse out pan before cooking vegetables.)
Melt ¼ cup of butter, or better, ¼ cup of salad dressing in pan.
Add vegetables (except tomatoes).
Cook for 5 or 6 minutes, stirring frequently.
Add tomato pieces.
Salt and pepper to taste.
Cook another 3 minutes.
Serve with liver.

For dessert: sherbet, which you can buy in individual serving size.

Note: If this vegetable dish sounds like too much food, or too much trouble, just cook the onion. Slice it thinly, **melt ¼ cup of butter at 300** degrees, add onion, stir and cook for 5 or 6 minutes.
Serve with liver, with a tossed salad, or sliced tomato, or whatever you have.

Chicken Breasts with Mushrooms

2 chicken breasts (sized according to how hungry you are)
1 bunch of scallions
1 small green pepper (optional)
1 pound of mushrooms
1 pound of rice (white and/or brown, long grain)
1 small can of corn (kernel or cream, according to preference)
1 package of frozen broccoli
1 large apple (Macintosh or Courtland)
Staples: if you don't have them, buy brown sugar and butter.

45 minutes before you want to eat:

Turn on oven to 350 degrees.
Wash apple, core and cut thin strips of peel from around the middle.
Put in a small baking dish.
Add ½ cup of brown sugar and 1 cup of water and sprinkle with cinnamon or nutmeg if you have it.
Put in oven, bake for 45 minutes. (Keep checking; if apple is small or soft it may take less cooking time.) Prick with a fork and if tines go in easily apple is done.

As soon as apple is in oven, prepare the chicken.
Season breasts with salt and pepper.
Turn frying pan to 375 degrees.
Melt ¼ cup butter in frying pan.
When butter bubbles, add chicken breasts.
Brown both sides (about 6 minutes on each side).
While chicken is browning, chop 3 scallions into small pieces, chop the green pepper, slice mushrooms.
Turn heat down to 325 degrees; add chopped vegetables.
Cover pan and cook for 30 minutes.

While chicken is cooking, prepare the rice.
Wash rice.
Bring 1 cup of water, plus ½ teaspoon salt, to boil in a pan with a tight-fitting lid.
When water boils, add ½ cup rice.
Turn heat to simmer, cover and don't peek for 20 minutes.

Remove apple from oven when done.
Cook vegetables you've chosen. If corn, it only takes 5 minutes; if broccoli, follow instructions on package.

When chicken has cooked ½ hour, remove lid, put breasts in oven on a plate to keep warm.
To juices in pan, add 2 tablespoons of finely chopped parsley. (If there's not much juice, add ¼ cup water or cream.) Stir, making sure you scrape all the bits that are stuck to the bottom of the pan. Salt and pepper to taste; pour over the chicken.

Rice will now be done. Serve with butter, salt and pepper. Drain vegetable and serve.

Andrew Allan on Nobody

I have a telephone answering service. Since I am out a good deal, I pay them a certain amount every month to hear my phone ring at their office and to answer it for me when I am away or gone to the bathroom. If anybody says anything, they write it down, and when I call the answering service, the nice girl looks in the box marked with my phone number and tells me what it says there.

The crown prince of Eppingstein has called to ask if I will join him at his hunting lodge immediately after the autumn equinox. The wife of the ambassador of Blotz wonders if I found a stray earring under the sofa cushion. The Gem Invisible Mending Service says my pants are ready. CBC TV wants to know if I will pretend to be an archbishop in a play – for money. CBC radio wants to know if I will say something out loud on the microphone on Friday morning. A

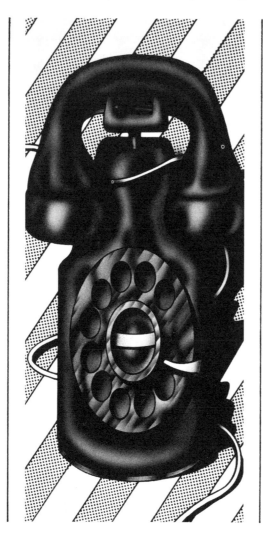

lady called Miss Rumplestiltskin phoned to say she had changed her mind – but wouldn't leave a number.

This is the kind of thing the telephone answering service is happy to report to me. And I, of course, am happy to hear it reported.

But life is not always that crowded with incident. There are times when the nice girl goes away to look in the box with my number on it, and comes back to say, in a sad voice, "Nobody called."

Nobody called. Nobody. The girl's voice tried to provide an edge of comfort. It's all right, really. Things will be better tomorrow – or the next day. But for the moment, "Nobody called." I am not wanted, not required. People can breathe without me.

But Nobody. The nice girl may not realize it, but I have become rather fond of Nobody. Even when there are no other calls, when the whole world is breathing away without the slightest thought of me . . . even on a day when not even a federal candidate has put a piece of literature into my mailbox to say that for the first time in several years I am indeed known to exist . . . even on a day when all is silence and the gods are slumbering heedless on Olympus . . . even on that day I have the secret satisfaction of hearing that Nobody called.

Nobody can be relied on. In the darkest moment, I can comfort myself with the thought that Nobody is there.

The White King asked Alice to look along the road and tell him what she saw. "I see nobody on the road," said Alice.

"I only wish I had such eyes," the King remarked in a fretful tone. "To be able to see Nobody! And at that distance too! Why, it's as much as I can do to see real people, by this light!"

I have always felt that the White King made a mistake. He confused "Nobody" with "Real People." The alternative to "Nobody" is not "Real People." The alternative to "Nobody" is "Somebody."

In a lifetime of looking along the road you will not descry any person more real than Nobody. Somebody may let you down. Somebody may become as sounding brass and a tinkling cymbal. Somebody may turn out to be no more than a cloud of dust in the twilight. But Nobody will loom out of the distance like a long-expected guest – like your fondest dream – like an angel in disguise.

My dear friends, let us raise our glass to Nobody. Even if the glass is empty, let us raise it anyway. It is better to raise an empty glass than to nurture an empty illusion.

No matter how empty the glass may be, we can rest assured that Nobody will Understand.

Conversations with Prime Ministers: Pierre Elliott Trudeau

The tone of the conversation I had with Pierre Elliott Trudeau in our Toronto studios in February of 1974 is characterized by the very first exchange of remarks. If you'll notice, I'm trying the old interviewer's trick of seduction, although, I hope, being very careful to imply that he *had* been a hero of mine, to allow myself room for what I intended to be some impolite questions later on. He responds with an instant reminder that he remembered the only other time we'd met, and implied by it that *I* should be on my guard, too.

Later on you'll see that I am trying to work him into something of a corner on Quebec. Virtually everything that emerged from the three series of programs we had done from Montreal and from Quebec City had convinced me that, culturally and linguistically, Quebec had already established itself as a separate and unique community by 1974, and that the sooner the rest of Canada recognized that fact and made moves to accommodate that specialness within a new framework, the better our chances would be of still being able to use that phrase, "the rest of Canada." If we ignore what has happened, what is happening, and what will continue to happen, I was and am convinced, Quebec will inevitably follow its cultural and linguistic uniqueness with political and economic separation.

These views had begun to dawn on me in the early 1960s, when I was covering Quebec for *Maclean's* magazine, and they had grown strongly throughout the sixties and had been strengthened and confirmed by my experiences with "This Country in the Morning." I remember at one point talking with Alex Frame about a television program we might someday do called "These Countries." I wanted to talk to the prime minister of Canada about what I had learned. In our conversation, though, as you will see, he cuts off this attack with a brilliant gambit; he uses the phrase "Toronto separatist." Just *uses the phrase*. My attack is stymied. For however real the information and impressions on which I want to base my next series of questions may be, those questions are asked under the cloud of the phrase he has used. More than any other interview I ever did, this one resembled a chess match. And that surprised me, for what I had been trying to elicit was a sense of this most mysterious man, a man who at the end of this conversation feels that he has somehow bared his soul. Curious.

PG: I welcome this morning the Right Honourable Pierre Elliott Trudeau, prime minister of Canada, and a hero of mine in 1960. . . .

PET: Is that when you interviewed me for *Maclean's*?

PG: I wrote a profile of you for *Maclean's* magazine – you were a tough interview then, a tough person to write about because. . . .

PET: I wasn't sure I wanted any publicity.

PG: I don't think you did. The. . . .

PET: Contrary to today.

PG: You certainly didn't want any personal publicity. That sense of privacy that you've maintained through your political career was already evident when you were a teacher of law at the University of Montreal. I felt like an intruder when I was in your house trying to interview you.

PET: Did you come to my apartment downtown? I think you did.

PG: No, it was your parents' house in Montreal. And the man I knew then was very quick, very involved – in fact I think the article that ran in *Maclean's* was called "Portrait of an intellectual engagé" – we talked about *Cité Libre* and the people who were there, and I could sense your intolerance of foolishness and your intellectual gifts. It has often occurred to me since then, watching you in office, that there must be many frustrating things for you in that office. I wonder, do you like your job now?

PET: Yes, I like my job. I think I answered that question for myself when I decided to get out of the university into politics; that I'd have to play new rules and accept compromises, and I'd have to try to govern in a way that was acceptable to the majority of the people rather than in a way that might seem best in the absolute. It's a transition that was difficult when I made it, but having accepted this new set of rules, I live very happily under it.

PG: Your occasional flashes of temper — which I would think might be more noteworthy for their infrequency — but every time you say something in a moment of anger, it becomes front-page news. If you were on the steps of the House of Commons again, would you have told the truck drivers, "mange de la merde"?

PET: Probably not, because I learned from that one what the consequences were. But if I were talking to some guy who was insulting me and bugging me, and if I knew that the press wouldn't play up my comment to him, I probably would say "mange de la merde." You know, I still say it to guys who bug me, but they don't go and tell the press and the press doesn't put it in the headlines. I'm sure you still tell some guys to. . . .

PG: Yes, but I don't pretend that I said fuddle-duddle after I do. I've never heard anyone ask you: what did you say on that occasion?

PET: Well, the truth is, I didn't say anything. That's the whole point. I didn't say anything and I explained that in the House of Commons. I moved my lips and people said, "Ah! but he moved his lips and this is what he was saying." You know, if they are going to begin to read your lips, they'll be soon asking what the nature of your thoughts are.

PG: George Bain broke a major barrier in the *Globe and Mail* the next morning by reporting what he understood you to have said.

PET: Well, George Bain was being very inventive, as he often is. He certainly couldn't have read my lips from where he was sitting in the gallery. Amusingly enough, just about two months ago in the House of Commons the complaint was that I wasn't speaking loud enough. You know, everybody shouts and groans and so on. I don't believe in raising my voice to shout louder than the guy who is shouting at me, so I just speak to the Hansard reporter and it gets reported. When they complain that they can't hear what I'm saying, I say: well, either be quiet and you'll hear what I'm saying, or else, if you're so good at lip reading, the way you were a couple of years ago, just read my lips.

PG: Do you wish you hadn't said, and I'll quote, if I may, "I think we should encourage members of the Opposition to leave; every time they do the IQ of this House rises considerably. When they get home, when they get out of Parliament, when they are fifty yards from Parliament Hill, they are no longer honourable members, they are just nobodies." Do you wish you hadn't said that about the Opposition?

PET: Oh, hell no. You know, Peter, you are putting me on. This was an adjournment debate, eh? We had been sitting for, I don't know, eleven or twelve bloody months and the Opposition had been keeping Parliament going on and on and on. It's a very simple fact that Oppositions like the House to sit, because that's when they get in the news. When the House is not sitting, they may be doing important work back home, they may be broadening their minds, but from the point of view of news in the capital, they don't exist anymore.

PG: Isn't that a kind of a sweeping generalization, Prime Minister, that insults men like John Diefenbaker and David Lewis, and — well, we can go on, but these are men for whom I'm sure you have some respect. . . .

PET: Well, they were the very people who were speaking against the adjournment, who wanted Parliament to sit all summer and all night and all day and all weekend because that's when they get the publicity. And once again, if they are hurt by that

There once was a baby named Justin,
Who said, "I don't like being cussed in
A bilingual tongue,
When I'm really so young,
And it's only your shoulder I mussed on."

Audrey Graham
Delta, British Columbia

50

kind of thing, why shouldn't I be hurt when every day of the week they tell me that I'm a hypocrite or that I've misled the people or that I'm a blabbering idiot or that I'm a fascist or I'm trying to abolish the monarchy or kill Parliament? This is the common currency of debate in Parliament.

PG: How is it possible to take personal abuse of the kind that you are talking about? Being called by labels which no rational man would be able to justify — fascist, hypocrite. I mean, we all err from time to time, but are you hurt personally?

PET: No, and that's why I object when the Opposition or the media blow up something I say. Every day of the week somebody in the House of Commons gets up and says I'm a hypocrite. But if it can't work two ways, it's just not my style. I like to hit back.

PG: How do you like Walter Stewart, who is becoming to you sort of what Peter Newman became to John Diefenbaker?

PET: I never read Walter Stewart. I don't think I've ever seen anything he wrote so I couldn't care less what he does or says.

PG: You haven't read *Shrug* or *Divide and Con*?

PET: No.

PG: . . . or his articles? Do you read *Maclean's*?

PET: No.

PG: What do you read, Prime Minister, may I ask?

PET: Cabinet documents, memoranda on various subjects.

PG: Do you have information prepared for you the way we read about the president of the United States having it prepared, sort of a condensation of the nation's press?

PET: Well . . . yes and no. I can't say that I look at a clipping service every day. But when my staff wants me to see the effect of a particular policy on public opinion, or the effect of a particular trip on the electorate, they will give me a series of clippings and I will read them. Or if I'm going to give an interview on a special subject — if you had a pet hobby horse, for instance, they would have said, Newman is strong on whatever it is, economic nationalism or. . . .

PG: I'm Gzowski.

PET: So, in this sense I get briefings on specific subjects, but I certainly wouldn't lose my time reading second-hand observers like the ones you mentioned.

PG: Can we talk a bit of politics. . . .

PET: . . . I didn't mean second-hand, I meant second-rate.

PG: The country has changed a great deal since you came to power; would you agree that it's becoming more regionalized?

PET: Yes, but I think that the swings of the pendulum are rather frequent and brusque in Canada. I certainly got into federal politics because I felt that the central power was getting too weak. The present direction, as you say, is towards decentralization, but I'm rather certain that the pendulum will swing back again very soon. Perhaps it's beginning to do that over oil. People are realizing that if you let one province, on such a basic issue as energy, dictate what is good for Canada, then you begin to see the country itself erode as a state.

PG: Is that a fair analysis, that people will see the weakness of regional power? Would it not be equally true to say they'll see the strength and value of regional power? You could say that the West is where Quebec was ten years ago, could you not, in its sense of dissatisfaction and regional identity?

PET: Yes, I think you are as right as I am. You will recall that in the fifties I was in favour of more provincial power for Quebec. It was only around '62 or '63, when I thought Quebec was going too far, establishing embassies abroad and so on, that I felt it should be pushed in the other direction. I think it's true with the western

There once was a baby named Justin
Who found his dad's looks quite disgustin'.
He said, "It's so grim,
That Dad won't get a trim,
I'm not sure if he's Sorab or Rustim!"

Dr. A. Hare
Swift Current, Saskatchewan

provinces, too. I suppose generally, over the years, they probably didn't feel they exercised enough provincial autonomy, and they're in a period now where they are doing it. All I'm saying is that that isn't going to last forever, because people will realize that if the country is to remain united, at some point people must choose Canada over their province.

PG: How are you going to get popular in the West? How can you get over their anger? James Gray says the West is not separatist; it is simply fed up. You have seven members west of the Ontario border. And unless you perceive signs that other people don't perceive, you're in trouble in the West.

PET: Well, I'm obviously in trouble in terms of politics; the last election showed that. But I think there are two things that might be kept in mind. The first is that, for Alberta, where we don't have a single Liberal sitting in the House of Commons in Ottawa, you must look at the history of politics in Alberta since 1905. It's been against the federal government whatever its colour — Alberta has consistently elected its members to the Opposition, generally overwhelmingly and for long periods of time. So this is not something new. That's point number one. Point number two is that, you say: what am I going to do about it? Within days after the last election we decided to have the Western Economic Opportunities Conference, which had never been done before, a federal-provincial meeting of a regional character. It's literally true that the whole apparatus of the federal government for four or five months just bent itself to that one task, trying to solve the problems of western alienation, problems of what you call its anger. I didn't expect suddenly to produce results at one conference. They're naturally skeptical, and it's a matter of seeing over a period of time how we implement some of the obviously very good intentions that we expressed there.

But, it's much more than a question of political alienation — the West is alienated from Toronto in a business sense, indeed, in a cultural sense. You know, the CBC Toronto — I'm sure I don't know about the Gzowski program — but in the West they don't recognize Toronto productions as something expressing their desire for their own culture. When we have the Canada Council or other cultural agencies, the Film Board, the CBC and so on, making decisions that seem good from the point of view of those who make them, people out in Vancouver or in Edmonton say, well, you know, these are made down in Toronto or Montreal. . . .

PG: They're right, aren't they?

PET: Well, all I'm proving is that it's not Pierre Trudeau and the Liberal party who haven't been able to knit this country together. If what you say is right, it's the whole of Canada, it's the industries, the head offices of corporations, it's the people who complain they can't find housing or jobs in Metro Toronto. They can find them in Saskatchewan, if they want to move there.

PG: Can we talk about Quebec?

PET: Sure.

PG: We talked about pendulums being the pattern of Canadian history. Do you reject outright the people who say that the tide of independentism is simply growing and swelling as each new age group comes into the voting population?

PET: It will depend on how the country is governed. Nationalism or separatism is always the product of some failing in the institution that is being attacked. It's been my thesis that the federal government for a hundred years has failed to understand the proper needs of the Quebec people — you know, the way we've dragged our feet on bilingualism for so long. And so long as we haven't solved that and the problem of participation of French Canadians and the problem of Hull and so on, we're going to have new waves of separatism which will have to be fought.

There once was a baby named
  Justin,
With energy he was a bustin',
He was born with no hair,
But then so was Pierre,
So he won't need a haircut,
  just dustin'.

Joyce Rous
Paris, Ontario

When we were talking of western alienation, it's this phenomenon. If, after fifty years, Alberta feels alienated, some people will have to work to make that province understand that it can have its role in decision-making, just as a few French Canadians decided to demonstrate to Quebeckers in our time that French Canadians could have a damned important role in Ottawa. Which they did, with the result that some people thought there was too *much* French power. Well, now I wish some people would work so hard in Alberta that the people would begin to think there is too much Alberta power in Ottawa. But if they're always electing people to the Oppositions of whatever government happens to be there — this time it's my government, but some years ago it was against Tory governments — they'd be electing Social Crediters and so on.

PG: But if you, Pierre Elliott Trudeau, man of reason, eminent negotiator, willing to look at all these things rationally, if for six years you have seen the growth of regional identity, would there be any validity whatsoever to an argument saying: we ought to take a look at the constitution now, to allow for some variations, before these things get out of hand and the country does break down in some real and formal way? Why not sit down and discuss it now, while we can still talk, on the grounds that perhaps a generation from now we will not be able to talk with Quebec, perhaps with the West?

PET: Sit down now and discuss what, Peter?

PG: Discuss greater powers for the provinces and specifically, a special status for Quebec, which has a growing cultural identity and a great sense of excitement, a great sense of itself.

PET: You know, we sometimes talk about the Toronto Eskimos. I like to talk about the Toronto French Canadians who have discovered that the way to give justice to Quebec is to give it special status. This is what you've just said, I take it.

PG: I said it was not necessarily my. . . .

PET: All right, you're talking for. . . .

PG: I'm talking for all the people I talk to in Montreal. . . .

PET: . . . Toronto separatists.

PG: . . . the way I used to talk to you. . . .

PET: Who are your friends, Peter? I mean, I'm interested in keeping the doors open to Quebec. Special status means that you're beginning to close the doors. Therefore, I can understand a lot of English-Canadian intellectuals rejoining many of the Tories who say French is for Quebec and English is for the rest of the country. And the sure way to achieve that is either separatism or special status. Give more powers to Quebec and you certainly won't have men of meaning coming to Ottawa — they'll say: we'll do our work in Quebec.

Take the example of communications. Do you think you'd have a Juneau or a Picard working in federal institutions if we were to give way to provincial demands to put all communications in the hands of the provinces? The answer is no. It's a simple process of analyzing where the power lies. And if you're going to give all the power under the constitution to the provinces, or most of it, the people who want to exercise power are going to go there. That's a kinky solution: if we can't make federalism work, let's go for separatism. But you know my options; I think we can make it work.

I can't understand why people sort of wring their hands about what's going to happen a generation from now, with all these young French Canadians being born and believing in separatism. They'll swing the other way. One generation of intellectuals will go in one direction and the next one will go in the opposite, and I'm sure that the sons of today's separatists will probably smirk at their fathers' retro-

There once was a baby named
  Justin,
Whose father said, "It is my
  custom,
To keep from the press,
Any leaks, any mess,
I can count on you, I am
  trustin'?"

Audrey Graham
Delta, British Columbia

grade ideas. So what's new?

You know, I was talking to a Quebec audience about three weeks ago, and it's strange to see how the separatists have been quiet in the past three months. Why? They haven't got any oil in Quebec. If they had to pay world prices for oil, where would Quebec be? Quebec would be paying – I calculated the figure – it's half a billion a year more for its oil. But whatever new prices come in, Quebec may be putting a third of its whole provincial budget into the increased price of oil. So the separatists are not saying: good, we should be independent so we would have to pay this to the Arabs. The separatists are, well, being quiet. It's the federalists who are saying: oh, we've got to find some schemes so that we equalize the price across Canada.

PG: Did Canadians expect too much of you as a man in 1968?

PET: Oh, I suppose they did, collectively. If you take each Canadian individually, they'd be pretty reasonable about understanding the limits of any human being, certainly mine. But collectively there was a kind of phenomenon – people thought it was going to be a great new age. You remember, I spent half of that election telling people to cool off, that I wasn't going to work any miracles, I wasn't going to be a Santa Claus, I was just going to try and govern as best I could.

PG: But you couldn't stop the press, us guys, you couldn't stop people from having great expectations. . . .

PET: And I can't stop you from tearing me down now.

PG: Do you feel that people are trying to tear you down now?

PET: Oh, well, who was it you named earlier?

PG: Walter Stewart.

PET: Well, is he or isn't he? I haven't read it, but I understand he is.

PG: His books are critical – I may say that without fear of exaggeration.

PET: Well, that's fine. Now look, Peter. You say they were building me up in 1968. I suppose it's true. Are they building me up now? I suppose not. Are they tearing me down? I suppose it's a matter of whom you read.

PG: Have you changed at all, Mr. Prime Minister?

PET: No. Tel qu'en lui-même l'éternité le change. You know, one grows older, but I don't think I've changed my basic principles. I hope I've matured. Perhaps I should ask you what you mean, have I changed?

PG: It occurred to me in 1970 that perhaps if that kind of crisis had occurred while you were still a law professor – even though you were a centralist, you were a radical and a shit disturber and a man of outspoken views – you might have been put in jail in October of 1970.

PET: Peter, a lot of people conveniently forget that I was a defender of democracy. I believed in the power of the state, of the elected representatives of the people, to govern for a period of time. I've always told the separatists that if they don't like federalism, they should stand up on a box on a street corner and fight against it, talk against it, agitate against it. But change it democratically; don't use violence against it. Now what happened in 1970, apart from the violence, which you might say was just some kooks? What happened in 1970, I suppose, was that the largest possible group of strong and respected opinion leaders opted for a position against the democratically elected government. They said, the government must give in to terrorists and release what they called, quote unquote, the political prisoners. You remember this manifesto?

PG: Yes.

PET: Well, name the names if you want, but just choose about any respected opinion leader in Quebec, whether it be from the university or the press or the trade

There once was a baby named
    Justin,
Whose coming was angrily
    cussed in
Conservative caucus
By members who raucous-
Ly prophesied grief on the
    hustin'.

Patrick Watson
Carleton Place, Ontario

unions. They had meetings, they sat down, they signed. They signed statements saying: we must give in to the terrorists, we must save Pierre Laporte and Cross and, in order to do that, we must give in to their request, which is to release, quote unquote, the political prisoners. Peter, if I'd been in the Quebec universities then I would not have signed that. I would have said: if you don't like the Bourassa government, or the Trudeau government, if you don't like federalism, okay, let's continue campaigning against them and it. But let's not support those who have used kidnapping and eventually murder, in order to get people out of prison. I think that all those intellectuals and union leaders and academics and journalists and so on were not only manifestly wrong, but they were really on the verge of destroying the civil society in which we live. And in that kind of situation, no Toronto separatist will make me change my mind. I wouldn't have wrung my hands about civil liberties. I would have said, democracy comes first.

PG: Let me try to clarify the point I was trying to make before . . . it seems to have been insulting to you, and it was not intended to be.

PET: I didn't take it as an insult. I just suggested it was based on a misapprehension.

PG: Well, my suggestion was based on the fact that a lot of people who do believe in democracy, who do believe in freedom, who do believe in the kind of politics that you believe in and have stood for and fought for, went to jail innocently. I'm not talking about the people you yourself have described as a bunch of kooks. Or perhaps even the people who signed those manifestos. I'm talking about people who were arrested wholesale, and one of them could have been you because you were that kind of figure. People were arrested wrongly.

PET: If that's all you are saying, then perhaps you're right. I had Karl Marx in my library and perhaps I would have been arrested and gone to jail. I don't think I would have bitched about it. I would have bitched against the guys who created the kind of climate in which the state, the elected representatives of the people, in order to defend the authority of the state, had to use strong measures. I would have bitched then as I bitched before against people who were rejecting democratic means and who created a climate of oppression in which I would have been caught up and victimized, as you said. That's my position.

PG: Okay, one final question, Mr. Prime Minister. Participatory democracy, Just Society — those phrases imply that we're all going to get together and work things out. Then, in 1972, "The land is strong." I guess the implication there is that things have been worked out. Was that what "The land is strong" was intended to mean?

PET: Well, I'm not a great believer in slogans or labels. I suppose they are needed. I don't reject that one; I don't make a great defence for it either. What was it intended to mean, Peter? It was intended to convey a feeling that I had, that we were on the way to solving our most divisive problems. I was thinking of those issues on which I had campaigned so strongly in 1968. The answer to separatism, through federal participation. The answer to regional alienation, through the Department of Regional Economic Expansion.

You know, dammit, this land *is* strong, Peter. You just have to look at any other country and then look around at the tremendous wealth of this country and the energy resources — the only industrial country except perhaps Norway that is self-sufficient in oil. The boundless provisions of all kinds of natural resources. A small but highly educated population. It may not have been the right slogan, but it certainly is the truth; the land is strong, if people only want to believe it.

I was visiting a place where fifty Italian immigrants were getting their citizenship papers a few nights ago, and they believe the land is strong. They came from Italy to Canada and they asked to be citizens of this country, and you hear them cheer

There once was a baby named
 Justin,
Whose nocturnal wails were
 disgustin'.
But said Papa Pierre,
"I really don't care,
'Cause I know that he's just
 filibustin'."

Anne Wadge
Toronto, Ontario

55

is for "eh,"
and to it we owe thanks,
For whenever we say it,
they know we're not Yanks.

Judith Berlyn
Montreal, Quebec

whenever you say something like the land is strong. So I won't suddenly say the land is weak just because Pierre Trudeau didn't get his majority in October 1972.

Now, presumably, it was the wrong type of slogan. Why? I don't know; I'm not a slogan-maker and I don't know why it appeared ridiculous. You were asking about other things, participation and so on. People said I didn't make it work, but certainly I was close to the people. To those who say I was hedged up in the ivory tower of the East Block — just think of wheat farmers throwing wheat at me in Saskatchewan, and the armoury in Vancouver with the great demonstrations. You know, I was in the middle of a lot of demonstrations between 1968 and 1972. There was a hell of a lot of participation. I have no regrets. It just didn't click in 1972 and I don't think it's because we made a lousy campaign. It didn't produce the results we wanted. So, let's just go on and govern. As I've said, we'll go on with the minority we have, and we'll run the full term if we can get our legislation through.

PG: So, I should not infer from the fact that, since we've been trying to get you to come on this program since the program started, and you finally agreed to come on it, that there's going to be an election called?

PET: Heck, no. I suppose if there was going to be an election called I probably wouldn't have come. I wouldn't have wanted to indulge in this kind of introspection and soul-baring. I'd probably be on fighting programs where I'd be answering SOBs and telling them where they were wrong and so on.

PG: Maybe just mouthing words. . . .

PET: Maybe just mouthing words and moving my lips and having bright interviewers say, "Aha! I know what you meant."

PG: The Right Honourable Pierre Elliott Trudeau, thank you.

The Great Canadian Novel #2

There once was a baby named
    Justin,
Who followed the family
    custom,
When cooed at by lasses,
Who charged him in masses,
He shrugged as he charmingly
    bussed 'em.

Leah Cohen
Toronto, Ontario

Once upon a time, many years ago, an old prospector sat by his campfire throwing his oreless samples, one by one, into the silent blue sea. He did this every summer. It was a life he knew and loved.

He observed, after a while, that a shape, much bigger than most common fish, swam regularly in the area into which he threw his rocks. He became obsessed with the desire to discover its identity, and, one day, unable to control himself any longer, he rolled up his trousers and waded out to the spot.

At his feet lay a most beautiful mermaid.

The prospector and the mermaid became great friends, *more* than friends. They met every day. He would bring her tobacco to chew, whisky, chocolate, apple pies, beer; in fact, everything he could find to delight her. He showed her how to string bottle tops to decorate her neck and her hair. She, in return, would sit on his knee, lovingly caressing his brown,

wrinkled face, playfully tugging at his bushy brown beard. He even managed to teach her a few words and he loved to lie, staring up at the blanket blue sky and have her whisper these words in his ear. It was a summer of ecstasy but autumn brought changes. Bloss (as she had been christened) grew fat. Lack of exercise dulled her skin and her scales began to shed like acute cradle-cap. She was often drunk and would thrash about in the shallow water like a frenzied whale about to be landed.

The prospector, sensitive to the fact (as it undoubtedly was a fact) that the magic of their relationship had withered along with the charm of Bloss's appearance, saw no reason, when it was put to him in an equally sensitive manner, to refuse a career for her with a travelling circus. Months later, the procession could be seen jogging its way along the hard, crusty winter roads, Bloss's aquarium encircled with neon lights like a winking, mobile lighthouse on a black sea, within it Bloss, sloshing and lurching, a cigarette in her mouth. She had become gross but it was her very size that was to bring about a twist of fate.

En route to yet another town her lurchings

became rhythmic, just as a solid weight will do in a washing machine. With one oversize rock on the road to add momentum, the whole aquarium capsized; the lighthouse light went out forever.

They searched for Bloss without success. They were on the banks of the Mackenzie River; hundreds of miles to the north lay the open sea.

Years later the prospector was reminded of his lost, one-time love. A young fisherboy, it was reported, had seen a strange object leaping out of the turmoil of the Mackenzie as it meets and mixes with the open sea. The boy insisted that he could hear it shouting, over and over again, one short, obscene request. The object was lithe and smooth, he said, like a beautiful woman.

The prospector needed no more convincing; he was overcome with grief at what he'd done. Even today, you can see his boat combing the meanders and inlets of the great Mackenzie River, tirelessly following its course to the open sea, backwards and forwards, year after year.

Who is to tell him that the object of his search has gone forever? Who is to explain that all that is left is a dream, the reality of which he once had and destroyed? Not I, little children, not you, nor me.

Mrs. Christine Ellis
Pine Point, Northwest Territories

Found poetry (against my better judgement) from an old *TV Guide*

1) The NHL hockey playoffs (1)
 time
  to be announced
   time
    to be confirmed
     to be announced
      the bold ones
       to be announced

 The NHL hockey playoffs (2)
 time
  to be announced,
   time tentative
    temperatures rising,
     Let them live!
      The reluctant heroes.

2) it takes a thief
 going places
  outdoors, the
   untamed world,
    the challenging sea.
     Call it courage,
      People who sing together.

3) The American Revolution
 fourth
  of six parts.

4) when michael calls
 a woman
  is terrorized
   by phone calls from
    a child, bill moyers, world religions,
     the adventurers, city magazine.

5) Civilization to be
 announced
  at the pub,
   country-style,
    from the horseshoe tavern
     a touch of grace,
      the dream of instant riches.

Diane Lynch
Pickering, Ontario

Newfoundland Recipes

Sangria

1 bottle Spanish red wine
1 bottle Spanish brandy (available under the name Duff Gordon)
1 bottle Triple Sec or Curacao
1 lemon
1 orange
sugar
1 can Canada Dry or Schweppes Bitter Lemon

Slice the orange and the lemon and put them in a large glass or stone pitcher. Pour in the wine and the sugar to your taste (anywhere from ¼ cup to a full cup). Next shake in the Triple Sec and the brandy (also to taste). Stir. Chill. About ten minutes before serving add the can of Bitter Lemon and a tray or two of ice cubes. Put in refrigerator until ready to serve.

Note: Initial cost will be roughly $16.00.

Salt Fish Casserole

In Newfoundland, fish means "codfish." All else is salmon, or halibut, or trout, or whatever. So when the term "saltfish" is used it means dried, salted codfish.

Melt ¼ cup butter in a heavy saucepan. Brown 3 large onions in the melted butter. Very slowly add 3 cups warm water to the onion mix. Simmer 15 minutes.

Thicken with flour and water mixture (some people like this dish very thick — others prefer it somewhat liquid). Add 4 cups cooked, flaked saltfish. Serve as a main dish with potatoes or rice or on crackers as a cocktail snack.

This is very versatile as it can be used as a main dish or for a late-night snack. We once froze a gallon of it and took it to serve in Nova Scotia!

P.S. Newfoundland salt codfish must always be soaked in water overnight, the water changed the next day and the fish cooked for about 20 minutes.

Bacalau from Portugal

Cook and flake enough salt cod to make 2 cups of fish. Fry 2 cups of chopped onions in olive oil (corn oil will do). Add flaked fish and mix to heat. Push mixture to one side of frying pan and break 3 eggs into the other side — chopping them as they fry.

In another pan fry 2 cups chopped boiled potatoes. Mix the potatoes into the fish mixture; serve with chives and black olives on top.

It is worth a trip to Portugal just to try their delicious saltfish recipes — so different from the traditional Newfoundland ones, yet adding some interesting variety to salt codfish. With this you serve a chilled Casal Mendes rosé wine to keep the Portuguese flavour to the meal, and the traditional Iberian dessert "flan" at the end.

Cod au Gratin

Layer 4 pounds fresh cod fillets with 2 pounds sliced sharp cheddar cheese in large casserole dish.

Prepare 2 cups of medium white sauce and pour over fish mixture. (Diced onions may be added to the white sauce while cooking.)

Grate sharp cheddar over fish mixture and sprinkle with bread crumbs. Bake for 45 minutes at 375 degrees.

This dish may also be served as individual dishes for an appetizer. We prefer it as a main fish and serve it with a glass of chilled Canadian Sauterne. Bakeapple (cloudberry) parfait finishes off the meal in style.

Fisherman's Brewis

"Brewis" is made from hard tack – ship's biscuit – a dry, unleavened flour and water product called "hard bread" in Newfoundland.

Soak 2 or 3 cakes of hard bread overnight and dice when soaked.

Cut 1 pound salt fat back pork in slices and render out in a large heavy pot. Put into the hot oil 4 pounds of fresh cod fillet (any white fish may be substituted). Add 4 large onions – chopped. Salt and pepper to taste.

Cook for 30 minutes (do not stir). Keep covered. Drain hard bread. Add to fish and stir to mix well. Serve immediately. (Makes a delicious fish stew without the hard bread.)

This is our very favourite fish recipe! This dish has been served to hundreds of people over the years and requests for seconds (or even thirds) are usual. Try a glass of homemade blueberry wine with it and partridgeberry tart afterwards.

Fish and Brewis

Soak overnight, boil for 30 to 40 minutes, and flake:
    4 pounds salt cod
Soak overnight and bring *just to a boil* in the same water:
    2 cakes hard bread (brewis)
Chop fish and brewis together or serve separately. Serve with "scrunchions."

This is the traditional Newfoundland dish. "Scrunchions" are small bits of salt fat back pork fried crisp. Both the diced pork and its oil are used as a garnish for fish and brewis. Some of the other condiments lavished on top include white or brown sugar, molasses, raw onions, butter, an onion sauce called "drawn butter" and, in recent years, both ketchup and mustard.

If salt codfish is unavailable in your area, we suggest that you write to the Canadian Saltfish Corporation, Royal Trust Building, St. John's, Newfoundland, and ask how you can obtain some.

Elizabeth Reynolds and Margaret Kearney
St. John's, Newfoundland

Blizzards

This may sound pretty dumb to those of you who live in less temperate parts of Canada than I do – temperate in climate, that is – but the highlight of this Canadian winter for me, in an outdoor sense, has been the one time it really snowed here in Toronto. It was the Thursday between Christmas and New Year's. It had started to snow during the night and just refused to stop. By noon the streets were jammed; that evening, a lot of people who commute by car were making arrangements to stay in town overnight; it took me over an hour to drive home, a trip that usually consumes only about twenty minutes. We got something like eight inches of snow – good, heavy wet stuff that really drifted and hung the way honest Canadian snow should.

What on earth could a normally sane – I like to think – man find to like in that kind of mess? Well, first of all there was the driving itself. Like most people who take the same route to work and back every day of their lives, I am bored by driving. It is one of the times I am most grateful for radio. And the chance to turn it back into an adventure – even though that adventure was only one of skidding and sliding and slipping and getting stuck – the chance to make it an adventure was one I enjoyed seizing. That's the key word, really: adventure. There was a kind of anarchy in the air that day, a hint of the same feeling that people remember from such other real emergencies as a power failure or a crucial strike. For once in our too-routine lives – too routine physically, I mean – we had to find a way to cope; to rely more on each other. We shared our difficulties and our discomforts and out of our common problems arose an accompanying sense of common friendliness. The driving may have been arduous, but the drivers were a heck of a lot nicer than they usually are.

Like almost everyone who grew up in Canada, a great many of my childhood memories involve the winter and being out of doors. A big dog that wouldn't stop chasing my sled. Soakers from a winter creek. Making angels in the snow. The way the snow matted in your hair and around the edge of your parka. Just being cold, the exquisite pain of nearly frozen toes and fingers, and the equally exquisite relief from a warming fire. Hot chocolate and sleigh rides, snowball fights and skating across the fields, endless hockey games and a whole fantasy life about the Arctic – some of the imaginary adventures I had on my way home from school made Duncan Pryde's stories sound like girl guide hikes. Later on, trying to get a goodnight kiss when it was fifty below and then walking

A woman got on the Newfie Bullet in Port aux Basques. Halfway through the trip she called to the conductor, "Stop, I have to get off!"

"Lady," he replied, "I can't stop the train here."

"But I have to get off. I'm going to have a baby."

"You shouldn't have gotten on the train in that condition."

"I didn't!" she replied.

There once was a baby named Justin,
Whose parents with pride were near bustin'.
They formed (with some piety)
The Justin Society
Which was silly, but quite interustin'.

Marian Mann
Guelph, Ontario

home across a northern Ontario town because the buses had all stopped running . . . cold, clear nights, and brilliant days. Most of my memories, as I say, are physical, related to the elements, and there are days now when I would just like to run out and make angels, but have instead to go to work or to a meeting that cannot be missed.

Canadian winters, as Percy Saltzman explained a while ago, are not getting milder or shorter; but to those of us who live in cities they seem less – winterish. The snow is more often gray than white; the chances to go out and romp with kids and dogs, with sleighs and toboggans are increasingly rare. Although there always is enough snow to shovel or scrape – or so it seems – there is never enough for a snowman. It is possible, of course, to *go* to winter. But somehow there is something wrong with climbing into a car and driving fifty miles or so just to find an open field – not wrong, exactly, and I know a lot of people enjoy doing just that – but it is at least artificial. The reality of outdoors in winter is still the children rushing out to taste the cold of the year's first snow; still a six-year-old coming home an hour-and-a-half late from school, his clothing invisible under a solid layer of snow. He looks as if he rolled home, as well he may have done, but his cheeks are red and his eyes are shining. Now, *that's* winter. And if the only way we can get back to those elementary experiences requires an unexpected blizzard – well then, let all us city folk pray for more unexpected blizzards.

Among the people who agreed with me about the pleasure of blizzards was Mrs. C.V. Hart of Toronto who wrote:

Dear Peter:
About four years ago, we had such a beautiful unexpected blizzard here in Toronto that the schools were closed for the day. My then kindergarten-aged daughter and my three-year-old and I spent the whole glorious day tramping up and down the *middle* of streets, dropping in on friends for lunch. Since then, I have been hoping and praying for such a thing to happen again. The day of that particular blizzard, the streets were full of people dressed in brightly coloured ski clothes – none had been able to get to work, or school. There was a real holiday spirit of friendliness and conspiratorial glee. When I heard you this morning wishing for such a blizzard to happen, I was so happy to hear that someone else felt the same way as I do. Tonight, when you take your last look out the window to see if, just maybe it will snow, my children and I will be joining you in the Big Blizzard Hope. . . .

Word Games

Password

Password is a word-association game; the object of the game is to communicate a secret word to your partner by giving him one-word clues that have some association with the secret word. For example, if the secret word is "angel," some clue-words might be "heaven," "wings," harp."

rules: Four players, in two teams of two. One player of each team agrees with the other on a secret word, unknown to the other two players. Toss to decide who goes first; after the first round the winner goes first. If you are scheduled to go first in a round you may pass, but only on the *first* play of a round.

No proper nouns may be used, either as clue-words or as the secret word. You may not use a variation of the secret word as a clue; for example, if the secret word is "angel," you may not use "angelic" as a clue-word. Try not to use obscure words.

scoring: You may gain ten points on any given round. Only one team may score on each round. The person who guesses the secret word earns the score for his team. The round ends when the word is guessed or when ten guesses are used up. You begin with a possible ten points and subtract one point for each incorrect guess. The game ends when one team has twenty-one points.

Ghost

This game has been called Hangman and many other names, but the principle is to complete words by having players add one letter at a time. The title of the game, whatever you decide to use, may be used to keep score.

The object of the game is to *avoid* completing a word of four letters or more. The first player (draw lots to determine who goes first) says a letter. Each player then adds another letter in turn, so that the sequence of the letters forms a part of a word (not a proper noun). Letters may be added to the beginning or end of the existing sequence, but the new sequence formed must always be part of a real word. If a person adds a letter which forms a three-letter word, he does not lose the round; the next player goes on to add another letter. If, however, a player adds a letter which forms a four-letter word, he automatically loses that round. From then on, anyone who completes a word loses that round.

A player who cannot think of a word from

which to base his played letter may add a fictitious letter in the hope of bluffing the next player. If the next player calls the bluff, the bluffer loses the round; if the next player is bluffed and attempts to complete the fictitious word, then fails, he loses the round. Bluffs may prolong the game until the last bluff is called.

Players who lose a round (i.e., complete a word or cannot think of a letter to add to the existing sequence) have one letter of the word "ghost" added to their score tally. When one player has all five letters (g-h-o-s-t) on his score card, that player drops out of the competition until only one player, the winner, remains. (Obviously, if the players want to play more or less than five-point games, they must decide on another scoring word or another scoring system.)

example:
Following are the plays in a hypothetical game: (1) r, (2) ra, (3) rat, (4) arat, (5) arate, (6) parate, (7) eparate, (8) eparates, (9) separates. The player who added the ninth letter loses that round. Following are three variations of the above game:

VARIATION I: The player who added the fourth letter made the following play: (4) rate, and thus lost the round.

VARIATION II: The player who was to have made the ninth play in the hypothetical game decided to bluff and added an "r," forming (9) reparates. The tenth-move player called the bluff and when the ninth-move player could not come up with a word in which was contained the sequence "reparates," he lost the round.

VARIATION III: The player who made the bluff as in variation II, on the ninth move, succeeded in bluffing the following player. That player in turn added a "p" in a further bluff, forming (10) preparates. This move successfully bluffed the eleventh-move player. He could not think of a letter to add, but did not call the bluff, and thus lost the round.

Helpful hints on strategy: especially when two players are playing, try not to start with obscure letters or you are likely to lose. If you are stuck, always challenge the last player.

Dictionary

number of players: Any number over 3, preferably between 5 and 10.

equipment: One dictionary, the bigger the better; plenty of pencils and paper for everybody.

rules: One player is "It." He chooses a word from the dictionary (any word except a proper noun) which is so obscure that none of the players is likely to know the meaning. If any of the players knows the meaning, he must so declare before the round starts. He may drop out of that round or a new word may be chosen. "It" reads the word, pronouncing it as closely as possible to the dictionary's phonetics, and spells the word. "It" does *not* read the meaning of the word aloud at this point. Each player copies the word and then writes an invented definition for that word, making the definition sound as much as possible like "dictionary-ese." Each player then passes his definition to "It," not showing it to the other players. When all definitions are collected, "It" reads them aloud, numbering each of them, including the real definition at some point but being careful not to indicate its identity in any way. The players copy the definitions and their numbers. When all definitions have been read, each player must guess which definition is the real one. Players may give reasons for their choice in the hope of persuading other players to vote in a particular way. "It" keeps a record of the definition each player has chosen. When all the votes have been cast, the correct definition is announced and the scores are tallied.

scoring: Points are awarded as follows: ten points for guessing the correct definition; five points if someone else voted for the definition you wrote, and one point for voting for your own definition. The latter is a "safety" move, assuring yourself at least one point on the scoreboard. Voting for your own definition may also persuade others to vote for it, giving you five points for each vote.

example:
The word: jauk (pronounced "jock").
Definitions:
    (1) jauk: Noun; from Hindi; a triangular cotton head-covering worn by lower-caste women.
    (2) jauk: Adjective; from Norse; brave, hardy, virile.
    (3) jauk: Verb; Scot; dally, dawdle.
    (4) jauk: Verb; Gaelic; to shrug.
    (5) jauk: Noun; Medieval; an earthen well-bucket.
Number three is the correct definition according to Webster's *New Collegiate Dictionary*.

Ding dong.
"Go away. Avon to be alone."

Michael McLaughlin
Edmonton, Alberta

On each of my lawns, I'd invariably find
Attestation of the wandering canine.
To an early demise it drove me you've heard
Damned if they didn't at last get me interred.

Herb Fears
West Vancouver, British Columbia

Harry Bruce on November

There was a misty, blowing, heated fragrance in September but it is as dead and distant now as the tan on the perfect arms of a summertime girl you will never see again anyway. October's blazing times have run out — and so has all hope of a really hot fluke of an afternoon to fool you (if only for an irreplaceable afternoon) into believing that the season is not moving.

The afternoons off, for football games, they've run out too. And the cheerleaders. The unshakeable memory of the warmth their legs seemed to promise still inspires impossible reveries but, if the chance to touch the soft surge of their cashmere belongs to anyone now, it is not to you.

The pairing-off, the taking of steadies, the exchanges of pins, they're set forever. The rituals of October have established the things that matter, and all the eager fear and freshness and laughter and discovery of going back to school has settled into an endless and remembered dreariness, remembered from other years in a crash of boredom and tension and despair, the dreariness of blackboards, chalk dust, pointers, Bunsen burners, tests, projects, books, maps, projects, lectures, smelly lockers, class bullies, the odour of disapproval, and darkness in the early afternoon.

You know now which teachers you will be able to tolerate and, unless you appear to change, which teachers will not be able to tolerate you. They are already nattering at you about Christmas exams, putting the fear of failure in you; but the ecstasy and brief freedom of Christmas itself, of the Christmas break, are distant beyond all hope. There's no light at the end of this tunnel. It is too long.

It is November. The leaves are slimy, and the rain is falling.

November has stripped the trees and now you can see more of the sky than you could even last week, but so what? What is there to see up there except a pall without end? It's too soon to skate. It's too soon to find Her at the rink. It's too late to lie in the sun. It's too late for everything. It is November.

And fathers, mothers, teachers, and the grumpy, contemptuous adults who run the corner soda-bar, and the ageing thug who polices the pool hall, these older people are all closing in on you because life has moved indoors and under the yellow lights that *they* control.

The rain and the cold wreck all the meetings out on the grass with the friends who understand you, and get your jokes; and life is an eternal round trip between house and school and, even aboard the steamy limbo of the streetcars, the lights burn in the daytime. It is November.

Hallowe'en ushered it in, and there's something *right* about that. Surely it is the grubbiest, meanest, sickest of all our folk festivals and, since the Hallowe'en sock hop brought you nothing but the usual pangs of unrequited yearnings and a long ride home by yourself on an empty streetcar, you know that Hallowe'en can interest only small, greedy children. It's a time to train kid sisters and brothers not only in the arts of beggardom but also to get playful about skeletons, corpses, caskets and blood-sucking bats. Welcome, November. Hail to thee, black spirit.

And right after that, Remembrance Day. Two minutes' silence. The long, dim service in the school auditorium, which smells of varnish and old wax. Oh God, our help in ages past, save us from November! And save us, too, from the Sadie Hawkins Day dance. Will anyone ask you? What if she's ugly? Will the Arthur Murray lessons you bought with your paper-route money really save you from hideous embarrassment when the time comes to dance to Glen Miller's *String of Pearls*? Save us from November.

Well, my flashback is over. But the mood lingers on. A Toronto high school set my attitude towards November a quarter-century ago and, although the high-school kids of the seventies may revel in it, I still know that November is the barest month. The nothing month. I think we might try to inspire the nations of the world to declare a six-week October and a six-week December. Almost overnight, we could wipe out at least the name of November, and that would be a beginning.

The Great Canadian Novel #3

"Being Pierre Trudeau Means Never Having To Say You're Sorry" (The title has nothing to do with the plot, but I couldn't work that phrase in anywhere else.)

The time is election year in Canada. It is an election year like any other election year in Canada. The people without jobs are too busy looking for work to worry about the unemployment issue. Canadian businessmen, trying to woo the United States dollar, are too busy to worry about the American takeover of Canada. Overflow crowds of up to thirty-seven people gather in local Legion halls to listen to the candidates debate the issues. The election date is June 27, cunningly calculated by the government in power as the day when most Canadians will be on holidays anyway. The only unusual thing about this election is that the Communists, in light of the friendly negotiations between China and the U.S., have decided to field a candidate in every riding.

As election night draws near, the CBC and CTV networks, having consulted IBM (Canada), decide not to bother covering the elections as the computer has already predicted an overwhelming win for the government in power. Thus, it is a shock to discover the next morning that the Communist candidates in eighty-five percent of the ridings have won, thanks to the 472,379 Canadian voters who decided to cast a ballot. The news is so shaking that it even gets coverage in the New York *Times* on the same page as the results of the California kumquat harvest. Since President Nixon doesn't read the *Times*, he doesn't know yet of the Commie threat on his back doorstep.

The scene shifts to China some time later where the new MPs have been invited for a tour of the country. To show their respect for these great Canadians, the Chinese give the MPs autographed pictures of Lin Piao and treat them to a sumptuous banquet of sweet and sour spareribs, egg rolls and chicken fried rice, ordered from a local take-out in Peking. Meanwhile, visiting American journalist William S. Huckley, from the Akron, Ohio, *Journal*, out for a stroll and trying to wear off the stuffiness of a forty-eight-course Chinese dinner, runs into the Canadians and learns the reason for the visit. He exposes the fact that Canada has gone communist in his hard-hitting weekly.

This news is immediately picked up by the U.S. president who decides that the only way Canada can be saved is to send in troops, throw out the Commies and make Canada safe for democracy. But, of course, since he is so busy with important wars, he can't send in his top-flight fighting men. Instead, a group of veteran volunteers, the Green Billies, are ordered to attack.

Armed with a French-English dictionary, the advance guard moves in on Toronto. Speaking in halting French (every American knows that all Canadians speak French) he warns the populace that they are being invaded. Unfortunately, the guard arrives during rush-hour traffic, is rudely shoved aside and told to go back to Quebec if they can't learn to speak English. They go to Quebec and try again, but this time nobody understands them because they are using Parisian French and everybody knows that French Canadians can't understand Parisian French. Finally they make themselves clear and take over the best hotels in Canada's main cities — Toronto, Montreal, Vancouver and Kamsack — where they are charged double rates because they are Americans. The invasion seems to be a success.

However, they haven't reckoned with Canada's youth. A group of unemployed musicians apply for an Opportunities for Youth grant (all government programs are still in effect because the Communists are so surprised at winning that they never bothered getting any new programs together) to set up a guerrilla unit in Saskatoon, Saskatchewan. That city has been left alone because the Americans couldn't pronounce the name. They receive a grant on the conditions that they do not make a profit on the guerrilla movement and that they use no dirty words in their campaign to drive out the Americans.

Here will be a sub-plot, the love story between Megan Kowolski, the Ukrainian head of the Louis Riel chapter of the IODE, and Bill Smith, an American draft dodger who doesn't really like Canada that much but is willing to show us how to do things.

The guerrilla group attack the Americans, but unwisely choose the day of the Grey Cup celebrations to do so.

They try to get into the Royal York Hotel to fight the Yankees, but are turned back by the Toronto police because they don't have a key to a room in the hotel. The Americans, meanwhile, are not aware of the Grey Cup annual celebrations. They hear the noise and the hollering and the shouting and the whooping, look out the window and see the maddened throngs. Fearing civil insurrection, they rush from their rooms where they are attacked, mauled and kissed with beery breath by the celebrants.

Having never seen such a spectacle, they decide that they can never subdue such a wild

is for flying,
why must we pay more
To fly here at home,
than to some distant shore?

Eileen M. Purvess
Toronto, Ontario

race and rush out, surrendering to the guerrilla group who are still arguing with the cops to get into the hotel. Canada is saved.

But wait. Is Canada saved? The country's businessmen are furious. The invading troops were paying good money, jobs were found for everyone in servicing the invaders, and now that the guerrillas have defeated the Yanks, where will the money come from?

In desperation, they ask to reopen negotiations and President Nixon sends his most able diplomat, John Connally, who agrees to talk only if the Canadians will include a few Japanese on the negotiating team because he doesn't want to hurt the feelings of the Japanese, who are after all the U.S.'s best customers. The

Americans agree to win the war if the Commies will give up their seats. The Commies are weary of running it all anyway as it was more fun complaining about the conditions than doing anything about them.

The guerrilla group is retrained at a Canada Manpower center in various jobs such as cake decorating, and another election is called.

Canadians have learned their lesson. At least fourteen more people turn up at the polls and Canada is ruled once more by a dynamic, apathetic government and everyone is sort of happy.

Pat Sherbin
Dartmouth, Nova Scotia

Christmas Gifts for the Teenaged Girlfriend

This is the time of year I used to break up with girls. A little earlier than December 21, I guess, but around now, just before Christmas. This was not, I hasten to point out, any part of the Christmas blues, or any of those other psychological phenomena that social scientists have recently come to associate with Christmas. It was because I could never figure out what kind of present to give my girl friend. And what was worse, it was easier to give than to receive: I used to live in terrible fear of getting from some*one* I liked some*thing* I did not, or what might have been even worse, something I did like, but which would be a lot better than whatever it was I would have given her, because I never could, as I say, figure out what to give them.

I'm talking now about being – what? – about thirteen, or maybe through most of my (and those girls') early and middle teens, so I'm talking about *serious* love, real *crushes*, as opposed to the kind of love that leads to deeper love and, in my own case at least, to marriage. The only girl I *ever* gave a real Christmas present to, in fact, was Jenny Lissaman, and I married her before the next Christmas came round, although I don't think – I really am quite sure – that that was one of the reasons. But the girls I had gone steady with in high school – and come to think of it, this lasted through university too – I used to break up with as diplomatically as I could about four o'clock on the afternoon of December 18. "It's not that I don't like you

any more, Jane . . . it's just that, well, I think we each ought to go our own way for a while."

I realize I'm leaving the impression that I was some kind of Holden B. Lothario or something. I wasn't. It wasn't very often I was able to get close enough to girls to be able to break up with them, and more often, when I did get closer, it was they who broke up with me. "It isn't that I don't like you any more, Peter . . . it's just that . . . " and so on. There weren't that many of them, either. I think, in fact, that I broke up with the same girl on December 18, 1947, as I did on December 18, 1949. And I think the reason I broke up with her in '47 was that in '46 she'd given me this wallet for Christmas and I, well, hadn't been able to think of anything to give her, and I had this awful moment at home on Christmas morning, when my mother asked who the wallet was from and I blushed and shuffled my feet and hemmed and hawed and finally told her, and she asked what I'd given the girl and I said that I, ah, that I had, well, actually I hadn't given her anything. And then my mother made me phone her to say thanks. And that was really fine, I'll tell you, phoning this girl while your mother listened to make sure you were polite.

I mean, what was there to give? A charm bracelet? They already had a charm bracelet. Who'd go *out* with a girl who didn't have a charm bracelet? A sweater? What size? You couldn't *ask*. I know this sounds easy, but you just think about being thirteen years old in 1947 and trying to figure out what size sweater your girl friend wore. Parents were no help either. "Why don't you get her a nice book, dear?" A book, for God's sake. You might as well have given her mittens. That was another thing, I

red leather, yellow leather
red leather, yellow leather
red leather, yellow leather

Mary Charbonneau
Dartmouth, Nova Scotia

suppose. Gloves. Once I even got up to the glove counter in one of the big department stores in Galt, Ontario, but three guys I used to play basketball with came by and I had to fake to the right, pivot and pretend I was picking out a pair for myself. Earrings? She'd have looked silly in earrings. Barrettes? Skate guards? One of my first loves was the greatest figure skater in the GCI & VS and, in my view, in the world — but you still couldn't give skate guards to someone at Christmas time. That was the whole problem. If it was useful enough—"why don't you give her a nice warm scarf, dear?"—it just wasn't the sort of thing Humphrey Bogart would have given Lauren Bacall, and if it was that sort of thing it was too soppy to give to anyone in case someone else found out. So I used to break up with the girls in late December. This left me with problems for New Year's Eve, of course, but somehow they seemed to get solved. "Jane? Hi. I know we're not going steady anymore, but listen, next Friday night is . . . and, well, you know, Rhonda's having this party and, well, if you're not going with anyone . . ."

I've got a couple of daughters now, and the oldest one at least is exactly the kind of girl I used to break up with. As a father, I'm still having difficulty trying to figure out what to give her—the boys are easy. I'll solve it, of course, and I promise her, if she's listening today, that it won't be mittens. But I can't help wondering if somewhere there isn't some young guy sneaking around the glove department and hoping like mad no one from his basketball team shows up.

I'm entering my fourth month. Things are finally beginning to speed up. I've felt such a peculiar thing that's hard to describe. It's sort of like a plastic bag floating in water. . . . I don't think I'll really be able to feel the baby until the end of the fourth month.

I don't feel too comfortable in pants any more. My husband and I went on my first trip to a maternity shop—my God, I've never seen anything like it in my life. Horrible, horrible stuff. Lots of hot-pant outfits, not quite appropriate, I'd say. And besides, all their things were for women eight months' pregnant; I just looked ridiculous. It was so bad.

I've been thinking again about the baby's name. . . . Now there's a good chance, if it's a girl, she's going to be called Katya.

Apparently the baby now weighs about four ounces; he's fully formed and measures six to seven and a half inches. It's hard to imagine.

I woke up terribly depressed this morning. I'm bored with being pregnant, just damned fed up with the whole thing.

I was talking to a girl friend and she's very close to the end. She told me she's very frightened of the whole thing, very afraid. She hadn't been to any classes so I'm hoping that my classes will help me.

I finally have been violently ill from being pregnant. Touch wood it never happens again.

I'm oiling my stomach and bust every night after my bath and checking very carefully to see if I'm getting any stretch marks. So far I haven't found any.

I think I grew enormously this past weekend. . . . My husband thinks so, too. And I felt funny things inside. I felt as though I'd been running very fast and could feel my heart beating very hard in my stomach. And later I felt something like little bubbles bursting inside. Maybe this is the beginning of real movement.

I'm worried a lot about smoking while I'm pregnant. My doctor said it would be better if I didn't but he wasn't absolutely strict about it. . . . I wish I could quit. . . . At least I can cut down.

I'm tired and cranky at work now, but people there seem to be very understanding and don't mind too much. It's really a help, when you're feeling low and someone says you look marvelous.

Back to a little girl or a little boy again . . . I hope it's a girl.

I've decided I'm going to be a perfect mother, despite everyone telling me over and over that I'm going to spoil the baby rotten.

Somebody said to my husband, "She's going to stop work? I worked up until the last minute! She's just going to go home and be bored." I don't know why I got upset but I did and began to cry about the whole thing.

Tonight the baby made a movement like a frog jumping. That's the only way I can describe it, sort of like a frog kicking its legs out when it swims. Today is the beginning of my fifth month, so I guess it's right on time.

Pollution in Pincher Creek

November 1971: Day One

Last summer, two major oil and gas companies which operate in southwestern Alberta – as well as a lot of other places – settled out of court a suit for $700,000 filed by fifteen families who had launched that suit in 1965, claiming damage to their property and their health from air pollution. In spite of the size of the award, and the dramatic confrontation between a group of citizens on the one hand and government and industry on the other, that case has received little national attention. Today, "This Country in the Morning" begins a five-part examination of it. We do so with a couple of things in mind. The first, of course, is simply to inform people of what went on in the Alberta courts (had a similar case occurred in the East, I'm sure there would have been at least one hour of network television time devoted to it and heaven knows how many major magazine articles and newspaper stories). But we also feel that the Pincher Creek case, as it is most handily known, may well hold some lessons for all of us about the way we as a country are legislating against pollution, and about the very difficult choices each of us has to make about the balance between ecology and the economy.

The Pincher Creek case is not a simple one; if most stories have two sides, this one has at least five, and we're going to present all of them here. I would ask you not to pick all your heroes or all your villains until you've heard all sides. For myself, having read thousands of words of background and news coverage (such as it was), I see no single group of villains – not industry, not government, not the press, not the citizens, and certainly not our legal system. I should also point out that, in spite of the size of the award, it was an out-of-court settlement; that is, no court of law has ever judged the two oil companies involved, Shell and Gulf, guilty of air pollution or of causing any damage. The settlement was a voluntary one, made after more than six years of litigation.

That litigation began when a group of fifteen families in Pincher Creek, Alberta, found they had no recourse outside the courts. Pincher Creek is a community of 3,200 people, about 130 miles southwest of Calgary. Until the late 1960s, it had been almost entirely a ranching community, where cattle and pigs were, as they still are, bred and fattened for market. In 1957, Shell Oil and Gulf, or British American as it then was, erected gas-processing plants in the Pincher Creek area. The purpose of those plants is to remove the sulphur from the sour natural gas found in the area. That sulphur is reclaimed and sold – an important point, because it means that it is in the industry's *economic* interest to get as much of it out as possible. But the important product, of course, is the gas itself, gas without which the Trans-Canada pipeline probably wouldn't have been feasible. In the processing, however, in the flaring of the natural hydrogen sulphide, extraneous gasses are produced, principally sulphur dioxide. And sulphur dioxide is not a pleasant thing to have around, as you will hear in a minute.

Today, I'd like you to meet Mrs. Edith Macrae, who was secretary-treasurer of the Pincher Creek citizens' committee that eventually filed suit against Gulf and Shell. Later you'll hear from the newspaperman who wrote most of the coverage of the Pincher Creek case in the Calgary *Herald*, from the lawyer who handled the citizens' action, from spokesmen for both the oil companies involved and finally, from an official of the Alberta government. When it's all over, I'm not sure what conclusion you'll have come to – but you will know a great deal more about the issues that are involved, and the practical questions at stake when citizens take action on their own behalf.

PG: I wonder if you could tell me what it's like for you and your family to live on a farm where that stuff is pouring out over you?

EM: Well, it's a most depressing thing. One of the symptoms we noticed in connection with the fumes was that it did have a depressing effect on people. . . . We have often been referred to as having psychological symptoms. I know that when the fumes were present, the children would sit and cry for no reason; they just really felt miserable. When things were particularly bad they would vomit; diarrhea was a very common symptom. They suffered nose bleeds, eye irritations, skin allergies and would break out in rashes.

PG: Were there doctors who actually said that this was a result of the sulphur dioxide?

EM: Yes, there were doctors who thought so, but it seems that they weren't listened to. This is one thing I've often wondered about; why weren't professional opinions recognized? I believe that the oil companies felt that the doctors were family doctors, in many cases friends or acquaintances of the people involved, and that they couldn't give an accurate, unbiased professional opinion. Consequently, the oil companies didn't really accept their opinions. I was also really upset that at the time we were trying to gather scientific evidence, the medical officer for the municipality was unable to get the names of certain chemicals that were used in plant processes because they were a trade secret. He was trying to see if there were other substances that could be causing our problem, but he was unable to get the names of those chemicals.

PG: Was he someone acting on behalf of the committee?

EM: He's hired by the provincial government as health officer, and he was acting on our behalf. He was really very concerned for us.

PG: How was your livestock affected?

EM: They're affected in much the same way people are, although I think to a lesser degree because we noticed, on days when the fumes were really bad, that all the cattle would be lying on the hilltop; you wouldn't find them resting and grazing in the valleys, in low areas. They seemed to have enough natural instinct to know where the better air was. We noticed that cattle confined in the fumes would often go off their feed if they were being fattened, even with the use of things to aid their digestion and to improve their appetite.

PG: And that, of course, was the business you were in.

EM: Yes, this would be a setback in that they would cease to gain. The beef business is based on rate of gain per day, and there were many days when the cattle didn't do very much gaining. If anything, they would fall behind. There were a number of families who previously had raised a considerable number of pigs, but it seemed as though the young were affected very badly. The litters were very weakened; our little piglets seemed to die as soon as they were born and quite often were born dead. It had never been a problem before. Some families that have moved away are successfully raising pigs again. A provincial veterinarian did some tests on pigs to try to determine what the trouble was, but they didn't reach a conclusion. They did find out that either a sudden, large amount or a sudden, small amount would kill the pigs, but even large amounts given over a period of time wouldn't bother them nearly so much. So this is still a mystery.

PG: In 1958, you and your family were living about fifteen miles from Pincher Creek on a rented farm on which you raised and fattened cattle. Why did you feel you had to leave that farm?

EM: In 1957, when the B.A. plant had just gone into production in that area, we became bothered for the first time by pollution. It affected most of the family and when my fifth child was born, the doctor wouldn't allow me to take him home because they had already sensed that things weren't right. So I stayed in town with the baby while my husband stayed at the farm to run things.

PG: To stay in town with the baby was a short-term solution for you. What did you do about the fact that your house was in that kind of area?

EM: Well, we still had occasional problems, and when we had an opportunity to buy a small ranch just about three and a half miles away, out of the prevailing wind and the area that was being affected by the operations of the B.A. plant, we relocated and began building a new farmstead. At this time, Shell hadn't built wells to the west and there was no indication whatsoever that the second plant would be built in the area. We had just built a new house when we learned that Shell had found some very rich wells in the mountain area and was planning to build a plant. As it turned out, the plant would be directly southwest of us, which meant that the prevailing wind would bring the fumes in our direction.

PG: In 1967 you moved again, this time into town, did you not?

EM: Yes, the children were unwell and we were just getting nowhere trying to convince people that there was a problem, so we decided to take the family out of the area. We were very concerned about one child in particular. We have been grateful ever since that we made the move, because she's a different child; she just improved tremendously within a few months.

PG: Can you tell me how she seemed to be affected?

EM: She was the baby of the family and she was the only child at home; the rest of the children were, by this time, all in school. The children who went to school daily were out of the area, and while they started off to school in the morning feeling wretched, by afternoon, quite often they felt much better. But the baby was in the gas a good part of the time and she had just simply stopped eating from the time she was about a year and a half old until we moved in November 1967. She hadn't gained any weight; she weighed thirty-one pounds and even, at one time, lost a pound.

PG: Thirty-one pounds at what age, Mrs. Macrae?

EM: From the time she was one and a half until she was three and a half. We moved into town and within four and a half months she gained five pounds. Her appetite improved and she's just a very healthy, active girl now. But I worry about what would have happened had we not made the decision to move.

PG: Obviously, at this point other people were concerned by the amount of pollution. When was the committee formed?

EM: During the opening of the Shell plant and for a period following that opening, pollution was really very bad. After much publicity in the newspapers, the provincial government called an inquiry in the courthouse in Pincher Creek, which was attended by cabinet ministers, officials of the Health Department, municipal council, ten of the farmers being affected, and the oil companies. We were given a chance to make representations at this inquiry. After the inquiry, the government set up a committee of experts in Edmonton to study our problem. One of the things we had noticed in our contacts with the Health Department was that, whenever we talked about things that had happened or mentioned reports of complaints, it just seemed that they were unaware of it. They either hadn't heard about it or they just weren't getting the information. So we decided that if information was what was required, well, we would collect all we could and forward it to them and perhaps this would bridge the communication gap.

PG: That would have been some time in 1963?

EM: Yes. Early in 1963 we formed a committee and we began to collect data from different families, anything from our observations of wind direction and smokestacks or anything that was in any way connected with our problem. This was all compiled and forwarded to the provincial Health Department.

PG: At what point did the group of you together decide to act, to sue Gulf and Shell?

EM: A scientific advisory committee was set up by the government following that Pincher Creek inquiry. When we saw the report that was compiled, we realized that the government felt that most of our complaints were of a psychological nature. There just seemed to be no hope that they were going to take action of any kind, so we decided to retain a lawyer, but not with a court case in mind. We obtained the lawyer to make further representations to the government, to see if he couldn't convince them that we did have a problem. This went on for many months, nearly a year, and then at the end of that time we were still unable to convince the Health Department that something should be done. So we notified them that as a group we were no longer going to send information to them, that we couldn't accept their findings and that we were hiring a lawyer and we were probably going to court.

Day Two

One of the reasons we're looking back into the Pincher Creek case is that, although it was pretty well covered in at least southern Alberta, it has not had anything like the national attention it would have received if it had occurred in, say, a major city in the East. In spite of its lack of a formal conclusion, of a judgement by the courts, it is one of the most significant cases yet in Canada of citizens – and, to be fair, industry and government – trying to cope with the struggle between everyone's desire for more dollars and everyone's desire for cleaner air. One exception to the media's lack of interest in the Pincher Creek case is John Schmidt, agricultural editor of the Calgary *Herald*. To bring our knowledge of the case further along from where we left it yesterday, I asked John Schmidt:

PG: How did you first find out what was going on in Pincher Creek?

JS: In 1965 I attended the annual meeting of the Alberta Farm Regime, now Unifarm, when a delegation of Pincher Creek farmers came into the meeting and asked for financial assistance to take this case to court. They asked the farmer's union to put out an appeal for funds because it was going to take an awful lot of money to fight this case and they just didn't have it.

PG: In the end, I think they got $5,700 from the farmer's union, didn't they?

JS: That's about right, through contributions that ranged from $1.00 to $500 from farmer's union locals, Four-H clubs, municipalities and even labour unions. They figured that there was something going on down there and they wanted to have it brought forward.

PG: In that period, provincial regulations required that the plants achieve 93% efficiency; does that mean they're allowed to leave 7% of the sulphur dioxide in what is coming out of the chimneys?

JS: No; it means 7% of the hydrogen sulphide can be left in but this in turn must be flared off. When you flare it off, by incinerating it to 1000 degrees Fahrenheit, it turns to sulphur dioxide. This is what's sent up the plant stack.

PG: Those regulations have become much more severe since then, have they not?

JS: I believe it's now 95% and I think they are going to 97%. In the spring of 1960, the ranchers in the area of these processing plants began complaining about air pollution from heavy concentrations of sulphur dioxide. They were suffering eye irritations which were diagnosed as being chemically caused. Other illnesses were vomiting and nausea, severe headaches and loss of appetite, night awakening – kids woke up in terror, crying. And I understand the headaches were really splitting; they just about blew the top of your head off.

PG: In talking with Mrs. Macrae, we heard some dramatic stories. Have you ever talked to a doctor yourself who has said that these symptoms were directly related to the chemical irritants?

JS: No, I haven't talked to a doctor directly, but I've read the transcript of the provincial hearings set up in November 1962 on this and Dr. L.B. Collins of Lethbridge gave evidence of this, that it was a chemical irritant. Also, the Veterinary Services Department of the Alberta government carried on some experiments on animals. The sulphur dioxide affects the animals by breaking down their lungs. I asked a federal animal-health man here in Calgary if this would affect the animal's meat and he said not to the best of his knowledge; they have never been able to demonstrate that. However, he did say that meat is not tested for sulphur, although it is tested for other minerals.

PG: As this situation began to develop in the early sixties, the citizens began to complain to the government, right?

JS: They complained to the government and they also complained to the owners of the plants and they raised hell with a few MLAs, but the plant management steadfastly maintained that they were running pollution-free operations. Possibly they were, under the government standard set up at the time. There were several government inquiries and the government also set up a scientific advisory committee which imported a so-called pollution expert from California. Their final report cost about $300,000. At the end of that report the conclusion was reached that these people were not suffering from anything they could put their finger on but psychological illnesses, if you can imagine that!

PG: That must have frustrated the farmers terribly!

JS: Well, they realized they weren't getting anywhere, so they set up a committee of their own. It was called the Pincher Creek Industrial Pollution Committee. They started keeping records of everything that happened, like who got sick, the nature of the illness, the time, date, place, direction of the wind and the severity of the odour. All the farmers and ranchers in the area reported, so they had a complete record of what happened to them down there. And when they figured they had enough evidence they went to Premier Manning and presented it to him. But eventually they had to go to court.

PG: Have you been back to Pincher Creek recently?

JS: Yes, I went back to talk to several of these farmers when the settlement was reached. From what I was told then, there still seems to be some trouble at the plants when they shut down for cleaning — some problem getting back on stream. I was told that the air was still pretty rotten at those times; they would get some really heavy doses of gas. I don't know whether it was in my mind or not, but I had a heck of a headache the day I was down there. I don't think it was in my mind.

PG: Totally psychological. . . .

JS: Well, if I listen to the government it was purely psychological.

PG: John, does any kind of a financial settlement, even $700,000, really solve the problem?

JS: Well, it did temporarily for the fifteen families involved, because quite a few of them had to move. One man had to move into Pincher Creek and he now commutes nineteen miles a day to his ranch. But I think the whole thing must be discussed in the context of the petroleum industry being an instrument of society, created by society for society's own use. Having said this, we must realize that society has an obligation to protect innocent people from instruments of its own creation. These people must be compensated for property damage and their health must not be impaired. And they must not be held up to ridicule by disbelieving public officials.

Day Three

Today, we continue our examination of the Pincher Creek case, talking to the lawyer who handled the citizens' complaints — complaints that eventually resulted in that $700,000 out-of-court settlement. The lawyer's name is William Geddes, and he spoke to us from his office in Calgary.

PG: After the results of the study prepared by the scientific advisory committee became public, and having tried all other routes, the citizens' committee decided to proceed with some kind of civil action. . . . Is that correct?

WG: That is correct. The government hadn't taken any drastic steps at that point. In my own opinion, the plaintiffs would have been better off if the inquiry hadn't been held – certainly, since they didn't do anything in a legal way for approximately two years, the whole process was set back that much longer. They finally decided that the only course left for them was a civil action for damages and an injunction against the plants which would, in effect, limit the amount of effluent discharged into the air. This was a very difficult point in the lawsuit, and the defendant had very different views as to whether or not an injunction could be obtained. This would be about 1964 or 1965.

PG: How do you decide how much money you're going to sue for?

WG: Well, in this case, I think you could almost say that you throw a dart into the air and see where it lands. The figures were just very unsophisticated guesses.

PG: What were the figures named in the suit?

WG: I think the total was a million and a half dollars. When you start this kind of action, the main thing is to achieve some kind of remedy, to control the actual pollution. That's what the people wanted. They were interested in improving the environment, but since the only damages a court will award is money, it had to be that way. I mean, you don't have a nuisance if you don't sue for damages.

PG: Were all the committee's records available to you?

WG: Oh, yes; they turned them over to us early on. As a group of lay people, none of whom had ever been involved in lawsuits before they started this, they did an excellent job of mustering evidence, which is the thing you must have, as a lawyer, to continue this kind of suit.

PG: What kind of evidence, from your point of view?

WG: The only evidence that they could give, really, was of their experiences. They were trying to describe times of day and the type of odours that they had noticed and how it affected them. You'll appreciate that of forty adult people, one person has a very sensitive nose and at the other end of the scale someone has a very, shall we say, tough sense of smell, and in between is everybody else. Of the forty people who experienced the same environment, one wouldn't notice a thing and somebody else would be quite upset. Anyway, they would make notes of their experiences or just tell you about them; some were a little extreme and some of them bent over the other way. It was a difficult job of averaging, I suppose you'd put it that way.

PG: What sort of records had Shell and Gulf been keeping through this time, and were they made available to you?

WG: They had kept – and they were pretty good about this – very good records of complaints and individual experiences. They were only made available as a result of the litigation because in a lawsuit both sides must show any record they have that affects the lawsuit in question. Fairly early on, the defendant oil companies saw certain of our records and we saw their records.

PG: In volume, how many of their records did you see?

WG: Well, I would estimate in the order of ten filing cabinets for each defendant.

PG: It must have taken you a day or two to wade through that amount of material.

WG: The whole process – and the defendant lawyers had an equal task because they had to read their own clients' records, too – took about a year. It was a difficult job for the defendants to gather some of this information together because some of it was stored in Pincher Creek, some in Calgary, some in Toronto. But reading the documents is just the first step. Next is the examination for discovery. Here the usual procedure is for the plaintiff to examine the defendants first, and then the defendants examine the plaintiffs. We had actually started the examinations for discovery.

PG: At what point was the figure of $700,000 decided on?

WG: I think it was about 11:30 in the morning of December 18, 1970.

PG: Approximately. . . . ?

WG: Yeah. . . . After about eighteen months of negotiating back and forth, trying to get all sides to agree, we finally hit on that.

PG: How much did Shell pay and how much did Gulf pick up?

WG: I have no idea. They decided that together and then dealt jointly with me.

PG: A curious thing has happened here. . . . But do you think this case is really resolved?

WG: Firstly, I'm satisfied that the situation has improved, but I think it's more the responsibility of the companies to do this than any tightening of provincial regulations; I think this is a private thing. Secondly, people have received money, but this is, in effect, compensation for the fifteen years of difficulties some of them have had. You wouldn't think it fair, I'm sure, if the remedy were that the plants be shut down . . . a very unwise thing to do, I would think.

PG: Do you think there's a general lesson for society in the Pincher Creek case?

WG: Yes, I do. I think that the people there showed amazing courage and patience in continuing the lawsuit. I think those who were involved in the lawsuit have a far better appreciation and respect for the whole legal system — except for the usual criticism that it's too slow and we all would like it to be faster. But generally I think they have a lot more confidence in the fact that the courts will protect the little man against the big man.

Day Four

Yesterday, when I suggested to William Geddes that one of the reasons the air seemed clearer at Pincher Creek now was that government regulations were stricter, Mr. Geddes quickly pointed out that a bigger reason was the policy of the industry itself, the oil and gas industry. It is from that industry that we'll hear today. No one will name the amount each of the two companies involved — Gulf or Shell — paid to the families of Pincher Creek, so today we'll talk with both of them. First, speaking for Shell Canada, Mr. Reg Anderson, gas manager of the company's exploration and production department and also, it's worth pointing out, president of Alberta Sulphur Research Ltd., and a member of the Environmental Conservation Committee of the Canadian Petroleum Association.

PG: Reg, I think it's important for people to realize that there are economic forces and forces of environmental control at work in the Pincher Creek case that don't necessarily mesh with one another. How many jobs are involved there, and what has the development of gas around the Pincher Creek area meant to that part of the province economically?

RA: When Shell first moved in, the general area where the plant is was considered to be a depressed area. Since that time, of course, the industrial development of the plant has taken place, and payroll in the area directly from our operations amounts to a couple of million dollars a year. One can see that this has had a dramatic impact on the economy of the southwestern portion of Alberta. I think it's probably noteworthy that many of the small towns in the prairies are shrinking in size, whereas Pincher Creek is actually expanding; I think that the economic stability of the area is guaranteed for years to come as a result of the economic activity of the gas plant.

PG: When people first began to complain about what they maintained was pollution of the air, in 1960 or perhaps even earlier, they complained to the government and they complained to you, did they not?

RA: Yes.

PG: And the report of the scientific advisory committee on air pollution, released in 1964, said that all measures that could be taken really were being taken. Was that your understanding of the report?

RA: Yes, I think generally that was the understanding that one gained from the report.

PG: Now, seven years later, you and Gulf have together paid out $700,000 to those people. So you have obviously come to believe that some damage had been done to their livestock, and perhaps even their health?

RA: I don't think we're saying that at all, Peter. It would be foolish for us to deny that we put sulphurous gas into the atmosphere, but it was a very complex procedure and at one point in the litigation we concluded that the plaintiffs and the defendants would be well served by settling the matter without a long and bitter court battle. Obviously the plaintiff felt the same way; we think both sides were very much better off to settle than to proceed with litigation.

PG: But in paying out $700,000 which, even for Shell and Gulf together, is a great deal of money, I would think that, by implication, you have said, yes, some damage was done.

RA: Well, Peter, there has been no legal adjudication of damage by a court and I can't add much to what I've already said.

PG: Have any of your own employees ever reported the kind of symptoms we heard Mrs. Macrae of Pincher Creek talking about? Nausea, vomiting, headaches, depression, anything like that?

RA: We have people from our own company living in the same area and no, they haven't been complaining of these kinds of problems.

PG: Are you totally satisfied that your own records have always been correct about the amount of emission, which can vary from day to day?

RA: There is no doubt that we improved our measuring techniques dramatically over the years, both in the area and in the plant itself. I'm sure that we and the government are both in a better position today to measure and monitor the gas plant than we were in 1960.

PG: So if the air were polluted in the early 1960s, if people did suffer damage, it would be a lot less likely to happen now.

RA: Well, if indeed there was a problem in 1962. . . . I think it's safe to say that there is certainly less of a problem or there is no problem today.

PG: There is no air pollution?

RA: Well, there is always a certain amount of sulphur dioxide in the atmosphere, but it's well controlled and well monitored, and well within the requirements that are imposed upon us.

PG: Reg, as well as being a senior executive of Shell, you're also active in a number of environmental-conservation committees in Alberta. I'd like to ask you about how you see the general implications of the events in Pincher Creek, but at the same time I would like to point out that Shell and Gulf have, in a way, been fingered by the press, and made to look worse than they really behaved. I understand that the man who did most of the reporting of the Pincher Creek case, with whom I've talked on the program, didn't talk to you before he wrote his five-part series.

RA: Well, that's true, we were not asked to comment before that series was created. But I'm personally very happy that the litigation has been settled. After all, the objectives of the people of Pincher Creek and our own are very close, and I'm looking forward to a more neighbourly relationship between us all, now that this is out of the way.

The second spokesman for the industrial side of this multi-sided story is Mr. William Winterton of Gulf Oil of Canada. Mr. Winterton is associate general counsel for Gulf and is pres- ident of the Canadian Petroleum Law Foundation, an organization doing research into the legal aspects of the oil and gas industry.

PG: Mr. Winterton, one point that has come up as we've looked into this story is that, if it were purely a question of dollars, the extracting oil and gas companies would take out 100% of the sulphur because this is something they can sell. So there's no profit at all in putting sulphur dioxide into the air.

WW: No, I think you must appreciate that the technology is not that perfect. A sulphur plant may attain, say, 92% or 93% efficiency, but to try for 100% efficiency is almost impossible. . . .

PG: Because the last few drops cost a higher amount?

WW: Yes. It may cost you as much as $8,000,000 to squeeze it up another 2%.

PG: What percentage are you now in the Pincher Creek area?

WW: Well, I think we're roughly around 91 to 92%. It's my understanding that we're not expected at the Pincher Creek plant to attain 97% efficiency because of the size of our plant. I think you should know that this plant was originally designed to process six hundred tons of sulphur a day and that, since 1967, the amount of gas we've been producing has been greatly reduced, so we're emitting less than half of what we're authorized to emit.

PG: Mr. Winterton, increasingly in the future, society and business and government will have to make decisions involving the environment against the economy. We've been discussing one such decision here, and I think it's important that people understand how much the gas and oil industry has done for that area.

WW: I don't think people generally realize the considerable importance of the industry, not only for the province of Alberta, but nationally. It wasn't until Gulf committed itself to building a plant here that the Trans-Canada pipeline got off the ground. I believe that that helped Canada to a certain degree of independence in the area of gas supplies. . . .

PG: In point of fact, most of the gas now goes to the United States, doesn't it?

WW: No, actually, I think most of it goes down east. They may trade it out, but it was originally designated to go to Ontario. Furthermore, our plant was built in three stages, so that during the course of construction there may have been as many as a thousand men at a time employed there, which has benefited the local merchants and the businessmen. Since that time, of course, we have had a staff of about fifty people.

PG: You're a lawyer and you will have a proper response to this. Having settled out of court for $700,000, Shell and Gulf, to my layman's interpretation, have somehow implicitly admitted that there was pollution and there was damage done to those people. Now that concept doesn't hold up in law, does it?

WW: No, it really doesn't. Of course we never denied that there wasn't some pollution. We think it's primarily a business decision, considering the situation in which we found ourselves — primarily, we just wanted to get on with the job of producing gas down there.

PG: The settlement also involved some easement rights given by those same families, did it not?

WW: That's correct. As part of the settlement, the plaintiff agreed to grant to the two oil companies an easement permitting these companies to continue to allow the effluent to cross their land, providing it stays within the permitted levels set down by a regulatory body. The companies would only be liable for any damages that might occur as a result of effluent in excess of permitted levels.

PG: So, in effect, they're saying that you can continue to do the same thing?

WW: That's right.

PG: How do you feel, generally, about provincial regulations, and how has Gulf got along with the government over these?

WW: We've got along well. The oil industry has been given a lot of attention here, and the industry itself has provided a lot of the data and the techniques and expertise, which is improving all the time. . . . It's not perfect, but generally I would say that we've been able to live with the standards set because we think they've been realistic. The difficulties start when you have a lack of knowledge, a lack of technical experience and data, which brings about the establishment of conflicting standards and improper criteria.

PG: Could I pick you up on that one point? In its report published in 1964, the scientific advisory committee on air pollution said that everything around Pincher Creek was just as it should be. Everything, every measure of control that should be taken was being taken. And yet we have, seven years after that, an out-of-court settlement. What changed between 1964 and 1971?

WW: I don't think anything changed, basically. The scientific advisory committee was made up of very qualified people and they conducted a study for a year; they had a lot of data available and as far as we're concerned their report pretty well confirms the results of our own studies. We had put people in the most sensitive area in a trailer for several months, along with recording devices, and their report was pretty well the same as the committee's. We also feel that part of the trouble down there was the fear of the local people: they thought they were being poisoned. Now, we had several meetings with the residents. We tried to explain to them exactly what was going on at the plant, and tried to allay any fears they might have had about what was going up the stack. But I'm afraid that they didn't believe us and subsequently they didn't believe the report. They just didn't like the tone of it, I guess. But I really think it was quite accurate.

Day Five

We turn today to a government spokesman, Eugene Kupchanko, who, in his capacity as an engineer for the Alberta Department of Health, followed the case from the beginning. Today, he speaks from the perspective of his new job, director of pollution control in Alberta's newly formed Department of the Environment.

PG: Mr. Kupchanko, as far back as 1961 or '62, the Department of Health was receiving a fair number of complaints from the citizens of Pincher Creek, wasn't it?

EK: Right, and it was our duty at that time to investigate all complaints, to find out what was causing the situation.

PG: At that time, did you have technical monitors in the area?

EK: Not at that time. Back in 1962 the whole pollution field was pretty new, but when we started the advisory committee, we brought in a consultant from Los Angeles, Larry Shakes, probably one of the top people in air pollution, and he got us going on a complete monitoring program.

PG: And then through 1963, some very intensive tests were done by the Department of Health, now the Department of the Environment?

EK: Right. During the next couple of years an advisory committee was formed, composed of experts in various fields — chemical engineers, veterinarians, field observers, a metrologist and our own personnel, who were experienced in the chemical-engineering aspects. There were also several medical doctors on the committee.

PG: And in March of 1964 that scientific advisory committee published a report that came down pretty definitely, saying: "The concentrations of pollutants that have been measured are well below the levels where an adverse effect on a person's livestock or vegetation would occur." It also said that: "The continued intensive investigation in this field carried out during 1963 is not warranted." Can I sum up that report as saying that every measure of control that ought to have been taken was being taken in Pincher Creek in 1964?

EK: No, not completely. You can appreciate that the technology of gas-plant engineering increases and the technology of pollution increases. Then we as a government ultimately impose more stringent regulations on the plant. We didn't just stand still in 1964.

PG: Those statements I read are direct quotations from the report. It seemed to indicate that things were okay.

EK: Not completely. It said that there was no adverse effect on health. Now, it didn't deal with any of these odour situations that have developed, or the problem of corrosion. This is where, I think, the whole problem started . . . the anxiety of the people due to the odours in the area, which they associate with some sort of toxicity.

PG: I see. Because it smells bad, they were sure that it was poison.

EK: Right.

PG: Now, from 1964, the people in the Pincher Creek area carried on their fight in spite of this report. They continued to complain to the government and then they found it necessary to launch the civil suit we've been talking about. Did conditions in fact change in Pincher Creek?

EK: I think that conditions probably did change for the better, because of better operational procedures in the plant and less venting of the odours. I think the action brought about by the citizens in the area was the result of conditions around 1963. Certainly, the amount of pollution during the next couple of years had decreased quite significantly.

PG: The suit took six years. At the time it was launched, the people there were keeping daily diaries of what they took to be the concentration of sulphur dioxide in the air. Their records eventually became a factor in the litigation, so I can't quite believe that the people felt they were acting on past injustices.

EK: I don't know how they could keep their own sulphur dioxide measurements, because the only people doing sulphur dioxide and hydrogen sulphide measurements were ourselves, the Department of Health, and the two companies involved. At that time the measurements were quite low; in fact, the measurements were lower than they are now — even, at that time, lower than in Toronto or Montreal. So it's not these particular compounds that were causing them anguish; it was the odorous compounds.

PG: In your attendance at those hearings and your examination of all kinds of testimony, have you ever heard a medical doctor say that anyone had suffered any medical damage?

EK: For the life of me I can't remember if anybody said that there was medical damage. Well, let me answer that in a different way. We actually exposed animals, ten pigs, to very high concentrations of sulphur dioxide and hydrogen sulphide over extended periods of time. These were concentrations a thousand times higher than what we monitored in Pincher Creek, and we found no evidence of damage within the lungs.

PG: How does that compare with the statement we heard from a number of people, that the pig industry around Pincher Creek has in fact been wiped out by the presence of the gas?

EK: Well, it certainly can't be justified by our veterinarians here. There's nothing really to affect the pigs or the cattle. If you can raise pigs in Toronto or Montreal, you should be able to raise them in Pincher Creek, because the hydrogen sulphide concentrations are of a comparable nature.

PG: Were your measuring instruments always in the right place topographically?

EK: We made every effort to try to get these instruments in a site that we considered had the highest pollution potential. Initially, the instruments were put in the yards of those people with the complaints. Subsequently, we did go to some sites where we thought we would find the highest concentration.

PG: The oil and gas industry talks favourably about the Alberta government's regulations advancing at about the same speed as the technology itself. How do you feel, as a civil servant, about the oil and gas industry in Alberta and its willingness to respond to regulations?

EK: I think generally they've been very cooperative. But you can't come to an industry and say, well, tomorrow you've got to have $5,000,000 worth of this sort of equipment. That just can't be done. We give the industry a fairly good lead time in which to install new equipment or come up to more stringent standards.

PG: And they respond?

EK: They respond, right.

PG: Should industry be held responsible for damage that industry is alleged to have caused, or should that perhaps be society's duty, to repay people who allegedly have been damaged?

EK: No, I think the onus should be placed on the industry if they damage other people's property or other people's livelihood. I see government's function in monitoring and regulating, to see that pollution limits are not exceeded. If there is a continual offence, with no apparent action being taken, then certainly government should step in.

PG: What do you think the long-term effects of the Pincher Creek settlement will be? First of all, do you think it might encourage people to go around government regulatory bodies and pursue their own civil actions?

EK: I think that it's the responsibility of a regulatory body to keep the environment in a reasonable condition, and this is representative of the demands of the people. If we have a lot of complaints from an area like Pincher Creek, then we must go to the companies and tell them: look, you've got a fair amount of complaints, how about tightening up? Certainly this is the attitude that we take.

PG: Do you think one other effect of the Pincher Creek case might be just a little more attention to pollution control by industry as a whole?

EK: Oh, I think so; certainly the onus has always been on industry. If they cause the damage, then they must face the litigation.

That completes our evidence on the Pincher Creek case. What you have heard, I should add, is only the very surface of some of the deeply contested facts at issue. As just one example, Mr. Kupchanko spoke today about the contradictory figures on the amount of sulphur dioxide in the air. The people of Pincher Creek, he said, weren't capable of making the kind of technical measurements required; the only really adequate equipment belonged either to the government or the companies. And yet, one day in March of 1962 – the period the dispute concerned – John Marcellus, one of the citizens who was involved in the suit, read on his Drager gas detector an amount of more than 100 parts per million of sulphur dioxide in the air near one of the plants. The company's own machine that day registered 13.5 parts per million. A level of 25 is considered "toxic." Admitting the discrepancy, no one argues that this is too much poison in the air – and one of the measurements was made by a citizen.

Here is a quotation from a brief to be submitted next week to the Alberta Department of the Environment by Dr. Don Gill of the University of Alberta Department of Geography, a brief describing environmental pollution in southern Alberta. Dr. Gill is describing conditions now, when, from all that the parties to the Pincher Creek case have told us, conditions have improved. "Monitoring of the stack emission is performed once annually, usually over a four-day period. . . . Three out of the seven sampling periods (June 1966, July 1967 and June 1969) show emissions of sulphur above the provincial board of health limitation. If this occurs during a pre-warned sampling run, then emissions could conceivably be different during other periods. The emissions of sulphur dioxide from the stack samples are of such a volume that concentrations of the fumes caused by the topography or wind currents could be toxic."

Or on the simple matter of the gas itself: sulphur dioxide smells bad; no one argues with that. But what does it do? You've heard that there are questions about whether there was any real medical damage caused to the citizens of Pincher Creek. But were the symptoms described by Mrs. Macrae – nausea, headaches, loss of weight – were they all imaginary, brought about by a bad smell? Or were they direct, chemical results of the gas? To the people who suffered those symptoms, I don't suppose it matters. Nausea is nausea.

And what about the livestock? We've heard that the pig industry around Pincher Creek has virtually collapsed. As long ago as 1962, the Lethbridge *Herald* quoted a veterinarian in Pincher Creek as saying that almost the entire district had gone out of hog production because of pollution. Yet Mr. Kupchanko's researchers say that pigs have survived as much as a thousand times the amount of sulphur dioxide that was in the air during the worst of times. I quote from an experiment cited by Dr. Gill: "Sulphur dioxide in concentrations of 10 parts per million or more for 3½ to 7½ hours produced (in hogs) lung damage, respiratory tract problems, and impaired growth rate. It was shown that these symptoms corresponded to those of hogs examined at one of the ranches in the polluted area. There is no evidence that any formal action was taken by the provincial government following this report."

But these are all questions of fact and, since no court of law has ruled on those facts, they all remain open to debate. Perhaps a more important point is that both sides in the litigation, the fifteen families of Pincher Creek on the one hand and the two oil companies on the other, have reached an agreement that is satisfactory to each of them. If indeed wrong was done, they have agreed, then it has been redressed, and the companies, as you've heard, now have easements from the citizens to carry on their business as usual.

Are there deeper questions involved? I think

there are. And from the evidence of the Pincher Creek case, perhaps they are questions we should all be asking ourselves.

For one thing, is it really necessary, with the amount of anti-pollution legislation we now have on the books in virtually all our provinces, in many of our municipalities and in Ottawa itself, for citizens to have to act on their own behalf to the degree that the fifteen concerned families of Pincher Creek, Alberta, acted? If they do not act, what is going to happen to citizens who suffer from damage by pollutants, who don't have the kind of resources, energy and courage the Pincher Creek families have?

Is it really all that healthy when we hear, as we have heard, such mutual praise between government and industry, when a senior civil servant can speak with pride of his department's "understanding with all industry," can say that government understands that it must give an industry what it calls "lead time" — time to install the minimum equipment? Or should *all* regulatory bodies be cracking down as hard as they can when there is any scrap of evidence of pollution? Should there be more tension between public regulatory bodies and private industries?

I don't know the answers to these questions, and in asking them in the context of the Pincher Creek case, I do not mean to point a finger at any particular industry or even at industry in general. For we are all of us polluters, from leaf-burners, car-drivers, cigarette-smokers, up to large government institutions or public utilities that turn energy into produce. But if we are all polluters, so are we all being polluted. Taken at one level, the Pincher Creek story could be seen as a dramatization of something that is happening to all of us — and are all of us, I wonder, as strong and as capable as the fifteen families of Pincher Creek?

I Resign from My Lawn

Dear Lawn:
I've had it; enough, I say, enough. I quit, I resign, I terminate our relationship herewith.

It is customary, I suppose, in letters of resignation, to list with delicacy one's reasons for resignation. Well, I cannot find phrases delicate. Only a catalogue of ills that you have subjected me to over the past several years.

You haunt even my winters with memories of the past summer's ills, and insane visions of those I can expect in the summer to come.

In early March you have me as the village idiot: tramping about on your hard-frozen surface, numbing my extremities in the course of spreading your spring feeding. Your allies, those garden "experts," demand this labour of me, in order that you shall spring forth green and lusty with the first warm rains of April.

April, that unspeakable time of taunting. How many hours do I spend in back-breaking labour attempting to drive my mowing machine through the green and lusty jungle I've created, only to find that the better portion of that jungle is weeds?

Once again, out comes the spreader and on with the weed-and-feed stuff. I swear you must be in cahoots with the weather, for no sooner do I spread twenty dollars of this muck on you, than along comes a thunderous cloudburst to wash it all away.

Then, of course, you retire to spend the summer alternately burning to a miserable brown and blushing with the green and yellow polkadots of dandelions.

In late August you lull me into a sense of false security by just lying there all coloured a nice green. Then I awaken one fine morning to find you covered everywhere with the purple fog of ripened crab-grass seeds. Naturally, the pods have split and a billion or so nice fat seeds have already embedded themselves in preparation for next year's attack.

Finally, to add insult to injury, you cordially invite every dog for miles around to use you as a lavatory, knowing full well it is I who must perform your distasteful ablutions.

For your information, I have been to see my banker this very morning, and at dawn tomorrow, the men with the green cement are coming, and I've bought a can of gold paint for the lawn mower.

D.G. Bremner
Mississauga, Ontario

is for Greene,
whether Nancy or Lorne,
One's still Canadian,
the other's gone foreign.

Barbara Greeniaus
Toronto, Ontario

Dear Mr. Bremner:
Ungrateful cretin! You think to resign from me, do you? You dare to catalogue that libelous list of so-called ills! All this you expect me to take lying down, as it were? Not bloody likely!

Allow me to tally mine own manifest of grievances! You and your progency have stamped about on my back these past years with magnificent contempt for my finer sensibilities. In spring you, your neighbours and especially that overweight postman insist on continuing use of that short cut even when the ground is a soggy sponge. Then, come summer, you berate me for not growing. So tell me — who can grow when packed to the density of reinforced concrete?

Following the advice of other non-thinkers

of your ilk, you irregularly shower me with all manner of odious chemicals. Thank God for the cloudbursts! They are the only things that save me! Have you ever heard of manure?

Crab grass indeed; you wouldn't know crab grass if you fell into it. That so-called purple fog of yours was not crab grass, you twit! It was your usual Saturday-morning hangover!

As for your green concrete man, a pox on both your houses. I've just sold myself to the Midnite Sod Company and by 2:00 A.M. I'll be packed and gone!

You can't quit from something you don't have!

Yours truly
Your Lawn

P.S. Ever tried chewing a blade of concrete?

Bumbershoot

March 3, 1974

Dear Mr. Gzowski:

A rush of memories as the years rolled back to hear the word "bumbershoot" on one of your programs some weeks past. How well do I recall the Anglican minister, Canon Taylor, walking down our village street on a wet day carrying a huge black bumbershoot to protect him from the falling rain; and what a great source of interest to the village children was the neat little square window cut out at the front of the umbrella, covered with isinglass.

How well I remember my mother's dinner parties when Joe Paul, the famed Indian runner, each year borrowed my father's shotgun and always returned with deer steak to grace the table. I recall small place cards brought from China by a friend. They were little white unpleated fans and had beautiful watercolour sketches thereon and tiny black ebony handles.

My mother's built-in china cabinet: one drawer with bridge talleys, beautifully coloured pencils dipped at the end in a thick, wax-like substance, and on each end, waving, gorgeous silk tassels — deep purple, bright pink, buttercup yellow — lovely, lovely shades. Also my mother's calling-card case, suede with a water-silk lining: I can close my eyes and bring to mind the scent of cedar as I opened each drawer.

School: in the center of the room, a pot-bellied stove. One boy was delegated weekly to bring in the short lengths of wood to keep us warm, and on Hallowe'en we would decide among us, with the help of the teacher, who would donate the ingredients with which to make fudge on top of the stove.

Jones' Lake: alongside our school in winter we could skate for quite a distance and we would don our warm socks and skates in the little skating house, which was situated at the top of the lake. One February 14, I received a very lacy Valentine from a boy whom I admired; I was twelve or thirteen years of age, I think, and was teased to such a degree by my schoolmates that I took it over to the lake after school and hid it among the alder bushes, planning to reclaim it later, only to return and find a most unkind and thoughtless breeze had blown it away. I shed my first tears.

The post office: we had to cross over a bridge to reach our post office in order to collect mail, as there wasn't door-to-door delivery, and I was always terrified to look down and see the mighty rush of the waters of the Sissabo River.

Cappy Granville's store: a delight to the heart and eye — hunkey doreys, ladies' choice, sheets of pink and blue candy buttons attached to strips of paper, honeymoons, bags of popcorn — the kernels were numerous, but there was always a ring with a coloured stone to reward us for our purchase. "Chaws of tobacco" licorice, suckers in the shape of nail kegs, maple, lemon, grape, orange and raspberry. We would run down the hill from school at recess with our money clutched tightly in our hands and try to decide as quickly as possible what we would like to buy. Often we went further, over the bridge to Lent's Meat Market, where we could buy one slice of bologna for one penny. But the shorter walk to Cappy Granville's store was still our favourite, for we could munch more leisurely on our way back.

The Dunbars: my dearest friends, Oressa and Annie, ages eighty-four and eighty-five respectively when they passed away, one within a week of the other. One would see in their front parlour wreaths in deep frames, glass protected, made by removing strands of hair from the heads of family members. Here I learned to play the zither, or what today is commonly named the auto harp.

My treasure of those happy, wonderful days is a small Jenny Lind doll given me by my long-departed friends. The Dunbar girls, as they were affectionately called, to the day they passed away wore long, black, rusty-looking gowns complete with petticoats and pantaloons and black ruched bonnets. I can still see the strings of dried apples hanging on nails in their back

Can you cook a kipper quicker?

Mrs. Neighbour
Scarborough, Ontario

80

porch and the little chair in the window of the front room upon which the younger generation rushed to sit. It had once been a small nail keg and was covered and padded with pink and white rose-patterned chintz. On the headrest was a white bit of linen and the words "Come and Rest," which, I presume, one of the sisters had embroidered, in red, with great patience.

In closing, a little verse told to my sisters and me by the Reverend Donald Farquhar's wife, a close friend of the family.

Once a pigmolicepin
Met a biddy lum
Sitting on a curbstone
Chewing rubber gum.
Said the pigmolicepin
"Will you give me some?"
"Ninny on your tin-type"
Said the biddy lum.

Barbara H. Hanright
Moncton, New Brunswick

The Great Dishwasher Disaster of 1973

A saga of a night of terror and adventure on the high seas (which takes place in prairie Saskatchewan)

On your dear mother's recent visit to her sister in Alberta, she discovered that her sister and brother-in-law had purchased a new-fangled kitchen device which, it is claimed, washes your dishes at the touch of a button. She came home full of news of this machine and it seemed she would not rest until she, too, owned such a machine. The decision was finally made that we would purchase one in the near future; a few days later, after purchasing a copy of the *Consumers' Report Annual* at a local newsstand, I confirmed that one particular brand would be a wise buy. (I have now, of course, lost all confidence in *Consumers' Report*, but you will see why as the story unfolds.)

Lo and behold, a week or two later a flyer arrived at the house telling of a sale of the products of this particular manufacturer — of course there was a great buy on a dishwasher, and we were hooked. The deal was consummated on Friday and arrangements made to deliver the thing on Saturday. I will now list the events chronologically as they happened — you must keep in mind that your mother and I would be quite long in the tooth now, if we had any, with a certain fear and suspicion of new mechanical devices and, of course, quite utterly devoid of any knowledge of things mechanical.

Saturday: 1500 hours
Ship's crew in particularly good spirits — why

shouldn't they be, the drudgery of doing dishes is over forever. Much good-natured bantering going on such as "it's coming," and "it's not coming," etc., etc. The weather is beautiful, sun shining, water running in the streets, spring is just around the corner. No premonition of what lies ahead. The galley by now is piled high with dirty dishes, last night's supper dishes and lunch dishes plus this morning's breakfast dishes and dinner dishes. What the hell! The machine will do them; on with the fiesta, so to speak.

1530 hours. As I lay abed in the captain's quarters, there was a commotion at the front door. The thing had arrived. It was lugged in by what I took to be mere schoolboys; they placed it in the kitchen and gave the first mate (mother) some perfunctory directions re how to hook it up to the sink and were gone in less than two minutes.

1600 hours. The two instruction booklets that came with the thing were read and re-read. Let me say a word about instructions; it has always been my contention about these instructions, whether they be for a child's toy or an automobile, that there is an unwritten law that the person who writes the instructions must be highly knowledgeable of the intricacy of the item he is writing about, but at the same time he must not be above the third-grade-school level in composition and English. I have known about this for some time now and nothing has come along to change my thinking.

1620 hours. The countdown has now begun, the first mate has loaded the machine with dishes to the scuttlebutt (whatever that is), including some dishes that are clean.

1730 hours. Supper is finished and the dishes piled in; countdown is proceeding in an orderly fashion and we are now approaching blast-off with great anticipation.

Sis mixed six sweet Swiss biscuits.

She made a proper cup of coffee in a copper coffee pot.

Dave Birley
Edmonton, Alberta

1810 hours. Ten, nine, eight, etc., etc., three, two, one and it's hooked up and at the same time, mark you, the hot water tap, which is connected to the machine, is turned full on. The salesman told us the cycle would take forty-five minutes so we settle down to await the completion of this cycle. The machine is making some rather disturbing noises, but presumably that is to be expected, part of today's living, so to speak.

1900 hours. Machine still operating full blast, hot water tap still full on. Booklet says the dial will turn around to the "off" position and the machine will shut itself off when the cycle is complete. The noises now sound a bit more ominous. I decide to go to the front room to watch the hockey game – you see, a captain must be careful to show an outwardly calm countenance no matter how bad the actual conditions are, much akin to the orchestra, you might say, which kept on playing as the *Titanic*

was sinking. I turn on the TV but actually have one eye on the kitchen and one eye on the front door. The first mate stays in the galley, watching this dreadful machine and nervously chain-smoking.

2000 hours. As we exchange tension-filled glances back and forth between the front room and the galley, we both realize something is very wrong. The machine is still operating, and making what now seem to be even more ominous noises. The whole crew is drawing closer to panic.

2030 hours. I decide to take some action, and approach the galley with some caution. The first mate is still sitting, watching the machine, on her fifteenth cigarette since supper. I give the order to advance the control button a few notches, and go back to the front room to watch the game, although I still don't know which two teams are playing.

2100 hours. Situation remains tense, machine now emitting a slight aroma of wires burning or something. We are now taking some water in the galley as the machine is leaking, noise becoming more menacing. I decide to issue further orders to the first mate. Now, from the doorway of the galley, instructions to further advance the control knob. As you probably know, there must always be someone of some competence left in command, so could not gamble by actually entering the galley.

2130 hours. Machine is now making loud sloshing noises; we are still taking water. First mate now busy placing rags, etc., on the floor around infernal machine to hold back the flood. Now decide to send out a distress signal. Enter galley at great personal risk, phone out to the dealer's house, phone rings busy. After a few more tries with the same result, return to the front room, then tell the first mate to phone (good thinking). Phone call is answered but it is a girl child that answers. "No, Daddy is not home." Does she know the repairman's name? "Yes, and he lives next door, but [and this is a big but] he doesn't have a phone." Is this 1973 or 1873, for God's sake? Hold the phone and she will run and see if he is home; she comes back to the phone and says his house is in darkness. Daddy will be home by 11:00 P.M., and she will give him a message.

2145 hours. It is now apparent I will soon have to give orders to "abandon house," although I have personally decided I will go down with the house if necessary. Give a last order to the first mate to turn the control knob full around to the off position. The infernal machine is silenced. Thank God.

2200 hours. The hot water tap is turned off. We both now realize that, since the booklet says a cycle runs through twenty-three gallons of water, and since not a drop has been pumped out into the sink, we have a machine full of God knows how many gallons of water plus whatever is left of our dishes. Machine still seeping. Crew getting tired, nerves shot.

2230 hours. Decide to have a cup of tea, but wait — what can we make it in? Our teapots are all in the machine. Tea is made, somehow (in a billy-can I think); neither of us enjoy it anyway.

2330 hours. Dealer has not called, or has he possibly met with some accident in his hurry over to our rescue? (The bastard never did phone; it is my guess he was out getting swacked from the profits he made on the machine.)

2345 hours. Decide there is nothing further we can do, will retire and try to get some rest; the first mate sets her alarm for 4:00 A.M., at which time she will get up and check the galley for further seepage. And so to bed. I take two sleeping pills which I figure should see me through the 4:00 A.M. alarm.

Next day

1000 hours. I phone dealer, he gives me a long-winded story which signifies nothing but during which he mentions that at no time would there be more than one gallon of water in the machine and possibly three at the most. Said he would come over. Mind you, he never did.

1015 hours. First mate opened the door, wonder of wonders, there were only a few gallons of water in the bottom of the machine, the dishes were okay except they were somewhat dirtier than when we placed them in the machine. Had a hasty breakfast, nothing to make coffee in, had to boil my egg in a pan with an ill-shaped lid, one dessertspoon and a stick to stir our coffee, etc., etc.

1030 hours. A very disgruntled crew sets about to hand wash and dry practically every goddamned dish in the house! I am aware I might be faced with outright mutiny over this development.

1300 hours. Dishes now done. Peace at last.

Wilf Garlick
Prince Albert, Saskatchewan

The Great Canadian Novel #4

Boutillier Whynott, last of the Lunenburg scallop fishermen, leaves his boat and goes to Halifax to find his daughter, Heather-Fiona, who has eloped with Odysseus Poulos, a young Greek sailor who jumped ship and is in Canada illegally. From the Greek community in Halifax, Boutillier learns that the couple has fled to Montreal, where Odysseus, who speaks no English, can go underground in the Greek ghetto.

Arriving at the Montreal bus station, Boutillier receives garbled instructions from a joual-accented floorsweeper and heads for the Greek quarter. But to Boutillier, all foreigners are alike and he mistakes the Jewish neighbourhood for his objective. He takes up with Seymour Popovitch, who invites him to a party where he may get news of the runaways. To kill

is for hitch-hike
the Trans-Canada Highway,
And the hundreds of cars
that aren't going my way.

Sheila Simpson
Corner Brook, Newfoundland

time, they go to a tavern and end up doing a pub crawl through the dives on The Main. In the graying dawn, they show up at the remains of a bar mitzvah feast, and Boutillier learns his mistake. He finally gets in touch with the Greeks, only to learn that Heather-Fiona and Odysseus have moved to Ottawa, where Odysseus has a job in his mother's godfather's wife's flowershop.

Boutillier hitch-hikes to Ottawa and finds Heather among the roses in the Olympian Flowershop. She refuses to return to Lunenburg.

Odysseus has been left in charge of the flowershop and has promised to deliver tulips for an important wedding. An Air Canada strike prevents the tulips from arriving on time. Odysseus, desperate to make good, decides to purloin the Dutch tulips along the Rideau Canal.

Boutillier follows Odysseus and catches up with him as he begins to cut. Odysseus hands Boutillier a bunch of tulips just as two police cars pull up. Boutillier and Odysseus flee and head west with Heather-Fiona.

They wind up in Drumheller, Alberta, where grain elevators and barns are overflowing with unsold wheat. Odysseus buys wheat cheap and begins to make, can, and sell a Greek sweet made of wheat-hearts and honey. Business booms, and the Pouloses and Boutillier become accepted members of the community. Heather-Fiona joins the IODE and Odysseus becomes an active worker for the Social Credit party. Years pass and Odysseus's business expands into a million-dollar operation. Boutillier's and Odysseus's mutual longing for the sea causes Odysseus to open a branch in Vancouver and they move there.

After fourteen years, Odysseus decides to apply for Canadian citizenship. His illegal entry, plus the old tulip theft, are brought up and his application is denied. He is ordered to leave the country and prepares to move to Los Angeles. Ottawa suddenly realizes that if Odysseus moves to the States, his Canadian business will become American-owned and operated. The decision is reversed, and Odysseus, at last, becomes a Canadian citizen.

Mrs. Patricia Murphy
Halifax, Nova Scotia

How to Build a Terrarium

materials:
1 glass container (clear glass with lid, e.g. fishbowl, cookie jar)
drainage material (gravel, sand, or charcoal chips)
terrarium soil, a mixture of potting soil and peat moss
spoon
spray atomizer
soft cloth
an old nylon stocking

plants:
small ferns, pepperonias, baby's tears, dracaenas, begonias, small palms, short moss, petunias, aluminum plants, or other small plants.

method:
For our terrarium we used a cookie jar 10 inches high and 8 inches wide.

Wash jar, making sure it is clean and dry.

Think of your landscape and plan where you want hills and other features. Place the drainage material in the bottom of the jar, making sure you are landscaping while doing this. You will use approximately 2 cups of the material (perlite is recommended). Use ½ inch of drainage material for every inch of soil. (Pepperonia roots are 1½ inches long, therefore you would use 2 to 3 inches of soil and 1½ inches of perlite at the lowest point.) Use the nylon stocking to separate the perlite from the soil, acting as a filter.

A thin layer of charcoal can then be used to keep the soil smelling fresh (note that the charcoal should be washed and dried before placing in the terrarium). If terrarium soil is not used, mix potting soil and peat moss in equal quantities. Make sure the soil is slightly moist and landscape again with the soil. Make sure you have enough to accommodate the roots of all the plants. For this size jar you will use approximately 4 cups of soil.

Use a spoon to dig a hole 2½ to 3 inches across to accommodate the roots.

To remove the plant from its small plastic pot, squeeze the pot, grasp the base of the plant and pull gently. Then loosen the earth gently so that the roots will fall free and intact.

Smooth the soil so that the base of the plant, once planted, is level with the soil in the bowl. Always work with the largest plants first. If your plants become too large for the jar they may be pruned to the proper size.

The soil should be fertilized every three or four months and only if you feel it is needed. Liquid fertilizer is preferable to pellets.

A sprayer should be used to give the plants the moisture they need. You can tell if there is enough moisture in the terrarium by the moisture on the soil and the lid. There should be just a thin layer of moisture on top of the soil and slight evidence on the lid of the jar.

reference:
The World of House Plants, Elvin McDonald, Popular Library.

Middle Age, Running Away and Dying: A Trilogy

Harry Bruce on Middle Age

My father died in Toronto almost a year ago. The other day I was walking on the patch of Nova Scotia coast where he was born and where he grew up, and I found he was on my mind. I was right down on the shore and a stiff little gale was crashing the waves on the stoney beach. It must have been blowing about forty — it tossed the tops of hundreds of silver birches and I kept stopping to let the amazing sound whistle through my head, and I speculated on the countless times in the years of his childhood that he'd hung around down here and heard it himself.

He knew precisely where the cottage should stand. Up on the bluff where you can see over Ragged Head and all the way down the bay to the open ocean. He knew where it should be but he never found the time to build it and, even if he had, he'd seldom have been able to spare even a week just to sit up there and watch the sea. He carried the sea and these sounds in his head all his life, and he let them spill out in the poetry he wrote 1300 miles inland; but he simply worked too hard, too long and too loyally ever to build the cabin in the place where he knew it should stand. It's there now. I had a man build it last spring. I'm sorry that, so far as I can know, my father never had a chance to see it.

The cottage reminds me that the strangest thing has begun to happen to many of the men I know who are roughly my own age. I mean men who have lived more than half the years they might reasonably expect out of one lifetime. Men of thirty-eight or forty, or forty-five. What's happening to them is that, in their own minds, if not quite in their actions, they're becoming social drop-outs. They've worked so hard themselves that they resent nothing so bitterly as they resent a twenty-year-old panhandler. But, at the same time, they've felt a stirring within themselves, a longing for the young bum's casual approach to life and jobs and careers. Now that it's almost too late for them, they sense that some of the kids may be on to something, some attitude that could just open them out in some great and still incomprehensible way.

These men do not like their jobs. They do not like their bosses. They do not like the goals of the companies, universities, publications and organizations that pay them enough to keep their families warm and fed. They do not like as many people as they did when they were younger. They may love their children, and some of them love their wives, but they do not like selling themselves to do right by their children and wives.

They are accomplished men who are good at what they do, but they no longer dream of shaking or improving society. They no longer dream of earning awards, honours, the widespread respect of other men. They no longer dream of becoming very rich. You could say there's nothing new in this, that men have always lowered their sights as age teaches them their limitations, but I think something else is going on in their heads. It's the growth of a feeling that, somehow, they're being had. It's the growth of a suspicion that, in some crucial respect, their own fathers may have been wrong.

Their fathers worked hard, usually for one employer, throughout almost all of their able years. They drove themselves to their highest positions during the final quarter-century of their working lives. When they were the age my friends are now, they were only beginning that long, final push to a vice-presidency, and the last thing that would have crossed their minds was dropping out of what they held to be an honourable rat-race. At forty, they were young men on the way up. At forty, their sons are puzzled men on the way out.

"Another seven years," says this friend of mine. "Another seven years and the kids will be through university, and then you'll see, I'm going to tell everyone to shove it. I've got this place back in the valley, and I'm going to sell the city house, I'm going to quit this sweatshop. I'm going to sit back there in the valley, and maybe write a bit, or maybe do sweet bugger-all!" He'll have a few thousand dollars, and he doesn't think he'll need much money to get by on.

I hear it again and again from my contemporaries. They're plotting their independence, right down to the last limited dollar. Some of their wives have already sensed the inevitable, and they're going back to school to get job training. These men are neither young nor middle-aged. They are just old enough to want to be free forever of people who have the daily power to tell them what to do. They want to see only the people they want to see. They want to retreat to the hills. They want to talk all night over a bottle or two. Some want to go to hotel rooms with strange women. Others want to go to hotel rooms by themselves, lie down and stare at the ceiling. They want to walk the beaches of mysterious islands. They want to think about their time. You might say they are just men who now know they'll never make it really big, and have simply lost their drive. I don't agree. I think they—I should say *we*—are part of the unacknowledged Lost Generation of the times and that, before we go, we'd like to find ourselves.

Read
Oct 17 1972

Vic Dardick
Box 321, High Level, Alta,
Oct. 11, 1972

Dear Peter Gotskie? hope I spelled that right
I know how you feel you should see the
fun they hav with my name I am also
a lousy speler.

I listen to your program when ever
I can mostly becaus CBC is about all we
get hear. HE! HE! But seriusly I do like your
program some times you get a little beyond
me but its different and I like it.

I herd your program today and you
reed a powem about a feletu ~~leeving~~ his
citefid asst hill typ job and taking off for a
cotage in the woods I wonder how meny
men have don that. I have don it
I lived in Welland Ont for 15 years and ~~work~~
worked in just about all the factoryes that
I married a girl there had 4 chilldern
but after pining for my praire hom for 15 yr.

Vic Dardick on Running Away

This letter, the first of many we were to receive from Vic Dardick, is reproduced in its original form; otherwise, it would be hard to believe that anyone could spell and punctuate so badly and yet express himself so lyrically. The pencil marks that score the letter are mine—they helped me to read the letter aloud on the air.

I finnaly took off for 2 years found this place in High Level it is the most northerly farming cuntry in Canada I beleaue and I have found my sele here (finally) but bt cost me dearly my wife took one look at this cold God forsaken Country and took off as fast as that old bus would tack her I sonatinas wais I had fosst her to stay but I love my freedom to mutch to foas my will on eny one ebs freedom I miss them verry nautch so I work like hell cleaning th baush off th land burning roots bracking new land with a 24 in bradcys plow . and work it is . only 4 out of 10 peopl stay in this cuntry . But I have promised my silf I would stay I have quit so meny good jobes that I would be emberest to tell how meny . I figer a fellas ight to make a stand sooner or latter you cant run for ever .. but I share wish my family was here with me . but if I went back thare I would only be thincking abaut this place .

87

All the time I was in them smokey factories I used to think of the open prairies, the free blowing wind with not a house in sight. When I come back I drove out in an old 51 ford ½ ton and I drove night and day. The second morning I was in Saskatchewan it was in the spring the wind was blowing the ducks were mating, and the antelope were trotting across the prairie I stopped the truck and I took a deep breth of freedom I never felt so close to God in all my life and that was when I said to my self. there aint enuf money in Ontario to make me stay there.

I have a new family her. I have a family of bares living on the south west quarter. She dug her den right under my corner post and it's a real good one too. I get a wild stalion that comes to visit every now and then and a wesel lives uner my shack. the little devel stole my duck the other morning. there is also a pure white wolf that comes threw here every week or so to chick on me. Walks right threw the yard but I hardly ever see him but I shure see his tracks they are larger than

the palm of my hand. I don't have TV here but I wouldn't have time to watch it with all these wild critters around here to watch. Like how many people have seen the mating dance off the hill crane or watched a wild stalion making love to a spirited little filly or seen the wheat fields in spring with so many ducks and geese you couldn't count them all or watched all the beutifull colers off the sunsett at nite. I have read the paper at 11.oclk at nite here many times. I have driven the tractor all night with out turning on the lights this is a verry exciteing country for those how are young at hart. It is the last fronteer. I don't know why I am telling you all this except to say that a man only lives once and if he is brave enofe he lives it the way he likes and likes it all the time he lives.

Yours Truly
V. L. Dardick

PS. I shure hope you can read this mess.

Hugh Sinclair on Dying

The two preceding essays, one from my old friend and colleague Harry Bruce in Halifax, and one from a man who was to become my friend, Vic Dardick of High Level, Alberta, brought one of the most singularly moving letters I was ever to receive at "This Country." I'd like you to read it the same way I did, just one letter among the morning's mail:

March 20, 1973

Dear Peter:

I was very much interested in the follow-up item on your program today about middle age. Being a working man, I missed the earlier item(s), and perhaps got a bit of the wrong slant, but there came through to me a general sort of malaise surrounding the fact that we all do get so soon old.

This is something we've been taught here in North America for entirely too long. From birth we're taught that *young is beautiful* and that old age is something that is either ugly or doesn't exist. The "now" generation owns the world. Even after we die, the undertaker (now called the funeral director, or some even more euphonious name) pretties up the remains so that the "bereaved" need not admit that anyone has died, passed away, etc.

The danger of all this was very strongly brought home to me some six years ago, when I learned that I had cancer. Inoperable, incurable, but painless. At thirty-three, I was about to die.

After about six months of getting used to the idea of dying, I began to live. Don't get me wrong. I'm no brave specimen. Nor do I yet much relish the idea of "going to my reward." Simply, I have come to recognize that death is at least as inevitable as taxation, and that the time between birth and that final event had best be used as well as possible. Today is the most important event that can happen.

Peter, for the last six or so years, the sun has never shone so brightly, the food has never tasted better, our children have never given my wife and I so much pleasure, and the world around us, for all its troubles, has never been so good. We've travelled from one end of this country to the other. And we've all had a great time. Last year, I even travelled around the world. And do you know what? Canada is still the best place under the sun.

Anyway, I'm going to die. Not this year, I hope, because we're moving to B.C. soon, and there are so many things that I still want to do out there. Maybe not even next year, but that, of course, is in the hands of God. But when it comes, I'll at least have lived. And that's what it's all about.

Yours truly

Hugh Sinclair
Ottawa, Ontario

That afternoon, I telephoned Hugh Sinclair. I told him how much his letter had moved me, and how it had made me think of my own death, and of whether I was living each day as well as he was — you may be beginning to understand now why I can say my years on "This Country" made me think differently about myself — and that I had realized I damn well was not. And then I asked him if, along with his wife, he would come on the radio and talk about what he had written to me. After a great deal of hesitation — on all of our parts, for we didn't want to exploit his pain, only to share his strength — they agreed to do so, and a week or so later, the family drove to Toronto and we talked, both privately and publicly. The Sinclairs talked about the practical things involved in preparing for a husband's and father's death. They talked about how they were gradually transferring the financial management of the family from Hugh's hands into Nancy's, because she'd never done any of that stuff before, and about how they'd been able to talk about things many of us never get a chance to face — how, for example, they each felt about the other remarrying in the event of a death. The people who heard them met a strong couple, who had faced adversity and wrestled it to a draw. Later, Hugh wrote me about what had happened since we talked.

September 6, 1973

Dear Peter, Alex, et al:

I'm going to try and do something now that I've never tried before. That is to write a letter carefully. You asked me to write when we were settled out here and let you know how we were making out. Well, we're here, if not completely settled, and since each day is a unique experience, I can only tell you how things have gone, without prognosticating.

We left Ottawa about the end of June, all full of high spirits, with the hockey sock full of money for the trip and the car full of gas. There was quite a scene on the street when we left, what with the kids crying to see the end of their friends and the people we left behind proclaiming how good we'd been as neighbours. Some five seconds after we disappeared around the corner, the tears dried up, the neighbours were discussing the new people moving into our place, and the car coughed in anticipation of a long trip.

Weather was fine and kids well behaved until we got to Longlac, which is somewhere in northern Ontario. Then it rained. Then the kids started to wonder when we would get to B.C., and I started to wonder which of them would be the first to be strangled. But we persevered, peering through a streaked windshield until we got past Winnipeg. And it came to pass that the sun shone, and we decided to camp rather than stay in motels. We had intended to tent all the way, but rain put an end to that. Anyway, we spent that night north of Winnipeg at Riding Mountain National Park under canvas. Damn near froze. Ah, that's life, knocking the ice out of your boot in the morning after shivering in a too-light sleeping bag all night. It doesn't matter, though, for that afternoon, just past Yorkton, the rain came down again and we were able to suffer the ignominy of motels until we woke up just outside Jasper to a pleasant sunshine.

And so to Prince Rupert, where with one hundred inches of rain annually, there's not much time for anything else. If you're wondering why we were there, you don't know that the ferry ride down the little passage to Kelsey Bay on Vancouver Island is just about the most beautiful boat ride in the world. I will accept that fact as an act of faith because B.C. Ferries tells me that it's true. But it rained and fogged and blew things that looked very much like snow and a bit of hail in my face, and I didn't see a thing. I had a good time; for the money, I had better have a pretty good time, but I didn't see a thing. We had a riot in the cafeteria when all the kids wanted something different for breakfast, and the orders got a bit mixed, and it took rather a firm hand and a loud mouth to get them back on an even keel (you can use nautical terms like that when you're on a boat), but I didn't see a thing.

We arrived in Kelsey Bay without too much trouble. The car had decided to spew oil because a new filter had not been tight, and I could not find a wrench to tighten it, but that's hardly a serious problem. And the trip down here to Nanaimo was without incident of any sort. The sun even reappeared to cheer us on the last leg of our journey.

We were greeted like Masters and Johnson (or is that Radisson and Co.?) when we got here. While my relatives were glad we'd made it safely and we had some fine old talks into the wee hours about childhoods and what not, the real-estate agents were ecstatic. I never knew people could be so friendly when they smell even what little money we had (notice the past tense). Little did they realize just how much lower the market is out here than the one we left. And so we bought a house.

The neighbours are about the nicest people you could wish to meet. Some of them came up to see what nuts had bought that big house on the hill, and some of them came to see who were the parents of those bad $%*&*# kids that moved in, and some of them were simply curious and friendly. But I don't think there's a mean bone in the lot. They brought frozen salmon (marvelous) and smoked salmon (you wouldn't believe how good) and flowers and vegetables and valuable information and most of all, their open friendship. Great place.

And finally, the job. I came out here with the intention of enjoying this place as far as work is concerned. I found instead that it fits like an old shoe. Some of the operations are a bit different, but the process of acclimatization is already finished and I'm treated as if I'd been here since day one.

So am I happy? You bet your sweet something or other. I don't give a damn if I never see the mainland again, because what they have there I don't need. Food here is abundant. Climate is perfect. People are ideal. Fishing is nowhere in the world better. No keeping up with the Joneses. Social pressures are nonexistent. Almost no traffic to battle. Petty politics — none at all. I don't even remember what my problems were back east. They've all evaporated.

It just occurred to me that someone might think we came out here to run away from my cancer. Not true. We came here to be comfortable for as long as I should continue to be able to enjoy life. I still expect to die of this. I still have not turned the corner that leads downhill, and I still don't relish the thought of going. If anything, I want to live more now than I did last year. But, except at times like this, when the past floods in and it's necessary to talk about it, I rarely think about being sick, and can honestly say that I never brood about it.

So by my definition, I'm a success. As a matter of fact, I'm more fortunate than most of the people I know. They worry about what they're going to do. I know what I'm going to do with my time; it's a possible set of aspirations I have, and they have in large measure been realized. I could die today without regrets. That's success.

We still get dribs and drabs of mail about that interview. That disastrous interview. You know, we went there in the hope that we could help someone. With one exception, all the mail was from people who wanted to help us! I only hope that some of the people who didn't write got something out of it.

I don't expect that there will be any more mail. In any event, those who did ask for our address have doubtless forgotten all about it.

We're not much interested in giving out our address, although I'd be hard put to give you any kind of cogent argument why. Maybe the thought of trying to answer the type of letters we got is distasteful to me. Druther go fishing.

Caught my first salmon last weekend. Not big, but the six of us did not succeed in eating the whole thing at one meal. Looking forward to this weekend and more fishing. I've even bought Nancy a rod, etc., and when I get my boat and can go at will, we hope to spend a fair amount of time together on the water. Let the teachers look after the kids.

If you're ever in this part of the country, look us up. I mean all of you together, or each one individually ... especially if you like salmon.

Yours very truly

Hugh
Nanaimo, British Columbia

I hope he knows how many people he helped.

Ireland

For all that I had read, heard, seen on film or talked about in preparation for our trip to Belfast, Northern Ireland, I was not prepared for what I saw there. We drove up from Dublin on a fine bright morning, the road winding its way through the rolling hills and the old villages. The scars of battle still fester in the border area between the north and the south. The customs shed is now, I think, in its fourth location, the first three having been blown to smithereens by extremists.

The troops who stop you at the border carry their naked rifles at the ready. It is amazing how young they look, and how afraid, as I would be afraid, too. Where the British troops are stationed, and around the various stations of the Royal Ulster Constabulary, lie coils of barbed wire, and many of the most vulnerable buildings have been surrounded by high wire fences, higher, presumably, than a saboteur can lob a grenade. Again, on the roads in front of the military bases, high rippling bumps have been built into the macadam so that your vehicle must slow to a crawl. This to prevent hit-and-run bombers from escaping by car. In Belfast itself, the car can be a weapon; many of the most serious bombings have been set off by people rolling automobiles loaded with explosives into the target areas, setting a time fuse and then running like hell. If you leave your car parked and unoccupied almost anywhere in downtown Belfast, the troops will blow it up first — an explosion presumably less serious than that of the bomb it may contain — and ask questions later.

Most of the store and pub windows in the main downtown areas of Belfast have been blown out or boarded over, or both. The side streets are shut off by iron gates, and you can enter these streets only through a turnstile and only after being frisked by a trooper. Again, the purpose is to prevent the hit-and-run bombings of buildings. Frisking is as commonplace as shaking hands. Before you enter a store. On your way into your hotel. You may be arbitrarily stopped anywhere on the streets. And troops in armoured cars and open jeeps, with riflemen scanning every building top and high window, patrol almost constantly.

And yet there is a curiously casual air about it all. Much of the frisking seems almost perfunctory. I bought a bottle of Irish whisky in a liquor store, where the two troops who were guarding the till were casually eating sandwiches. Carrying it back through the barricade at the end of that short street, I simply held it aloft, still wrapped, while the soldier at the gate ran his arms over my legs, back and sides. He never asked what it contained. Even when we visited Tommy Herron's house — the heavily guarded home of a Protestant extremist leader — I could not help thinking that a fast man with a pistol could easily have got the drop on the young man who greeted us at the door with a shotgun at his side.

In many ways, of course, the people of Ulster have grown used to violence and its continued threat. In other ways, the tension is just too much to bear constantly. If people there were to think of nothing but the war they would go nuts. And they are not nuts. The people of Belfast I met in my too-brief time there are some of the warmest and friendliest I have ever met anywhere. And by far the majority of them are fed up with the violence, which is being extended by who knows how many extremists of both sides.

I never did meet Tommy Herron. This morning, though, I found out what he looked like. His picture is in the morning paper. He is dead. Two boys found his body in a ditch near Belfast. He had been shot in the head.

Tommy Herron, who was thirty-six years old when he was killed, was a leader of the UDA, the Ulster Defence Association, one of the extremist factions of the Protestant, or Loyalist, side in the struggle over Northern Ireland. I

think I should begin by saying that I do not like the organization he had come to lead. This is not a matter of choosing sides. Most of the people I talked to in both the north and the south do not think much of the extremists of either side of the battle of Northern Ireland, and Tommy Herron was an extremist. Even in Prostestant Belfast there were people who described the organization he led, the UDA, as not much more than a protection racket. For a fee, a couple of Herron's men would sit in a pub all night and assure the owners and the customers that no Catholic bombs would go off there and that no Catholic troublemakers would come in and start a fight that would wreck the place. It was said that if the publican refused to hire these men, his chances of trouble increased by more than the normal rate. Herron himself was a former shipyard worker and garage manager who was, when we were in Belfast, apparently supported by his UDA activities. He carried, legally, a pistol with him at all times, and in the back seat of the car he drove was a loaded shotgun. During the time we were in Belfast he did not go out by daylight.

We had arranged to interview him on a Thursday evening. The driver who took us from our hotel through the barricaded streets of downtown Belfast gave no outward sign of recognizing the address we gave him in a Protestant suburb, but when we pulled up at the door and asked him to wait, he nodded his agreement and then carefully backed his car up a full block from the front door.

Tommy Herron lived in a small, semi-detached house in a neighbourhood that might compare with, say, northeast Edmonton — prosperous working class. We had arranged our appointment in advance. As we walked up the steps to his front porch, the door swung open. "Are you here to see Mr. Herron, then?" asked a pleasant-faced man of about twenty, with long hair and an open shirt. We said who we were and produced, at his request, our passports. He gestured us into the front room. It was only then I noticed the shotgun he held carefully at his side.

Mrs. Herron, a perky little redhead, apologized for Tommy's absence — "He'll be here any minute," she said — and asked us to sit on a couch away from the window. The pleasant-faced young man sat directly in front of the window. A television set faced him, showing the day's play at Wimbledon, but the young man's eyes swept back and forth, back and forth, not following the flight of a tennis ball, but shifting between the TV set and the street outside, which he scanned at least once a minute, all the while

Betty Botter bought some butter, but she said this butter's bitter. If I put it in my batter it will make my batter bitter. So she bought a bit of butter better than the bitter butter and she put it in her batter and it made her bitter batter better.

Connie Pedersen
Brandon, Manitoba

Continued on page 94

Daddy was a ball player

Bob Bossin summer '12 ©

Daddy was a ball player, Momma had a radio, I used to stay up till I heard his name, he'd come in off the road with his cap in his pocket and stories I wasn't supposed to hear. I got a little older and I hung out at the stadium; I heard a lot of stories and they weren't about baseball, my Momma sang praises, Daddy stole bases, singin nobody plays like me. Sittin on a riverbank practisin my banjo, singin bout the old times, livin in the new. Wonder if the river runs down to where I dreamed of, wonder if I'll always dream of you. There's some played harder and there's some played smarter but there's none of em plays just like you.

Daddy worked the ferryboat over to the island, my Momma sang hymns and she made good tea my Daddy came home with his hands in his pockets and the
Daddy had an oil well over in Saskatchewan, Momma had a radio my brother and me — Daddy came home with cash in his pockets and the
Sweet smell of gasoline. I got a little older and I hung out at the island, I
Sweet smell of gasoline. my father was the keeper of the Eddy stone light and my

92

wore white shoes to the Saturday dance, take her on a ferry ride
Momma was a mermaid on the wine dark sea, Daddy played the horses and he

just to see her smile, and kiss her if I ever got the chance Sittin in a
brought me home the banjo 'and no-body plays like me Sittin in a

river bank, practisin my banjo, singin bout the old times, livin in the new.
coffe house, practisin my banjo, singin bout the old times, livin in the new.

Wonder if the river runs down to where I come from, wonder if I'll
Wonder if the coffee house runs to where I dreamed of, wonder if I'll

always dream of you. There's some played harder and there's some played
always dream of you.

fine —

Smarter, but there's none of em plays just like you. Bridge

D.C. al fine.

J.A.H. May '74

is for Indians,
the original Reds,
They've left warpath
for courtroom
to challenge the Feds.

E. Arthur Harris
Vancouver, British Columbia

carrying on a running and well-informed conversation with me, another Wimbledon fan, about the chances of the British favourite, Roger Taylor.

Along one side of the Herron's small living room was a shelf of high-priced liquors. Favours from friendly publicans, I wondered? On the other side, among other souvenirs of recent times, were six of the rubber bullets the British troopers in Northern Ireland use for mob control. All the while, as we waited, there was a steady parade in and out of the room of the Herrons' five young red-headed children and their friends. The pleasant-faced young man at the window opened his shotgun and began playing absent-mindedly with the shells. There was a phone call. From another room, mysteriously, appeared another soft-spoken but authoritative-looking young man to say that Tommy would be delayed.

On a table near the TV there was a small collection of cards that took away any temptation to laugh at the comic-opera situation we were in, sitting in a pleasant living room that was under armed guard. The cards were expressions of sympathy. Less than a week before our visit, some men — no one knows who they were — arrived at a door, put a pistol to Mrs. Herron's pretty red head, and went upstairs and shot her brother to death in the bed in which he was sleeping. No one even knows if they thought that man was Tommy Herron.

We waited another hour. Another phone call. The authoritative young man said Tommy would be delayed indefinitely. He'd be out on patrol all night, and there was no use waiting. We said our goodbyes and added that we'd try again tomorrow. I never got to meet him; our schedules never meshed. But I saw what he looked like this morning, going bald at thirty-six, a man, to judge from the small picture that ran with his obituary, with angry eyes and no smile on his mouth, part of history now.

September 17-20, 1973

Perogies and Holubtsi
(Ukrainian potato dumplings and cabbage rolls)

Mrs. Kolosky's Everyday Boiled Perogies (Varenyky)

Potato and Cheese Filling

5 medium potatoes
1 cup dry cottage cheese
2 tablespoons butter
1 small onion
salt & pepper
1/8 teaspoon dry dill weed

Boil and mash the potatoes. Set them aside.

Melt the butter in a heavy frying pan on low heat.

Add the onion, chopped fine, and stir until the onion is light brown in colour.

Mix the butter, onions, and cottage cheese into the mashed potatoes. Season with salt, pepper and dry dill weed.

The filling should be made first, so by the time the dough is finished, it will be nice and cool.

If the filling is made the night before, to cool in the icebox, it is even easier to handle.

Mrs. Kolosky's Dough for the Filling:

2 cups all-purpose white flour
1 teaspoon salt
2/3 cup cold water
1 egg

In a small bowl, mix the water and the egg with a fork.

Sift the flour and salt into a medium-sized pot or large mixing bowl.

Make a hole in the flour and slowly stir the egg and water mixture into the flour with a wooden spoon.

If you don't have a wooden spoon, use a potholder to hold the blade end of a breadknife and stir dough with the wooden handle of the knife.

Sprinkle some flour on the kitchen table for the dough.

Using the bottom part of your palms, knead the dough with a pushing motion until the dough is smooth and shiny.

Divide the dough into three parts, rolling out one part at a time. Cover the dough not being used with a dishtowel to keep it from drying out.

With a rolling pin, roll out your piece of dough about one-eighth of an inch thick and cut it into two-inch squares.

Put a square of dough in the palm of your hand.

Place a teaspoon of filling on the square and fold it over to make a triangle.

Seal the perogies by pressing the edges of the dough together.

For half-moon perogies, cut the dough with a round cookie cutter or a water glass and fold the dough in half over the filling, sealing the edges to form a half-moon.

Drop the perogies into a large pot of boiling water.

Keep the heat on high. Stir the perogies gently with a wooden spoon or knife handle to prevent the perogies from sticking to the bottom of the pot.

When the perogies come back to a boil, they will float to the top.

Now, allow them to boil three or four minutes.

Drain the perogies. Melt one-quarter cup of butter and pour a small amount into a wide-bottomed serving dish. Alternate layers of perogies with the rest of the butter.

Shake the dish. (To fry yesterday's perogies, melt a quarter cup of butter or lard in a heavy frying pan. Brown the perogies on both sides, on low heat.)

Serve potato and cheese perogies with sour cream.

Mrs. Holub's Cabbage Rolls (Holubtsi)

What you need for the outside:

1 medium-sized head of fresh cabbage
1 cup tomato juice
¼ cup melted fat

Choose the cabbage carefully. Avoid cabbages with pointed heads. A cabbage with a flat head has smooth, wide leaves, perfect for rolling holubtsi.

What you need for the inside filling:

1 cup rice
½ teaspoon salt
1 cup boiling water
4 tablespoons fat
1 medium onion
½ pound ground beef
½ pound ground pork
½ cup tomato juice
salt and pepper

Wash the rice in cool water and drain it into a sieve.

Add the washed rice to the salted boiling water and bring to a fast boil. Let it cook a few minutes, then, with a cover on, reduce the heat to low, and let it simmer until all the water is absorbed. The rice will not be thoroughly cooked.

Melt the fat in a frying pan.

Add the chopped onion, ground beef, and ground pork. Stir with a fork until the meat is light brown.

Add the tomato juice to the meat mixture.

Combine meat, rice, salt and pepper. Be generous with the pepper.

Cool the filling in the icebox for a few hours, or better still, prepare it the night before making the holubtsi.

Put a kettle of water on the stove to boil. Now, prepare the cabbage. Remove the core of the cabbage by cutting around it with a sharp pointed knife. Leave the cabbage whole.

Place the cabbage with core down into a deep pot. Pour the boiling water over the cabbage to cover the cabbage completely.

Cover the pot and let the cabbage steam on low heat. As the outer leaves soften, they will come away from the core of the cabbage.

Carefully, take each leaf out of the pot. Keep the cabbage steaming in the water until all the leaves can be loosened.

When the leaves are cool enough to handle, cut off the center rib of each leaf, trying not to cut into the cabbage.

Line the bottom of a wide pot or small roaster with cabbage leaves or use the center ribs that you cut off the leaves.

Put a teaspoon of filling on each leaf and roll lightly. The ends can be left open or tucked over at each end like an envelope.

Place the rolls close together side by side in layers. Between the layers, sprinkle a little salt and pepper and the melted fat. Don't be afraid to salt and pepper the holubtsi. In the cooking the cabbage will absorb much of the seasoning.

When all the layers are arranged, pour a cup of tomato juice over the top.

For holubtsi with a real sauerkraut taste of sour cabbage from the barrel, omit entirely any tomato juice from the recipe. Instead, alternate the layers of cabbage rolls with layers of drained, canned sauerkraut.

If you wish, cover the holubtsi with a few cabbage leaves. Put a tight lid on your pot or roaster and bake the rolls for 1½ to 2 hours in a 325 degree oven.

When the rolls can be easily pierced with a fork through the cabbage, they are cooked. These holubtsi, containing rice and meat, are a meal in themselves.

(If you add a layer of cabbage leaves to the top of the pan, you may wish to remove these before serving as they will be quite blackened.)

Maara Haas
Winnipeg, Manitoba

There once was a baby named Justin
Who cried, "Caucus boys I'm not trustin',
To suggest one my size
Should permit compromise,
And be used to draw votes is disgustin'!"

Ruth Miller
Calgary, Alberta

Hopscotch . . .

It's clouding over in Toronto today, and apparently cooling off, but yesterday was one of those March days that could make even Victoria jealous. The newspapers had their obligatory pictures of girls in short skirts — I'm not knocking those pictures, you understand, just pointing out that they're obligatory, just like the pictures of kids throwing their books in the air on the last day of school. There were people out in parks, on driving ranges, and just ankling around the sidewalks. It even smelled nice, and you could see green where a week before there had been mud or snow or bare branches.

And some of us, I suppose, went a little silly. My own car has been in hospital for a few days and when I got home from work about five o'clock it was by taxi — the old harried businessman trick. In the driveway of our house was a game of mixed singles hopscotch, and I put down my homework and settled in to watch it for a while. The players were a nine-year-old boy named John and a twelve-year-old girl named Maria. John was ahead, throwing a set of keys that he'd found somewhere (stones bounce on pavement and don't make good markers) at the seven, which was on the left of the second arm of the hopscotch pattern. I don't know if there are regional variations on this, or temporal ones, because for the life of me I cannot remember the details of how we used to play hopscotch, but the 1974 Toronto rules are as follows.

On the ground you mark off this pattern: three single squares in a row, then a double, which consists of squares number four and five, another single, a double — seven and eight — and at the far end a semi-circle which is space number nine. You throw your objects — John's keys, for example (Maria was using a chain bracelet she wears, which has terrific stopping powers on the pavement) — into, first, square number one, and then you hop over that into square two, three and so on, using one foot only except on the doubles — you may straddle four and five — and so on up to the other end and back. Then you throw into square two and repeat, and you keep on with this operation until you fail either to hit your object square with your talisman or to hop cleanly through the prescribed pattern. There is no butterflying, which is balancing on the ball of your foot and wiggling the heel to achieve balance, and no touching the lines. You may — and this surprised me — touch the ground with your hand while reaching over to retrieve your object while you

are balanced in the square with the next highest number.

There is one other rule which was unfamiliar to me. After the first player has successfully got through nine and, so to speak, come out the other end, he or she begins at the top and works backwards to number one. *But* – and how about this, sports fans – that player may pick one "lucky number" and chalk it in. From then on, he or she may land on that square in any way

that seems fitting – two-footed, wiggling or anything else. It is sanctuary for him, or her, but it is also forbidden territory for the other player or players. This means, for example, that in a three-handed game, after two of the players have each made nine and are working their way back, a third player is given some incredible feats to perform.

By now, you will have guessed that the game in our driveway last night did have a third player, a thirty-nine-year-old, slightly over-weight cigarette-smoker who had arrived home in a taxi, and who was using for his throwing piece a quarter which, dammit, bounced too much until I got the hang of it. John blocked off square number six, the one between the two doubles. Maria took three. This meant that at one point, when each of them had a talisman on one arm of the first double – and you cannot land on a square where your opponent's man is – I had at one point to go bippity, boppity (that's one and two) and then hurl myself Nureyev-like towards the farthest flung double. I almost did it once, but kids draw squares for kid-sized feet and I was just about to try it one more time when. . . .

Well, we have this fairly stuffy neighbour who lives down the street a way. I do not know his name, but I do know he has no children, and he does have a front yard that is bowling-green clean, and that whenever our dog chooses to relieve herself illegally she aims at his hedge, and that whenever a road-hockey ball goes out of bounds it seems to end up on his lawn, and whenever . . . well, no one can do anything wrong without it somehow affecting him. And there he was, standing at the end of our drive-way, watching me bicker with a nine-year-old over whether the nine-year-old had linesies or not.

I wish there were a Gregory Clark ending for this or something. I wish the old coot had come and joined in the game too, and I could report that to you. But he didn't and I can't. I just stood there feeling sheepish, and scratching my hair, and feeling as if I were nine years old with my hand in the cookie jar. And then I thought, you know, on a day like today I *am* nine years old, and I wish I had a worm and a roller-skate key in my pocket, and the biggest problem I would be facing over the weekend was a soaker. And I liked that quite a lot, quite a lot indeed. So up yours, neighbour, I said to myself, and we finished the game. John first, Maria second, me trying to hit the damn eight.

I went inside to join my wife for a pre-dinner drink, and the real kids stayed on. But after dinner, when I was stretched out with a book, Maria came in and said, "Hey, Dad, do you want to play hide and seek?"

There once was a baby named
   Justin,
Who came just in time to give
   rustin'
Mod swinger Pierre
A new family-man air
And an image more voters may
   trust in.

Mardi Bastow
St. John's, Newfoundland

is for Jackson,
be it A. Y. or Russ,
One wore a smock,
the other a truss.

Barbara Greeniaus
Toronto, Ontario

... and Jacks

Dear Peter:
My mother tells me you don't know how to play the exciting game of jacks, and want to know how. Well, I'll tell you the game as I know it.

A set of ten jacks and a ball are used.
Any number of people can play.
The idea is to complete the game in as few turns as possible.
The first person to complete the game wins.
A turn lasts until a person "blows it," and then it's the next person's "go."
A game is made of six sets:
   1. Plainsies
   2. Cherries
   3. Knocksies
   4. Grabsies
   5. Double Bouncies
   6. Catchies (or Throwsies)
Each set is made of ten rounds:
   1. Onesies – pick up one jack at a time.
   2. Twosies – pick up two jacks at a time.
   3. Threesies – pick up three jacks at time for three times then just one.

Got it? So the rest of the rounds work that way too.
   4. Pick up 4 jacks, then 4 more jacks, then 2.
   5. Pick up 5 jacks, then 5 more.
   6. Pick up 6 jacks, then 4 more.
   7. Pick up 7 jacks, then 3 more.
   8. Pick up 8 jacks, then 2 more.
   9. Pick up 9 jacks, then 1 more.
   10. Pick up all ten jacks.
Simple! Then you go on to the next set.

Now to see who goes first, everyone must "toss up." What this means is that you hold the jacks in your palm, throw them up in the air and try and catch as many as you can on the back of your hand. The person who catches the most goes first. When it's your turn, you hold the jacks and the ball in the same hand – and throw the 10 jacks on the floor. Once the jacks have been thrown out you cannot change your sitting position.

Now, you start on the first set plainsies, on round onesies. (If you are left-handed reverse the following instructions.) Bounce the ball with the right hand – pick up a jack with the right hand, catch the ball with your right hand (hold up the jack), and then transfer the jack to the left hand and repeat. When you have picked them all up, you go on to twosies.

The rest of the sets are:
   1. Cherries: This is the same as plainsies except the transfer from the right hand to the left is done before you catch the ball. (The name comes from ancient Greece where they played this with cherry stones. This set is also called "cherries in the bowl.")
   2. Knocksies: same as plainsies only you knock on the floor with the right hand before you catch the ball each time.
   3. Grabsies: same as plainsies, only you do not transfer the jacks to the left hand at all. You must keep them in your right hand the whole time.
   4. Double bouncies: same as plainsies, except you let the ball bounce twice before you catch it. (Also called "double boresies" 'cause it's so boring!)
   5. Catchies (or throwsies): same as plainsies, but the ball doesn't bounce. In fact it can't touch the floor. (Note: The trick is to throw the ball up not down, allowing more time.)

Then of course there is blowsies. This is when you make a mistake or really mess up: if you miss the ball, disturb any of the jacks you aren't picking up, etc. Lots of things cause blowsies. That's when you lose your turn. When it's your turn again, you start where you left off. If you "blow out" at plainsies, on foursies, then that is where you start off – at plainsies, foursies.

O.K! Those are pretty well the rules as I know them. But I don't see how you can call this a children's game.

Tony Trask

The Great Canadian Novel #'s 5 & 6

Rails

The story takes place on a CPR transcontinental passenger train in late February. The characters are thus cleverly introduced each time the train stops, and unwieldy ones can be conveniently dumped in the same fashion once they have served their purpose. The main characters are, in the order of their appearance:

Victoria Verygood: a buxom eighteen-year-old Nova Scotian student nurse with slightly protruding front teeth and an industrious nature. She is going to Vancouver to study advanced occupational therapy. (Her brother, Victor, an auto mechanic with rippling muscles, gets on the train with her to protect her virtue, but, conveniently, is only going as far as Toronto, where he has an appointment with Don Shebib.)

Marguerita Meadows: a thirty-eight-year-old American female supremacist anthropologist of Spanish descent, who has been studying Eskimo social customs in northern Quebec. Six months in the wilds has left her — a practising bisexual nymphomaniac — strong, healthy and horny.

Jean-Claude Joseph Marie Henri Pierre MacPherson Fortier: a twenty-three-year-old separatist poet and rock singer on the run from the law and the irate Westmount parents of a fourteen-year-old girl whom he impregnated as a political gesture. He is attracted to Victoria for political reasons at first. . . .

Harry "Blades" Drab: a fifty-two-year-old B.C. MP and ex-professional hockey player on his way back to his constituency. There has been an emergency, and since the airlines are on strike, he, an impatient man, is forced to travel by rail. He spends the first part of the trip locked in his private drawing room, sending out periodically for spruce beer and salmon-salad sandwiches, until forced to relate to the others through dramatic circumstances.

Each in his separate compartment, they hurtle towards their destiny. The first 413 pages are spent in flashbacks, establishing the identities of the characters and reviewing Canadian history, and in brief dining-car encounters with other, minor, characters. (A priest, travelling from Rivière de Loup to his new parish in St. Boniface; a stockbroker from Toronto; a troupe of acrobats and freaks who missed the circus train; an elderly drug commissioner who shares his roomette with pot-smoking sixteen-year-old twin sisters and a performing dog; a prairie farmer returning from his brother's funeral; a drunken but dashing bush pilot; three Red Power advocates on their way back from a conference at Montebello, and a researcher working for Pierre Berton — or maybe Pierre Berton himself.)

Suddenly, between Sault Ste. Marie and Thunder Bay, the train stops, and the passengers are turned out into the snowy dusk. Parliament has finally granted its permission for the CPR to discontinue passenger service. A CPR executive, who has been flown in by private helicopter, makes a moving speech, and the train moves off slowly, tooting a mournful farewell.

The final 746 pages of the book deal with the attempts of the passengers to make their way to civilization. Many perish in the attempt, and their bodies are eaten by the survivors.

(There's a lot of good wilderness lore in here, which makes it a handy book to take on a camping trip.)

Finally, only three make it to Capreol as spring comes to northern Ontario: Jean-Claude and Victoria, married by the priest (just before he died) in the bush, and Marguerita Meadows. She found true love with Harry, who died of exposure in the previous chapter. She is softer, somehow, and more feminine, because she knows that in the quickening stillness of her hitherto barren womb, she carries his child. Jean-Claude joins the RCMP, and is decorated by Her Majesty for heroism and courage.

Alison Gordon
Ottawa, Ontario

The Maple Leaf Forever

The novel takes place in the near future. Our nation is torn apart by two factions: those who would see our interests sold out to the insidious needs of giant U.S. corporations; and those who would see our country remain one sovereign state . . . from the Atlantic to the Pacific . . . from a hundred miles off the Arctic shores to the Great Lakes and Manitoulin Island.

For the moment, the crisis has temporarily healed deep rifts between French and English, East and West, and NABET technicians and the CBC.

As the novel begins, Canada has been forced to cede the province of Alberta, with her oil and tar sands, to U.S. interests. Canada's ageing prime minister, a former international playboy, had no choice. For, if he didn't hand over Alberta, the largest hamburger drive-in chain in the nation, with its offices located on Wall Street (where else?), had threatened to pull its "stakes" (no pun intended) out of Canada. Without these drive-ins, millions of car-driving Canadians would starve to death. Urged by monied pro-U.S. factions at home, the prime minister handed over Alberta, oily gem of the prairies. Where would it all end? Some suggested with the ceding of Quebec. But wiser men knew U.S. corporations would never accept.

The anger of the Canadian nationalists is quick and effective. Demonstrations by white-shirted rowdies topple the government. A young premier from the Maritimes narrowly squeezes into office. U.S. corporate businesses are new to him, none ever having located in his province. His task: to bring Alberta back into Confederation, to appease strong U.S. factions in Ottawa, and to rescue further slices of Canadian life going south of the border, such as the NHL, Anne Murray, the economy, etc.

February 24, 1972
Dear Winner:
I'm in this embarrassing position.

I hope you know by now that you're one of the prize winners of our limerick contest. My problem is that I said the prizes would be copies of *The Lure of the Limerick*, only I said it before I'd read it. Now I've read it. It's a — well, the truth is it's a dirty book. I guess I should have known, but I didn't.

So, I'll send it to you if it won't offend you. I'm pretty sure it won't, since people who like limericks tend to be, let's say, broad-minded enough, to enjoy other limericks even when they're naughty.

Will you let me know what you think? Congratulations, and thanks anyway.

Best wishes
Peter Gzowski

Dear Mr. Gzowski:
You mean to say you thought there could be a whole book of *clean* limericks?

Best regards
N. MacKenzie
Willowdale, Ontario

Dear Peter:
Thank you for your letter explaining your problem. After two minutes' deep thought, I have decided that if you are old enough to read *The Lure of the Limerick*, then I probably am too.

Yours sincerely
Ruth Miller
Calgary, Alberta

Will the new prime minister save the country from southern avarice? Will he rescue the Dominion from the greatest threat to its unity since Russ Jackson won two Schenley awards in one year? Read on and see how the youthful PM crushes Big Business covetousness once and for all, enjoys a few romantic flings on the side, and restores Robert Goulet to his rightful place – singing on Canada's ARC recording label.

What the critics say:

" . . . it just makes me want to quit."
   – P. Berton, CBC
" . . . say, where is Canada anyway?"
   – New York *Times*
" . . . sensational; a must on everyone's reading list." – J. Hanlon
" . . . at last, the truth about what goes on in the nation's bedrooms."
   – I.M. Lurid, *Obscene* magazine
" . . . it is novel."
   – Alphonse DeBris, Obscure Publications Ltd.

John Hanlon
Edmonton, Alberta

Marjorie Harris on People's Liberation

If "This Country" changed me, it *revolutionized* at least one of its regular contributors, the Toronto free-lance writer and broadcaster Marjorie Harris. This is her own account of one of the most controversial and fascinating series we ever did.

When "This Country" went on the air, the women's movement was tucked away in little corners all over Canada, faltering a couple of years behind the sisterhood in the U.S. There wasn't much communication between any established groups. Women's studies programs were just being launched in universities, and the press usually referred to feminists as bra burners. When Alex asked what I'd like to do for the show, the most natural thing for me at that moment was women's liberation. I was a nice, middle-class, closet feminist, pretty confused by the issues being raised. I agreed with the social aspirations of the movement: day-care centers, equal pay, equal rights. But I'd been meeting real

feminists: politically committed women who went far beyond social issues. They seemed to be questioning everything in our way of life. I wanted to learn about that aspect of the movement in a systematic way, and maybe, in the process, pass along useful information.

"Okay," said Alex, "how would you do it, what would you call it and how much time do you need?"

"Well," said I, "I'll do interviews, have readings and make comments; call it People's Liberation – it's not only going to affect women; and give me at least twenty minutes a week."

It seemed very simple. It'd be a consciousness-raising session on air for both Peter and me. Damn the consequences. I certainly wasn't an authority on the movement, but I got support from feminist friends who said there aren't any authorities. It's just that some women know more than others right now.

My memory of that summer of research for the first ten weeks of the show is one of being rattled with insecurity, and, at the same time, of being completely happy because I was spending so much time working on a subject that was rapidly becoming my favourite.

The image of women's liberation then was rotten: a bunch of steam-rollering dames in army fatigues out to de-ball men and destroy one of the basics of society – marriage. Men seemed to hate women's libbers, as they called them so contemptuously; most women were scared of them too. Me, too, in a way. But I was also very annoyed. The feminists I knew didn't fit any of the press clichés. They were attractive, intelligent, most of them were married and they sure didn't have an out-and-out hatred of men. They were, instead, angry about a male-dominated system that was faltering. They felt it had to change so that a better, more humane one could evolve.

I thought I was being pretty crafty calling the series People's Liberation. I didn't want to scare anyone off. And I believed then, as I do now, that anything removing the unjust stereotypical roles from women would benefit men and children, too. I was as anxious to make a better place for my son as for my daughter. And since my husband had got me interested in reading the movement literature in the first place, when he was researching an article on the New York feminists, I wasn't bucking any prejudice at home. It seemed very rosy that summer.

The first show terrified me more than anything else I've ever done, before or since. It wasn't just being in the studio. It was the subject matter. As an introduction to the series, I used long definitions, filled with personal experiences, of the catch-phrases being thrown around: male chauvinism, sexism, the difference between feminism and women's liberation. I packed a lot of emotional content into that show. I got at some of the subtle forms of oppression I'd encountered (Why bother with university, dear, you'll just get married?); we had some historical readings; and it lasted for an hour, a format that stayed for the whole series. My nervousness was about all the personal stuff – Hey, out there, this is *my* experience, not universal, but maybe we can draw some things from it that apply to a lot of women.

Peter was agreeable to the idea of doing it on such a personal level, at least as a beginning, because he was struggling with his own male chauvinism. The second week I dealt with role stereotyping; the following week, how to create a perfect female for a male chauvinist. That was fun: I hauled out all the jokes and standard lines about little girls and lumped them together. Little girls, I said, should behave in a feminine way. They should be passive, observant. They should not be tomboys (deviant behaviour). They should learn as quickly as possible how to get around daddy, how to be a flirt, to be coy, to get their own way. Both Peter and I had to admit we'd made errors in the way we'd handled our kids: boys take out the garbage, girls set the table. That kind of thing starts role definition right from the beginning. Dad works, Mom stays home.

We got a lot of mail right from the first week. I was astonished both by the amount and the quality. The letters addressed to me personally were terrific (the negative ones were addressed to the office or to Peter), most of them from women who'd had similar experiences or who were offering ideas and lots of support. After one show about how women are treated in advertising, I received this letter:

I get outraged every time I turn on the TV and see *me* represented as a clumsy, dim-witted cleaning woman, or a thing used to sell their cars or booze. Every one of them is organized by a man; the voice of authority is a man. I get the same feeling when I see women in bras and girdles plastered all over signs and ads in buses and things. Do they really think we are so useless and stupid?

There were a lot of cries of pain and anguish in those letters.

Apart from the letters, a lot of other good things were coming out of the show. Most of the material I was digging up for the readings was all new to me. I'd never read Mary Wollstonecraft, or finished anything by Simone de Beauvoir except *The Mandarins* or, God knows, tried to tackle Kate Millett. I read and

read and read and still there was more. I had no idea of the huge body of literature that had been written by women (the perfect product of a male-oriented education).

By the end of the first month, I was in a bit of a bind. Several listeners felt cheated because I'd mainly talked about women and this was supposed to be People's Liberation. Some of them thought I was hysterical, bitter, unhappy, frustrated, gushy, and maybe just a bit of a lesbian. I was merely stating the facts of my life, I hoped a little objectively. I certainly wasn't bitter about things. My feminist friends, the real radicals, thought I was much too wishy-washy. They saw Peter as the archetypical male chauvinist, patronizing me madly, and why didn't I *do* something about that. I felt completely torn in my desire to please everybody but came to the only conclusion possible. I had to please me first and move slowly from point to point.

About the same time, a group of fourteen women, including me, decided we should organize a proper consciousness-raising group. Some of the topics we talked about were close to the ones on the show. But we didn't spend one hour on sex-role stereotyping. We spent a month. We were from twenty to forty, married, single, divorced, generally intelligent, some brilliant . . . an all-round terrific group of people. My kids hated the meetings held at our house. We'd sit around, have a beer, talk. And, according to the kids, we made too much noise laughing – a little ironic, given the dour image of the movement. But there is *something* about a group of feminists. We laugh and laugh.

In spite of all the gruesome stories I heard from women about how they'd been affected by men, I never got up a good steam of hostility about them. Certainly not towards the most important men in my life – my husband and son. My son was, by his own admission, a male chauvinist. Everyone knows men are more intelligent, superior in every way to women. Everyone knows. How? Just by being at school, looking at books and magazines. My daughter said she was turning into a feminist because most of the books she read made girls disappear when the action started. But they both said to me: "Do you have to go on about women's lib all the time? You spoil the fun." I was changing. I couldn't look at TV, or go to the movies, or read magazines with them without pointing out all the sexist junk I saw. It hit me in almost everything, everywhere. I was getting to be no fun at all.

I asked my husband recently what I was like in those months. "All I remember," he said, "is a person talking out loud all the time. A frantic person." I don't remember being frantic. I felt

A man is not
        liberated, until –
The lady foots half
        Of the motel bill!

Margaret Stapley
Toronto, Ontario

A man is not liberated until
– five P.M.
– the price of ammunition goes way the hell up
– getting laid comes *second*
– he stops kicking the dog
– he's unemployed
– he learns how *not* to look (that's a doubble ontundra)
– he understands that Germaine's on his side too
– he's dead

William Stark
Larry's River, Nova Scotia

A man is not liberated until he can:
– love a woman without idolizing her
– be dependent on a woman without being demanding
– expect neither more nor less of a woman than he would of a man.

Ann Anderson
Kentville, Nova Scotia

exhilarated, high, ridiculously happy and intense.

I tried to keep a light touch in the show, but I was finding less and less to laugh about. I got criticism from one woman with the CBC, an activist in organizing women. "Sounds too much like a cocktail party every week," she said. "It's too personal." I tried putting a clamp on that. (I was still trying hard to please.) But it was difficult, given the skills I had at the time. It seemed not only a history of women, but of myself.

The material on women and work triggered off a lot of reaction. One typical one was: "Why am I being dumped on because I'm a housewife?" I never did criticize women for staying home. It wasn't for me. But I learned that when you strike close to the core, some people will hear precisely what they want to hear, not what you say. And because I was passionately concerned about the conditions of working women, a lot of mail assumed that I was against housewives. My point then was that women, working or not, simply have to start thinking about each other. Women at home have to stop hating and envying those at work. And working women have to stop being contemptuous or envious of those securely at home. It got to be such a point that, whenever women and work came up, Peter would say, "Now, you aren't saying that women *must* get out and work, are you?"

The point I was trying to make in most of the shows is that women must be given more options. We should allow girls to grow up feeling that they can be fulfilled as human beings without being married or having children, if that's their choice. We must not produce women who are looking mainly for security. We must produce boys who can grow up to be emotional and weak sometimes, without feeling any the less male. Those seem like minor points today, because most of us accept those principles. To some people, then, it seemed hysterical.

I felt the women-and-work theme was an important one to hammer home. Close to three million women were in the work force (not including prostitutes, call girls, and cleaning women), mainly doing menial tasks. Only 4.2 percent of the total work force had women in management positions. As my consciousness was being raised by these facts, my reading of magazines and newspapers was changing. I hated the female image out there: that unattainable, glamorous, skinny person. Most of us just don't look like that — we haven't the time.

I was also getting lots of material out of government documents and statistics. And women were sending me examples of how they felt discriminated against. One woman was enraged when she and her husband bought a house together, only to find that there was a

signature space for *purchaser* and *purchaser's wife*. I kept hearing from women who'd stayed at home and felt they'd done a fine job, but didn't have two dimes to rub together. As one woman put it: "After twenty-seven years I still have to ask for money to buy a new pair of shoes. It's humiliating."

The show has such a wide audience that it was inevitable, wherever I went, that someone had heard the series. I spent a lot of time talking to women and came to realize increasingly how we're kept apart. From age zero, we're told we must behave in a *feminine* way to get male approval. We must compete with each other for that. Women are gossips, we're told, or when we get together we just talk about babies. It never occurred to us that this subject was a lot more important than football statistics.

One cocktail party really hammered things home. A man came up to me and hissed: "I've heard those shows you're doing. They stink. Don't you dare talk to my wife." I did. She, as it turned out, wanted to speak to me, to find out where she could get information about the movement. Were we being subversive because her husband disapproved? I suppose we thought so. I was explaining to her how to start a consciousness-raising group, and other women at the party just naturally joined our conversation. By the evening's end, they were on their way to getting a meeting organized. Not, as this woman's husband fantasized, to pick him to pieces, but to read and discuss their own history. Straight intellectual curiosity.

I got letters that began: "Just wait until a door isn't opened, a seat offered, a cigarette lit — then you'll scream." Only people who haven't been on public transportation or in a department store in the past twenty years could possibly see these as defendable amenities. Women had, for centuries, been pieces of property handed from father to husband. And the history of suffrage in this country didn't bring any cheer either. Women were recognized as people by the British North America Act in 1928. It must have come as an enormous shock for those women who'd been fighting for the vote for decades, to find out that they hadn't even been legal entities.

This was a glorious period as well as an angry one. I was seeing women as uncritically as is humanly possible. They could do no wrong. Our great humanity would save a failing society. Provided we all got together, that is. And I was certainly getting together with other women. There were Women for Political Action meetings, meetings to organize a Women's Place, the usual CR session; and loads of phone calls and mail. Since I was part of this maelstrom, wasn't everybody?

I was even attempting to apply some feminist principles at home. At that point, we had a housekeeper on a daily basis. I did the cooking and we lumped along. We started changing by sharing a lot more of the work that had to be done without a housekeeper. And it certainly improved my attitude towards cooking after a long day's work. I realized that, in my preachiness about the movement, the kids could hardly get a word in edgewise. I started to listen to them a lot more carefully. My son, who now considers himself a feminist, can hardly believe the neanderthal views he held then. But then, we've both had a couple of years of humanizing. He doesn't have to be a jock, and I don't have to point out any sexist innuendoes in his magazines or movies. He knows where they are.

My total involvement was having its effect on my style. Whenever we got to a really good, strong point in a reading or an interview, I'd raise my arm in the velvet-fist salute (clenched fist raised). It was definitely making both Peter and Alex nervous. In my permanent state of high, it no longer bothered me that I wasn't pleasing them. My love affair with the series could have gone on for weeks, since I had enough material for another ten shows. The crunch came on program fifteen, when I did a show about housework. I started out as usual by saying I was not putting down housewives. But they are the only people who say, "I'm just a housewife." Truck drivers don't say, "I'm just a truck driver." Neither do lawyers. I was making the point that this is a money economy and housewives are outside it. They weren't included in unemployment statistics. And if we were really serious, women at home should be paid salaries for services rendered: make it taxable, so both spouses could pay at a lower base income. Occupation: housewife, would indeed be recognized as an occupation, not something women put in time at for twenty years, and after which figure out how to recycle themselves. Well, I'd gone too far.

Both Peter and Alex reacted in the extreme. Alex even came rushing into the studio. Old wishy-washy had turned into a *radical*. The point seemed to me to be perfectly logical. The show came to an end a few weeks later, with relief on both sides. It was wearing me out, and I had a lot of other things to do in the women's movement.

Of course, since that time, we've had the sacrificial lamb of Irene Murdoch. That women's-libber prejudice is still with us, in spite of the fact that the movement is no longer considered a passing fancy. I now know a lot of women who do stay at home, who want some political and economic clout. They are changing their self-image as passive receivers, affecting

their kids and getting involved in political-action groups. I know a lot more women now who can really look at themselves and say: "I'm a person for me first, the rest will take care of itself." I know lots more women who read newspapers, look at ads and can spot very effectively how they are being fiddled and manipulated. I know a lot more angry women.

But there still aren't enough of them to make a revolution. I really thought that was going to happen a few years ago. It's going a lot slower than my fantasies at one time would have permitted.

It's a shame to see so many aspirations of the movement being twisted into endless government committees that meet endlessly to discuss what we've all known for a long time — that women get the short end of the economic stick.

One vast difference has taken place since the series was on air. A lot of well-known women have very publicly declared themselves feminists. They are models I'm so very proud of. People I can point towards as examples for both my children. Schools are helping a bit. They've thrown out a lot of blatantly sexist books. Girls are allowed to take Industrial Arts; boys can take Home Ec — not together, mind you; we wouldn't want to push them too fast. I know a lot more women who are keeping their own (well, their fathers') names. All small steps, but important.

A man is not liberated until he can converse comfortably with long-haired children and youths while he is ignorant of their sexual identities.

Peter G. Zimmer
Halifax, Nova Scotia

is for Klondike.
There's gold there for certain —
And most of it mined
by a writer named Berton.

R.E. Hainsworth
West Vancouver, British Columbia

A man is not liberated until he stops saying to male children, "Stop that crying like a girl," or, "You guys are skating around like a bunch of girls."

Kay Logan
Westwin, Manitoba

A man is not liberated until he is as proud to say "It's a girl!" as he is to say, "It's a boy!"

Anon.

103

I still believe the point of my last show: divisiveness among women has been a major factor in our lack of power. We're cut off at the knees as long as we're snide and distrustful of each other. We have to face ourselves honestly. Until women can present an alternative that is formidable and serious, men aren't going to be interested in liberating themselves from this system. Until men see that there are other ways of thinking, reacting and feeling, they'll just work up arguments to fend off incipient feminism. And none of us will get anywhere, except into a worse mess.

There's a feminist line that goes: "Who wants to be equal with men? Who wants to be equal with slaves?" What feminists want is real change, for everyone. And as this feminist sees it, people's liberation.

Hallowe'en

Something's gone wrong with Hallowe'en. I don't know what's caused it: television, nuclear tests in the atmosphere, fluoride in the water or what. But Hallowe'en simply isn't what it used to be. For me, Hallowe'en was soaping windows and ringing the door on the school principal's house before running madly away. It was standing on one side of the road while a friend stood on the other, and when a car came by pretending to pull on an imaginary rope. It was also, of course, ducking for apples and pulling toffee at parties, and trying to catch a rich, sticky, bad-for-your-teeth goody that swung on a string suspended from the ceiling. But all those things are over now. I even wonder if there's anyone left in the country who knows how to pull down a backhouse. I can just see today's kids trying to rip out the plastic shower curtain in their over-decorated, two-basin, fluorescent-lit apartment bathroom.

I don't think we can ever bring those old Hallowe'ens back, and I guess there are a lot of things about them I wouldn't want to bring back. But I'll tell you one thing. Any kid who shows up at my house next Wednesday with a plastic mask from Woolworth's and a shopping bag big enough to hold a week's groceries for the Dionne quintuplets is going to get one unshelled peanut unless (a) I recognize him or her, and (b) he or she is willing to come in and sing us all a song or do us all a treat. I think I might even wire up our jack o'lantern with a microphone so that I can bark those rude words to them when they're least expecting them.

What I'd like to do is put the Hal back into Hallowe'en. . . .

To which I received the following anonymous reply:

R.R. 3, Hallowe'en's Town
10:30 P.M., October 31, 1973

Dear Peter:
You are a bad influence on people. You were the cause of the misdemeanour I just committed. I just put the Hal back in Hallowe'en. I have this minute returned to my home after pushing over an out-house. I've never done such a thing in my life before. It is a wet, spooky night in the country. I went for my usual walk before bed, with no evil intentions, when suddenly I remembered a nearby out-house used by vegetable pickers and your exhortation suddenly possessed me. I could not restrain myself. I walked resolutely to the place and with one shove (never really expecting it to budge), it went tumbling into the ravine! What a glorious feeling for a woman of fifty to see her first out-house tumble. I feel I could push over the world next.

Yours sincerely,

A liberated woman

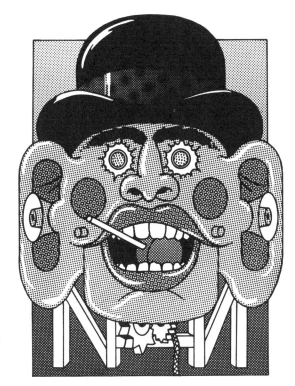

Hallowe'en Recipes

Puffed Wheat Candy Balls

1/3 cup butter
½ cup light molasses, honey, or corn syrup
1 cup brown sugar
2 tablespoons cocoa
1 teaspoon vanilla
7-8 cups puffed wheat
1 cup chopped peanuts and/or raisins

Melt the first four ingredients in a saucepan. Bring to a boil and allow to boil for 8 minutes; remove from heat and add vanilla. Pour this over the puffed wheat and peanut and raisin mixture. Form into balls or press into a greased 9″ x 13″ pan and cut into squares. If you decide to form into balls be sure to grease your hands well first with butter, shortening or vegetable oil.

Hobgoblins

1 eight-ounce package pitted dates
1 cup seedless raisins
1 cup dried figs
1 cup walnuts or peanuts (chopped)
2 teaspoons grated orange peel
1 tablespoon orange juice
½ teaspoon cinnamon
marshmallows, prunes or figs, almonds or cherries

Grind fruit and nuts coarsely in food grinder or blender. Mix with orange juice and cinnamon. (The mixing should be done with your hands — again, well greased.) When mixture is well-blended, form into balls; roll balls in icing sugar that has been coloured orange.* Put a marsh-mallow on a toothpick and stick into the top of the fruit ball. Then add a fig or large prune on top of the marshmallow and make a face on the fig or prune with pieces of almond or cherries.

*Easy method of colouring icing sugar with liquid vegetable dye: mix a few drops of dye into a small quantity of granulated sugar. Then mix granulated sugar with icing sugar (best method is with your hands as with pie-crust mix).

Honey — Sesame Seed Snaps

2 cups sesame seeds
per
1 cup liquid honey

Mix. Simmer in saucepan 10 minutes. Press into buttered pan. Cool and cut up.

Soy Beans

(One five-pound package costs about $1.20)
Soak overnight or about 8 hours; drain, dry, fry in hot oil for about 8 minutes. Drain. Sprinkle with salt. Alternative to frying: bake in 350-degree oven for an hour.

Stuffed Dates or Prunes

(I recommend dates — they're nutritious, much less expensive, and kids like them.)

2-3 cups dates or prunes
1 cup peanut butter
2 tablespoons honey
½ cup grated coconut
icing sugar or chopped nuts

Mix all ingredients except dates and icing sugar/nuts. Stuff dates with mixture, roll in sugar/nuts. Makes 40.

Maxine Crook

Conversations with Prime Ministers: John George Diefenbaker

We thought the best place to interview the Rt. Hon. John G. Diefenbaker would be in the old court house in Prince Albert, Saskatchewan, the court house where he had fought and won so many great battles before he emerged on the national scene as our prairie Messiah. We had heard of his great reputation as a storyteller and we thought that the physical associations of his old pre-political arena might trigger off some fascinating reminiscences from him. So, as we had done earlier with the Centennial Library in High River, Alberta, and as we were to do later with outdoor settings in Niagara Falls, and the University of Guelph, and in school gyms in Aklavik and Tuktoyaktuk in the Northwest Territories, we created a radio studio on the spot.

As it turned out, the trouble was worth it. Being home again did show one of Canada's master storytellers at his best. But before we got him there, all our trouble — for we had built a whole three-hour program around the core of an hour with Dief — almost went for naught. We saw Mr. Diefenbaker in Saskatoon, where we'd done a couple of shows. He'd just returned to the Hotel Bessborough from one of his morning strolls. I introduced myself to him and said I was looking forward to seeing him in Prince Albert. He looked at me strangely, as if he'd forgotten the interview, and then asked if we'd mind sending a letter of confirmation to him in Prince Albert. Nancy Button, who once again had masterminded all our arrangements, did so and included in her letter a sentence to the effect that we'd call him on the morning of the program to check again and to arrange transportation to the court house for him and, if she'd care to come, Mrs. Diefenbaker. When Nancy did call that morning, she encountered a furious former prime minister of Canada. She had, he said, not addressed the letter to the *Right Honourable* John Diefenbaker, and who did we think we were anyway? Who we thought we were was a bunch of people with a radio program to do and no featured guest. What a strange mixture: this great populist leader, master orator, statesman and politician ... yet offended by one unintended slight from someone who had worked so hard to set up a show especially for and about him.

In any case, it all worked out. Nancy apologized profusely, I put on a jacket and tie, and we talked.

PG: I've looked forward to this for a long time. How are you?

JGD: I'm always fine, I always feel well. I walk a mile and a half each morning at quarter to six and if you want to come along and can walk that distance in seventeen minutes, you're welcome.

PG: I can do it in about seventeen-thirty. . . .

JGD: Well, you see, that shows you've got to speed up a little.

PG: This courtroom must hold many memories for you.

JGD: Yes, it's a place that I appeared in continuously for many, many years. I was on the defence a great deal, although criminal defence never amounted to more than five percent of my practice. I also acted as a prosecutor, but I wasn't a good prosecutor because I forgot once the trial got underway that the crown never loses; in the stress of court I was inclined to forget that fact, and therefore my prosecution days did not continue very long. One court, I had nine defences in a row and there were nine acquittals over a period of two weeks. Then I prosecuted two and they were convicted, and the judge said to the jury, "You've been wrong for the last couple of weeks and you're still wrong."

PG: You were involved in the Grey Owl case here.

JGD: Grey Owl. . . . There was an extraordinary character, a character all by himself. He pretended for many years to be the offspring of Archie Belaney, an English remittance man, and an Apache princess. He came to Canada about 1905, married an Indian woman named Angele, who taught him Indian lore. Then he went overseas in the First War, became a sniper, was wounded, came back to Canada but forgot all about his wife. . . .

PG: It slipped his mind, did it?

JGD: Perhaps, perhaps. . . . Anyway, he went to Temagami, where he met a very charming and beautiful Iroquois girl whom he married on the top of a hillside as the sun rose, according to the ancient rites of her tribe. Although he'd been a trapper, he developed a sudden desire to become a conservationist and came to Prince Albert. I remember when he arrived, the Department of the Interior, as it was then called, represented him as a most unusual person. They said he was born on an Apache Indian reservation in Arizona and that he had such knowledge of the beaver that he had written a beaver dictionary — nobody has ever seen that dictionary — but it contained forty-nine words or expressions. He went up to the national park here where he continued to write magnificently, at all times pretending that until he was twelve or fourteen he hadn't known a word of English. . . . As a matter of fact, he was born in Hastings, England.

By this time Grey Owl had had his hair done in plaits, had moved the British people as they had never been moved on the question of conservation as he spoke on radio, had gone to the palace, the first time in all history that anyone sat before the king and queen. He sat and he conveyed the message to George V and Queen Elizabeth on behalf of their furred brothers of the earth and their feathered brethren of the air. He said, "I sit here; this is the proper method among the aboriginals to which I belong." He spoke on the dangers, the awfulness of fox hunting; he shocked the sensibilities of the fox hunters of Britain. He reaped in tremendous amounts of money, then he came back to Canada.

In the meantime, Angele had seen his picture and said, he's an Englishman, he's my husband. That's when he really moved. . . . Finding that he was going to get caught up — this was '31 or '32 — he applied for Canadian naturalization. He said, I bled for this country, but I'm not a citizen. In order to explain how he came to be in Canada, he said that he'd gone to England in 1905 with Buffalo Bill's circus; it went bankrupt and he had to make his way somewhere so he came to Canada. He set out all these particulars and he got his naturalization. And he served as a good Canadian citizen, a lecturer beyond anything I've ever heard.

I'll never forget the descriptions he gave when he came back, the second time, from the United Kingdom. I think it was 1938; I was over at the legion that night and the Owl had just come back with about thirty thousand dollars. He was called on to make a speech. He said, "Jest a minit" — he had a friendship with beer that was most unusual, an absorbability that excelled anything I've ever known — and after he completed his internal ablutions he delivered a speech, the like of which I have never heard in eloquence anywhere. While in the United Kingdom he spoke in Albert Hall, and I know what it is to speak in Albert Hall. I spoke there in 1958, introduced by the prime minister of the United Kingdom with nine thousand people there. He had just as many, although he had never spoken in public. This was the speech he delivered to the Legion here in Prince Albert when he finally rose:

"There I was," he said, "eight thousand pairs of eyes on the Owl. I'd never spoken in public before and I wondered to myself, and you'll pardon me for my lack of knowledge of the English language, whether I'd be able to articulate in a manner that would be understandable . . ."

"There I sat," said the Owl, "and just before I got up to deliver my speech, what did I see but this lady" — gesturing to his Indian wife, the one he married on the top of the mountain. "She looked up at me, but it wasn't that alone; every one of you, my comrades, was there. I saw you. I wasn't going to let down the Prince Albert Legion. But finally, as I was being introduced, what did I see?" — and here you must understand that Grey Owl had two beavers with him, Jelly Roll and Rawhide — "There sat Jelly Roll to my right and to my left, Rawhide, seated on their respective haunches. And again I apologize for the fact that my knowledge of English, as such, may not be conveying to you the finer touches and tints that you would like to have in language. But there they sat and they spoke simultaneously: 'Grey Owl, do yer stuff!' "

A great naturalist, a tremendous man in every sense of the word. A supreme charlatan and, in my opinion, the greatest naturalist that Canada ever produced.

PG: You're the great parliamentary orator of our time. Could you coach other people in the art of oratory?

JGD: Well, I'm not accepting your premise in any way. . . .

PG: You're not rejecting it, either. . . .

JGD: Well, I was in Saskatoon a couple of days ago at a graduation of grade twelve students. And I told them that it was there in Saskatoon that I endeavoured to be

February 17, 1974

Dear Peter:

I have a riddle for you that was given to a group of college students some twenty-five or thirty years ago to assess their ability to analyze objectively. There is a logical answer but it does take a sharp mind to develop the answer in less than an hour, and for most people it will probably take weeks, if they don't give in first.

A and B were two friends. They were walking down the street together. A was on the way to shoot A's wife. B fell down and broke his leg. B then shot A and the question is, why did B shoot A? The answer can only be developed by asking questions of someone who knows the answer. The one who presents the problem can answer only yes or no to questions asked. It is immaterial if B shot and killed A; it was not a lovers' triangle.

Garnet Boyd
St. Stephen, New Brunswick

able to express myself in a way that would be articulate enough so it would be understood without unnecessary interpretation. I tried and I tried but I was tongue-tied. I was very much like some of those people in the civil service who now go down to Quebec City to learn French. They stay for several weeks and when they come back, they're about as tongue-tied as they were when they left. Well, I had no opportunity like that. I simply had to try to speak in public. I tried in two oratory contests in the Saskatoon Collegiate and I failed miserably. My late brother received the gold medal that I never could achieve. And it was the same in my early days at university. I would try to emulate others, generally leaders of freedom: Temple, Sheridan, Pitt. I read their speeches; I tried to catch something of their philosophy of life, of freedom. When I was a boy on the homestead, Gibbon was a daily companion. Father insisted that we study Macaulay very carefully. It was a hard, long road to be able to express myself without a manuscript, which is essential to anyone in the law. And that used to be one of the requisites of Parliament.

PG: Used to be? Is there no one in the House now who approaches. . . .

JGD: Yes, when I first came in — oh, I would say there are a great many very able young men. I am very much taken with them. I came in at a time — in 1940 — when there were greats in the House. You might disagree with them, but you were moved by the power of their arguments and above all, their sincerity. The House of Commons is a place where you may disagree, but you form for those who sit opposite a deep sense of appreciation of their devotion to their country, so long as they speak in sincerity and truth. And that, I think, is one of the essential elements.

When I see people read their speeches — and this is outside Parliament, because you're not allowed to read a speech there, according to the rules — I'm reminded of that American senator you've heard about who achieved the highest position in the Senate, a seat on the most powerful Senate committee. The afflictions of time and re-election made me wonder how he'd get along. Well, he hired the costliest speech writer he could get. He didn't tell anybody about it. He read the first speech and his fellow senators were deeply impressed. They couldn't understand how he had concealed this magnificent capacity for language and thought and his knowledge of foreign affairs. The second speech was the same. Well, after he got those two speeches, he wrote to his writer and said, I wish from now on you'd write them in a little simpler language so I'd understand what I'm talking about. . . . That annoyed the speech writer no end. The next speech came along and the senator read it without looking it over. He got to the top of page **eight** and it said: "From now on, you old buzzard, you're on your own!"

PG: What do you think about Watergate?

JGD: I'm very distressed about it. Some say it's politics. Sir, politics do not consist of perjury, conspiracy, fraud, deception, destruction of political enemies or concealment of crime. It's one of the most serious things that has ever happened in my lifetime, the destruction of the faith which people have the right to have in those in public life. I say that because I'm grieved by what has been revealed. It's beyond anything that one could ever expect. But it shows what can happen when a praetorian guard surrounds the chief executive of a nation, when a lot of little men with the mental capacity of nonentities achieve a position of power, when they place themselves above the law. It also shows human frailties to be what they are: the greatest concern must be to maintain the decencies of life as well as the respectability that comes to those who endeavour in their lifetime to live according to decent principles.

I'm over-awed by what has taken place. Mr. Nixon is a friend of mine; I cannot believe that he knew. It's the greatest argument that can be given for the preservation of an executive that's above politics. If this kind of thing happened in our country, you wouldn't have a situation where the head of state and the head of a political party were one. The attacks made today on the president weaken the prestige of the United States everywhere in the world.

I'm also grieved by the degree to which, through television and radio, hearsay evidence is being spread all over the United States and Canada. Innocent men can have their reputations destroyed by scoundrels who simply say, "A told me that B told him that so and so took place." An investigation like that should not be open to the public. It should be in the nature of the hearings of a grand jury under our system. No one can ever get a fair trial in the United States after this kind of publicity because in the heart of the people, each one of them will have been convicted in advance, even on the basis of pure hearsay.

PG: May I ask you a dirty question?

JGD: You never can ask me that 'cause I don't indulge in that kind of thing.

PG: I meant sneaky, as opposed to risqué. . . . Did you ever get a guilty man off?

JGD: No, because if the jury found him not guilty, he was!

PG: Can I just throw some names at you and see how you react? Do you remember Harry Finkleman?

JGD: Oh, absolutely! Harry had a business here in town for years. A great fellow, that Harry, very fond of him.

PG: Did he bring you to Prince Albert, because Danny Finkleman said. . . .

JGD: There are several who say they brought me to Prince Albert. I don't object to anyone joining in the concourse. . . .

PG: Who did bring you to Prince Albert?

JGD: I brought myself. . . . I was practising at Walker and I used to be here all the time. Various people suggested I might come in here and finally, in 1924, after four and a half years of practice in Walker, I did. It's one of those things – the if's in life. If I hadn't come here, my life would have been quite different. If I had gone to Edmonton, as it was pressed on me that I should, how different my life would have been. And if it hadn't been, in 1952, that the three or four that are here at this moment and several others in particular were with me fishing up north – after all, business must take second place to following the precepts of Izaak Walton – it would have been quite different.

It was late one night and Fred Hadley said, now that your constituency has been wiped out completely in Lake Center – it was the third time they had operated without anaesthetic on it – why don't you run in Prince Albert? And I laughed about that because the only protection the Conservatives had at that time was under the game laws. But they all gave me their support and went to work. So if it hadn't been that I was fishing in 1952, that would have been the end of the road. As a matter of fact, this is one of the interesting stories that's not been told before: if they hadn't gerry-mandered my seat for the third time, I wouldn't have been a candidate in 1952 and I would have devoted the rest of my life to the law.

PG: I want to indulge myself with another name for you – may I do that? Sir Casimir Gzowski.

JGD: Oh, I know your name very well, that great Polish patriot. . . . He came to Upper Canada in 1834; am I right?

PG: Yes.

JGD: You're not telling me anything about that. My people were living right alongside your great-grandfather in 1836 in Upper Canada.

PG: I didn't know that. . . . But did you know that when Sir John A. Macdonald

Answer:
A and B are both psychiatrists. They are conducting an experiment in hypnosis to discover whether it is possible to make a person do something under hypnosis that would ordinarily be against his principles. B has hypnotized A, and, in the context of the experiment, has instructed A to shoot A's wife. B is accompanying A in order to stop A should A actually follow through on B's suggestion. But B falls down and breaks his leg.

retired, Sir Casimir Gzowski was the man who raised the money for the maintenance of the Macdonald household?

JGD: No, I didn't know that, but I've always had a deep and abiding respect for the memory of that man, who did so much for this country and hasn't received the place in history he deserves.

PG: I just wondered if you wanted a Gzowski to go out and raise some money for you and your political faith?

JGD: I have never objected to assistance. . . .

PG: To be a bit more serious. . . . You're a much honoured and beloved man, but you have been attacked from time to time. Have those attacks hurt you deeply?

JGD: Anyone going into public life, if he achieves the top, is the subject of continual attack. You're just like a goldfish in a goldfish bowl, but more vulnerable. I don't mind attacks, I don't mind criticism, I never particularly mind personal condemnation, but I do object to falsehood. I followed a course in life without which no one could maintain a sense of equilibrium; I always chose to believe that the other person has at least some reason for what he says, whether or not he has. I knew where I was going; I've always directed my life. When I was eight or nine years of age, I said I'm going to put an end in Canada to discrimination on the basis of race and colour. When I started into public life, anyone with a name like yours, regardless of the magnificence of the record of his family, was always in the hearts of many a second-class citizen. The first-class were those of English and French origin. I said I'm going to put an end to that. And when you have an objective in life, you don't allow yourself to be detoured from your purpose, for each one of us has something in his heart that nobody else has and that was in my heart.

In a lighter vein, I remember one day in the House of Commons when I had the floor and Martin, Pickersgill, Sévigny, with Pearson giving them an assist, were bombing me from across the way – I love that type of participation – and over here in left field at the very back was a young member who's going to remain unidentified. He always wanted to get an answer by interrupting me and he interrupted me this day. I paid no attention. He became annoyed and said, apparently the right honourable gentleman was a little afraid of the question he was going to ask. I asked the honourable member to repeat that and he did. I pointed this out to him: a big-game hunter with big game in sight never allows himself to be detoured by rabbit tracks!

PG: What would happen if Dalton Camp walked through that door?

JGD: Well, I think the courthouse would collapse. Everything he's ever touched has.

PG: What would happen if Peter C. Newman came in and tried to sell you a subscription to *Maclean's*?

JGD: I had Mr. Newman at the last meeting of the campaign. He was present for the purpose of seeing me wiped away because it had been said by one of my opponents that I was going to be washed down the drain the way you flush a toilet – they're changing plumbers now. Well, he was here to see the thing. He wrote a book – I endeavoured to get him the fiction award of the year – he should have had it. And I'm going to let you in on a secret that even he doesn't know we know. He was there with his hearing apparatus attached to him so that he knows what's going on, although the person who chats with him doesn't know it's there.

PG: You mean a tape machine?

JGD: I mean something like a wiretap attached to you. They have them now so small that a dentist can put one in your teeth and it enables you to hear half a mile away. I don't know whether he's that up-to-date or not. In any event, he was there and a collection was taken up. Generally, I never have collections but the people there decided to do it. The collection plate came along and there were a lot of dollar bills on it and Mr. Newman reached for a quarter. I think he was a little bit disturbed that he would have given the only quarter on the plate, so he gave a dollar instead. I've always appreciated that contribution to the campaign fund of 1972.

PG: Were you hurt by the cabinet ministers who seemed perhaps to desert you?

JGD: Well, I find it very interesting that when the cabinet ministers left Mr. Pearson, they did it on the basis of principle. Several of them have now disappeared in so far as Mr. Trudeau's concerned, but it's not regarded as anything serious. You know, it's strange how a few years make such a difference to the press of the country. What was regarded as evidence of weakness under me, is now considered as preponderant evidence of strength. There's no reason why any minister should stay on if he disagrees with the policy. But I will say one thing and you can interpret this as you will: the two ministers who claim that they left my cabinet because of nuclear power – I think they had other reasons.

PG: I think I'll just leave that alone, shall I?

JGD: I think you will because you might find an unusual name for an unusual person.

PG: Should I pry further?

JGD: No, we're not having a prying contest!

PG: Do you think that the great victory of 1958, the 208 seats, was a bad thing?

JGD: Yes, I've always thought that. I had such overwhelming support – mind you, St. Laurent had got 190 seats – that the press of Canada, because of the weakness of the Liberal party, became the party of opposition. No matter what came up, they attacked. And now in the light of events, where they write on nuclear weapons, where they write on the question of national development, where they write on the question of opening up the North, all the things they condemned me for, the heresy of my day has become the orthodoxy of today. . . .

There's something more to a political party than for the individual to be merely a pawn to be pushed around. On a question of principle they didn't want to support, I always allowed the members elected under me to vote as they pleased so long as they let me know. Otherwise, why elect them? And now then, when they say isn't it a strange thing that members don't vote with their party, do I have to recall to you that in the United Kingdom, three times Churchill voted against his party on massive matters and ultimately became prime minister? Do I have to recall to you that Harold Macmillan voted against his party and was almost out and became prime minister? And that Harold Wilson practically left his party in condemnation and later became prime minister? Now, members of Parliament are not required, in my understanding of Parliament, to park their consciences at the door when they come in to vote. And I never criticized members who changed their viewpoint because they believed in a matter of principle, providing it was principle they took that stand on and not their personal interest.

PG: Your victories were such very personal victories, victories of a man, not a party, in a sense. Is that a good idea?

JGD: You cannot build a political party unless your leader is able to inspire confidence among people. He's got to be able to catch the thought and the emotions of people. That's the greatness of leadership. Macdonald did it, Laurier did it, in 1968 our Mr. Trudeau was able to mobilize the emotions of people because they saw in him something that appealed to them. No, leadership consists of something more than simply an individual occupying a position. It requires something that brings to the heart of the average person the realization that here is an individual who's trying to achieve that which I believe is necessary for my country.

Andrew Allan on Christmas

It's time once again to send out our tinselled greetings, just as we have been doing for so many seasons now – Christmas greetings to all and sundry, to all sorts and conditions of men and women and children and small furry animals. The electronic circuits and the tall towers and microwaves through which we do it are a far remove from the holly and the ivy – even a comfortable distance from the mistletoe – but it's what we have and what we use. Even the most elaborate circuits come home at last.

A merry Christmas, therefore, to the homeless and the forlorn. A special urgent thought at Christmas time to the old lady who was standing motionless in front of a rack of Christmas cards, trying to think of someone – anyone – to whom she might possibly send a card. A merry Christmas, dear lady, and a whole post office full of bright mangers and of carol-singers bravely singing into the snowy street.

To the girl at the airport who was sitting by herself with an open letter in her hand and the silent tears on her face . . . the wish for a bright new morning.

A merry Christmas to moonwalkers, space-walkers, and jaywalkers, and most warmly to all those who feed the birds in wintertime. A joyous Yule to the rich, the overweight, and all those with cold eyes. To the old man on the park bench down by the frozen water, a bag of crumbs for the pigeons and a tender thought from St. Francis of Assisi.

To those who would like to sing but can't carry a tune, the gift of perfect harmony in the heart. To those who would write but can't find the word they are searching for, a Christmas song instead. To astronomers looking for a star, and to the friendly dog seeking a bone in all that white . . . a miracle at Christmastime!

To children who wake up with a tingle of anticipation, and then don't see what they were hoping to see . . . the assurance (though they won't accept it) that there can be more love in a hand-knitted sock than in a Lincoln Continental.

To the Man Who Has Everything, the comforting restfulness of Nothing. To the woman who is beautiful, the kindness that makes beauty perfect. To the woman who believes she is *not* beautiful, loving kindness at Christmastime.

To skiers on slopes, to all the maladjusted who feel they are on the skids, to the disappointed and the surfeited and the over-eager; to all who are human, and therefore vulnerable, a happy, happy Christmas and a New Year rife with promise.

To the farmer gazing across the frozen fields, a murmur of spring. To the businessman gazing across a frozen ledger, a murmur of Other Values. To all who keep the wheels turning and the circuits alive, to those who fly and sail, or merely only trudge, thoughts of home and a fireside and the scent of *evergreens* that can steal like incense into the lonely places.

To all who work in hospitals . . . to those in pain or confusion of mind . . . to the misunderstood, the misbegotten, and the misanthropic . . . a Christmas message of goodwill and gentleness.

May the world be now, if only for one little hour, "lazy with the love of God."

A merry Christmas.

Playdough

2 cups flour
¼ cup salt
⅓ cup vegetable oil
(this makes it smooth, and helps to preserve it)
water
½ cup cornstarch
(optional – this will help make the dough smooth, but it's not essential)

Using just enough water to get the dough to a workable mixture, sprinkle it on and work it in with a fork or your hands until the dough feels right for modelling.

Playdough will keep for a long time – just put it in a plastic bag or covered container and stick it in the fridge. It's a good substitute for modelling clay; you can bake it to hurry up the drying process, once you've modelled it, in a 250°F. oven for a couple of hours. It can be painted after it's dry.

Great Sports Boners

One of the guys with whom I coach hockey is also one of the people I most like sitting with when I watch hockey. He is a former very good player, and a fan whose enjoyment of the game itself, of its shapes and patterns and surprises, knows virtually no limit.

I had to phone him on Saturday to tell him about one tiny moment that had stood out in a game I had just seen between some seven- and eight-year-olds, one of whom is related to me. These kids play on half ice – meaning there are benches across the centre of the rink so that two games can go on at once – and what happened on Saturday was that for almost a full shift of three minutes, one of the players on the team opposing my son's team had been parked out in front of my son's team's net – he was doing, I figured, what older kids call goal-sucking. Anyway, he stood there, and eventually someone shot the puck to him – I don't think you could quite call it a pass. *This* was the moment. He trapped the puck with his stick, he aimed and he fired. The trouble was, at least from his team's point of view, that he had forgotten that it was his opponent's net he was standing in front of. In fact, I guess he hadn't been goal-sucking at all. He had been protecting the goal, and when he shot, he shot away from his opponent's goal and towards his own. The puck slid down half the length of our community arena, and had the boy's own goaltender not been alert, he might very well have scored on his own team. (I have seen shots going slower become goals in this league; in fact, I know one boy, to whom I am also related by parenthood, whose entire career as a goaltender consists of having ten goals scored on him in one game, in which there were only nine shots. He actually created one himself, by reaching around behind his own net, trying to clear the puck, and managing to drop it behind his back and over the goal line. Afterwards, I ran down to the dressing room to console him. I found him lying on his tummy while his coach was undoing his pads. He looked at me a little sadly and said, "Dad, I don't think I want to play goal any more." I told him I doubted if he'd be asked again, which he hasn't and which is okay with him.)

Anyway, Saturday I called my friend to tell him about the goal-suck who wasn't. He enjoyed that as much as I did, and together we began musing about people who would be remembered through their lives – by some of their contemporaries – for some great boner they had pulled, and often in the world of sports. I'm not talking here about the famous ones, the catcher who dropped the third strike in a World Series, or the guys who leapt off the bench to make a Grey Cup tackle or score touchdowns the wrong way in Rose Bowl games. I'm talking about mere mortals who sometimes rise above themselves in the glory of their boo-boos. I think we can all remember one or two. The friend I called, for example, had a classic, and although he could remember the hero's name – it is etched forever on my friend's mind, he says – I will keep it in happy secrecy here.

The town where they both grew up was St. Catharines, Ontario, and the occasion was the city intramural basketball final, some time around 1955. My friend's team was ahead 24-22 with only moments left, when the boy whose name he remembers so clearly, who was a guard on his team, dribbled and drove to his own basket, scoring against himself, my friend, and three other teammates to tie the game and send it into overtime. Because intramural basketball was played during the lunch hour, the game had to be settled by sudden-death overtime. My friend and his teammates spent the brief intermission telling the hero what he had done wrong, and issuing strongly felt suggestions that he not do it again. Tip off. The ball goes to the boy who had scored. This time, he knows what to do. He whirls, cuts, moves towards the basket at the other end of the floor. From eight feet out, unchecked, he lets fly a soft one-handed set shot. Swish. Game over. 26-24. The problem was that his teammates had forgotten to tell him that after regulation time the teams had changed ends, and the basket he had scored on, although at the other end of the floor, was still his own.

He has since become, my friend told me, a very successful man in his chosen field, which happens to be commercial aviation, and my friend still has the odd qualm about flying the airline for which his old teammate is a licensed pilot. But let us salute him and others of his calibre, the pullers of magnificent rocks; theirs were great moments in sports, and I honour their memory.

L is our land,
sea to sea, milk and honey,
We guard it with pride –
but we'll sell it for money.

R.E. Hainsworth
West Vancouver, British Columbia

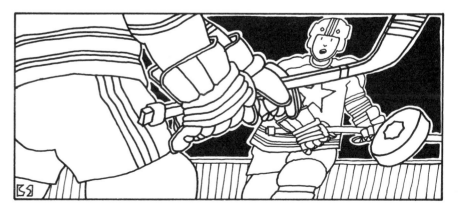

Vic Dardick on Welders

April 15th 1973

Hi Peter:

I would like to tell you about some of the men that work at the welding trade, some of them ordinary men who work every day and go home to thier family every nite and some who have no homes — just a motel room or a bunck house or wher ever they hang thier hat. Some have worked on every big job from coast to coast, from white horse to Seatel, in little mining campes in the bush — God only knows wher from the oil fields on the praries to the Artic and back again to the shipe yards of Vancouver to see the big city lights again and drink her good wisky and chase after her wimen to swap tails of thier venturs to one another. Of the men who died on the job's and meny of them who carry scars and broken bones to prove they're too dam tuff to die yet. like Tarable Jack McKraw. no one knows his real name so he's just Tarable Jack with a scar on one cheek and a broken jaw he had at one time but dosent talk about witch geves him a develish looking grin when he smeils and a partly disabled arme but one of the best welder's and fitters in the buisness. he drinnks too much

and genes his money to nogood wimen and when he comes to work all hong over and felling roff he neads two hands to steady his stinger but still putts on the welds as good as you ever saw. Big Fred McKay knows to night is not the night to push him because if the formen says one ward to him whyel Jack is working he would clime his form and eat him for dinner — all tho I have never seen Jack eat on the job exept once I saw him eat a hamberg that he had bin packing around for two days and she was some tuf he said and I beleoved him from the way he was chewing on it. but he mostly lives on coffe and sigarets and cusses himself for blowing his money on booze and bad wimen. theres little Frenchy who can climb steel better then a cat and if you geve him a ladder to come doan he jest hookes his heels on the side rails and slids doan it. when he welds he uses bigger rods. then enyone else and uses twise th heat. His welding rod stubs are glowing read hot when he throws them away and you realy got to husel to keep up to him. Why he says I can weld can weld enything

role doan ther nekers but never slacken thier pace as they make one perfect weld after another it makes you wonder why?

Yours truly

Vic Dardick

High Level
Alta

but a broke hart as the crack of dawn. thier's meny others Hans the Hun, little Joe the gooffy Newffy, big tall John, Dum Paul the polak, Fuggy McDuffy, Curly Moe who is ether a hippy or just hates barbers and shaves once a week wether he neads it or not. Blake Mack who gets dertyer then eny one els on the job. But thes men all have one thing in common they love to weld. they are artists with thier hands, as shur and steedy as a surgen. such rivelry among them selfs as to who is th best that I have never seen in eny other trade. Thair is little Barney who can gouge threw a 4" plate and find a fleck th size of a pin head that only a X ray machine could find, big John who could do things with a welding machine that the slide rule boys say is inposable. They have the pride and confodence of a Consort Pienest but are just ordinary werking men who know thier job and like to have a beer on Saterday nite. You will never see thier names on enything they built but with out them th slide rule boy's could all go to hell. But once you have watched thes men work and swett and coff the smoke of the welding rod fumes from thier lungs and see them squerm as the hot sparkes

I resign from obituary notices.

I will not read one more obituary extolling the lovability of an acquaintance who, to my personal knowledge, has behaved like a bastard all his life. I disassociate myself herewith from such chicanery.

Moreover, I announce herewith, the establishment of the Truth-in-Death Association. Its aim is simple. We will demand equal space on the obituary pages and publish an alternative and honest assessment of the deceased.

For example:
Old John Curmudgeon died today.
There's little cause for grief,
For all who knew or worked with him
His death's a great relief.
It's true he always paid the rent
And sent his kids to school.
But all admit: To know him well
Was punishment most cruel.
His kin agree to live with him
Required a saint's endurance.
The best that can be said of him:
"Thank God he left insurance!"

A.B. Acksiell
Toronto, Ontario

From girls, I hereby resign:

I hereby resign from taking girls out that just sit, drink and say nothing because the atmosphere bores them. I resign from visiting other girls with a girlfriend because the girlfriend would like to have an incessant chat with the girls to impress each other about nothing. I resign from going to the restaurant and ordering a small pizza because she doesn't think that she is hungry. Then when the pizza comes she is absolutely famished and eats practically the whole thing. I just say, "It doesn't matter," being a gentleman. Then going shopping with a girl and ending up carrying all the girl's packages. Also watching her try on an assortment of skirts and dresses that she will never buy. I also resign from dancing all night because the girl I took out suddenly develops a craze for dancing all night but then she doesn't mind if I wear my flat feet to the bone, does she? Of course I can't forget walking downtown with a girl only to be stopped by another girl to be informed on the latest gossip about someone that we know.

Until girls refrain from such things as these, I shall be forced to list girls as my number-one enemy.

Paul Sikorski
Mackenzie High School
Deep River, Ontario

Karen's Diary 3

People are beginning to ask me what I've got for the baby. Some mother I am; so far: a Winnie the Pooh bear and two pictures for the nursery. That's it!

The baby kicks all directions there are to kick, and she's found a way to tickle me – it's the weirdest thing. But I guess I have a lot more of that coming before it's all over.

I've been reading my book about natural childbirth again. The parts that have exercises in them are good, but I tried to figure out the one that's supposed to keep me from waddling like a duck – I feel like I am – and just couldn't.

I've been trying to find out from my books about intercourse during pregnancy. It seems as if that's something you're not supposed to know about – even the page seems to blush when they talk about it. It seems as though I shouldn't be interested in such things now, just like the middle ages.

I've stopped working, at last. I'm still unpacking stuff from our move, I don't know how many months ago. I'm getting more and more uncomfortable now . . . sometimes I can't sleep, which was really bad when I had to get up and go to work the next morning.

I can get so frustrated now just trying to get my stockings on. The first leg is all right, I can manage that. But trying to bend enough to get the second leg in is enough to make me cry – I just can't bend. It's so annoying – such an easy, simple thing, to put stockings on, and I just can't manage it anymore.

We went on a trip to Montreal by train and I think the baby really loved the motion of the train. She didn't kick at all. But when the train stopped and we got off, did she ever wake up and start kicking!

I've decided I need support stockings. I'm beginning to have, well, not real varicose veins, but they're beginning to show a bit and stand out if I've been on my feet all day. They probably aren't serious but they are becoming visible.

My husband is worried that when the baby kicks really hard, she'll hurt me. But it doesn't really hurt at all. It does make it hard to sleep or relax sometimes, though.

I stopped on the street today and had a really good look at myself in a store window. Right now, I'm still five-foot two, but I'm also approximately five-foot two in diameter, with wall-to-wall face. It really knocked me out because I had mentally made fun of some of the huge women I had seen at my doctor's office. I go and look in my chest of drawers once in a while just to look at an old pair of blue jeans that used to fit. I don't know if they're ever going to fit again. . . . I guess everybody reaches that stage. . . . Am I ever going to have a waist again? Will I ever get rid of this?

I'm going to ask my doctor tomorrow if I can go over to the hospital soon and see the labour and delivery rooms – I think it would give me more confidence. I guess I'm not really frightened, but I'd feel better if I had an idea about those places.

We went away for the weekend and I went skinny dipping. It was marvelous to swim again, with this big stomach. I'd like to finish my pregnancy in water!

I resign from adulthood.

I can see now that it was a very big mistake getting involved with this business. I do not have the temperament for it. In fact, I feel misled. When I was still involved with childhood and adolescent-hood, I allowed myself to be convinced that adulthood was really a big deal. The ultimate advancement. The station everybody wants to climb to. The privileges are unlimited! Liquor, cigarettes, sex, restricted movies, politics, marriage, cheaper car insurance, etc. And I believed it and put my nose right to the grindstone to get to that exalted position. And I got there – I made it! Right up there with the Biggies. Wow!

What a disappointment. I just didn't fit in. The epitome of the Peter Principle. I found, much to my horror, that I hated beer, couldn't get excited over whisky or gin, didn't even like coffee! Cigarettes gave me eczema; restricted movies seemed much like westerns, only more blood, and unerotic sex. Politics is all work and no play. Marriage is not too bad but there was

a babies and motherhood clause that was completely misrepresented. Cheaper car insurance – that part is true.

Sex is the only privilege that has lived up to the promotion, but I suspect that adulthood is not the only institution that has access to this.

But I tried, I really tried.

I was careful to read all bestsellers, I joined too many committees, bought some sensible shoes, kept my hair neat and short, had three children.

But it is no use. I just am not adult material.

So, I am resigning. I'm so excited. Just think, being able to drink milk in public again, bare feet in hot weather, long hair that doesn't visit a hairdresser every week – and children are not as hard for other children to tolerate. And no more bestsellers! Back to biochemistry, ancient history and the children's section at the library. Ah, it's been a long time.

Billie Boulter
Rosalind, Alberta

Chinook Day

January 15, 1973
Dear Peter:
My wife just called me to say that you were looking for some ideas with reference to a mid-term break during the winter months.

In this connection, I gratefully submit to you copies of correspondence on this matter with Ottawa last spring.

Hugh R. Franks
Toronto, Ontario

If I'd believed in Chinooks, the unseasonable and miraculously warm winds that are reported to sweep across southern Alberta just when they're needed most, there might never have been a Chinook Day, the very seasonable and equally miraculous holiday that, as of mid-February 1973, now sweeps its way across Canada each year just when *it* is needed most – the mid-week day (who needs another long weekend?) that falls precisely half-way between New Year's and Easter.

What happened was this: After our trip to Alberta in the winter of 1972-73, during which the thermometer had never risen above about twenty below and the winds had whistled continuously at about thirty miles an hour, I made some off-hand remarks on the air about the myth of the Chinook. It was, I said, something westerners made up for eastern grade-school geography books (which is where I first read the word), to convince normal people they weren't crazy to live there. Like dry cold. My wife, for example, was raised in Brandon, Manitoba, and never spent a winter east of Winnipeg until she married me, and still insists that twenty above on the Toronto lakeshore is less comfortable than fifty below on the corner of Portage and Main. And I know from experience that she is wrong. Even when the wind is

still at fifty below, your lungs freeze, the end of your nose dies and you can't walk three blocks without tucking your hands into your crotch.

Anyway, I said something disparaging about Chinooks on the air one day and it was as if I'd made a joke about Jonah and the whale at a convention of Baptists. I got letters, phone calls, newspaper clippings (all obvious forgeries), and petitions. People told stories. Jean Ockley of Calgary was one of my more temperate correspondents. She wrote:

About these Chinooks. We do have them, but in moderation. Any old-timer can tell you that they are nothing like they used to be when he (she) was young, and probably even we did not see them at their best. There is a story told by one of our most noted raconteurs of the time he left Morley (about forty miles west of here) to drive to Calgary with a team and sleigh. The sleighing was good when he left, but a Chinook blew in and he could see the snow would all be gone before he got to Calgary. He whipped up his horses and managed to keep the front runners of the sleigh on snow, but the back runners were in the mud all the way.

There was another story about some Indians who were going to attend a church service. The church was covered with snow except for a pathway shovelled in. They tied their horses to a post sticking out of the ground and went in. When they came out, there were the horses, dangling by their halter shanks from the steeple of the church and the snow was all gone. I don't really believe that one.

Lies, lies, obvious lies, and I said so. The barrage of mail increased. People sent aerosol cans of Chinook air. They sent sworn affidavits, family bibles, paintings, tapes of the sound of a wind, more newspaper photographs (all obvious forgeries) and invitations to come out and await a Chinook. By now, I knew I was on to a fraud. If I were going to be moved at all it would have been by this letter, which was from someone I had heard from before on other subjects and had grown, through the mails, to like and admire. But this time, I knew that even she had been taken in. She wrote, on January 4, 1973:

You don't seem to be able to believe housewives, ranchers and businessmen when they tell you about the Chinook. Perhaps you can believe a minister! There *are* Chinooks in Alberta. Sometimes they blow as far as Saskatchewan. During the fifties I lived at Cabri, Saskatchewan. While there I experienced many Chinooks. It's true that just twenty miles further east the winds swirled the snow around and created the same driving hazards as a blizzard. In Cabri, however, the water ran in the streets, men hung up their curling brooms, took out their clubs, balls painted red, and headed for the golf course. There *are* Chinooks, Peter. I hope you will be able to experience one very soon. For to be in a Chinook is a very joyous thing.

Sincerely yours,
Rev. Mary Haggart
Central Butte, Saskatchewan

Balls painted red, indeed! And in *Saskatchewan*. I maintained my integrity.

My conversion actually came about through a more devious route, and it started in the office one day just about the time the Chinook argument had reached a stalemate. The person who triggered it all was Herb Johnson, one of our producers who was born, perhaps not coincidentally, in Skiff, Alberta, the heart of Chinook country. On this particular January day, Herb was feeling grungy, and he said he just didn't think he could make it to the next holiday, Easter. There was an instant wave of agreement in the office — Canada, possibly more than any other country in the world — *needs* a mid-winter festival. As Janet Murray of Halifax was to

write when I shared our office feeling with the listeners:

Dear Peter:
Yes, we do need a holiday in the middle of February, and for what better reason than that it's half-way through the winter. After all, the feast we now know as Christmas was originally a "half-way" holiday, Saturnalia, and although the Christian Church has attempted to give it a Christian connotation, most people still tend to celebrate it in the pre-Christian way. The Church itself has half-way feasts . . . half-way through the sombreness of Lent, it celebrates "Laetare" Sunday, and half-way through Advent, it celebrates "Gaudete" Sunday, with bright vestments and a liturgy of joy and hope. So why not celebrate February 15 as our "Half-way Holiday," the day when our Canadian winter is half-way finished. (Those who ski may, if they wish, go into mourning.) And February 14, with its connotation of love and lightness, would be just the right day.

If our government, being too busy with making unpleasant remarks about each other, does not get around to declaring it an official holiday, why don't we "This Country in the Morning" people start a grass-roots movement and celebrate it anyway, and celebrate it in our usual "This Country in the Morning" way . . . getting to know each other from coast to coast.

The problem was, what to call this new day. I asked, and the listeners responded. There are a lot of Canadian historical events that occurred in February, and nearly all of them were nominated. My own favourite of these came from John Rutherford of Scarborough, Ontario, who wrote:

February 15 is about mid-way between January 1 and Easter and also happens to be Flag Day, the day that the Canadian flag was first officially flown.

I have to admit that this idea is not original. I believe that Gordon Sinclair, whose birthday happens to be on February 15, has promoted this idea for a number of years. But, as Gordon Sinclair has so few good ideas, I think one should give him credit wherever possible.

Louise Cochran of Delisle, Saskatchewan, whose birthday falls on July 20, thought it would be a good time to honour people whose birthday falls on December 25, as does that of her youngest child, and Bruzz Bethel of Edmonton wrote this:

February 24, 1972
Prime Minister's Office
Ottawa, Ontario

Dear Sir:
I would like to put forward the suggestion that the weekend of February 14 be declared an official statutory long weekend, for the following reasons:

1. Mid-winter break between Christmas and Easter.
2. As an advent to spring, revert back to daylight saving time (daylight the same length as that of October).
3. It is time for winter carnivals — Mardi Gras, Quebec Winter Carnival, etc.
4. Flag Day — February 15.
5. The beginning of Reading Week at the universities.
6. Valentine's Day — February 14.

I have discussed this suggestion with many of my friends and they welcome the idea. I'd be very pleased to hear your reaction to this suggestion.

Yours sincerely
H.R. Franks

P.S. Furthermore, I saw a crow today.

Office of the Prime Minister
Cabinet du Premier Ministre
March 10, 1972
Dear Mr. Franks:
On behalf of the Prime Minister, I wish to acknowledge receipt of your letter of February 24, proposing that February 14 be made a statutory holiday.

I am taking the liberty of forwarding a copy of your suggestion to the office of the Secretary of State, for consideration.

Yours sincerely
T.W. Trousdell
Assistant Correspondence Secretary

P.S. Only robins count.

Dear Mr. Franks:
The office of the Prime Minister has forwarded to the office of the Secretary of State, the Honourable Gérard Pelletier, your letter of February 24, 1972, in which you propose that February 14 be made a statutory holiday.

Please be assured that your suggestion will be given every attention by officials responsible for matters of protocol within the department.

Yours truly
Suzanne Perry
Correspondence Secretary

March 29, 1972
The Office of
the Secretary of State
Attention: Suzanne Perry
Correspondence Secretary

Dear Sirs:
On the matter of my proposal that February 14 be a statutory holiday, I should like to point out that the emphasis is on a holiday weekend, in which case it would be the second Monday in February each year.

Yours sincerely
H.R. Franks

c.c. Office of the Prime Minister

If people still got their tongues frozen to pump handles, you wouldn't hear about the winter-time blues.

I remember when a January wouldn't go by without somebody getting stuck to a gate or a pump handle. Then, in the butcher shop, people wouldn't be saying, "Oh, I feel very blaa today." Instead, the talk would be, "Did you hear about Mrs. Johnson's boy? He got froze to the pump handle." "Yes, and Mr. Johnson was afraid the well was going to freeze so he kept pumping until they brought some warm water. Now the poor boy's tongue hangs down to his belly button."

I only recall one winter where it looked like the town would be shut out at the pump. Fortunately, we were saved in mid-February by my friend Wilfred. He didn't think it was cold enough to get stuck so he licked the railroad track while we were waiting for the train to bring our papers. It took four of us paperboys to pull Wilfred off the track. However, the 6:10 did run over a little bit of his tongue. He still has a lisp but at least he doesn't have the blaas. Maybe we could get a day up for Wilfred's tongue?

And Marion Dunk, of Dundalk, Ontario, in

helping to give us some idea of how to celebrate it, wrote about how she would spend what she called Karma Day:

I would start off by thanking my husband for the cup of coffee he brings me every morning. Better still, I would get up and make him a cup.

I would wrap my arms around Andrea and Hamish, instead of saying "Come on — get up now, it's 8 o'clock." Yes, I think a hug would be much better than yelling at an eight- and ten-year-old.

Then I would go to the window and thank God for my eyesight. Instead of complaining about the seven-foot drifts, I would thank God for the chickadees, grosbeaks, bluejays and sparrows. Instead of complaining to the children because of the noise, I would thank God again, for my hearing. After my orange and french toast, I would listen to what the children are saying, instead of worrying about the mess in the kitchen.

When I walk down to the post office, I would thank God for the lovely clean air of Dundalk, rather than grumble to myself because I am fifty miles from a plaza.

And now I'm off to our little post office with this note. A day to spread Karma would be great, to tell people you love them, to tell people they are *people*. To hold a hand, pat a back, smile at those you love.

But in the end I relied on people like Kathy Lynn of Vancouver and Minerva Tracey of Wolfville, Nova Scotia, and Johanna Wenzel of (once again) Edmonton. Kathy Lynn wrote: "Southern Albertans should carry the responsibility for sharing their special relief with the rest of the country." Minerva Tracey wrote: "Everywhere in the east we have 'thaws.' In British Columbia we have 'unusual weather.' But on the prairies — where I have lived half my life — we have Chinooks." And on January 9, Johanna Wenzel wrote:

So glad you are still pulling the West's leg by denying that heart-warming wind's existence!

But, you know, I'm afraid no one can post you a sample, because it's like *love*: it's different things to different people, and if you have no sensitivity to it you will always be left out in the cold.

That's what distinguishes easterners from westerners. We believe in it so strongly we can actually feel it.

In the meantime, the land is cold, but the glow lingers on.

So Chinook Day it became and Chinook Day it remained and, I hope, will remain forever, the most appropriate mid-week day falling on the median between New Year's Day and Easter Sunday. From everywhere, from listeners, from our own imaginations and from Homemade Theatre, a group of slightly mad improvisation-alists, we collected a number of excuses for getting the day off from your usual respon-sibilities, home, office or otherwise socially useful. Then we decided how Chinook Day ought to be spent. On Chinook Day One I wrote this:

In spite of the truly excellent and useful advice that Homemade Theatre offered here yesterday – one of our own people called in a few minutes ago to say she couldn't come in because her nose had fallen off – I realize that Chinook Day is still too young a phenomenon in this country for everyone to be able to celebrate it totally. I mean, even *I*, one of Canada's most ardent Chinookians, have come to work today (wait till next year, CBC) – so I know some of you will have at least that problem, although I would point out to you, you harrassed, overworked, underpaid, winter-bound office workers in that car pool just pulling around the corner, that it is not too late to turn back. If you do have to go to work, I mean if there's *no* way out of it, or if you're there already – if you're there already turn your radio up a bit – I do suggest you take it easy. Spend a lot of time (a) at the water cooler, (b) at the coffee urn or (c) near the desk of the person of the opposite gender whose desk you have secretly wanted to spend a long time next to since last November. If you're at home, the first rule of this first Chinook Day is also to take things easy. The following things have been outlawed by the rules committee:

a) Housework – especially for those who really enjoy it. The more proud you are the rest of the year of the immaculate look of your house, the more stringently the rule applies today. Lie down on the rug.

b) All committee meetings, except those for totally useless purposes.

c) Good manners to people who call you on the phone or knock on your door for the purpose of conducting commerce.

d) Clean language, ditto.

e) Self-doubt, about anything whatso-ever, from age to beauty, from wisdom to your success as a parent. Today, you are a perfect person, and some of the things I suggest that perfect person do are:

1. Take a bubble bath.

2. Take another bubble bath.

3. Phone the school right now, tell them you need your kids and will pick them up in half an hour . . . then go do something with them you've never done before.

4. Leave the kids in school, phone your husband and tell him you need him, then go do something with *him* you *may* have done before.

5. Go on back to bed.

6. Take ten bucks, make a list of people you want to buy presents for – people you *owe* presents to are disallowed – go out and buy the presents and deliver them today.

7. Phone your first love.

8. Go to your nearest travel agent, tell him you have $2,000 and thirty days and you've never been more than twenty miles away from home before and get him talking. It's his own fault he's working on Chinook Day.

9. Take another bubble bath.

And finally, there's one thing that you almost *certainly* have done before – if you're over the age of, say, eighteen – that everyone wants to do on Chinook Day, and I want you . . . to go out . . . and *do* it!

And it worked. In our studios we had flowers, balloons, live music, games, celebrities and a

Why I Can't Go to Work Today . . .

Mrs. Karen Pratt of Ottawa, Ontario, has become possessed by the devil. The only way she can get rid of him is to run naked down a deserted beach in the Turk or Caicos Islands.

Carolyn Smith of Dartmouth, Nova Scotia, is going out to find her dog – she just let him loose in her favourite park. If you don't have a dog, she adds, borrow one.

Dinny Holroyd of Calgary has found her old friend Carolyn Smith's (Dartmouth, Nova Scotia) dog, and she is taking it back to her.

Someone has dug a bayou around Sylvia Bubb's house in Hampton, New Brunswick, and filled it with alligators.

Mrs. Ving of Windsor, Ontario, who has kept house for twenty-seven years, says the dust can have its way for just one day.

Mrs. Letty Hearn from Hampton, New Brunswick, has a neighbour who won't have to work on Chinook Day. He's a sheep farmer and, this time of year, he usually spends some time assisting ewes to birth their lambs. However, knowing that Chinook Day was probably coming up in mid-February, he gave his rams a day or two off last fall.

That will give him Chinook Day off tomorrow.

George Maryfield of Woodstock, Ontario, won't be in because he's planning to have a new member of the family in mid-November.

Neither Ross Ramsey of Halifax, Nova Scotia, nor his wife can go to work because they live in an attic apartment and someone stole the stairs.

Terry Evans of Amherst, Nova Scotia, says his wife and baby were arrested for sunbathing in the nude and he has to appear in court as a character witness.

Michael Hawke of Toronto can't go to work because he's trying to get over a cold, and both his hands are stuck in his bottle of vitamin C pills.

Mrs. Elizabeth Cook of Pickering Village says her doctor's sick, so she's going to pay him a house call.

Mrs. Tomlinson of Valleyview, Alberta, says her mail-order husband is coming on Chinook Day and she's staying home.

Sheila Davidson of Seton Portage, British Columbia, says her grape harvest is ripe and she has to stay home and tramp out the grapes.

Mrs. Judith Wilensky of Willowdale, Ontario, is going to leave a note for her husband to say she's out because she went to the library and they stamped her hand instead of her book – she's due back on the 21st.

On Chinook Eve, Susan Epps of Bury, Quebec, is going to get out of bed and take a bottle of wine, some cheese and liverwurst, her Jeanette MacDonald and Nelson Eddy records, her favourite books, and lock herself in the spare room. On Chinook Day she'll

mood of giddiness I don't think we ever matched on any other day. Mel Profit, a towering football player from the Toronto Argonauts, made a puppet out of plasticene. Bernie Braden sang a naughty song. Tommy Hunter's mother told stories about his boyhood, and we brought in old and new friends from all over the country. The first year we flew Vicki Meacham in from Milne's Landing on Vancouver Island to meet Mrs. Mary Slaney, a tough and marvellous widow from Ferryland, Newfoundland, and Mrs. Slaney said her only regrets about coming to Toronto centered around the fact that, after a lifetime on the shores of the Atlantic, she couldn't sleep in the Four Seasons Motor Hotel because it was too quiet. The second year Vicki and John Meacham came down on their own and both years, after the program itself, Vicki cooked up a batch of B.C. oysters and we all ate them and drank wine and got chinooked out of our minds.

We gave things away – in Halifax we threw a surprise reunion for the mayor's old high-school class – and accepted some of the goofiest and most appreciated gifts ever to have changed hands. Across the country, a lot of people seemed to share our mood. Their celebrations ranged from simple coffee parties to chartered-bus excursions to go skiing. On Chinook Day Two a bunch of people, whose names I know but will never reveal, sent up balloons reading "BLOW UP YOUR TV . . . HAPPY CHINOOK DAY" before hearings of the CRTC over

whether or not the CBC television network should have its licence renewed.

For most people, in other words, it worked. Peter Powning, of Sussex, New Brunswick, wrote this to me:

It was a beautiful, cold clear day today. I made a conscious effort to do something I'd been meaning to do for a while.

I'm a potter and because I was firing my kiln this morning, I wasn't able to leave the pottery until mid-afternoon. But I did have to make a quick ski to my neighbour's to borrow a drill bit and discovered what a nice day it was. They live in a log house half a mile away across our fields, without access by a winter road (and no noisy snowmobile), so I am afforded the pleasant necessity of an overland journey whenever the need or desire arises, which is often. They have no phone so pony express or footpower must suffice. Back to our beautiful day.

In the afternoon Bob (the neighbour), Beth (my wife) and I put on our skis and waded our way up the high open hill overlooking our valley. As we approached the top we saw fox tracks leading to a place where the snow showed there had been a scuffle.

We went and examined the spot and deduced from the evidence (many tracks, droppings and the still-warm stomach of a rabbit) that a fox or two had had a Chinook Day feast – at the expense of the rabbit, I'm afraid. We followed the fox tracks away from the site of the banquet to see if we could discover where the hare had been caught.

It was an easy trail to follow because, in addition to the fox tracks, there was an impression left by the bunny as it was dragged through the snow to the lunch appointment. The trail led us for several hundred yards into the wood on the top of the hill to a dense thicket of spruce, where there were hundreds of rabbit tracks, nibbled maple shoots and an abundance of what we called as children "bunny grunts." There we lost the trail. But the fox had led us back into an unexplored part of the woods and we continued our trek through unknown territory. Among other wonders, we found a porcupine's dwelling in the base of a huge dead maple. He looked very cozy and content. It was a rewarding hike on an exhilarating day. We had a fast ski (with two spectacular falls) down the slopes to our homes and promised ourselves that we would do it more often.

And there were dozens and dozens of similar letters. But into each life, I suppose . . . and into each Chinook Day as well. This is from someone who signed herself Lottie Crump, but who gave no return address and who, for all I know, may not even exist.

Thought you might be glad to hear that I took your advice and made today a holiday. Nice, bright, sunny day here so first thing I went out to ride the horse. It was just admiration of the weather that made me take down the top bar of the corral gate before the bottom one, so the mare jumped, hit the bar and neatly squashed my hand against the stable wall. It only took ten minutes to catch her, but in the process I slipped in the mud.

You had been on the air for some twenty minutes when I came inside the house again — the first thing I heard was your advice to take a bubble bath — then take another one. Well: I surely needed a bath, and I haven't had a bubble bath in years, so I turned up the radio and went to hunt for the materials to make the bubbles. . . . I fetched a box of laundry soap. I beat the water vigorously with the back-brush and raised a mass of bubbles, and when they were level with the top of the bath, I got in. Unfortunately the dogs, thinking the bubbles were a solid surface, all got in too. I was flinging frantic dachshunds out on to the bathmat when the phone rang, so I groped around for the last dog, tucked it under my arm and went to answer the phone.

Standing in the kitchen, with a dripping dog under one arm, chatting to a friend who wanted to tell me all about her holiday in Hawaii, I realized that there was someone standing at the french doors. I was in the kitchen and there was absolutely no cover from windows or doors, no mats on the floor to cover myself with — only a portion of a very grubby blanket that was a dog's bed. Attired in dog blanket and shower cap, I opened the door an inch or so and informed the caller that I was not at home; but he had just come to tell me that the hydro was to be turned off at 10:30.

Being very dirty from the blanket, I returned to the bathroom only to find that, in the schmozzle of getting the dogs out of the bath, the plug chain had somehow been pulled, and the bath was empty of all but bubbles. I had a cold shower. By this time the power was off, and destined to stay off until 2:00 P.M.

Now when the power goes off here,

everything goes off and as we were all shivering, the first thing to do was light a fire in the fireplace. As is usual when one requires a fire for heating purposes, the lack of incendiary materials is startling; there was an abundance of newspaper and several large logs — nothing to be done but to go out and saw up some appropriately sized wood. I am not much of a hand with a saw. When I got inside again I found that the dogs had taken a kapok-filled cushion from the chair in the den and torn it into pieces on the living-room carpet. While lighting the fire, I had the den door open to bring in the wood and to give a good draught from the chimney — and the puppies went out to the corral and each brought in a nice fresh horse ball. Lunch was accomplished with the aid of a spirit stove and eaten in disapproving silence over the mess — the puddles, the kapok, the horse balls — and spouse left before 1:00 P.M. for a more congenial atmosphere, asking me to let him know next time I was going to take a holiday.

At 3:00 P.M., when a semblance of order had been restored to the house, I decided to follow your other suggestion and buy somebody a present. I threw all the dogs into the back porch and headed for the village, where I purchased a mickey of rye, a bottle of brandy and a bottle of wine. Time was pressing, and it was easier to

tell her family she can't come out and do her writing or look after them because during the night a rat broke into the house and bit her, giving her the black plague, so she'll have to put herself in quarantine to protect them.

Marjorie Fox of Regina, Saskatchewan, is going to be treading water on (frozen) Wascana Lake.

Joan Bishop of Caledonia, Ontario, says she can't go to work because the sparrows and the bluejays are having a hockey tournament on the birdbath and she has to referee.

John Martin of Toronto says he went for a drive with his girl friend and they went farther than they expected.

Carolyn Kirkner says that the baby has locked the bedroom door from the outside and swallowed the key, so she'll have to stay in bed.

Mrs. Doreen Rosen of Burlington, Ontario, has sprouted white wings and is going to fly above the clouds and follow the sun all day.

Mrs. Brika Eisenhatten of Whitehorse, Northwest Territories, says that last night Picasso came down from heaven and complained that the angels don't make good models, so he asked her to be his model. He redid her body and she hasn't learned yet to walk with one leg sticking out from her shoulder and the other from her belly button.

Mrs. Nadine Asante of Terrace, British Columbia, says that it's been raining violets in Terrace, and the scent is so overpowering they have to keep all the doors and windows closed.

Twelve years ago, Peter Barrington of Ottawa, Ontario, was cursed on the day of his birth, thus: if his name should be called five times on Chinook Day, he would turn into a werewolf. He can't go to school because he never gets yelled at less than ten times a day.

Les Turvey of Essex, Ontario, says his belly button fell out and he won't go to work until he finds it.

Vern Smith of Tappan, British Columbia, who has to drive his two boys three miles to the school bus, says that a big brown bear has just given birth to a cub in the back seat of his VW, and he doesn't feel he should disturb her.

Glenys Catterson of Binbrook, Ontario, has left a note for her husband and kids: "I pricked my finger while I was dusting the spinning wheel, and I am overcome by a desire to go to sleep . . . "

Ted Greenwood of Chatham, Ontario, who is over forty and is taking things in moderation, decided to have sex only once a year, and Chinook Day is the day!

REGRET I CANT BE WITH YOU ON CHINOOK DAY STOP ITS THE DAY I SOCK IT TO THE HARPER VALLEY PTA STOP

JOCK SUTHERLAND
CHARLOTTETOWN. PEI

LEAD DOG SUFFERED A FLAT PAW STOP UNABLE TO ATTEND WORK STOP (SENT VIA MOCCASIN TELEGRAPH)

JOHN FAIRBROTHER
FORT SIMPSON. NWT

Dear Mr. Math Teacher:
I have an awful toothache today and the dentist says to fill my mouth with water and sit on the stove until it boils.

Yours truly
Norma Stromburg
Williams Lake, British Columbia

make all the purchases in one place. With the remainder of your suggested ten dollars, I bought paper, ribbon and cards and wrapped my purchases.

On my first visit I found nobody at home, but was bitten by the dog in my effort to put the present inside the back door. On my second visit I was welcomed with open arms and my dog bite was doctored with my present, both internally and externally. I was sent gaily on my way to deliver my third gift and really didn't mind a bit when I got the car stuck in the mud half-way to the house. Again I received a rousing welcome; husband and sons were called out to deal with the car and we all had a nip or two from the bottle of brandy to fortify ourselves for the effort. We all had coffee afterwards, laced with another nip, because nothing enlivens coffee so much as a drop of brandy. The conversation was becoming hilarious when I noticed that it was getting dark and I was past due at home to get supper. I was waved on my way, with a couple of nice steaks, bidden to take the "old road" out as it wasn't so muddy. They were quite right. It wasn't muddy as nobody had used it and I rounded a corner to be faced with an expanse of snow, discovering as the car sank slowly that it was a hollow. I extricated myself with steaks and handbag, but had to go back to turn off the lights. It wasn't very far to the road and I galloped along thinking about the salad to go with the steak. I was very lucky and got a lift almost immediately, as a police car came along. For some reason the corporal didn't think the situation was funny, but he was very nice and in the end agreed to drive

me right up to the house, where my family was waiting for me on the doorstep.

They were quite nice to me in the end. My spouse, after having said he thought I should sleep in the back porch, has put himself to bed in the spare room; so I'm just going to take a little nip of the cooking brandy in the kitchen cupboard to put me to sleep and climb into bed with the dogs.

Ah, well . . . it was a holiday anyway, and for a last word on what it really means I'd like to turn again to Janet Murray, who was, you'll recall, one of the people who helped us most in learning how to celebrate it on the day we designated. This is what Janet wrote to me after Chinook Day Two:

My husband and I and our children learned a fundamental truth about Chinooks today . . . you take them when you find them. As time has gone on, it has become apparent that we would not be able to think up an excuse, feasible or otherwise, to take Wednesday off; our schedules of appointments, meetings, interviews and patients were just too overwhelming. I was sorry about that because I had really enjoyed Chinook Day '73. But I knew that I would have to pass it up.

Then, we woke up today to find that twelve inches of drifting snow had snowed us in. My husband had patients to see in Pictou, one hundred miles away, and he made an attempt to get out, but the snow was too deep, our little street wasn't plowed, and besides, his car battery had died, and so had mine. School was cancelled, and so we were unable to do anything we were supposed to do today.

First he helped some friends get unstuck from the snow, then he came in and we had two breakfasts together. I curled up with him and the Lewiscraft catalogue, and planned all the crafts I will do next fall and winter. The kids got up one by one. They got their own breakfasts, whatever they wanted; then our oldest daughter, Shannon, put a sheepskin rug in front of the TV and did yoga while she watched the game shows. Seven-year-old Brian, who complains that school wastes too much of his time, went out tobogganing with his friends, and had the "funnest" time. Nine-year-old Suellen took breakfast and a mystery book back to bed with her. Eleven-year-old Bruce eventually crawled out of bed, and dragged his blankets and pillow to the rec room where he could sleep among friends.

My husband and I had another cup of coffee, and then set up the slide projector and looked at our last summer's Spanish vacation slides, and picked some others to send to a slide exhibit. The phone rang and someone answered it and forgot to put it back on the hook, so we were cut off from the outside world for the morning. My husband and I advanced to hot mulled wine, and talked vaguely about going out later to shovel snow or maybe take some pictures, and he said he thought he'd work on some research papers later, and I said I might do something too, but I really felt like I had a cold coming on, so maybe I'd just have some more hot mulled wine and read something, like the Lewiscraft catalogue or the phone book or a cook book.

Suellen just surfaced long enough to take lunch and another mystery back to bed with her. Two neighbourhood girls arrived at the door to ask if Bruce was coming out to play in the snow. "My God, he's growing up," I thought and poured some more mulled wine. Shannon is standing on her head in front of the TV, and Brian and his friends have left to throw snowballs at the boys down the street shovelling snow. And so it goes.

My Chinook arrived today, came on the icy blasts of a February storm, but it did what it was supposed to do. It gave me time to stop in the middle of a winter that has been too long, too busy, too full of worries and responsibilities and problems . . . time to bask in the warmth of the things and the people I love. And it taught me to take my Chinooks when they come.

And now back to my hot mulled wine.

Lynne Surette of Dartmouth, Nova Scotia, who is suffering from carbon-monoxide depletion, has to go downtown to inhale some city air. Her husband, therefore, has to stay home with the baby.

Bob Hatfield of Rothesay, New Brunswick, can't go to work because he's started labour pains.

A Garden Plan

A. Spinach. Sow spinach early. After cutting, clean up roots and plant early cabbage.
B. Swiss chard. Swiss chard will grow back after cutting and will give greens all summer.
C. Peas. Plant early peas. After harvesting peas, clean up plants and sow spinach in late summer.
D. Bush beans. Bush beans will produce until late summer.
E. Beets. Sow beets early and thick. Beet greens are an excellent vegetable. Thin beets to about two inches apart.

F. Tomatoes. Before planting tomatoes, sow radish. Plant tomatoes among radish. When plants grow taller and heavier, radish can be gradually picked out.
G. Carrots. Use summer carrots.

N.B. Many of our listeners have suggested that lettuce and green onions be included in this plan. They could be substituted for the spinach or for the early peas.

Tony Van Dam

vegetable garden: 8' x 15'

Key

A — spinach
B — Swiss chard
C — peas
D — bush beans
E — beets
F — tomatoes
G — carrots

Bi-country
in the Morning

You started it all – to rhyme's a temptation
The family screaming – switch off that damn station.
But you mentioned a book – did you say Tri-lingual?
I'm looking for one to help immigrants mingle.
The Yanks had a book as part of their kit
Of phrases to use – or *not* in Great Brit.
I'm asking for help – my plea is quite valid
Save me blushing red – my friends blanching pallid.

When I buy an anorak I'm asked "What is that?"
"Oh, you mean a parka, with a hood not a hat."
A vest is a waistcoat, just now they are in
In U.K. a vest is worn next to the skin.
My son's underpants have now become gaunches
That is the garment men wear 'round their haunches.
Sweaters you say – we call them jumpers
Cars don't have fenders because they have bumpers.

Trousers are pants – this will cause snickers
For pants in U.K. we simply say knickers!
Now this we can cope with and laugh till we bubble
It's the next lot that really get us into trouble.
There are so many – here's a few of the worst
It's vital that these be clarified first.
I'll illustrate here and I won't pull my punches
What I *feel* as an immigrant my biggest crunch is.

They'll be rated adult so turn down the wireless
Correct that to radio – hope my typist is tyreless!
Wrong again – my stenographer is bursting with laughter
She's my youngest girl saying "Mum, you get dafter!"
My intention is not to offend – not at all
But the bluer they come the harder we fall.
I'm like my backside if you call me a bum
But to pinch a girl's fanny in U.K. is not done.

A stupid mistake – that's a big boob
Big boobs in Canada is frightfully crude.
A carpenter, a joiner, but never a chippie
Our one word in common appears to be hippie.
You wish to rise early then ask for a call
Don't say knock me up – no never at all.
The next I can vouch is a real party wrecker
Say keep up your chin but never your pecker.

The ad said quite clearly four dollars a shag
In a barber's shop window?!!! They've got to be mad.
How about this – half-price shag carpet
Good heavens above – what a product to market.
It works vice versa and could happen to you.
In U.K. be careful who you ask for a screw.
Before you get nasty and say so quite tartly
Think how you'd feel in a mixed company party.

I've prayed oh so often when out for a sup
For the floor to just open and swallow me up.
You can't blame the English language we use.
It isn't the language, it's language abuse.
Because we speak English we become quite indifferent
The words sound the same – but the meaning's so different.

On Merv Griffin's show, Mr. Peter O'Toole,
When challenged for swearing looked dumb as a mule
Whatever he said 'twas a bleep for the nation
Though he assured Merv "That's not *our* connotation."
Not wishing our native tongue to relinquish
It's essential we learn Canadian English.
To those who are shocked and start to get shirty,
My words are all clean – and your mind must be dirty.

"Mrs. Limey"
Edmonton, Alberta

Mati Laansoo Tests
the Law of Gravity

Last year I tested the law of gravity for the listeners of "This Country in the Morning" by jumping off an aeroplane. People who heard the program might remember me talking about skydiving with instructors and parachutists — when I asked the students what they felt before and after their jumps, they said: "scared" and "terrific" respectively. And I'm sure listeners remember my terrified voice before and during the parachute descent.

The actual descent lasted less than three minutes. It took another three hours to edit the tapes for the radio show, and I must admit that I spent six long and difficult days trying to write it down on paper. But I didn't waste all that energy and effort merely to describe a few seconds, during which I encountered the most terrifying moment of my life. My purpose in writing this is to communicate something else — something rather interesting that I discovered, something that didn't come across on tape.

It was mid-October 1973 and I was in Vancouver when I agreed to make the jump. I had to take a parachute course first, and I had to take it in a hurry — even in Vancouver, the weather is getting tricky for a parachutist by October. There were other complications. My worst problem was how to get the jump on tape: I couldn't just strap my fifteen-pound Uher tape recorder on my chest, and even a cassette recorder would be too bulky. What I needed was an efficient transmitter and receiver, small yet powerful enough so that the receiver could pick up my signal from the air. When I managed to borrow one such unit from CBC television news in Vancouver, I discovered that the transmitter would stop whenever I turned my back to the receiver, connected to my tape recorder on the ground. If the equipment failed to pick up my voice during the jump, I'd have to repeat the performance.

So on that fateful day, I spent all my time fiddling with wires and antennae and cursing at the prospect of wasting all this effort. Even during the final briefing before boarding the plane (wearing a crash helmet, shod in para-trooper boots, clad in a jumpsuit, with a parachute harnessed to the back and a smaller one secured to the chest), while everyone was repeating their instructions, my mind was else-where. And that's why I was still desperately tugging at the microphone taped to my neck as we stumbled awkwardly from the clubhouse towards a tiny four-seater Cessna 180, idling noisily at the edge of a soggy pasture.

In order to make room for everyone, the interior of the plane had been stripped of every-thing except one seat, on which crouched a bored guy with a crewcut and thick bifocals named Jack, who was to be our pilot. Under the instrument panel, with his back crammed into an unbelievably tight niche, I discovered Jerry, our jump master. Jack proceeded to warn us to lean well forward, or the overloaded plane would fly straight into the high-tension wires above the end of the three hundred-yard-long field of mud. This statement scared the hell out of everyone, so we obediently bent over on our knees, with our heads pressed between our rumps and laps. There was a loud surge of noise and a terrible pounding sensation as the little plane bounced over boulders and across ruts; the straining engine performed a minor miracle, and we were airborne.

The noise was deafening; everything vibrated or rattled. After what seemed like hours, from my cramped position I could see Jerry yelling at me. I could see him yelling because his mouth was moving and the veins on his neck were bulging. He motioned to me that we were over the "drop zone," and that I was to jump first. My eyes followed his finger pointed at the target area, a tiny dot 3500 feet below us, where I must land. Suddenly there was a blast of cold air mixed with the roar of the engine as the upward-hinged hatch whipped open.

I won't bother the reader with my trivial thoughts as the pit suddenly yawned at my feet, as the sting of adrenalin filled my body. I will only describe precisely what I did next.

Carefully, I placed the boot of my left leg on to a twelve-inch pipe sticking out from the fuselage, and cautiously clamped my left hand around the diagonal wing strut. As I groped to clamp my right hand along the upper length of the strut, the wind force was so unexpectedly powerful that my right leg swung out behind me and the helmet banged against the wing above my head. And there I perched — frozen with fear — suspended in the slipstream, with the loose fabric of the jumpsuit flapping wildly around my legs.

At that moment, it flashed across my mind that, with all the worry and fiddling with the transmitter on the ground, I had omitted one crucial detail: I had failed to prepare myself mentally for the actual ordeal coming up. At that moment I also happened to remember from my high-school physics that, should you be unfortu-nate enough to fall without the benefit of a functioning parachute, you will accelerate at an increasing rate of 120 feet per second/per

is for my town,
good-old Mississauga,
The national trend —
two kids and a dogga.

Sharon Diachun
Mississauga, Ontario

126

second, until you attain a speed in excess of 120 miles an hour. You will also soon come to an abrupt stop – but only after bouncing a few hundred feet into the air, after the first impact with the turf.

So when Jerry slaps me against the leg and yells, "Go!" – I can't *move*. I'm stuck to that silly little pipe with one foot, holding on for dear life and staring wide-eyed at this madman whose obvious game is my demise.

The static-line has been cut! Somebody has replaced the chute on my harness with a backpack and, as I fall, a canopy does not appear above me because the backpack ejects a variety of cups and plates and thermal underwear! Too late, I see Jerry laughing hysterically and checking off another name from the list on his clipboard. My god, he's holding up a Jeroboam of champagne with the other hand! He's going to drink a toast with the pilot, who's wiping tears of mirth from his eyes. . . . You idiot, how could you be sucked into this madness?

But Jerry slaps my leg again, harder this time, and then this madness dissolves because I figure, what the hell. And all of a sudden, I am absolutely nowhere. In the distance I can hear someone screaming: "Arch thousand . . . two thousand . . . three . . . " (it's me doing the yelling, you see), and then all kinds of incoherent words are coming out of my mouth.

Then, ever so lightly (as the harness tightens around my thighs and shoulders), my fear turns to grateful relief and I descend into the perpendicular. A huge red-and-white-striped canopy billows overhead and the blue curvature of the Pacific Ocean sparkles ahead of me. The white-capped Coast Range looms to my left and the checkered quilt of miniature farms and fields is spread out below me. There is no sensation of movement. I hear a gentle whisper of wind through the shrouds. Soon the ground becomes larger. Reaching up for the steering toggles, I find them quite responsive. I can see the target (a fifty-foot circular mound of pea-gravel) which has grown to the size of a dime already. I make out the fluorescent orange of the drop master's coat, directing me. And I steer accordingly, letting the wind drift me nearer. Slowly turning, over the clubhouse – the ground is rushing up very quickly now – I'm going to hit a barking dog, staring up at me stupidly. And then: thump! I land on both feet and remain standing as the canopy drops over me – and it's all over.

Some excited people who have been around the tape recorder rush up to tell me that they heard me loud and clear. The drop master offers his congratulations. I landed only a hundred feet off target, and I'm grinning from ear to ear because everything had worked!

There was no cry of triumph, just some knowing looks from a few experienced skydivers. The sort of looks you get after an indescribable experience – only to be shared among the select few, as it were.

The last person I saw as I drove away into the sunset was an instructor lying on his stomach on top of a bench, demonstrating the position of arms and legs during free-fall. It occurred to me while I was negotiating the ruts on that same muddy field where a few hours earlier I had been bumping along in the other direction, that a lot of people would go on from here to real skydiving. This is falling free in a controlled spiral, and holding hands with other skydivers for a timeless moment like some strange ritual. Some people will repeat this performance thousands of times, and I know why they do it.

But just as I came to a stop to look for traffic, before driving up on to the paved road, I happened to look up into the sky. And way up above, I saw the little plane carrying another load of parachutists. I knew exactly what was happening inside. I could visualize the bored expression on Jack's face as he guided the frail craft upward through wide circles to the proper altitude. I could see his hairy arm reaching across the crowded cabin for the hatch handle. In fact, if I'd looked long enough, I'd eventually have made out a tiny little black dot for an instant before actually hearing the sharp crack of the canopy opening; then, the stationary circle of a little striped parachute, while the plane flew away. And as I pointed the nose of my old Chevy pick-up homeward, I got the picture that somehow, that first experience can never be duplicated.

It's like the song I heard on the car radio as I tore away down the highway. It was Alan Price, from his album *O Lucky Man*, and I turned the volume way up loud to hear the words. He was singing:

> There's no easy days
> No easy ways
> Just go out there and do it!
> And smile while you're making it . . .
> Laugh while you're taking it . . .
> Even though you're faking it . . .
> 'Cause nobody's gonna know . . .

's for the Newfie
in Tom Connors' tune,
He found it was cheaper
to live on the moon.

Diane Lynch
Pickering, Ontario

A Friend Remembered

March 27, 1974

Dear Peter:

Here's something that seems pertinent to what you're doing right now on "friendly overtures."

One of the most rewarding relationships I ever had was with a paperboy. When I was fifteen I was a scrawny, pimply, ugly adolescent. These things were not assets, even in the dull fifties, and no boy would look at me twice. Partly in defiance, with a sense of a "higher purpose," and partly out of sheer desperation, I decided to become a great violinist. I would get up early every morning and practise the violin from six o'clock to eight o'clock. One morning in February, I was working my way up and down the arpeggios when a snowball bumped the window. I went over and looked out. It was pitch dark, but down below me in the snow I could make out a bundled-up little boy, with a bag of papers over his shoulder. We looked at each other for a while, and then he waved. I waved back, and he went off down the lane. Every morning after that, about 6:30, a snowball would hit the window, and I would go over and wave. There we both were, up early and alone in a snowy world, two sparrows looking at each other. Then he would go on delivering papers, and I would go back to the violin. I never saw him in the daylight, and he disappeared with the snow in the spring.

I'm not a great violinist now, but I am a happy adult, and every now and then I think about that kid. What he did was pretty simple, really. He stood in the dark and heaved a few snowballs at a lighted window. I wish I could thank him for helping me get through that terrible adolescent winter.

Sincerely
Jean McKay
London, Ontario

Did you hear about the CBC announcer who bought snow tires?
They melted.

Geoffrey Burd
Kingston, Ontario

Siwash Racing Harness

Material Required: Approximately 10 feet of 1″ webbing, preferably nylon which can be sewn on a home sewing-machine. Nylon fleece for padding. 3-foot rope and swivel clip (as found on most dog leashes).

Method: Cut webbing pieces, allowing extra for adjustments. Typical measurements for Siberian husky: (see diagrams) A to C, 8″; A-B-D (2 pieces), 24″ each; C-F-C, 52″; E to E, 5″. A Samoyed would be bigger. Pin on dog for fit and double-check with harness off to see that harness is symmetrical. Refit with pull at F, simulating load. Double sew all joins.

Padding: Sew fleece on one side of webbing, then fold so that folded edge of fleece projects approximately ½″ beyond edge of webbing. Sew again near edge of webbing.
Bring fleece to same distance beyond other edge, fold, and then roll under center of webbing to give extra padding. Sew close to edge. [Sew padding continuously from C to A to B (fold) to A and tuck under.]

Tugline: Make eye splice (or a small, strong loop) at one end of the 3′ rope. Attach swivel clip to other end. Attach at F.

To harness dog, put head through from bottom into loop A-B from back to front. Put front legs through loops A-B-C-D. When harnessing two dogs tandem, attach one end of a neck line approximately 18″ long to each collar.

sled-dog organizations:

Nancy Scarth
Secretary
Arctic Sled Dog Club of Ontario
R.R. 4, Osgoode, Ontario

Dave Hobbs
International Sled Dog Racing Association
Box 144
Ontario, New York
14519 U.S.A.

dogs and equipment:

Hall Sleds
5875 McCrum Road
Jackson, Michigan
49201 U.S.A.
(sleds and harnesses)

Platt Sleds
Murray Hill Road
Youngsville, Pennsylvania
16371, U.S.A.
(sleds)

Kelson Kennels
Box 149
Como, Quebec
(complete line)

Fred Robertson
Stanstead, Quebec
(sleds only)

Zima Kennels
Box 57
Kila, Montana
59920 U.S.A.
(complete line plus dog training)

Mrs. Nancy Scarth
Osgoode, Ontario

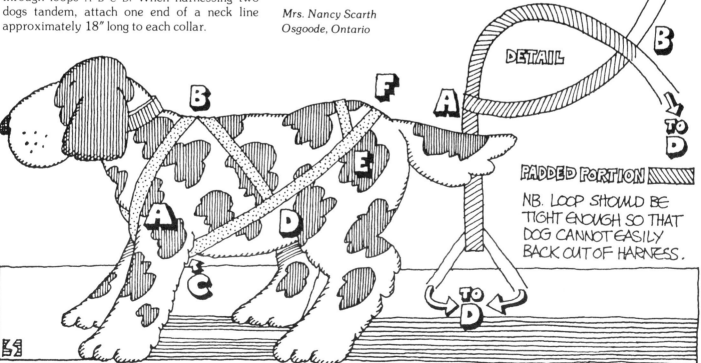

DETAIL

PADDED PORTION

NB. LOOP SHOULD BE TIGHT ENOUGH SO THAT DOG CANNOT EASILY BACK OUT OF HARNESS.

Andrew Allan on Hot Spells

I've been wondering what ever happened to that man who always fried an egg on the sidewalk. Every time we had a heat wave he did that, and always (strangely enough) had a news photographer nearby when he did it.

His only competition was the giant thermometer in front of the lumberyard. That was the thermometer that always burst. It stood full in the afternoon sun, of course, and that's why it burst; but also the lumber company never did get around to calibrating it for a heat wave. When you get your name in the paper every time your thermometer bursts, why argue with fate?

The lumberyard is gone now, and so, apparently, is the man who fried the egg on the sidewalk. The lumberyard has moved to the suburbs, where it sells artificial wood, with which suburban husbands fashion things of great beauty: namely, rumpus rooms.

And the man with the egg? I have my own theory about *him*. He is, at this very moment, escaping from this very heat wave in an air-conditioned bar, breaking his egg into a toddy.

The bar is, geographically, only a few yards from the downtown site of the man's erstwhile outdoor culinary conquests, but historically, it is a million light-years away. Any man today who breaks an egg on the scorching sidewalk isn't making news; he's just making a mess. And anyway, what's the use of it when the news photographer is already inside the bar enjoying the coolth?

The air conditioner is the Great Divide between the wicked old egg-frying era and today's beautiful new world of synthetic climate.

The wicked old era had ice wagons. Men cut blocks of ice out of the lake in winter, stored them in sawdust, and then had the iceman come down your street in summer and sell you just the size you wanted or your icebox would hold — although you had to allow a certain amount of loss through drippage between the wagon and your back door or the dumbwaiter. If the iceman was the most popular man in town during a heat wave, he was also the hottest. He was also the victim of small boys, who clambered on the back of his wagon when he and his tongs were delivering, boys who crammed their mouths and pockets with chips of his coldness and ran them over their brows and eyes and down their necks.

In a hot spell, then, you lay on top of the sheets and tried to breathe. You sat in the cellar when you could — and everyone asked you if it was hot enough for you, and you said it was.

When air conditioning finally arrived, it went first of all to the movies. When you couldn't stand the sidewalks any more, you ducked into a movie and watched a lot of head-shrinkers steaming it out on the Amazon, and you shivered delightfully. Some lousy features got boffo ratings when the temperature outside hovered around ninety.

By this time the ice man had been supplanted by the electric refrigerator — so you could stagger the few blocks through the fiery furnace to your house and lie in a cold bath with ice cubes floating all around you.

Restaurants — especially those licensed to placate the inner man with booze — were next to install the new-fangled cooling systems. And this meant you could sit in comfort, watching your lamb's curry simmering down in the icy blast.

In the wicked old days you would see downtown office girls frumping out of the buildings in their enveloping cottons, looking for all the world as if they had been prisoners in a steam bath with all their clothes on. Today the daughters of those same girls leg it blithely through the temperature in miniskirts and halternecks — cool in their hot-pants — freshly released from air-conditioned offices and on their way to bars and restaurants so icy the girls have to rent fur coats from the management.

Even your home can be air conditioned now if you're getting your relief cheque at regular stated intervals. And there are people baking in summer cottages at this very moment, yearning for the day when they can get back to town and cool off.

She stood at the door of Burgess Fish Sauce Shop welcoming him in.

Doreen Butler
Vancouver, British Columbia

Hockey in Humboldt

April 17, 1973:

Tonight, in Portage La Prairie, Manitoba, there will be no hockey game. In Humboldt, Saskatchewan, there will be no hockey tonight, tomorrow and conceivably, just conceivably, there might not be *any* hockey, for a long time to come.

I know – we all know here – that occasionally you feel we pay too much attention on this program to hockey. In spite of that feeling, we are devoting a substantial part of today's program to this story, because it is a story about values, about the way we think of ourselves and our children. If hockey is, as many people believe it to be, as clear a lens as exists through which to perceive our national character, then this is a story about that too. It is also an extremely interesting tale.

Terry Henning is a young medical doctor who practises in Humboldt, Saskatchewan, a community of some thirty-five hundred, a little more than sixty miles east of Saskatoon. He also coaches hockey. He has won provincial championships at three age levels, coaching boys younger than juniors, whose maximum age is nineteen. And he is the man the town of Humboldt turned to three years ago when its citizens decided to return to the ranks of competitive junior hockey, tier two. In years before that, Humboldt, with a junior team called the Indians, had played a rough, rollicking, aggressive kind of hockey that had won them a lot of games but lost them a lot of friends, including people in the Humboldt district itself. Attendance fell off. The Indians moved to Estevan.

Under Dr. Terry Henning's coaching, the newly named Humboldt Broncos turned that pattern around. Playing clean, fast, exciting hockey, the Broncos went to the provincial finals in their first year, won the provincial championship in their second, defeated Dauphin, Manitoba, in interprovincial play, and were defeated only by Red Deer, Alberta. At the same time, Henning was bringing along younger players – two of his players this year are fifteen and one is fourteen – and making certain, among other things, that their academic records stood up. This year, provincial champions again, they began interprovincial play against the Portage La Prairie Terriers, a bigger, tougher team, which Humboldt beat once and lost to once in Portage, then lost to twice in a row at home, and then, in the third game in Humboldt, the fifth of the series, beat again, 7-4.

It was this game, the fifth in the series, with Humboldt now down 3-2, that provoked the situation that had to be ruled on last night.

What follows is a list of the penalties from that game, played before a crowd of fifteen hundred in Humboldt on Monday night.

Game Number 5:

first period

Portage	5 minutes	spearing
Humboldt	2 minutes	hooking
Humboldt	2 minutes	cross-checking
Portage	2 minutes	high-sticking

second period

Humboldt	2 minutes	high-sticking
Portage	2 minutes	tripping
Portage	2 minutes	tripping
Portage	2 minutes	holding
Portage	2 minutes	too many men on the ice

third period

Portage	2 minutes	tripping (9:46)
Portage	2 minutes	roughing
Humboldt	2 minutes	tripping
Portage	2 minutes	roughing
Humboldt	2 minutes	roughing
Portage	2 minutes	slashing ⎤ (17:56)
Humboldt	2 minutes	slashing ⎦
Portage		misconduct ⎤ (18:03)
Humboldt		misconduct ⎦
Portage		fighting and game misconduct
Humboldt		fighting and game misconduct
Portage		fighting and game misconduct
Portage		fighting and game misconduct
Humboldt		fighting and game misconduct (19:42)
Portage		fighting and game misconduct
Portage		fighting and game misconduct
Humboldt		fighting and game misconduct
Humboldt		fighting and game misconduct
Humboldt		fighting and game misconduct
Portage	2 minutes	charging
Portage	2 minutes	high sticking
Humboldt	2 minutes	high sticking
Portage	5 minutes	spearing (19:57)

That final spearing call, incidentally, is reported to have occurred this way. With four seconds left on the clock, the referee dropped the puck for a face-off and the Portage player, ignoring the puck, speared the Humboldt player in the belly. Another brawl threatened to break out. Fans poured on to the ice. The referee called the game.

Following that game, Terry Henning and his manager announced that they had had it. They were forfeiting the series. Rather than, as they said, risk serious injuries to their boys, they would concede to Portage.

Which, you might think, would have been simple enough. Let Portage go on and play the Alberta champions and Humboldt could stay home.

Except that, first of all, Terry Henning and his manager, Dr. Jerry Rooney, an optometrist, have been suspended from hockey. And second, Humboldt, Saskatchewan, with its community-owned, almost all home-grown, clean, fast,

131

junior team, may be out of the Saskatchewan League for good.

The situation today is this: the sixth game of the series was originally scheduled to have been played in Portage La Prairie last night. After saying that they would forfeit the game, Humboldt could not, of course, get to Portage La Prairie in time to play last night. But the head office of the CAHA had ruled that there would be a twenty-four-hour postponement in order to give the people of Humboldt time to think over whether they would go back and play against the Portage La Prairie "Terrorists." Right after that decision, we talked with three people who live in Humboldt: Kelly Kidd, who's the president of the Broncos hockey team; Mrs. Pat Miller, Mary Miller, who is a fan and a supporter of the team; and Mrs. Dick Leggett, who has a boy on the Humboldt team. I began by asking Kelly Kidd about the kind of hockey that the Broncos play.

KK: A fast game and entertaining hockey, that's what our crowds here seem to enjoy. We have been bringing in a good crowd, and more every year, and that's the reason. We found that with our old team, the Indians, the crowds started falling out — they just didn't go for that hack-'em-down style of hockey.

PG: The people of Humboldt have responded, then, to Terry Henning's kind of hockey?

KK: That's right, and it is very entertaining hockey.

PG: Mary Miller, you are involved in this just as a fan, or is one of your boys on the team?

MM: No, no, I'm just a fan.

PG: What attracts you to the Broncos?

MM: Well, my whole family watched the Broncos and I sort of got carried along with the enthusiasm. I'm just like a kid with a new toy right now — I really love that club.

PG: How did you find Terry Henning as a coach? What did the kids think of him, Mrs. Leggett?

Mrs. L: Oh, they're very glad that they have Dr. Henning as their coach; they've learned a great deal, and anywhere Dr. Henning has taken them, he's always been complimented on their hockey ability, and the way they manage themselves off the ice as well as on.

PG: Mary Miller – as a fan, how do you feel about the team's decision?

MM: I feel that it was the right one, definitely no question. And I think that Kelly should go over it with those boys.

PG: Mrs. Leggett, as a mother of one of the players, how do you feel about this decision? It's the end of the season – the boys will never get the chance to prove whether they could have won the whole western championship.

Mrs. L: Well, we're very happy with what the boys have done this year, and I think that rather than have them hurt, I would rather see it as it is, as the management is doing it.

PG: How would it make you feel, if they closed down hockey in Humboldt? From everything that you've told me, hockey is a very important part of life in your town.

KK: Well, I'd hate to see it happen here but, after all, kids are a lot more important than hockey.

PG: I go along with that. Mary Miller, how do you feel?

MM: Well, we want hockey, Peter, but we want our kind of hockey and it's just as simple as that.

PG: Mrs. Legget?

Mrs. L: Yes, we want hockey, but I don't consider this incident a tribute to hockey.

The future of hockey in Humboldt is certainly in doubt, and the man who has had to make the decision, really, is Dr. Terry Henning, the man who took the team to the championships and, with his friend and manager, Jerry Rooney, decided this week to pull them out. Dr. Terry Henning, you're the man on the spot right now?

TH: Yes, I guess I am.

PG: Terry, is there any way whatsoever that you would play the final game against Portage La Prairie?

TH: That's a really difficult question. I myself, with my own principles and my own beliefs, I would say no, but Peter, this is a bigger problem than I can handle myself. This is up to our board of directors, and up to our manager and up to the hockey players. I will tell you one thing, though: if I've got anything to do with it, we won't go back. Before I would let the team go back I would request that the board of directors and the players and myself meet and talk it over. I feel very strongly about it.

PG: Kelly Kidd, the president of the Humboldt team, has told us that after the decision you and the management made – and it was a two-man decision at first, was it not?

TH: Correct.

PG: . . . that after that he checked with the board and they voted unanimously to support you in your stand.

TH: Yes, I know that. It's unbelievable to me, really, the pressures that have been brought to bear in the last twenty-four hours upon myself and Dr. Rooney, by people associated with organizations, or so-called organizations, so-called organized sport in this country. It's something you've really got to participate in yourself to appreciate.

PG: What kinds of pressures? Could you talk about some of the things that you have experienced in those last twenty-four hours?

TH: Yes, but I think probably you should understand just exactly what our hockey team is. They used to have junior hockey in this town and it was killed, by a fellow who is now coaching in the so-called tier one hockey in the bigger leagues. They just wrecked hockey in this town, according to people who were here before, because he was willing to go along with the type of thing that we're running into now. I can say, without any hesitation at all, that the Broncos have always been an extremely clean hockey team: we've always played extremely good hockey and we had fantastic fan support. Statistically, we've played some hundred and eighty-five games, or something like that over the three years, and we've been involved in three brawls – two of those have been in the last five games. There has never been a spearing penalty, as far as I can remember, against our club; there has been a butt-ending penalty, but I think over those hundred and eighty-five games that we've had, I would imagine, about five or six misconduct penalties.

PG: Jerry Rooney has written to the CAHA that he will forfeit the series, is that right?

TH: That's correct. When that brawl broke out, we just said no way. There is just no way, as a physician, that I could ever live with myself, saying to myself that I put kids on the ice and somebody lost an eye, or was seriously injured. I've got two kids on crutches right now, and I've got three or four kids with bad face lacerations.

PG: Are those the results of the five games against Portage?

TH: That's correct. Yep.

PG: After that game, did you talk to the boys at all before you decided about the forfeit?

TH: No, I didn't.

PG: You, you and Jerry Rooney decided against it?

TH: No, I told the boys that that was it and there was no way that I was going to take them down, and I said stay in the room and talk it over, you let me know. And the only thing I can say, Peter, is that they said they were behind me, that's all.

PG: We have talked already to people in Humboldt, and I don't know how representative they are, but it sounds to me as if the town is behind you. Do you feel that?

TH: Well, I hope so. That's all one can do in a situation like this – we don't think that anybody can read how the situation is going. All I can think is that basically I am doing the right thing. I hope that people are behind me. You know, my wife put a very good question to me, and I really found it difficult to answer. She said: what would you do, if you had a boy and you had to tell him to go out there and take that sort of thing, and I found it very difficult to answer. I've used that question a lot of times since, to a few different people who have been trying to put a little pressure on me.

PG: I want to find out about that pressure, but I wonder, is junior hockey beyond the guys like you and me, who believe in the way you talk and think about hockey?

TH: Well, it's got to be. There's just no doubt about it, Peter, I know that it is beyond me. . . .

PG: But you're a guy who has won the bantam championship, who has won the midget championship, who won juvenile and junior B – have I given you too many titles?

TH: Yeah, one too many.

PG: Okay. But you can coach kids, you can win hockey games, the Russians can win hockey games. . . . You do not have to intimidate to win hockey games. Last year, against Dauphin, Manitoba, you ran up against the same situation, yet you beat them.

TH: Yeah.

PG: Well, isn't there something left yet, to prove that your kind of hockey can be their kind of hockey?

TH: But is that ever going to make up for somebody getting injured? I'm not talking about the lumps and bumps that you take in sports, because, heck almighty, I went through it, I played football and hockey all the way through school. I took my lumps just like anybody else — I got a concussion, I had a fractured cheekbone, I lost some of my teeth. But as a physician I just cannot understand that this is necessary, really, and I don't know what all the hell, pardon me, but that's what I mean, what all the hellabaloo is about. It just doesn't mean that much to me and I know it doesn't mean that much to the kids, because the kids know that they have proved a point, really.

PG: What is the hellabaloo, what are the pressures that are being put on you? Is there an attempt to kill hockey in Humboldt?

TH: Yeah. There's no doubt about it. I don't know exactly how it will be done — I mean as far as them doing anything to me, I'm not worried about that. This is my decision alone, and I'm not trying to be a martyr or a hero. But somebody has to take the responsibility and I feel that I'm the one who should be doing it, and Dr. Rooney feels the same way. But there are all sorts of things that can be done. They can suspend me, and suspend Jerry — well, that is nothing too great. I don't think that they can do anything to the kids — I hope they can't. There are questions about revoking the franchise in the Saskatchewan pre-amateur junior hockey rink; there are fines that could be given to our club; there are also CAHA developmental monies that could be withheld from our league because, when you commit yourself to go into inter-branch play, which means interprovincial play, then it's a question of holding back monies, if these are not honoured. Nobody came out and said this; we've heard about thirty-five ways of doing it, but then again these are all things that we know can be done, and there's a possibility of it being done.

PG: But there is no threat big enough to get you to show up in Portage?

TH: No, there isn't. The only way, Peter, that I would go down there, is if my board of directors and my manager and my hockey team said, "Dr. Henning, we want to go." Now that's the only way, and I don't think that people are going to bend, at least I hope that they aren't. You know, there's been a lot of static over the last twenty-four hours, but there are two or three people who are very, very dear to me, and both of them have said, you have stood up, you have been counted, you have established a principle; for God's sake, don't back down.

Dr. Henning's action, and the results of that action and that decision, pose some questions that seem to us here to transcend hockey itself. Is winning, as Vince Lombardi once said, the *only* thing? Is the price of winning, if you have to win, violence? With the kind of physical price that we've heard some of those kids have to pay, are our value systems really set? Do guys like Dr. Terry Henning have no place in organized sports and nothing to pass on to our boys? Should you take a team like that from a community like that, and say you can't play anymore, because you don't want to play hockey of the other kind?

I guess by now you will have chosen sides — there's good guys and bad guys — but, as few stories ever are, this is not a case of simple black against white. There are two sides. Murray "Muzz" MacPherson is the coach of the Portage La Prairie Terriers, and we wanted to hear his appraisal of what Terry Henning had done. Yesterday afternoon, with the outcome still in doubt, I talked with Muzz MacPherson.

PG: Well, Muzz, I've heard a lot about your hockey team as we've been phoning around. What kind of a team are they?

MM: Peter, we've got a fine hockey club here. I'm disappointed about the remarks coming out of Humboldt — there were no complaints coming out of games one and two, when they had the split heading home, and they had not lost a home game at all in the playoffs up until Friday night, when we went in there and we beat them, and then we did the same on Sunday afternoon. We heard no complaints or anything there, Peter, and I'm shocked. After the game on Sunday, Dr. Terry Henning, as he was leaving the ice, reached over and shook my hand, and I thought then that there was no problem. Monday night there was a brawl, if you want to call it a brawl, and each hockey player on the ice got into it, from both teams — it takes two teams to tangle — but we're not complaining about our scars, Peter, we've got a few under the sweaters. A couple of fingers have been lost; there's one person just about lost his complete finger by being bit by one of their people. . . .

PG: Being bitten?

MM: That is correct, the second game here in Portage La Prairie. During the fight he got his hand in the fellow's mouth; he closed down on it, and he nearly bit it completely off. The nail was hanging when he went to the penalty box. It's a rough series, to the point of hitting, and they're getting their sticks up. In the last game in Humboldt, Peter, I thought that the refereeing really favoured the Humboldt hockey club. This is one of the reasons they don't want to come back, because they know that they are playing a better hockey club.

PG: Do you think they're intimidated?

MM: I think maybe they are, but I wouldn't want to use the word intimidated, I think they are. . . .

PG: Do you think that group intimidation is a part of hockey?

MM: We try not to have that, Peter. We are not trying to intimidate anybody. But when we went into their building, I don't believe that they were expecting to get beat. And I think that made it a pretty hard situation for them, to come back to Portage La Prairie, because they would have to wing two hot games here.

PG: Yeah. But did they win the game before they pulled out?

MM: Oh yes, they did, they won the night they pulled out — if they *have* pulled out — I believe that at eight o'clock tonight they will be here.

PG: They're not leaving, I'll have to tell you.

MM: They're not leaving?

PG: Well, if there's any chance at all, it's that they'll play Thursday night.

MM: Well, we won't play Thursday, Peter, I'll tell you that right now. The CAHA set the league dates and we're not going to vary. We're going to dress our hockey club tonight at eight o'clock and if they're not there, we're making wagers that we go west.

PG: I would like to hear your side, too, of the incident that touched off the final brawl in Humboldt. This is the way it's been described to me: that with four seconds left in the game, and the clock stopped, as the referee dropped the puck for a face-off, your boy speared the Humboldt boy instead of going for the puck.

MM: He caught a spearing penalty there, but as Bobbie Miller said, as the puck dropped he just brought his stick straight up and that's when he made connection. Now I'll tell you another incident: the brawl in the penalty box was started when their player hit our player, and their time keeper grabbed our player, and there's no way that we're going to allow somebody to start beating up our hockey player without going in and helping him out. The only people that went, Peter, were the people on the ice; there was nobody from either bench.

PG: If Humboldt did show up, if somehow this could be resolved and there was a game, would it be as rough as that final game in Humboldt?

MM: I would say probably not, and then again I'm not going to say, because our style is to hit where we can with the body, and to forecheck where we can, and if we keep this club off balance like we did in their rink, I'm looking for a very successful finish.

The men we're going to hear from now are two hockey officials in western Canada. Ed Young is the president of the Saskatchewan Junior Hockey League, and the Humboldt Broncos are carrying the Saskatchewan banner – or were – in a series against Portage La Prairie. Frank Germann is the Saskatchewan representative of the Canadian Amateur Hockey Association. He lives in Wilcox, Saskatchewan, and it is through him that the reports have gone to the CAHA about the way the series has been conducted. The decision about the eventual outcome will be based on his report.

PG: Who has the power to take a junior franchise away from Humboldt? Is that you, Ed, as president of the Saskatchewan Junior League, or you, Frank, as regional representative of the CAHA?

EY: There are at least three or four avenues. One would be the league, another would be the Saskatchewan Amateur Hockey Association, and another would be the CAHA and then a council under the CAHA called the Junior Council, which I'm sure will not look too favourably on this kind of thing.

PG: Why would you want to take the franchise away from the town?

FG: Well, why do you give speeding tickets?

PG: He wasn't speeding, he just forfeited a hockey series. That's the best junior team in Saskatchewan, right?

EY: I would have to agree, yes. And my honest opinion is that, if we lost Humboldt, if Humboldt lost its franchise, I think it would affect the league a great deal because they've been a real drawing card in the league.

PG: Why?

EY: Because they're an awful good hockey club. And they seem to give out a good brand of hockey, the type that we like to see in this league.

PG: I think I'm right in this or close, am I not, that $2400 goes to each of the eleven clubs in the league from the CAHA?

EY: Yes, the money is given to the league and we in turn disperse it to the clubs in equal portions.

PG: So the CAHA has got a big weapon if they want to use it.

EY: I would say yes, that it's a weapon and they would use it. I don't hesitate in saying that.

PG: Frank, this is a classic confrontation we've got here. We've got a stylish, well-coached hockey team. Everybody who talks about that team admires it. They're in a tight series, and it's only 3–2 with a team that is by all accounts an awful lot bigger and rougher than they are, and plays a dirtier, more aggressive style of hockey. It's a classic confrontation. Who's right and who's wrong?

FG: Well, I don't know whether that's really a fair question. I think they're both right. In no way, of course, can we tolerate dirty hockey. There's no doubt they are a big club, they're a tough club. They like to play it rough, I suppose, or at least hard, but I can't see anything the matter with that.

PG: Have you got any sympathy for Terry Henning as a hockey man?

FG: I have a lot of sympathy for him.

PG: If you were him, would you go back to Portage and play?

FG: Well, not if I was him. But *I* would go back.

PG: Why? What's the difference between your outlook and his?

FG: Oh, I've played an awful lot of tough hockey games and I've never really backed out of one. He's worried about his boys getting injured. I think I'm probably that way all the time myself, but we played seventy games all winter and then suddenly we don't go and play because we're worried about injuries?

PG: He is a physician. He says that his boys have had more injuries in those five games than they have in all the other games they've played this year. He's got two boys on crutches. He's got a number of kids with lacerations around the eye. He's really worried about a serious injury and he is a physician as well as a demonstrably good hockey man, and he doesn't want to go back into Portage and play that team again. But you say you would go in.

FG: Oh, sure I'd go. I guess I'm not a doctor.

PG: I guess you're not. Ed Young, would you go back?

EY: Truthfully?

PG: Yeah.

EY: I would say no. I wouldn't either if I was a doctor. As a hockey man, I may think different. The only reason I think he should go back is that he has an obligation to the league. I do sympathize with Terry but he does have that obligation: he's committed to continue the series. I do feel he should get some support, and I'm speaking of referee and police protection. If they could guarantee him that protection then I think he should go back.

PG: He says there's no way that could be guaranteed.

FG: So how *do* you guarantee it? Put twenty referees on the ice, one for each hockey player, maybe? We can't make a farce of the game, either.

PG: Where is Terry Henning's obligation? You're talking about obligations to the league and an obligation to the town, but what about his obligation to the boys he's working with and coaching?

FG: Well, say you were a member of the hockey team, and this was not how you wanted to bow out of a play-off. Do you want to admit that this guy is tougher than you, that he's a better hockey player than you are or that you didn't allow him to beat you? And you quit? Sure, maybe there is some intimidation. I never bothered about a team that intimidated. I always played to win on the scoreboard, and if they want to take penalties by dirty tactics, fine, as long as I could score goals while they're shorthanded. All you need is a bunch of boys that can take it. That's another lesson in life; I say that, because in thirty years I've never done what Terry's doing and I don't assume I'd ever do it.

PG: I'm really baffled here; I've heard about a team that deliberately goes out to injure. I've heard the referees criticized. You have talked about the possibility of match penalties, so the rules aren't being enforced. You have talked about the game sheets going off to Ottawa instead of going to somebody who can take action. What I want to know is, who the hell is responsible?

EY: It's probably just that this is how it was done and this is how we do it.

PG: But is it right or is it wrong?

EY: Well, it's a task to try and work yourself towards Dominion champion. I think it's beautiful if everything can move smoothly, but when something like this crops up, then it's wrong.

PG: So it's wrong.

EY: Well, we have rules in our book — if you pull your team off the ice in the second period, you're going to be reprimanded for it. Now, what if you pulled it off because some of your kids got hurt — does that stop you from being reprimanded? If that was the case then we'd all have kids getting hurt and we'd all be pulling our teams off the ice. So I don't know. Where do you stop, where do you begin?

The president of the CAHA is the man who had to make the final decision. He's Joe Kryczka, a Calgary lawyer, and I talked with him yesterday while the outcome of the game and the series was still in doubt.

JK: The last time I heard from our representative, who is Frank Germann,

Humboldt was refusing to go to Portage La Prairie, and they'd been advised that I was prepared to delay the series for one day, subject to appropriate financial sanctions, in order to have the series completed. Failing that, I was going to have to exercise whatever other remedies are available to me, which basically means that I would have to suspend the management and ownership of that Humboldt team, hold back whatever monies they have coming from this series, and suggest to the Saskatchewan branch that they shouldn't issue any authorization for Humboldt to operate as a junior A club in the upcoming season.

PG: That pretty well boils down to the fact that if they don't go there on Thursday night. . . .

JK: They're dead ducks.

PG: They're out of hockey.

JK: Yep.

PG: Who will make the decision, if it is as simple as kicking Humboldt out of hockey?

JK: I will have to make that decision. Frank Germann and his representative, Bud Bessey, who is the referee and chief of the Saskatchewan Amateur Hockey Association and who lives in Humboldt, have told me that the series hasn't been that rough. What I find difficult to understand, Peter, is why they waited until the three games that were scheduled in Humboldt had been played before they made their squawk. It's so coincidental — being a lawyer, it makes me suspicious.

PG: Now, Frank Germann, on whom you're relying for your advice, has not seen a game in that series. Am I right?

JK: Right exactly, yep.

PG: You have not seen a game.

JK: I haven't seen a game and, again, this is why this morning I was in communication with Dr. Rooney of the Humboldt team and George Allard, who was in charge and saw both games that were played in Manitoba. I think that Dr. Rooney of the Humboldt organization is certainly prepared to concede that the officiating and the games played in Manitoba were fine, and that at least one of the three games played in Humboldt was fine. That's why I think that the key factor here is not to say that any one team wins a series by default. While certainly I admire the motives of Dr. Rooney and Dr. Henning in saying they don't want any of their boys to be mutilated or hurt, because that's certainly not the object of playing hockey, I'm not certain that their approach to dealing with that particular problem is the proper one.

PG: What could they do that they haven't done?

JK: Well, if there was this brutality or deliberate attempt to injure, then they should have been in touch immediately with Frank Germann or the vice-president in charge of junior hockey, who would have communicated that situation to me.

That was yesterday afternoon. Since then, the decisions have been made. Last night in Humboldt, the board of directors met again to re-examine their position. Once more, there was unanimous support for the position of Terry Henning and Jerry Rooney. Later on, the boys again offered their support to Dr. Henning. Joe Kryczka made the decision that he talked about yesterday afternoon. He has now suspended Terry Henning and Jerry Rooney from hockey. He has awarded the series to Portage La Prairie. He has suspended the owners of the Humboldt Broncos. He is holding back their share of the gate receipts from their series with Portage La Prairie.

Is Humboldt a dead duck? We won't really know that until a full investigation is launched, and Joe Kryczka has said that there will be a full investigation of that series. I guess all I'd like to say about it is that I hope the investigation includes one question, and I think that that question transcends the boundaries of hockey itself. I would hope the investigation of the series would include it. If there is no room in Canadian hockey for Terry Henning, who is there room for?

As it turned out, there was and is room for Terry Henning in Canadian hockey, and room for the Humboldt Broncos too. After a detailed investigation of the whole series of events surrounding the Humboldt-Portage affair, conducted by Joe Kryczka, the man who sounded so muddy when he was on the air, Terry Henning was totally exonerated. Humboldt paid a token fine for forfeiting the series, but the coach, the manager and the team were all fully re-instated. The good guys won. And as a final development, there was this news story, more than a year later:

The Humboldt Journal

HUMBOLDT, SASKATCHEWAN, THURSDAY, MARCH 7, 1974

Goaltender fined $400 on assault charge

Tye Langton, goaltender for the Portage la Prairie Terriers in the Humboldt Broncos-Portage playoff series in 1973, was fined $400 in magistrate's court Thursday for common assault causing bodily harm.

Al Hilton, defenceman with the Terriers, was charged with the lesser charge of common assault and was given an absolute discharge.

The Portage hockey players were charged after the April 16, 1973 game in Humboldt. They were charged with assaulting Ross Gilchrist, centreman with the Broncos.

Gilchrist testified that he was struck on the outside left knee by the goaltender, Langton.

"I fell immediately to the ice and couldn't get up," said Gilchrist.

Just after he fell, Hilton speared Gilchrist in the stomach and then kneeled on his stomach, pushing down with his stick.

The incident took place about 10 feet to the side of the Portage net.

Gilchrist said the injury caused numbness to his leg and he lost control of the foot.

Bronco coach Dr. Terry Henning testified that Gilchrist was not involved in the play at the time.

"The puck was moving to the Humboldt zone in the east end," said Henning. "Langton skated out of the crease and swung his stick with both hands with the heel hitting Gilchrist in the leg."

Henning testified the stick hit the nerve that controls muscles in the foot. The nerve prevents the foot from turning over.

Defence counsel Harvey Pollock of Winnipeg tried to establish that Henning could not positively identify Langton because he was wearing a face mask.

But Henning wouldn't budge.

"During the first part of the game Langton was on the bench," said Henning. "Mercer, the second goaltender, was replaced by Langton midway through the game.

"Besides," said Henning, "there were only 2 goaltenders listed on the score sheet and if they were changed everyone would have known."

Henning said he could also positively identify Langton because he was sitting only a few feet away from him on the players' bench.

Dr. Jim Morton, assistant club physician, said the play was in the opposite end when Gilchrist was struck by Hilton.

Pollock at this point tried to establish that Hilton was covering Langton.

"Absolutely not," said Morton. "This was a deliberate action and it was not an accidental collision. The puck was moving away to the Humboldt end."

Morton also said Gilchrist still suffers from numbness in his leg.

Magistrate T.G. Schollie, in handing down sentence, said he didn't want to send either to jail.

"However, Hilton's display was a cowardly act and I can't very well send a person to jail for being a coward," said Judge Schollie.

The charges were believed to be the first ever laid in a Saskatchewan hockey game. Very few have been laid in Canada.

Also in court was the Portage coach, Muzz MacPherson.

Appearing for the Crown was Henry Kloppenburg of Saskatoon.

That April 16, 1973 was the biggest brawl ever seen at a Humboldt hockey game.

A total of 44 penalties were handed out with Portage taking 12 of 20 minors, 7 of 12 majors, 5 of 10 game misconducts and another misconduct.

Late in the 3rd period of the game, Portage's Henderson and Humboldt's Daryl Hushagen were penalized and shortly after a fight broke out in the penalty box.

In seconds players and fans were involved in a brawl. Seconds later, Hilton speared Gilchrist and the game was called.

Bronco club manager Dr. Gerry Rooney and Henning were on the line for refusing to return to Portage la Prairie to play out the series. Both were suspended by the CAHA.

Later, in June, after public cries from across the country to clean up hockey and praise for Henning and Rooney, the CAHA lifted the suspensions and fined them $500.

Dear NHL. WHA, and any other super-leagues I am fortunate enough not to be aware of:

I hereby resign from any attempt to help my sons join your ranks.

While father sits comfortably in the home-coming traffic jam on the Lion's Gate Bridge, admiring the gorgeous view of the sun sinking behind the mountains, I am frantically searching the house for any or all of the sixty articles required to dress our two sons for the practise of Canada's most overrated pastime – non-believers see Appendix A for list.

Having arrayed my gladiators in all that finery, I now dress myself and baby in winter coats, bonnets and boots. We roast outside since it is 70°, but in that freezer where The Sport is played, we, who do not have the fervour of The Game to warm us, need such accoutrements.

At last the players are on the ice. I can relax slightly and feed the baby her delayed dinner as long as I make sure that I don't miss any of my sons' good shots. One son is a goalie so I am fairly certain where to find him, but the other boy – that is anyone's guess. Hold everything! There is an injury – a cut under an eye. Nobody notices since it isn't a player, just my poor, almost-one-year-old daughter, whose stroller collapsed with her inside it. Well, at least that is an improvement on the first practice of last season – that brought on the premature birth of said daughter. Be thankful for small mercies; the baby is a girl. If you get your hands on her, I'll resign from Women's Lib, too.

As I finally stagger into the house with the last stray glove and follow the trail of the other fifty-nine damp articles, I hear the triumphant cry from the TV – "Hockey Night in Canada!" And the unkindest cut of all – baby daughter cheering.

Pamela Clark
West Vancouver, British Columbia

My Son is Sweet Sixteen

I know David is sixteen because . . .

His ears noticeably sit up when "marijuana" is mentioned on the blur of radio news.

He rhymes off a list of liquors and beers longer than the roll-call at the local AA.

He is always going out with mysterious, anonymous "friends."

His friends include: a religious group, a rock group, and a group of five girls.

His bragging takes the form of a recently acquired love letter, casually left on the kitchen table.

His play-wrestling with his brother is a hazard to furniture, younger sisters, and the dog.

Last year I wouldn't trust him with my egg-beater. This year he drives my car into downtown Toronto.

Now, when I ask him to do something, I say "please" and cross my fingers.

He complains that we lack sufficient house-hold items, such as: TV sets, tape recorders, cars, and socks.

His summer earnings will be spent for either a school trip to Paris or a two-hundred-dollar camera, neither of which his father and I have managed to acquire.

And when we take his brother's or sister's side in a quarrel, David threatens to leave, "because I'm sixteen, you know."

. . . I know, son, I know. . . .

Phyllis Zelcer
Toronto, Ontario

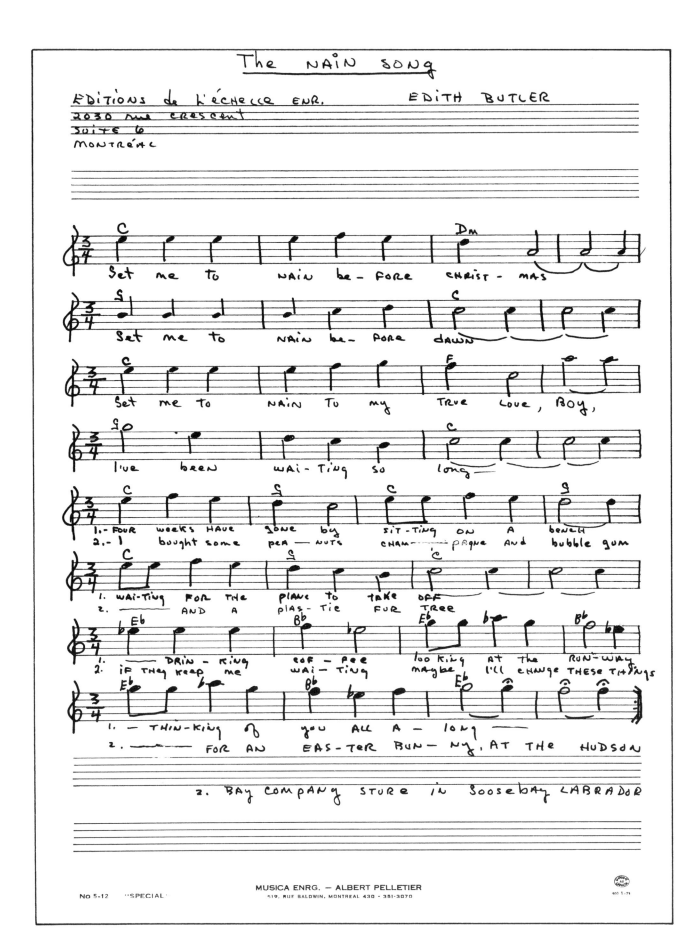

The NAIN SONG

EDITIONS de L'ÉCHELLE ENR.   EDITH BUTLER
2030 rue crescent
suite 6
MONTRÉAL

Set me to nain be-fore christ-mas
Set me to nain be-fore dawn
Set me to nain to my true love, boy,
I've been wai-ting so long

1.- FOUR weeks have gone by sit-ting on a bench
2.- I bought some pea-nuts cham-pagne and bubble gum

1. wai-ting for the plane to take off
2. ___ and a plas-tic fur tree

1. ___ drin-king cof-fee looking at the run-way
2. if they keep me wai-ting maybe I'll change these things

1. ___ thin-king of you all a-long ___
2. ___ for an eas-ter bun-ny, at the hudson

2. Bay company store in Soosebay LABRADOR

MUSICA ENRG. — ALBERT PELLETIER
519, RUE BALDWIN, MONTREAL 430 - 351-3070

No 5-12   "SPECIAL"

GORDON SINCLAIR

Read on the other Read on Air
Nov. 10

35 BURNHAMTHORPE BLVD., ISLINGTON, ONT.

Wed   March 8-72

Dear Peter   Czowski;

Maybe   blue   suede
xkixxx   shoes   are just for   ageing
Victorians like me.

I'm working on my second pair
of the past   7   years.   Got them in
Kitchener.

Salaam !

Gordon.

GORDON SINCLAIR

Nov   26-73

THIS COUNTRY IN THE   MORNING

CBC

Box   500

Toronto

About a   month   ago I   did   a   short
stint on the program and sogned a   cost
sheet   but   my   records show   no   cheque.
Could   you look into this?
I think it would be a   small amount   but
every   bit counts.

Salaam;

Gordon Sinclair

Everybody
% This Country in the Morning
CBC
Box 500
Terminal A
Toronto, Ontario
█Canada ✳█
M5W 1E6

Canada 8   1973

I knew that I would, sooner or later,
Depart from this world quite insane
From trying to explain to the 'phone operator
How to spell and pronounce my last name.

"It's COKE as in Pepsi, and KERR as in car,
With a hyphen between the two,
C-O-K-E dash K-E double arr."
"One moment Mr. Crockett," she'd coo.

I badgered and blustered, I'd plead and I'd shout,
I'd spell again and again 'till I shook.
But when St. Peter called and my flame went out,
It was misspelled in the Golden Book.

Derek Coke-Kerr
Edmonton, Alberta

John D. MacDonald

John D. MacDonald, who lives, I would imagine, somewhere in Florida, is certainly not the best writer in the world, but he is certainly not the worst either. Although he has sold millions upon millions of copies of his books, I somehow feel he is unrecognized – I don't think I've ever read a serious review of his work – and I couldn't let a program on how to get more out of the indoors go by without passing on to you some of my own pleasure in reading him.

Before I try to explain who he is or what he writes about – in case you haven't heard of him before – I should say that this is not necessarily a demonstration of how exquisitely honed is my own taste. MacDonald is an intelligent guy, and someone I would very much like to spend an evening with – or a morning, for that matter – but he is no challenge to the intellect. That's one of the reasons I like him. There are times in my life, quite a *lot* of times in my life, when I don't *want* my intellect challenged, when I don't want to think, don't want to contemplate the poetry that is the universe, don't want to spend time in the presence of the great minds of history . . . when I just want to be entertained.

What I am saying, I guess, is that however much we enjoy *great* writing, and however important that great writing may be to us – as, of course, it is – there still has to be a place in our lives for . . . well, if it's trash, then it can at least be good trash. I would find, for example, a diet of Saul Bellow or Norman Mailer or any of the so-called major writers of our time as difficult to live with as I would a diet of steak alone. There are days when I just want bacon and eggs – in fact days when it's *important* to me to have only bacon and eggs – days when I'm just not up to the enjoyment of truly great food. But I still like eggs cooked just so, and the bacon not too well done. Similarly with cultural stuff, if cultural it is. If trash plays, as I'm suggesting, an important part in our lives, and at no time more than when we're on our own, then at least let's have good trash: Dick Van Dyke as opposed to Lucille Ball; Cannon as opposed to Dragnet; Pogo as opposed to Blondie; Bugs Bunny as opposed to the Flintstones . . . and John D. MacDonald as opposed to nearly *every* writer of the same kind I know of.

MacDonald has written more than sixty books, and I guess by now I've read most of them. I've never seen or heard of any of them being published in hard cover, and nearly all the ones I own I bought for seventy-five cents a piece. They range from science fiction – books like *Ballroom of the Skies* and *The Girl, the Gold Watch and Everything* – to various attempts to do a kind of low-key Grand Hotel – I'm thinking here of MacDonald's *Please Write For Details*, or *The Crossroads* – but by far the majority – and I would say the best – involve crime and corruption and quite a lot of good, clean violence. There is also some sex – there's a *great* deal of sex – but none of it is any more explicit than your average TV show. No three dots, mind you, but nothing for the peeping Toms, either.

The best known of MacDonald's work, and the books that somehow characterize everything he does, are the eleven novels in the Travis McGee series. McGee is not quite a private eye . . . the back covers tend to talk about him as, for instance, "that free-lance knight in shining armour whose well-known nose for a dollar twitches at . . . " Well, the guys who write that kind of stuff aren't as good as MacDonald. McGee is a big, ex-marine who served in Korea, played a little professional football – linebacker – and now lives in a lavishly comfortable houseboat anchored in southern Florida. He makes his living by going after various scoundrels who have taken money from good guys, or, more often, good girls, and McGee's fee, which he very seldom seems to collect (he's too soft-hearted) is half the return. Like almost all MacDonald's heroes, McGee has gray eyes – size, about six-four or better, and

is for Ontario with
its freeways and tall towers,
Where one can sit in traffic jams
for hours and for hours.

Mary Simms
Halifax, Nova Scotia

gray eyes are a good way to spot the hero in the non-McGee books too – and a wandering eye for women, especially big women. If I were smaller, in fact, I'm not sure I'd get the same pleasure from MacDonald's writing – if Women's Lib has given us sexist, as in racist, then some short people might want to accuse John D. MacDonald of being a size-ist.

But the plots move well, the characters of virtually everybody in the books are surprisingly three-dimensional, and the dialogue is solidly realistic and entertaining. MacDonald doesn't have to rely on James Bondian gimmicks or John LeCarré's international intrigue to turn out an involving story. The Travis McGee books all have a colour in the title: *Bright Orange for the Shroud, The Deep-*

Blue Good-Bye, Nightmare in Pink, A Purple Place for Dying . . . and so on. But watch yourself if you get into John D. MacDonald, as I suggest you do, through McGee. There is at least one MacDonald book – *A Flash of Green*, which is not a McGee in spite of the colour in its title, and, now at least, MacDonald is always billed as "author of the Travis McGee series."

But you can't go very far wong; MacDonald is MacDonald . . . a total master of his craft, a storyteller, an enjoyer of people and of the senses, endlessly inventive, tirelessly imaginative. And on those days when I know I just want to sneak off to the bedroom with a hot drink and a turned-off phone, when I don't want to learn anything or be "improved," I am very grateful to him indeed.

is our Parliament,
pompous and proud,
Where insults are shouted,
both daily and loud.

Noel B. Daniels
Vancouver, British Columbia

Old Age

Old age is when "they" are forty and you are twenty . . . when "they" are sixty and you are forty . . . when "they" are eighty and you are sixty . . . and so on. So writes Mrs. P. Halls of Carp, Ontario, although she signs it "and others," and to Mrs. Hall goes prize number one in our contest on old age. To get all the prizes out of the way right now – because somehow prizes don't seem all that important in this contest – I'm also sending a book to a lady I can't name, because, as she says, "my friends might stop inviting me out in the evenings, and I don't like to go to bed every night at 10:30," for this epigram: "Old age is when you can play cribbage with your husband after breakfast." And lastly, a prize goes to Noel B. Daniels of Vancouver, for this poem:

Old age is when . . .
Vision is only the sight of one's eyes
And the glad cry of wonder has become just a shrug;
When the heart's a mere muscle within the ribs' cage
And the voice of the cynic speaks louder than love.

Those are the prizes. As in all our contests, the selection of winners is all mine and mine alone, and in this one so many people wrote and wrote so well that I'm quite sure I could have given several dozen as easily as I've given three. I had the feeling of a lot of people simply trying not so much to win a prize as to say something, and the most common things they were saying, I think, are summed up by the three entries I've already cited.

For the lady who plays cribbage after breakfast – isn't that a great picture, two people hurrying through the crunchy granola so they can get down to a little 15-2, 15-4? – the whole thing is very practical. For our winning poet – and there were a surprising number of very good poems submitted – it's a realization that old age is so much more a spiritual thing than a matter of years. And that's implicit, too, in the first winner I read. Time and time again, as I read through our several hundred entries, I came upon the very real theme that old age is something that happens to someone else, and not to you; when the forty-year-olds or the sixty-year-olds or the eighty-year-olds or whatever, become, as Mrs. Halls says in quotation marks, "they." Someone else; someone different. And that's a mistaken idea.

And that wrongful idea sums up exactly what's wrong with all of our attitudes about aging: the idea that somehow when we reach a certain age — and it really doesn't matter what that age is — we become somebody different; as if at some time in our lives we cross some mystical barrier that turns us into "them," instead of one of "us." That's a theme that's going to run throughout this program ... and if there's one thing we can accomplish in our special look at old age then I hope it's to convince a few people that in fact there is no such thing as "old age," that there is no greater difference between being eighty and being seventy than there is between being fifty and forty, or forty and twenty. We are all of us simply people, all at some stage in the long and continuous line between birth and death.

That is why, for instance, I did not name as winner any of the people — and it's interesting that more of them were young than old — who submitted romanticized versions of old age, however beautifully put those entries were. Anita Allsop of Edmonton, for example, who is twenty-three, sent a number of extremely well-turned epigrams ... "Old age is when one can be oneself and not lose face ... old age is when one thinks less of doing and more of being ... old age is when eternity is perceived and the lifetime of toil and endeavour becomes a small moment in time ... " and others. Elizabeth Frith of Ilderton, Ontario, writes: "Old age is like climbing a mountain; the higher you get, the more you can see." Or William Stark of Larry's River, Nova Scotia — who seems to send wise and witty entries to every contest — writes, among other things, that "Old age is when the world can crumble about you; and you can simply, quietly, shake your head ... always holding open the option to smile, or even to out-and-out laugh." Or, again from Nova Scotia — this time from J.J. Legate of Mahone Bay — a long and eloquent essay that includes this passage:

> Old age is when you wake to the realization that you are growing younger, when you become aware of a growing affinity with youth, when, like youth, you are free to sit back and look at the cockeyed world and laugh as you haven't laughed for a long, long time.
>
> Old age is when you acquire a new-found freedom to judge your past ideas, your past motivations, actions and accomplishments, and those of others objectively, and when you say to yourself, and to anybody else who will listen, "Wow! How unimportant are so many important things in life."
>
> Old age is when you begin to ask yourself questions that can be answered only in leisure and only with honesty.
>
> It is when you find yourself leaning more heavily on the past, not because you are a reactionary, but because you suspect that the future will not be better, nor perhaps as good, as the present, because you more than suspect that man will perpetuate his Disneyland and, in the doing, laugh less and less.

All of those are fine, and in not naming them or the dozens of similar entries as winners I'm not trying to say they're wrong. But what I don't think they're about is old age. I think they're about wisdom, and I am not convinced that wisdom is a function of years; I take it to be a function of humanity. If, in fact, I were going to name a winner in that vein it would be this, from Mrs. Judy Cornwell of Peterborough, Ontario:

> Old age is a time of gentleness, of tolerance and of peace; of leisurely conver-

sation and lasting friendships. A time of freedom from family anxieties and responsibilities, of satisfaction. . . .

How sad that it doesn't work out this way!

All this is not to say, incidentally, that old age is a time of universal happiness. Here are just a few of the entries that perhaps have a great deal to say about the way we treat the aged in our world.

From Sandy Cove, Nova Scotia: Old age begins when we are no longer of use to anyone else, when we have lost our loved one and our children are far away.

From Ottawa: Old age is when the only smile you receive all day is from a baby in a crowded supermarket.

From Saskatchewan: Old age is when your children would love to have you stay with them, but. . . .

From Halifax: Old age is when they expect you to love a geranium because your dog smells.

From North Vancouver: . . . when your daughter tells you she can't look after you any more. . . .

From Ottawa again: . . . when your children no longer come to see you at the senior citizens' home.

From Sherbrooke, Quebec: . . . when one regularly thinks, " . . . and now I never shall."

From Sasakipao, Ontario: . . . when all those you spent your life raising and caring for and loving; those you allowed to depend on you during their younger years; those that you prayed for in hopes that their lives would be successful – have forgotten about your sacrifices and regard you as a burden.

Or from Fort St. James, British Columbia:

Old age is when loneliness descends. When the trees and the flowers can't be seen because they are too far away. When the birds don't sing as loud and children don't play by your side anymore. Old is when you can't climb the stairs to your favourite room and the sidewalk is too rough for your feeble legs to traverse. Old is when someone giving friendship could make your day. Old is when your thoughts are all of yesterday because there doesn't seem to be a today and tomorrow is too uncertain.

But those, as I say, don't seem to me so much definitions of old age as comments on it. And the lady who wrote that last passage also wrote an incredibly joyous paragraph about the beauties of old age:

Old is when the wrinkles on a face become beautiful. Old is when the mind becomes more masterful than the body. It is when the time between sunrise and sunset can be so meaningful – a time when family and grandchildren can be fully enjoyed. Old is when there is time to really laugh and cry, to travel and enjoy a full mature love – to do all the things you never had time to do.

That's from Mrs. Lillian Willick of Fort St. James, British Columbia, and, come to think of it, I'll send her a book too. Again, if the purpose of our contest was to define old age then what I think it did was to point out how irrelevant is the number of years to a feeling of old. The saddest letter we got may well have been this one:

Dear Peter: I think old age comes when a person no longer becomes enthused about the things he wants to do or learn about. I feel old. I am thirty-three. Signed: A suburban housewife.

There was wit, too, in our contest, and I enjoyed it, and thank those who passed it along.

From David Ross in Fort Qu'Appelle, Saskatchewan: Old age is when you ask a beautiful lady to place your name on her dance program, and she agrees, for she knows what you're talking about.

From Bill Tiffin, in Wingham, Ontario: Old age is when you don't have to worry about avoiding temptation . . . it avoids you.

From Mrs. Russell Rayner, in Tignish, Prince Edward Island: . . . when a dashing young man can kiss you with the excuse " . . . you look just like my mother," and neither of you will be shot by friend husband. And don't laugh, writes Mrs. Rayner, who has more than a dozen grandchildren — it's true.

From Mrs. Edna Morrison of Dorval, Quebec (and I think about three others): . . . when you read the obituary column every morning to see if your name is there.

From John E. Lewis of Ottawa — I don't know why so many great entries came from Ottawa — : . . . when the hair on your chest turns white and you're the only one who notices it.

From Charlie Elkins of Shellbrook, Saskatchewan: . . . when a bird in the roasting pan looks better than a bird in a miniskirt.

From Donna Fine of Toronto: . . . when you preface, intersperse and end your comments with "these days."

From June Gallazin of North Vancouver: . . . when the people who complain that cops and sailors look pretty young are beginning to look pretty young.

From about five different people: . . . when you stop planting trees and begin planting annuals.

And from Lyle Walter of — good heavens, Ottawa again: Old age is when you can't remember the address to send your entry to old age is when. . . .

Next to references to the sex drive, the most common theme was the idea of first names. In one form or another, Jack Snyder of Montreal, Ava Larsen of Saskatoon, Sheila Davidson of Seton Portage, British Columbia, and — here's someone who didn't even sign her first name — Mrs. M. Kurcey of Saskatoon, among others, wrote that old age is when there's no one left to call you by your first name.

No. Actually, there was another theme that was more common than either sex or names. That was the idea of keeping your mind open to new ideas, of *exercising* your mind, of fighting against the physical aging process, and all of us here were impressed and moved by the number of people who wrote about themselves or about others . . . people who have, in *effect, beaten* old age. Old age, an awful lot of people agree, is simply when you lose interest in the things around you, Mrs. J. White writes from Richmond, British Columbia. Or, as Mrs. Goldie Thair, who was born in 1889, writes from Regina: Old age is when one is no longer excited by the *marvellous* changes taking place in the world, ideas and movements I never *dreamed* I should see in *my* lifetime.

And there was this letter, unsigned and with no address: I have the responsibility of three elderly people (in years, seventy-eight, eighty-four and eighty-seven) — but only the eighty-four-year-old is old. You are old the first morning you wake up feeling the world revolves around you — when you think first of "me."

No, as I've been saying, our efforts to define old age by years from your ideas of what it is didn't work out. There simply isn't any time in life when a person becomes old. Some people are born old; others can die young at 104. This is from Mrs. Gabrielle Philo, of Winnipeg:

I live alone and do not always like it. I believe that with all of us past that "certain age" – and, dear me, how certain it is – there are always great pockets of loneliness. Some of our friends have gone on; some have moved away. Friendships are a little more difficult to arrive at with the passing of time.

The cross which I have to bear is a greatly diminishing eyesight with the prospect of eventual loss thereof. Nothing more can be done with glasses. I still read part of the newspaper, part of *Time* magazine, some of the *Reader's Digest*. No more books, woe is me. I realize full well that there are crosses far harder to bear than loss of vision, but having always been an avid reader, some of the evenings seem long.

But, I make a practice of smiling even sometimes when I don't quite feel like it. It does me good and I believe it helps others. I take the best care I know of my health and my physical self, inasmuch as I regard it as an insult to the Almighty who gave me my body to do otherwise. Above all, I try very hard to live one day at a time.

I don't suppose it's a phrase many of them would use – although I'm not too sure – but the letters that got to me most were from old people who told it like it is. No romanticizing, no philosophies . . . just truths.

Old age is not, your letters have shown us, a sad time or a happy time; it isn't loneliness; it isn't serenity. It's all those things and others too. It's something some of us triumph over and something that defeats others. It's what Anne MacDonald of Saskatoon calls "the surrender of my individuality." Or what Anne Connolly of Montreal calls "building a Berlin wall around yourself" – and Anne Connolly, who obviously hasn't, is eighty-three. Professor John Stoker of Memorial University speaks for who knows how many people when he writes: "I am old and I am sixty, and I am young and I am sixty. I hover between them, dependent on the weather, and other things."

The Moose Jaw Band Festival

The Moose Jaw Band Festival is over and all the bands have gone home. The festival ended with a musical treat, the Saturday evening performance of Dynamic Sound by the RCMP Band. As on the previous occasions this orchestra had visited Moose Jaw, they gave an exciting, memorable performance. But even more memorable, perhaps, was the sight of hundreds of people applauding and asking for more. And after the performance we noticed numerous young people asking for autographs from men who, on other occasions, in other situations, they might have referred to as "fuzz," "pigs," and other unsavoury epithets.

Reflecting on the effect this band had on the audience, I came to the conclusion that perhaps the RCMP are overlooking an important tool in crime-fighting – that of music! As someone once said, "Music hath charms to soothe the savage breast." Perhaps then this theory could be put into practice. Imagine the pleasant surprise one would get when, having been waved over by an RCMP officer for driving a few miles over the speed limit, one was treated to an instrumental performance of "Slow down, you move too fast," rather than a lecture delivered in stentorian tones.

And those high-speed chases we read about in the newspapers, instead of being made ominous by wailing sirens, could be accompanied by a stirring rendition of the "Post Horn Gallop."

Crime suspects who were known previously to the police might be entertained by the song, "It seems we've stood and talked like this before," while their nefarious activities were being investigated. And I imagine desperados holed up in their hide-out could probably be persuaded to surrender upon hearing a serenade of the old song, "Lay down your arms and surrender to mine!"

Of course, the general public might be moved to respond in kind. Taking into account that this year is the RCMP's centennial, it would

's for Quebec,
where else will you see
Tel chagrin de ses fils,
et tel chic de ses filles?

U.S. Annett
Osoyoos, British Columbia

be appropriate to hear a few bars of "Happy Birthday to You," drifting from passing cars back to the officers sitting in their cleverly concealed radar trap!

But when criticism of the force arises, as it is bound to do from time to time, the policemen would be able to put their case forward through music. To the accompaniment of the RCMP Band, the entire force could gather on the lawn of Parliament Hill in Ottawa. Then, singing the immortal classic by Gilbert and Sullivan, which is as appropriate today as when it was written some seventy-five years ago, the RCMP officers and men could remind the people of Canada that "A policeman's lot is not an 'appy one!"

Peggy Halstead
Moose Jaw, Saskatchewan

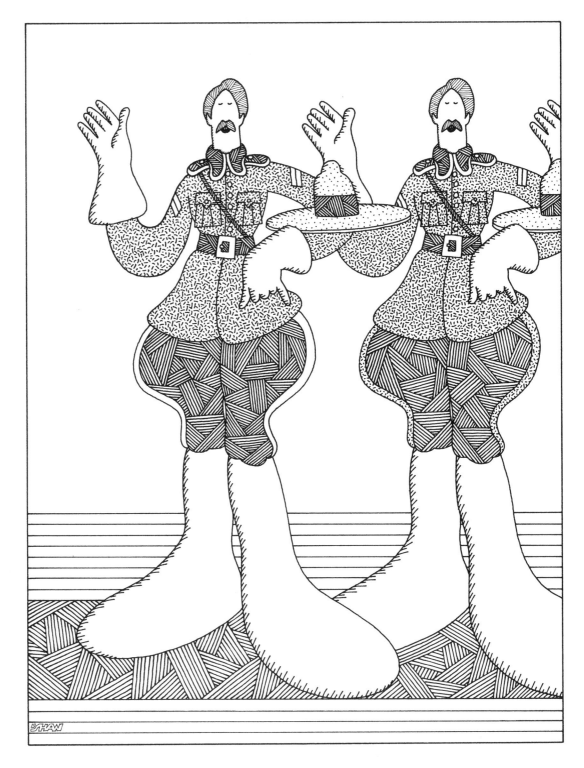

Likeable Lillian loves lovely luminous aluminum linoleum.

Norman Feakes
St. Norbert, Manitoba

On Flirting

And speaking of anniversaries, it's a little over a year ago today that we declared, well in advance of its official opening, the real beginning of spring. You may remember that program, with flowers and songs and a whole list of surprises for me, one of which was, ah yes, Debbie van Kiekebelt, the young girl track star on whom I have a long-standing public crush.

I would like to say at this moment that I am unequivocally in favour of flirting, and one of the very many good things about this job is that occasionally, as on last year's declaration of spring-day, I get paid for flirting in public. That "in public" part is important, for rule one of the art of enjoying flirtation surely is that it be one hundred percent safe. That is, that in their hearts, both the flirter and the flirtee know that nothing further is really intended. The best way to spoil a good honest flirt, I'm sure, would be to consummate it. You can *pretend* you have some serious purpose with that coy look in the corner of your eye, but if you *really* have, then you're doing something that is not flirtation, and that is not what I'm thinking aloud about today. I'm thinking about, for example, the way a guy who travels a lot can talk to telephone operators in different cities. Just the tone of his voice, or the smile in hers, is a pleasure for both of them, not *in spite* of the fact that they are a thousand miles apart but *because* of it. Both of them know from the outset that there can be no so-called serious purposes. Or sitting next to someone attractive on an airplane or in a train. When's that the most fun? When the person you really love is waiting at the other end of the trip. Or how about some of these situations? A wrong number that turns into ten minutes of innocent fun? Someone who catches your eye when you're taking the kids for a walk in the park? Or when you're stuck in a traffic jam and you just exchange glances with the driver of the next car over? What do they have in common? Simply this, I'd suggest: no chance of anything serious evolving. I'm not naïve enough to say that the kind of flirtation I'm trying to celebrate here is the only kind that exists, or that's pleasant. All I want to do on this spring morning – spring where I live – is to say that purposeless flirtation is a very nice thing indeed, that to flirt from time to time is not an insult to your husband or wife or anyone else you truly love. It may be, in fact, that the only people who can truly relax, flirt and enjoy, are those who do know the other kind of love as well.

Crunchy Granola and Things Like That

Crunchy Granola

14 cups (3 pounds) large flake oatmeal
2 cups wheat germ
1 – 2 cups coconut (desiccated)
1½ cups honey/brown sugar/raw sugar (not granulated). Use any one.
1 cup sesame seeds
1 cup shelled sunflower seeds/shredded almonds / walnuts / peanuts (unsalted) / pecans. Use any one.

Mix all together. Then add:

1 cup water
1 cup corn oil
1 teaspoon vanilla
1 teaspoon salt

Spread on a cookie sheet with a lip. Bake at 325 degrees about 20 minutes. Stir and turn to toast while baking.

Bran and Wheat Germ Bread

Ingredients

1 tablespoon brown sugar
¼ teaspoon ground ginger
2 cups warm water
2 packages dry active yeast
⅓ cup black strap molasses
2 tablespoons soft butter

3½ cups whole wheat flour
1 cup bran (whole or flaked)
½ cup wheat germ
½ cup skim milk powder (not instant)
2 teaspoons salt

Combine brown sugar, ginger, water & yeast. Let stand 10 minutes (should be bubbly).
    In separate bowl, stir together molasses and butter.
    Add yeast mixture to molasses and butter mixture.
    Add whole wheat flour and beat 10 minutes at slow on electric beater.
    Blend together bran, wheat germ, skim milk powder and salt in yet another bowl. Gradually add this to the beaten mixture.
    Cover with damp tea towel and let rise until double.
    Punch down and pour into 8″ x 5″ greased loaf pan.
    Butter top, cover with damp tea towel and let rise until double.

Bake at 375 degrees for 40 to 50 minutes.

Yogurt

To start, you take a small portion from a reliable commercial plain yogurt. Better still, obtain a live culture from a natural-food store. These cost approximately $1.75. Basically, what you are going to do is provide an environment in which the culture can grow. To achieve this, the culture is put in milk and must be kept at a constant body-heat temperature.

It can be put on an asbestos mat over the pilot light of your gas stove, or at 100 to 120 degrees F. in the oven. You can check the temperature with an oven thermometer which you can buy at any hardware store. If really dedicated, you can buy a yogurt maker, obtainable at local hardware or natural-food stores at a cost of $15.00 to $20.00.

If you have problems, it isn't always the heat or culture that isn't right but the milk itself. Because of homogenizing and pasteurizing, there may be no bacterial growth. Use non-instant powdered milk and you should have no trouble.

Start with a quart of warm milk (at room temperature). Stir in ½ cup of culture. Cover the container with a solid cover, not a cloth, and put in a warm place with regulated heat. Within 24 hours it should be set. Chill immediately to stop the bacterial growth. Otherwise, it will be too acidy. Before adding fruit, don't forget to take ½ cup out for your next starter. The starter will keep 5 more days or slightly longer. Yogurt can be used instead of sour cream and has an extremely low calorie count. So, for those watching their diet, keep it in mind.

Yogurt can be mixed with fresh fruit or jam. It can be served with maple syrup or honey as a topping. You can add carob powder, instant coffee and raw sugar, or vanilla flavouring. Can be mixed in with fresh fruit drinks in blender or used to make salad dressings or topping for baked potatoes.

Rayta (yogurt with cucumber and tomato)
to serve with curry

1 medium cucumber
1 tablespoon chopped onions
1 tablespoon salt
1 small firm ripe tomato, cubed
1 cup natural yogurt

Cut and combine cucumber, onions, tomato and salt in bowl. Let mixture rest at room temperature for 10 minutes. Remove excess liquid. Add yogurt, making sure to coat vegetables evenly. Refrigerate 1 hour before serving.

Banana and grated coconut with yogurt (can serve as dessert)

1 cup coarsely grated fresh coconut
    or unsweetened packaged type
3 bananas, thinly sliced
½ cup raisins
2 cups yogurt

Mix ingredients well and chill before serving.

For your complexion

If you don't like to eat yogurt, it makes a fantastic facial mask. Has lots of calcium. For oily skin, combine yogurt with fresh strawberries in a blender and put on face for 30 minutes. For dry skin, use yogurt alone.

Claire McLean
Montreal, Quebec

Whole Wheat Bread in Flower Pots

Use clay flower pots (must be clay). They range in size from 3″ to 7″. For a regular-size loaf use the 5″ size; you'll need 4 or 5 pots for a recipe.

Scrub the pots clean. Grease well with vegetable oil (*not* butter); grease several times initially since the clay is very absorbent, but not too much or the pots will smoke when heated. Place the pots in a cold oven, turn to 400 degrees and heat for one hour. Turn oven off and let cool. Repeat the entire process one more time and the pots will then be ready for use. Grease the pots (and the rims) well before storing and each time thereafter before baking.

Whole wheat bread recipe

1 cup lukewarm water
2 teaspoons sugar
2 packages of active dry yeast
2 – 3 cooked mashed potatoes
3 cups warm potato water
2 tablespoons cider vinegar
¼ cup melted lard or butter
5 cups of whole wheat flour
5 cups (approx.) all-purpose flour

Fill flower pots half full of dough (don't worry about the hole in the bottom of the pot – the dough will seal it). Let rise, punch down and let rise until dough is up to the top of the pot and gently rounded.

    Bake at 375 degrees for the first 10 minutes to brown the crust.

    Reduce heat to 350 degrees and bake 50 minutes more.

    Remove from pots immediately to avoid sweating, and cut bread across so you get round slices.

Lentil Sprout Salad

2 bunches of fresh spinach, torn into pieces
1 large red apple, unpeeled and sliced thinly
1 cup of lentil sprouts
½ Bermuda onion, sliced thinly (if unavailable
    try shallots)
3 tablespoons of olive oil
2 tablespoons of lemon juice
1 teaspoon of herbs, either oregano or basil,
    depending on the taste preferred.

Add vegetable salt to taste (this is sea salt with all sorts of vegetables that have been dried and added to the salt).

Toss the spinach, apple, sprouts and onion together. Mix your vinegar, lemon juice, herbs and salt together. Pour over the salad and toss well.

Claire McLean
Montreal, Quebec

is for Regina,
Queen City of the plains,
The breadbasket of the nation;
this, if it rains.

Mrs. E. Emerson Payne
Weyburn, Saskatchewan

Children on Fire

Quick! What do you do when you've just settled down in a hot bath and you hear a little voice floating up from the depths of the house, saying, "Let's play fireman! You be the fire, and I'll put you out."?

Do you leap from the tub and rush down a flight of stairs, pausing only long enough to rush back up a flight of stairs to retrieve your towel? Do you wrench the heat vent from the floor and shout down through the pipes, "Anyone setting fire to himself down there will be in big trouble!"? Or do you decide to wash your hair, sinking low enough in the tub for the water to cover your ears, thus blotting out sound?

I only ask because, although I have on my bookshelves two or three worn copies of Dr. Spock, two copies of *The Gessell Institute Book of Child Psychology*, and a yellow folder of all the columns Dr. Haim Ginott ever wrote, nothing in them even comes close to events as they happen around here. The trick is, I'm told, to apply their theories of child management to your home situation. Thus, Dr. Spock:

"Let your child set fire to himself. After a few tries he'll discover it really isn't a pleasurable experience, and he'll stop. All by himself."

The Gessell Institute:

"Setting fire to oneself is really very common to this age group. Many mothers have worried needlessly because they didn't realize how common it really was. Remain calm, and in six months he will have swung the other way and be dousing your lighted cigarettes with buckets of water."

Dr. Ginott:

"Hand the burning child a note which reads: Self-immolation is unacceptable to me. It makes me fearful. It even makes me panic. I know how difficult it will be for you to comply, but please try to put yourself out."

If none of these solutions appeal to you, there's always the homespun advice of Ann Landers:

"Dear Panic Stricken: At least you know he's not out holding up milk stores. Count your blessings. Some mothers don't even know where their children are tonight. Send for my free booklet, *How to keep your child from spreading to the rest of the house.*"

Actually, I spanked him, and sent him to his room. No wonder there are hardly any child-care books written by women. They're too busy coping with reality.

Diane Lynch
Pickering, Ontario

A few green seasons here with us
But this Birch was deciduous,
And now beneath the mouldering sod
He waits the springtime touch of God.
But be assured, all scoffing men,
The sap will surely rise again.

Paul Birch
North Vancouver, British Columbia

Here lies Scott,
Wrapped in a blanket,
His corpse as cold as lead.
He boiled all his water
Before he drank it . . .
His electric kettle killed him dead!

Scott Strong
St. John's, Newfoundland

Kennedy

I know, as I am quite certain you know, exactly where I was, and with whom, and how I learned about it. I can tell you the restaurant where I was — because it was the lunch hour in Toronto — and what I was eating, and even the name of the waiter, which was Ray. Ray said that they had shot the president of the United States, and we didn't believe him, and then he said it again later, and then someone turned on a radio, and the important business we had been discussing over lunch didn't seem important any more. I went home. I was, in fact, on holidays. I was doing some writing on commission, and when I went in the door I asked my wife if she had heard, and then I realized I didn't have to ask because the television was on, and we sat and watched it together for a while.

Being away from home today, I can't ask him, but I wonder if my oldest son, whose voice has changed now, and who plays right wing better than I ever could and who can beat me at chess but not yet at arm wrestling — I wonder if he remembers that that was the first time he saw his father weep, and I wonder if he can remember how I tried to explain to him why I was doing that.

I was twenty-nine then, and there are a lot of things that are different about me now. Both my hair and my ideas are more gray. I am not quite as smart today as I was ten years ago. But I am still intrigued by the fact that there is no other event in public history — not V-E Day, not the beginnings of the October crisis in Quebec, not the first landing of mankind on the moon — that stands so clearly in my private memory.

I have come to learn since that he was not the great president I had believed him to be. I have come to understand, perhaps, that no one can ever be the man I once thought John F. Kennedy to be. But I can't help thinking today, ten years after Lee Harvey Oswald shot him, that the world might, just might have been a better place if he had lived. He was, as someone has said this week, a man who could learn. Maybe he could have stopped the obscenity of Vietnam. Maybe. Maybe he could have understood what the young people of the later sixties were trying to tell the people in power, and maybe he could have responded to them in a way they needed to be responded to. Maybe, I say, because we will never know anything except that the men who followed him into an office that affects us all did none of those things.

It's curious, isn't it? As I'm sure you would, I began these reminiscences today about private things, about where *I* was when *I* heard, just as

I'm sure you know where you were ten years ago today. Private memories of one of the most public events in history. And yet I wonder if it was so much history — the history of public events — that was changed as it was our private selves. It meant something different to each of us. The world changed and it changed for the worse. But we changed too, didn't we? Our perception of the world is different now. I don't know if I could ever be as profoundly moved by a public event as I was by what happened on November 22, 1963. In truth, I hope I could be, and yet I doubt it. If they, whoever "they" are, could do that, what could they not do?

I guess there are two things that I hope for the son who saw me weep that day. The first is that he will understand why. And the second is that, if something should happen to him, the way it happened to all of us, that he will weep too, and survive.

November 22, 1973

Karen's Diary 4

We went to the introductory class and it was really, really great. There were about twelve couples all stacked on the floor with lots and lots of cushions. The teacher seems marvelous. My husband asked a lot of questions, sort of funny, some of them. He seems to be getting very involved now. But we found out that all that oil to prevent stretch marks is useless. We went through that exercise for waddling that I couldn't figure out and it seems to be helping my backaches already.

It's really funny how pregnant women look at each other on the street, sort of saying to themselves, I wonder how far along she is, is she bigger or smaller than I am? It happens at my classes too — everybody just sort of checking each other out — it's funny.

I went and got a pair of workman's overalls; the man who sold them to me thought I was out of my head. But they're the best thing in the world to wear around the house: they don't bind and just expand with me.

I'm so huge now I asked my doctor if I might have twins. He said no, that I'm really not big enough for twins, and it's too soon to tell, anyway. I gained more weight, but don't have to take as many iron pills . . . thank God.

I tried to convince my doctor that we had miscalculated by a month and that I was actually due in a month, not two months. He just laughed at me. . . . But I wish it would hurry now.

The hardest thing in classes has finally happened — the movie of a baby being born, colour and sound, close up, everything. My husband and I were cool and collected but afterwards I was pretty upset and felt really worn out. I think everybody was a bit uptight afterwards. I think I may have gone a little bit overboard the last few weeks, sort of like over-studying for an exam. Now that it's so close I seem to be having a harder time coping with the whole thing than I did earlier.

Apparently the baby is quite big now, with its head down in the birth position. She weighs about five pounds now, I guess. I really wouldn't mind if she decided to be born now — two months more seems forever.

Lately I've had very strange dreams about the baby, which I guess is normal for a pregnant woman. In the last one I had given birth to a little girl, I knew that much, but it had a full set of teeth. And it came with all kinds of instructions pinned to the pillow in the carriage. Maybe I'm just worried because I'm not sure I can change a diaper.

We talked about the drugs you get during labour today. One girl agreed not to have any unless she asked for them. I guess I feel pretty much the same way. The medical terms were confusing and I didn't know half the names of the drugs they mentioned, but I know I don't want to be doped up during the delivery.

I've had my hair cut — just getting ready for later on. I want it to be wash-and-wear. I'm too heavy now to spend a lot of time on it and I don't want to have to after I'm in the hospital and get home with the new baby.

Continued on page 158

Johnstown Boogie

by Kenzie MacNeil
Arr.: Shauna Doolan

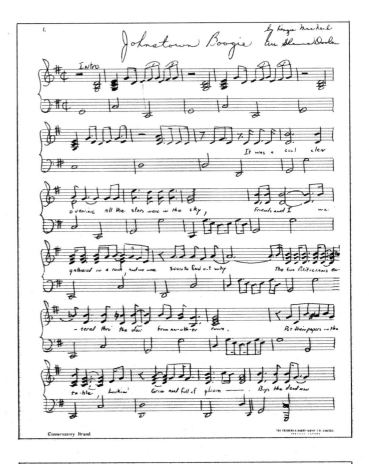

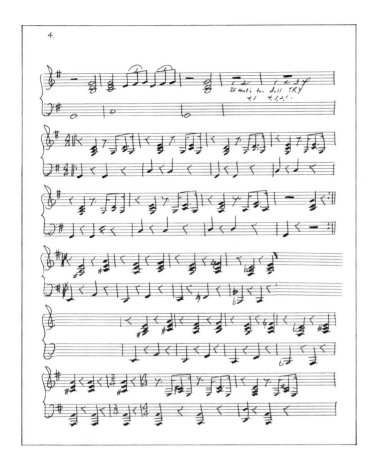

We all hit the panic button in class. Up until now it's just been breathing exercises and we're pretty confident about that part of it, but this time we were told about a stage called transition which is just when the baby's head is about to show. It's supposed to be a time of confusion and depression and can last anywhere from two contractions to two hours. You're just not interested in anybody or anything, not even the baby or getting the birth over with. It sounded frightening and confusing and I have given it a lot of thought.

I'm ready to burn all my books on pregnancy. I was reading one, going through all the breathing exercises again, and I had to put it down. I was getting really frightened. There are two more classes and I will go to them, but I'm sure I won't know how anything is going to turn out until I'm actually at the hospital trying it.

Maara Haas on Japanese Beetles

Among the many things I am grateful to Paul Hiebert for is his introduction of Maara Haas to our program. He brought her to us on the first broadcast of our final season — a warm, round, stately, slow-voiced PhD in literature from Winnipeg. After we heard her talk, we asked her to tell us some more stories on tape, and virtually every Monday thereafter, Maara told such stories as this one, about growing up in Winnipeg in the 1940s.

Anyone who knows my father, the druggist, knows better than to come within smelling distance of the White Cross drugstore on a Monday afternoon.

Monday is the day for cooking Japanese beetles, the basic ingredient of a hell-fire liniment guaranteed to cure the worst kind of chest cold, providing the smell of the linament doesn't kill you first.

Other days, the smells in the pharmacy are strange, but strangely pleasant. All year round, the air is choking with camphor, a kind of furry, ice-cube smell that goes up your nose like a hot-pepper icicle. Not as strong as the camphor, but always present, is the pungent lemon-oil smell coming up from the wooden floorboards of the drugstore, and holding down the oil in a fine, choking dust that shrivels your throat, is the smell of chalky brown cascara, hard to swallow. At any time, breathing is hard in a house that's part of a drugstore, divided by a green curtain dispensary.

Being born to it doesn't make it any easier when the stench of Japanese beetles rises from the kitchen stove. Stoic peasants, my mother and I put on our World War I gas masks, preparing for the ordeal. Metka, the cat, has already made her escape to a secret hiding-place behind the sauerkraut barrel in the cellar.

"Be brave," says my mother.

The heavy sound moving towards the kitchen is not the horse brigade of the RCMP. It's only my father wearing Salvation Army boots with this year's iron cleats.

"Where is the white enamel roaster for cooking beetles?" asks my father, looking dangerously creative as he stomps into the room.

Wham, slam, bang, he throws the pots and pans out of the cupboard. Last week it was the green and ivory cabbage pot. Another week, the earthenware flowerpot for baking Easter bread. Whatever pot he chooses, it has to be a pot with something in it.

My mother hugs the white enamel roaster to her chest. "It's full of holobtsi, the only pot smelling clean. I'm sick to death of camphor perogies, camphorated pigs' feet and oil of eucalyptus mushrooms. Stinks, stinks, everything stinks! And now the crucifixion — Japanese beetles. I want at least one pot for cooking."

"Take out the holobtsi," threatens my father. "Take them out or I'll toss them to the ceiling."

In a mild show of temper, he jumps up and down like a mountain chort exorcised by holy water. The stiff, pointed forelock of his black hair gives him the look of the devil himself.

"What is more important? Eating or creating?"

"Creating, creating, creating," says mother, who talks in the straight run of a railroad track, no end in sight.

"Creating music for the church — do we get a discount on the pew or a special seat in heaven? Creating poems for the Spanish guitar — and how many spaniels are buying Tus-Kee-Kee, your all-cure Indian remedy for lumbago, croup, distemper, bunions, itchy scalp and female disorders? Why creating and creating magic potions for the old people with bad blood on credit? The old people are dying off fast and the young people are not for lightning outhouse cascara or hell-fire linaments. Why can't you be modern, modern? Mr. Ph.D. Shumansky is doing; Dr. Vanderspiegel is doing; Samuel made-to-measure Rothstein is doing; even the Leonard Britannia fishandchips is doing. Everyone is making money — doing — and what kind of doing are you doing? Trading medicine for cabbages and carrots."

My father opens the oven.

Sizzling, crackling in their brittle skins, the Japanese beetles are oozing out a curdled amber-black juice, radiating infinite heat and stinging power.

"Better than old-fashioned capsicum seeds," he explains.

Now for a couple of pounds of sheep grease

to smooth it down, a gross of cool white jars and a gold, highclass label, printed in black letters

THE WHITE CROSS LABORATORY

"Mamma, be expecting a sack of carrots from Mr. Pikoosh, Porcupine Mountains, payment for the box of rose-hip medicinal tea, no mailing charge. And six turnips, payment for a bottle of Sex-All, Mr. Hinkel, Rabbit Hill, who can't seem to do it anymore."

Ignoring the invisible axe in my mother's eyes, my father takes the pot of beetles and returns to the mystical green curtain dispensary to meditate on the ills of humanity.

Tomorrow, Babka, the ancient grand-mother, is coming to the drugstore. Before she agrees to any medicinal treatment, she must hear the chant of exorcism in high Mass.

From my bed, I listen to my father rehearsing the magic words that are certain to destroy the evil witch sticking pins and needles in the Babka's ear:

Spiritus Camphorae
Aqua Camphorae
Mistura Camphorata
Capsicum
Capsicum
Capsicum

Perpetual Motion Button

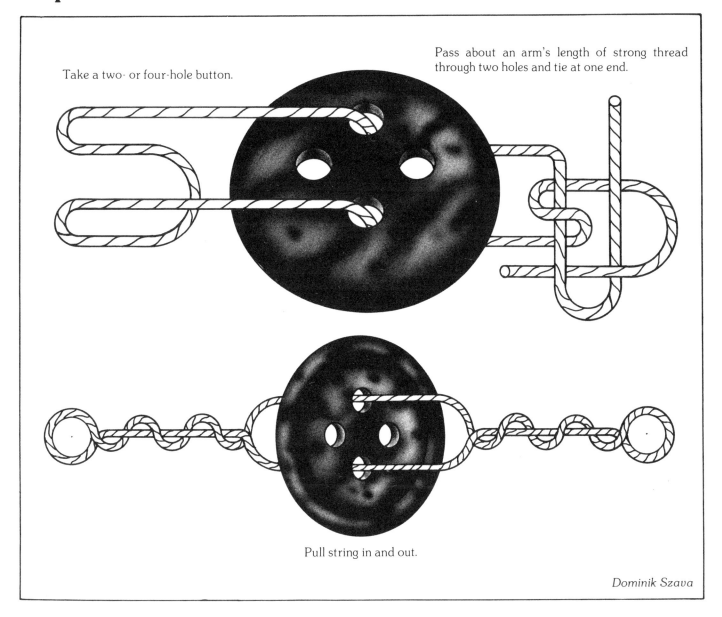

Take a two- or four-hole button.

Pass about an arm's length of strong thread through two holes and tie at one end.

Pull string in and out.

Dominik Szava

Newfoundland

It is less than a week now since the four of us from this program who went to Newfoundland returned to our home base, and though I cannot speak for them, I suspect that they all have some of the same feeling I have this morning, which I can only describe as a sort of homesickness. For me, this is a rare phenomenon. As I'm sure I've said before on this program, I've spent a lot of my life, both before I became a journalist and, partly because of that, after I went into writing and broadcasting for a living, travelling around Canada. A list of the places I've lived or worked over the years, including the thirteen months or so since this program began, sounds remarkably like the lyrics to a song by the Travellers. Toronto, or at least southern Ontario, is my home, of course, and while that doesn't necessarily mean I think it's the best part of the country — as a matter of fact, I don't — it does mean it's where I live. Yet I still have felt, everywhere I've gone, *at home* — in a way I could not, for instance, in Cleveland, Ohio, or Bayswater, Georgia, or Kingston, Surrey, England.

I once wrote a long essay in *Maclean's* magazine about how Saskatchewan was the most Canadian part of Canada — yet even that doesn't mean I think it's the best. What is the best part? Or, for that matter, what is the most Canadian part of Canada? I'm sure I don't know, but I do know that I have never enjoyed a week of travelling quite so much, or, for that matter, felt so instantly at home, as I did in Newfoundland last week. I haven't said anything about this until now because I wanted to make sure that when I talked about Newfoundland I was not still high on the hospitality of the people we met there or the sheer and — for me, at least — surprising physical beauty of the place. But since we left I've been kind of turning over in my mind what happened to us there and what seemed to us at least to make Newfoundland a province not like the others.

As I turn that thought over, the picture that keeps coming to my mind is a group of people, ourselves from Upper Canada, but mostly Newfoundlanders, sitting around over a glass of rum one afternoon — not screech, either, *rum* — and just gabbing. The gist of this conversation was about the difference between pre-Confederation and post-Confederation Newfoundland. Confederation, for God's sake. To those of us who grew up in other parts of the country, or indeed in other countries, Confederation is a dull, dry, abstract word that conjures up, if it conjures up anything, tricky and uninteresting questions on history examinations, or the formal picture of a group of men, all obviously holding too still too long for an artist. But to Newfoundlanders who are no older than I am, it is living politics, or at the very least living and very recent history. They *experienced* it, during the long, bitterly fought debates of the 1940s, and on all of their lives — from a lawyer I talked to in Cornerbrook, who many people think will one day be premier of Newfoundland, to a tough and gentle old lady who lives by social assistance in the outport of Ferryland, and who entertained us for an afternoon — on all of their lives it had a direct and specific effect. For us, history; for Newfoundland, reality. And because of that, I think that Newfoundland, which is at once our youngest and our oldest province, has a sense of its own past and traditions that the rest of us lack. I guess in a way I envy Newfoundlanders that sense, but even in a week it is possible to share enough of it with them to carry it around for quite a while. Newfoundland may have got the baby bonus by joining Confederation in 1949; but the rest of us, I'd suggest, got something quite a lot more important from them.

Someone asked me yesterday if, because of the way the program has been moving around — and will continue to move, incidentally, beginning in Alberta early next month — if because of that I had a particular vision of Canada. I'm afraid I was fairly rude in answering the question, just as I'm sure Newfoundlanders, if they are indeed capable of being rude, would be if someone asked them about their vision of their own island. The more I continue to get around this country, the more I realize that, whatever it is *Maclean's* magazine and the CIC are now talking about, if you can articulate it, you don't understand it. Show me a man with a pat definition of what makes Canada and I'll show you someone who doesn't know what he's talking about. You can make points about Canada, to be sure — just as you can say of Newfoundland that it is non-plastic, human, vital, exploited, harsh and incredibly lovely — but you have come as short of *defining* it as you would fall short of defining love by saying it's a good healthy roll in the hay.

So these brief reflections are intended to say nothing at all, except that all of us here are still glowing from what we learned in Newfoundland, that we are glowing just as much at the prospects of the places we'll be going next month and after, and that this country in the morning or any *other* time of day is just *some* place to live, my sons, and there's not a great deal wrong with that.

is for sandbanks,
but soon they will pass,
And turn up as cement
to smother more grass.

Eileen M. Purvess
Toronto, Ontario

Conversations with Prime Ministers: Lester Bowles Pearson

I don't know what I can say about my conversation with Lester B. Pearson. It was one of the last interviews he ever gave, and I think that one of the reasons he was so open on the radio was that he knew he was dying when he talked to me. We broadcast it on December 28, 1972, the day following his death. This is how I introduced that broadcast:

From all parts of the country today, and from all over the world, tributes are being paid to Lester Bowles Pearson, a great man and a good one, who died last night in Ottawa. Mr. Pearson meant something special to those of us who work at "This Country in the Morning," as, I'm sure, he meant something special to everyone who had a chance to share the pleasure of his company. I had that chance earlier this year when he came here to talk about the first volume of his memoirs. It was one of the most enjoyable hours I have ever spent on the radio, and it was the way I, for one, remember Mr. Pearson now: witty, warm, informal. I share with many people today the feeling that I have lost both a friend and a hero. I mourn that loss. But I cherish the memory. What follows, then, is our tribute – a very special talk with a very special man.

PG: *Mike: The Memoirs of the Right Honourable Lester B. Pearson*; PC, CC, OM, OBE, MA, LLD. Have you any idea what those stand for, Sir?
LBP: Oh, if I put my mind to it, I could probably identify them.
PG: How many honorary doctorates have you got?
LBP: Well, I have fifty, as a matter of fact, but a great many of them are from universities outside Canada and, as we used to say in the army about certain decorations, they came with the rations. As secretary for External Affairs and as prime minister and leader of a party, I was a natural for honorary degrees.
PG: Some of your degrees are real, though, unlike some people. . . .
LPB: Well, yes, I've earned some.
PG: This book is the first of three volumes, and I guess it's a little more informal than the others will be. . . .
LBP: Let's say very much more so. This one just takes me down to my entry into politics, and during most of that time I was a civil servant in External Affairs, at the beginning quite a young one, without the responsibility that I later had. In the early days, I had only a kind of worm's-eye view of the world. . . . Of course, the first part is my family life and early life and my schooling.
PG: I knew you were a great hockey fan and I knew, as everyone must know, that you played some basketball and hockey in your youth. But I had no idea what a jock you really were as a young man. . . .
LBP: Well, I love games. It's a very genuine passion which I shared with all the members of my family, with my father and even my grandfather, and I played at really every game. I loved baseball – I wasn't a distinguished participant because the four years that I might have been playing games in senior leagues in Canada I went overseas, and it wasn't till I got back to Oxford University as a student that I had two years of really intensive participation.
PG: But before you went to Oxford you dropped out of law school to go and play baseball. . . .
LBP: No, I dropped out of law school because I couldn't face the possibility, after being out of college for so long, of two years as a law student, reading books like *The Social Contract*.
PG: So you'd rather go and throw a piece of leather around?
LBP: Yes. But it was my brother Vaughan who was an absolutely first-class ball player, and I think I've cashed in a bit in recent years on his reputation.
PG: Ah, you've got better in retrospect.

LBP: That's a law of compensation: you get worse in some other respects.

PG: From my reading of the book, there you were, a successful history professor, casually tempted by the Department of External Affairs when you heard that there was a vacancy for first secretary. You don't seem to have expected to pass the examination – but I love the way you found out you did get the job. Could you tell us about getting the telegram?

LBP: Well, it was summertime and I was in the old Baldwin House doing something or other when a telegram arrived for me there. I'd just been to the doctor about my eyes – he had put those drops in that make it difficult to see; and here I knew the telegram was from Ottawa and that it was important. . . . Well, I couldn't read it. I went down into the cellar because somebody had said that if you have belladonna in your eyes you can read better in the dark, but I couldn't see anything, so I walked across the front campus to the university library. I found a little girl who was behind the library and said, do you mind reading this telegram to me – she must have been a little startled – and it was to the effect that I had been selected as first secretary.

PG: Is it true that right after that you were offered the job of coaching the football Blues and coaching lacrosse at the University of Toronto?

LBP: That's right. I was very tempted. We liked the university life – my wife especially liked life on the campus – and I got this letter from Dr. Hendry who was the chairman of the advisory athletic board asking me to be director of athletics, to coach one of the football teams. I could also have kept my academic interests alive by remaining assistant professor of history without giving so many lectures, and that was a very, very tempting offer. It was even as much money as I was getting in Ottawa.

PG: Think of how much Canada's history would have been changed! But the Blues might have won a few more football games.

LBP: Ah, well, they did pretty well in those years. These things happen in everybody's life.

PG: Your book shows a great love for England and a great love for Oxford, where you spent two years that were obviously very happy and satisfying ones for you. Would you tell about your arrival at St. John's College in Oxford?

LBP: You're right about my love for the old country, England and Ireland and especially Oxford, where I had the happiest two years of my life. I remember when I got a fellowship to go to Oxford, I didn't know what college to go to – I didn't know very much about the college system, but I had a friend who had just come back and he'd been at St. John's, so I applied for St. John's.

He told me – I'm a very, well, a sort of extrovertish gregarious type, I suppose I still am, more or less the same with everybody – and he said, now look, don't be *too* friendly, don't rush up and slap everybody on the back when you get to St. John's. It's a very formal place; it's been going for four hundred years and they have their hierarchical dispensations there, so be, ah, be a little more dignified than you are hanging around the fraternity house. So I had this in mind when I arrived. He had also told me that the porter is a very important man at a college and to get on good terms with him, so I went up to a man who I thought was the porter – he was standing by the lodge and he looked like a porter and he was dressed like what I thought a porter should dress like – and I drew myself up in my Canadian dignity and the dignity of a freshman at St. John's and I said, "My name is Pearson and I've just arrived. My bags are outside; take them out of the taxi and can you show me to my room?" He looked me up and down and he said, "Oh yes, Pearson, oh yes, we know about you coming," he said. "Let me introduce myself. My name is

Paul, I'm the senior tutor of the college." He was a very distinguished classical scholar, a very important man – and he had a sense of humour.

PG: Did he get your bags?

LBP: He didn't, he called the porter, but he dined on that story for a long time.

PG: A question that occurred to me as I read your book – it has such a nice, quiet reflective style – would you have rather been a British gentleman than a Canadian?

LBP: Oh no, I could never have been . . . I couldn't change my accent. There was no possibility of me ever being mistaken even superficially for an English Englishman – I love the country, of course, and the people, even though it seems a thousand years away, that kind of life, now. But the idea that I could settle down and live there was quite impossible. I was a Canadian, glad to get home.

PG: You remember so many people – you remember undergraduates at Victoria College, you remember all the men you served with in the war, but there's one especially moving paragraph in the book, about Norman Young. . . .

LBP: Yes, he was my brother-in-law. Norman and I married sisters in Winnipeg, we were married at the same time, and Norman and Grace went off to what was then the Gold Coast, where he taught in Achimota College. When the war began he got a commission in the Camerons and I used to see a lot of him in London in the early days of the war. He shouldn't really have been a combat officer; he was about my age and he had at that time four children, young children. But Norman, who was really a pacifist by instinct, became a crusader against Hitler, and when he became a crusader for or against anything he was a genuine one. He landed at Dieppe and he was one of those who never returned from Dieppe. His regiment got in, I think, farther than any other, and he was the front man in the front company.

PG: That was the Second World War.

LBP: Yes. The First World War also made quite a dint on my friendships – more so, I suppose, than the second.

PG: I noticed the number of men whose names appear and then disappear.

LBP: It was a bloodbath. I think that was when I first got my passionate horror of war and my belief in international friendship, however difficult that may seem to bring about.

PG: I'd like to talk to you about some of the famous people you met as a young man – a worm's-eye view is your phrase, certainly not mine.

LBP: Maybe we can call it a bleacher observation.

PG: Mike: you got that nickname in the services, would you say?

LBP: Yes, it was tossed at me by my squadron commander when I was in training in the old Royal Flying Corps, because I had ambitions of becoming a fighter pilot and he didn't think Lester was a very good name for a potential fighter pilot.

PG: Neither did you, did you? You say in the book, "I left Lester gladly behind."

LBP: Yes. I'm not enamoured of the name, because there was a comic strip in those days – maybe there still is – called Lester the Pester, and I was a little, ah, sensitive. It's a family name, it's a good respectable name, but Mike appealed more to me.

PG: This is another one that just pops into mind – what did people call Mackenzie King? You have a paragraph in there where, is it only Mrs. Roosevelt who ever called him Mackenzie?

LBP: Well, President Roosevelt called him Mackenzie and perhaps Mrs. Roosevelt. His intimates called him Rex, and that may have been a family name. I've heard Mrs. Massey and Mr. Massey call him Rex, but I've never heard anybody call him Mac.

PG: Or Willy.

LBP: Ah, he may have been called Willy, but Mr. King was not the kind of person who encouraged nicknames, you know; and William Lyon Mackenzie is a pretty trio of names anyway, without nicknaming them.

PG: You, of course, as a young man called him nothing but Mr. King.

LBP: I called him Mr. King with great respect and a good deal of awe.

PG: You met so many of the great figures of our time in your service in the diplomatic corps as ambassador to Washington, in your work at Canada House in London. When was the first time you met Churchill?

LBP: It was at one of those dining clubs that are so common in London, where you get together and have dinner and somebody talks; each member can bring a guest and I was brought as a guest to this one — it was 1938, I think, or '37. Churchill spoke to us that night about what was happening in Europe, after an extremely good dinner which would have put a normal man to sleep; he talked for about an hour and that was the first time I was exposed to the magnetism of his personality and the convincing eloquence of his words. He told us that war was coming and there was only one way of avoiding it, and that was to arm quickly and to arm completely.

After about forty-five minutes of this, with a glass in front of him, he stopped and said, "If I'm to go on talking, I have to have some sustenance," and he asked for a cold beef sandwich. After that dinner, he wanted a cold beef sandwich! Then he went on and I remember thinking at the time, this man is almost irresistible when you are exposed to him in this way, but I can't help but believe that he might be wrong — if we arm to the teeth at this particular time, perhaps we may be provoking the wrong kind of reaction. But he was right.

PG: You say that your first emotional reaction had been to become an out-and-out Canadian isolationist. So you had to fight that tendency within yourself?

PG: Yes, because up until the middle thirties, certainly I thought that nothing could be more horrible than a second world war, that there was a very real danger of it being brought about by European power politics, and that if Canada as a member of the Commonwealth had to take part in that kind of war, that was too high a price to pay for membership in the Commonwealth. But when I realized what was happening to Czechoslovakia, what was happening to progressives inside Germany and what was happening to the Jews inside Germany, then I came to the conclusion that Naziism and everything it stood for was degrading and evil, and that Hitler's ambitions and power would bring about war unless he was stopped. And around 1938 I was quite willing to go as far as anybody could go in advocating resistance to Naziism, even if it meant fighting.

PG: I want to ask you about one more man, because of all the historic names that echo through your book, most of them are written about with respect and with a word that so characterizes you — decency — all except Harry Truman. Oh, you're looking somewhat taken aback.

LBP: I had great respect and admiration for him when he became president, but not when he was vice-president. When I called on him, the vice-president, as ambassador, I had the rather startling experience of being ignored as a Canadian representative and then treated in a very sort of cavalier, Missouri-political fashion, and I thought, good gracious, this man is standing between a sick man and the presidency of the United States.

PG: You were sitting in his office and he invited in some other crony from the Senate. . . .

LBP: A couple of senators, and we all sat down with bourbon and water — and this was a formal visit from the ambassador of Canada to the vice-president.

PG: We can't have that.

LBP: Well, but I thought, this man doesn't really know how to carry on foreign relations, at least. If I were a sensitive Latino or a sensitive European I would have made an issue out of this. It didn't bother me as a person and I found his informality quite easy and refreshing, but then I saw him later at a press-club dinner when I thought he gave a very vulgar speech. He sat down and played the "Missouri Waltz" with an actress sitting on the grand piano, pulling up her skirt almost to her knees, and that was terrible in those days. But I had great respect and admiration for him when he became president. He really showed himself a man of quality and decision and determination then.

PG: Except where music critics were concerned.

LBP: Oh yes, yes.

PG: I keep saying the Honourable Lester B. Pearson, and you're in fact the Right Honourable Lester B. Pearson.

LBP: Well, it's shorter, Honourable — you can even call me Hon., if you like.

PG: Do you ever wish that there were a different kind of honours list, that you would now be Lord Pearson or Lord Mike?

LBP: Oh, no!

PG: You saw R.B. Bennett in London when he was Lord Bennett, and he had lost interest in Canada in some way.

LBP: Well, he had, but he talked. I saw a good deal of him during that period. It was the period of the blitz and he was reminiscing a great deal about Canada and the past. I think he was uncomfortable and rather lonely over there.

PG: Is it true he would talk to you because you were a civil servant, and therefore non-partisan, but he would not talk to Vincent Massey?

LBP: He didn't get on at all with Mr. Massey. And that wasn't Mr. Massey's fault at all; he did everything he could to establish friendly relations with Lord Bennett. But Bennett was suspicious of him as a former Liberal and an appointee of Mr. King, and still Mr. King's representative in London.

PG: Not Canada's representative?

LBP: Well, he would admit that he was Canada's, but he also thought that he was Mr. King's representative. But he was kind to ask us down to the country at a time when living in London was sort of rackety. And it was interesting to hear him reminisce about the old days. When he did reminisce, it was always about Canada, and the earlier days, Calgary.

PG: Did you ever see Lord Beaverbrook around?

LBP: Once or twice, because he lived beside Lord Bennett. But I really didn't know him. And I don't think he had a very high opinion of me, even in those days. I think perhaps he thought I was too much of a Canadian nationalist. And perhaps too much of a Mackenzie King-Vincent Massey Canadian nationalist. I don't know, but I didn't get to know him at all. Fascinating person he must have been.

PG: During the Second World War, you were at Canada House as a diplomat. And I love the way you pointed out the contrast between the official and unofficial communications. The way it comes up in the book, of course, is about the increase in the price of oatmeal by a penny. Can you explain that, how it works?

LBP: I suppose my ironical treatment of this kind of bureaucratic correspondence is due in part to the fact that I am a very informal person myself. And this kind of stilted diplomatic correspondence, which goes away back to the eighteenth century, used to arouse my amusement. You get these dispatches that begin: Sir, I have the honour to report . . . and then a long rigamarole about something the Canadian army was doing wrong — charging not enough, or charging too much, for supplies from the British. And then it would end up: I have the honour to request, Sir, that you take this matter up with the Canadian authorities; I remain, Sir, Your

Excellency's most obedient servant. A letter like this would be addressed to the high commissioner. He'd toss it over to my office, and then I'd get hold of the quarter-master general of the Canadian Army and say, the British are sore because you're charging too much for oatmeal. Or too little for oatmeal. And what are you going to do about it? And he'd write me back a couple of one-liners — it would be very forthright — telling the British to go to the devil, or something. And I'd send that all back. I always tried to get an extra sentence over the British, you see. That was one of my little diversions. They don't do that so much now.

PG: Has some of the elegance of the age of diplomacy gone?

LBP: Oh, yes, very largely gone, and quite rightly. Diplomacy has to reflect the manners of the age in which it is carried on. Now that we're in an age of popular participation and control, to go round in knee-breeches looks a little silly. It's a shirt-sleeve job now, because we live in a shirt-sleeve world.

PG: I cannot quite discern your own attitude towards pageantry and pomp from the book.

LBP: I like it! I like it when it's genuine. When it is indigenous. The trooping of the colours at Whitehall. The opening of Parliament. The lord mayor's inauguration, or initiation. All that kind of thing has a genuineness about it. It's part of the folk lore, and the history of the country. And when it's done well, it does add to your feeling for the country, if you belong to the country. I laugh at, and I have no use for, contrived pageantry.

PG: Can you think of an example?

LBP: Oh, when you try to manufacture a tradition at once, you see. And you surround it with a kind of drill. I can think of this sort of thing in Washington. We have some good indigenous national pageantry in Canada. I think, for instance, of the Calgary Stampede — that's Canadian. I can get a thrill out of that.

PG: You had a little difficulty with the sword you had to wear to the coronation of Queen Elizabeth.

LBP: Well, I was always uncomfortable when I tried to be part of natural pageantry in England. Because I was over there, I used to be asked to do some of these things, and I liked doing them, it was fun, you know. During the coronation I was an usher at Westminster Hall. Of course, they didn't call me an usher; they called me a Gold Stick-in-Waiting. I had to wear court costume for that. But it gave me a chance to see what was going on, and it was amusing. I attended the court ball as an attendant.

PG: Wasn't there some problem when you arrived at the court ball, and you had to get your sword off. . . .

LBP: That's right. You know, it's a complicated uniform. You have a heavy black coat with gold braid, and you have brass buttons from your neck right down to your middle, about thirty of them. And it's quite a job buttoning them and unbuttoning them. Then you have a sword in the side, underneath this coat, and nothing else, because it covers you up and it's very heavy. I was going to a dinner before the coronation ball, when the butler — a very distinguished-looking man, the most distinguished-looking man there — said I'd be more comfortable without my sword. Which was quite true. But I had a feeling: how can I get the sword off without unbuttoning the thirty-two buttons, with only my BVDs underneath; this is going to be very difficult. I was starting to do it, though, when he looked at me. And he knew I was a Canadian — that covered a multitude of protocol sins. He was very kind to me. He said, "Look, Sir, you don't have to do all that. Just unbutton the frog button down there and the sword will come off, and your belt will be all right." Now that was a kindly deed on his part, especially as other guests were about to arrive.

PG: For CBC fans, would you describe what happened in the taxi, yesterday?

LBP: Oh. . . . Well, I got in the taxi with our daughter, and this taxi driver heard my voice and he looked behind and he said, "Are you Max Ferguson being L.B. Pearson, or are you L.B. Pearson?"

PG: How do you enjoy Max's version of you?

LBP: Oh, I enjoy it very much. He's a wonderful mimic and quite a person. I enjoy listening to him.

PG: In writing about these years, and thinking again about your days as an undergraduate, as a professor, as a baseball player and, of course, as a diplomat, have you ever regretted becoming a politician? Taking a buffeting in the public arena?

LBP: Oh, there were times, I admit, when I looked back with some nostalgic longing for the days when I was immune as a civil servant from criticism. But if you go into politics you have to accept this. It's not a high price to pay. Remember that I went into politics as secretary for External Affairs, and that wasn't a very partisan or controversial post. I never expected to be anything more, and during those ten years I was very fortunate. All parties were agreed on the principles of our foreign policy. I'm sure that some of my colleagues must have thought I had a very enviable portfolio indeed. I didn't take any buffeting then.

PG: In fact, you took a Nobel Prize.

LBP: Well, I got into a little controversy over Suez in 1956. But that was a legitimate difference of opinion on a question of high principle. I didn't mind that. It was only later, when I became the leader of the party, when I was right in the middle of domestic controversy. I had a very controversial time.

PG: Can you really not fix anything, Mr. Pearson? Are you as impractical around the house as. . . .

LBP: I'm afraid I am. And, thank goodness, my wife is not. She's the general manager of our household, and has been since an hour after we got married.

PG: So you can solve international crises, you can hold a political party together, you can work among the greats of the world, but you cannot put a new washer in a tap?

LBP: No, but I can change a lightbulb correctly, five times out of six. . . .

PG: A final question, Sir: who's going to win the World Series?

LBP: You know I. . . .

PG: Now, you've never stepped back from controversy. . . .

LBP: Well, I'll go way out on a limb, and I'll say that. . . .

PG: Don't be a diplomat now.

LBP: Cincinnati's going to win!

PG: Good, good, me too! I'm a big Johnny Bench fan. A big Lester Pearson fan. It's such a pleasure to talk to you, Sir. Is volume two coming out next year?

LBP: Yes, next year. It's about half through now. And then volume three, probably about six or seven months after that.

PG: Will you come back?

LBP: I would be delighted to.

PG: Thank you, very much.

A Music Box

materials
bobby pins
a cylinder of wood (diameter of at least 3″)
two small pieces of wood (approx. ½″ x 1″ x 3″)
a wooden crate (an orange crate will do) with the
    top removed
nails
two large nails or screws

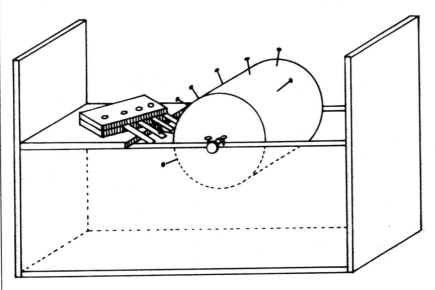

instructions:
Hammer the bobby pins flat.

Slide the bobby pins in between the two small pieces of wood one at a time, adjusting their length so that when you pluck them, they give you the note you want (I made a scale of eight notes).

As you put each bobby pin in place, hammer a nail beside it. This holds them securely.

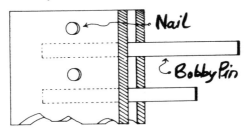

Measure the circumference of the cylinder of wood (put a piece of paper around it and measure the length of it). Take the piece of music you want to play (make it as short as possible) and count the number of beats to it. You want to divide the cylinder into that many spaces, so divide the number of beats into the circumference of the cylinder. The answer is the

distance between each beat. For example, the first line of "Mary Had a Little Lamb" has eight beats:

If the circumference of the cylinder is 16″ then the space between each beat would be 2″.

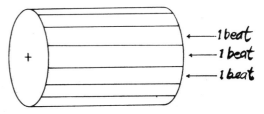

Draw a line around the cylinder where each bobby pin would be hit. The nails you will hammer into the cylinder will be on these lines, so that they will be sure to pluck the bobby pins.

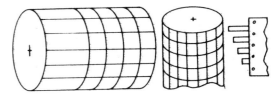

Hammer in the nails according to the music you want played, making all the nails the same length.

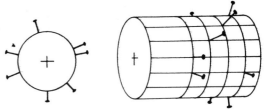

Nail the bobby-pin box to a wooden platform (the top of the crate does perfectly). The bobby-pin box should be put on an angle so that the ends of the bobby pins are parallel to the edge of the platform.

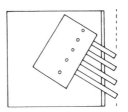

Nail the platform to the top of your box.

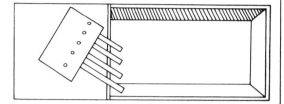

Hammer the large nails into the center of the ends of the cylinder to act as an axis. These are to balance the cylinder on the orange crate. Rest the cylinder on the box so that the nails overlap the bobby pins just slightly. Keep the cylinder in place by putting a nail on either side of the large nails.

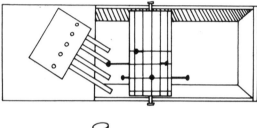

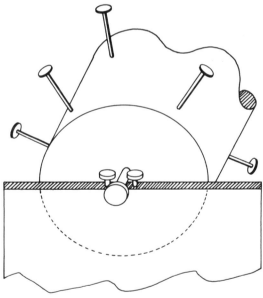

When you turn the cylinder forward by hand, the nails should pluck the bobby pins to play your song. You may have to shorten some of the nails so that they pluck the bobby pins evenly.

Jane Johnson
Ottawa, Ontario

Andrew Allan on Nervous Breakdowns

I was passing a bookstore the other day. That was a striking event. I seldom pass a bookstore. Usually I go in. But, although my withdrawal symptoms were as high as the humidex, I kept on walking.

Half a block away I did what in theatre parlance is called a "double take." The book *couldn't* have been called that! *Nobody* could have written a book called that! There was no such book!

I had seen it in the window of that bookstore, though. At least, I *thought* I had seen it in the window of that bookstore, nestled there — bright and hopeful in its dust jacket — among all those "how to" books ... *How to Build a Dog House, How to Build a Bird House, How to Build a Cat House, How to See into the Future, How to Forget about the Past, How to Avoid the Issue* (a political handbook), *How to Avoid the Issue* (a book about planned parenthood).

I *thought* I had seen it there. But *had* I? It was too good to be true. There was nothing for it but to about-face and look in the window again. I did that.

The book I thought I had seen — whose title had blossomed so slowly in my subconscious — was *How to Enjoy a Nervous Breakdown.*

If ever a book was *needed*, that is the book: *How to Enjoy a Nervous Breakdown.* Compared with a book like that, books like *How to Build a Castle in Spain without Speaking Spanish* or *How to Do-It-Yourself Even if You Don't Want To* are nowhere. Or soon will be.

How many people do you and I know who are having a nervous breakdown? All right then ... how many people do we know who are *enjoying* a nervous breakdown? Ah! — as Hamlet may have said — there's the rub! I venture to say that there are millions of people at this very minute who would have a nervous breakdown immediately if they could be assured they would enjoy it.

"Nervous breakdown" is an unscientific name for a condition in which the neurons have come unstuck. It is, you might say, a neurological disorientation. (You *might* say it, but I advise against it.) "Disorientation" means you don't know where the sun is going to rise and don't care whether it *does* or not.

The condition is brought on by fatigue, tension, or thinking about the wrong person for hours on end. It may serve you right (as people say), but it's also (as Hamlet *undoubtedly* said)

is for telephone,
a real national thing,
Just as you get in the bath:
ring ring ring.

Peter Gower
Maxwell, Ontario

a consummation devoutly to be wished.

Everybody around Elsinore said Hamlet was having a nervous breakdown . . . well, actually they said he had gone mad, because in those days they didn't have the advantage of our expanded vocabulary. But Hamlet made a lot more sense than his prospective father-in-law, Polonius, who believed the night followed the day, when every sane man knows the day follows the night. Hamlet's only blunder was coming to his senses long enough to fight a duel and get killed. If he'd kept on with his breakdown, he might be alive yet.

A fringe benefit of having a nervous breakdown is that no one expects you to make sense. If anybody asks you what you think of Gay Lib or when the election will be or what is the square root of minus one, you simply say "Fiddle-dee-dee" and you're off the hook. You can sit on the grass all day staring at a flower, and nobody expects you to be off making money or a speech, or shooting something. If you heave a rock through a window, they simply take you to a psychiatrist.

Some of my best friends are psychiatrists, and nearly all my best friends think they are.

I suspect that half the population would be having a nervous breakdown if it weren't for that little hobgoblin called Guilt. Would it be fair to the family? Would it be fair to the shareholders? to the brains trust at city hall? to the picket line? the tax assessor? medicare? the guy in the car behind? With your head full of guilty questions like that, you may *get* a nervous breakdown all right — but bedamned if you're going to enjoy it.

Oh . . . about that book in the bookstore window! When I got back and looked *in* at it, my heart submerged. It wasn't *How to Enjoy a Nervous Breakdown* after all. It was a piece of predictability called *How to Avoid a Nervous Breakdown*.

The great book remains to be written. If any publisher wants to make me an advance on it, he has only to address me in care of this program.

And that's Hamlet's cue to come up with his customary tag line: "The rest is silence."

Skating

This weekend, like 400,000 other boys in Canada, two of my sons played hockey. The older one, who has just turned thirteen, has been playing organized hockey for five or six years now. He enjoys it and plays it fairly well, if I say so myself. The younger one is just eight, and Saturday was only the third game he has played in his life, but he had fun, and I'm sure will have more, and will play it fairly well too. But I couldn't help thinking as I watched each of them that something has gone out of hockey for boys . . . at least in the towns and cities . . . and with it something essential about the Canadian winter.

Neither of my sons, and I wonder how many of the other 400,000 kids on 20,000 teams across the country, has ever played a hockey game in his life without shin pads, hockey pants, elbow pads, shoulder pads, a tinny, gloves, helmet or mouthguard . . . without a referee and a timeclock, without a coach and a dressing room. I am not going to do a number on you here about how much better it was when we had old *Liberty* magazines stuffed down our pants, and used frozen road apples for pucks. Nor how nice it was to change into our skates outdoors — I've frozen my toes too often for

that — and whether you froze your toes in 1911 or 1934 or last week, frozen toes hurt just the same. In many ways I envy my boys their numbered sweaters and their official goals-and-assists records. But there is one day I'll bet they'd envy me, too, and for me as much as anything that day symbolizes everything I love about Canadian winter.

A bunch of us were still in the early stages of our usual Saturday six-hour, shinny game, outdoors, in a boarded-off part of the ball-park in the small city where I grew up. We were about ten or eleven years old. It was late in winter, and the night before a freezing rain had fallen on top of the snow, and had frozen there. After half an hour or so of the game, someone shot the puck over the boards and someone else climbed over to go after it. To his amazement, he found that his skates didn't break the snow; the sharp morning temperature had hardened the frozen rain into a solid crust, and instead of walking to get the puck he was able to glide. Tentatively, he shot the puck farther across the park. It slid for at least the length of a hockey rink, and he called to us, and one by one we clambered out of the enclosed rink and out across the frozen snow after him, laughing and yelling as we found that we too could skate across the open.

And away we went, swooping out across the area where the fall fair had been the September before and out over the football field.

Then up a hill, and – wonder of wonders – down it, our skates still not cutting the snow. And out of the park we went, across city streets and down lanes and out into the country . . . as untrammelled as birds in the clean crisp air, winging our way across hills and around trees, down into a valley and then side-stepping up the other side.

We skated miles that day, going anywhere we wanted to, sometimes leaving the puck behind, sometimes playing hockey with half a mile between the goals. It was a rare phenomenon of nature, something that I have since learned has a scientific name, when the rain freezes fast enough on top of the snow to make the whole world one outdoor rink. I don't want to know that technical name. It is the freedom I remember, the freedom and the laughter, and I sometimes wonder if I, or my sons, will ever be that free again.

Trapped Housewives

Early in the gloomy spring of 1972, Herb Johnson, one of our producers, had an idea that it would be good to ask three women – not "experts," just women – to come in and talk together about some of the contrary forces they were experiencing in the light of, for example, what Marjorie Harris had discussed on her "people's liberation", series: pressures from the media to be "more than housewives"; pressures from their husbands to stay home, or, in some cases, to get out and become a "more interesting person"; pressures from their background to raise their children as a full-time job, or simply pressures from within themselves not to let the good years of young adulthood slip away.

We found three such women, and they talked well and honestly, and then the next day we had their husbands listen to the tape and respond in public to their wives' public comments. We found that the women had said some things in public they might not have said directly to the men they loved and lived with – and vice versa. The two conversations obviously struck a chord. A lot of people wrote about what they'd heard. We decided to initiate yet one more contest. The rules were simple: we weren't seeking answers to the problems of the trapped housewife, because we realized that there are no simple answers, and we certainly weren't offering what turned out to be one of the few substantial prizes we gave away (usually people entered our contests just for the fun of it) for the best whiner. We wanted only an honest and personal statement, and for the best one, which was selected partly by me and partly by the three women who had started it all, we did offer a reward.

I said in the introduction to this book that one of the things I learned about my profession through "This Country" was how many people who had never been paid before were as capable as writers as many of the big-name professional journalists in Canada. I offer the winning entry in our trapped housewives' contest as proof.

March 8, 1972

Dear Peter:

Mark, eight months, is dirty; Brett, three years, is quietly flooding the bathroom; Jan, four, is skating on the baby's stacking rings. When this letter is finished, however, two hours of work will restore some semblance of order, and I will have gained that most precious possession, an hour to myself. Any trapped housewife will tell you that those hours are rare. I have known two women who are totally fulfilled in their wife-mother-housekeeper roles, and have frequently envied them their liberation. But it's not my bag, and this year – the first in six years of marriage – a fear of being trapped has frequently threatened to engulf me. There are reasons aplenty – perhaps a look at how I escaped the feeling in the past is a key to explaining today's reaction.

Our oldest son was born in Frobisher Bay. At home for the first time in a cold, isolated climate, I was prepared to feel caught up in drudgery, but I never actually did. The child-oriented culture sustained us – everywhere the Eskimo people gathered, children were welcomed and enjoyed. There was always someone to hold the baby if I wanted to dance, or just have a rest from him. On the rare occasion when we did have a sitter, we would come home to find her asleep with our son on her back, and her son in our crib. Whenever it was necessary, my husband could take the baby to work. Doctor appointments were social happenings. I found a part-time job which I did at home, and I even flew into two settlements I'd never have seen otherwise. Life that year had its hassles, but we were richly compensated, and we were sad to leave. However, the impending birth of Brett forced us to be realistic – there was room on my back for one baby, but two in a parka is more than company, and nine months indoors is an uninviting prospect.

After Brett's birth in Prince George, I had the beginning twinges of "trapped-ness," which intensified with the burgeoning publicity around women's lib. So when a six-week job as a hospital social worker presented itself, I grabbed it gleefully. A retired foster-mother who had cared for two hundred children in her time came to mind the children, so there were no concerns on that score – I knew she knew more about kids that I'd ever know! The job was fun, it was satisfying, my co-workers were interesting and helpful – and at the end of the six weeks I was glad to quit. For the first time in three years, I was truly content to be home, because I *chose* to be there. And with surprising speed, activities I considered relevant – tenants' rights, SPEC, women's rights, native rights – engulfed me. Suddenly drudgery was a mindless routine and I no longer even noticed I was washing floors and changing diapers. I was tired a lot, but the trapped feeling had vanished.

With the move to Winnipeg, the scene changed . . . again, barefoot and pregnant. This time, our population-conscious friends suggested abortion; the less vehement commented daily on my expansion rate, and dourly predicted twins. But the task of setting out roots in a new city precluded brooding about the state of affairs in my head. Summer provided three months in Campbell River – an oasis of greenery, friendliness and sanity in contrast to urban growth and grubbery.

This winter, though, arrived with a vengeance on October 31, and with it came my sensations of being boxed in, caught up in roles which should have been subsidiary but had completely dominated the essential *me*. Finances are tight; as we hoard pennies for a summer trip to England, the luxury of a babysitter is rare – besides, the baby makes strange, and no babysitter with knowledge aforehand would come near! Since it did not seem possible to do justice to any volunteer work on a regular basis, it seemed better to do none. I reconsidered going to work, but I still feel that the reasons for my decision to quit in Prince George are valid: a maternal hang-up I don't want to shed. I feel that there are few enough years in which to teach our three the values we consider to be important. We have invested considerable time and energy arriving at these values and, while we hope they will be questioned later on, for now we wish to make them known, as only we can do.

There are, of course, satisfactions – some vicarious pleasure from my husband's endeavours; some direct satisfactions from the way the children are beginning to cope with life; refuge in enjoyable craft sessions and time to learn a few new things. Still, I am nervous and irritable, and less tolerant of the screaming self-expression children resort to – while I depend on it more and more myself. I, too, am desperately searching for a sign of spring! So we are purchasing season's football tickets and I am off to see about a regular volunteer job.

It seems to me that we may be caught up in a basic fallacy. Our child-centered culture is largely child-centered in terms of *tasks* – perhaps we could learn a lesson from the Eskimos, who are less hung up on tasks and more centered around enjoying life in the company of the entire family. When we first came south, I think we had a more basic sense of what mattered, but it is eroding as other values have impinged: if I worried less about table manners, I'd have more time to enjoy the imaginative and messy games which spice the boys' meals!

The nuclear family has, it seems to me, greatly increased the trap we housewives find ourselves in. After two weeks of sleepless nights, I long to dump my kids with a grandparent or an aunt and sneak home for a good rest. Friends can and often do provide welcome relief, but it is unrealistic to expect them to be as involved as you are with your family.

Because I alone bear responsibility for fulfilling the immediate emotional and physical needs of four other people, it is sometimes impossible to find time to meet my own individual needs – the hunt for myself, which only I can make. I know too, that my husband at times finds it difficult to meet the needs of his family despite his very loving and unselfish nature. Perhaps this is what lies behind the resurgence of communal living, and we do consider it from time to time.

In all this, one single thought sustains me. This is, after all, a temporary state. In a few years the children will have become in large measure independent; I will be able to search out a lifestyle that is creative and individualistic while leaving room to meet the needs of my family, which is, through it all, an important piece of my life. I am really only temporarily detained by a detour I chose, and I am constantly reminded that my trap is a tender one. The problem is that relatively few women have such a happy future in store. If I were untrained, or had a husband who felt that my "place" was in the home, or if I lacked confidence in my ability to "make it" in the world, the trap would be terrifying.

For me, however, there is a trap that is larger and more fearful than even that one. We all are caught in a society where we are less and less, it seems, able to control our own lifestyle. This is nothing new, I guess – but now that I'm in my early thirties and have experienced more defeats than victories in the power-to-the-people scene (but haven't reconciled myself to defeat), there seems no way out. I feel much like Piglet must have felt as his sweater unravelled on that blustery day, and there seem to be few acceptable answers to "Where am I going?" I don't feel that a cop-out is the answer – surely there has to be a way to effect constructive changes in our system and style of life, and I expect that I'll keep trying to find it. In the meantime, I wonder if the family trap we so often deplore is not really a symptom of a larger trap we feel completely inadequate to change. Surely, if we paid more attention to the quality of everyone's life, the quality of each individual family's life would improve immeasurably.

Suzanne Hudson
Winnipeg, Manitoba

Suzanne's prize, as I said, was a substantial one. We offered to send her, with or without her husband, to any place in Canada she'd like to go for a vacation. She chose to go to a place I'd like to visit, too. She also chose to go with her husband. After her trip she wrote:

173

September 12, 1972

Dear Peter:

The trip to the Queen Charlotte Islands was nearly all we had hoped, but it was four months too short! The north island (which was all we really saw, due to the lack of transportation among the southern islands), is a microcosm of B.C. — enormous sand beaches reminiscent of Long Beach, copper-hued rivers from the interior, the plains of Dawson Creek country, mountains, Caribou-like hills, and rain forests of Cathedral Grove stature. Unfortunately, the loggers have been carelessly at work; large tracts of land are scarred with scrubby debris, abandoned after the giants were logged out — ugly.

In four days we hiked a lot, and got lost once for a short time in the woods. We camped on the North Beach, carefully enclosing our hiking tent in plastic, but woke drenched because the heavy dew had risen to the underside of the tent and poured down with sufficient force to make a thunderstorm proud. We stayed in a magnificent new hotel constructed mainly of native materials — stone and cedar; we slipped and slid up the hill at the northern tip of the island to see Alaska and the sweep of North Beach; we visited an archaeological dig; we stopped at the old village of Haida and imagined what life must have been like in the

1800s; we lost the lid of our only pot to a curious, marauding raven; we ate dehydrated food and found it tasty.

Mostly we talked — uninterruptedly — to each other for hours about the good and bad things in our relationship and family and about alternative lifestyles for us. Should we chuck all the education to the wind and go commercial fishing? Tempting! Should we stay married? Yes! Should we adopt a child? Maybe. Do we want to go back to the land — a full-time, purist life? No. How do we encourage Ian to like school, which he hates? No answer. We walked and talked, we drank beer in the pub and talked. We reached no earth-shaking conclusions, but we're more aware of where we stand in considering alternatives.

Also, we talked to the people on the island — Mrs. Brown, who runs the store at Skidegate; a fisherman from Queen Charlotte City; an Indian girl coming apprehensively home from Vancouver for summer vacation; the craft-shop owner who shut up shop to drive us to the place she suggested we camp; the doctor who treated Pete's ballooning, red-streaked, blackfly-bitten arm; a fellow who was going back to the land; an old-timer who remembers greased roads and thought we were crazy to plunge into the woods looking for a dugout canoe; the Kellys, who were camped near us and came from Prince George, where we were married; two ten-year-old boys camping alone for the summer; an armed-forces family moving to Inuvik.

We welcomed the absence of eager attempts to pander to the whims of tourists — no neon signs, no maps of hiking trails, no drive-in restaurants. The weather was good — we had jetted in, but found it too incongruous with the history and background of a canoe-building, sea-mastering culture, so we were happier to fly out on a single-engine Otter, at an altitude which really allowed us to see the northern coastal area.

After a night in Prince Rupert, we came through the inside passage on the B.C. ferry to Kelsey Bay. We missed the much-acclaimed grandeur of the passage because of the fog, but we were delighted to sight two killer whales sporting in a channel. Several American passengers were sure they were dolphins! Together with many other back-packers, we slept in comfort in the lounge and chatted about our holidays — a pleasant end to a much-dreamed-of holiday.

Thanks again

Sue Hudson
Winnipeg, Manitoba

Cold Soup Recipes

Peter's Gazpacho

2 large, ripe tomatoes, peeled and seeded
1 large sweet green pepper, chopped
3 cloves of garlic, peeled and chopped (or to taste)
½ cup olive oil
chives (to taste)
parsley (to taste)
basil (to taste)
3 tablespoons lemon juice
1 can consommé + 1 can cold water
1 large mild onion, sliced thinly
1 cup diced cucumber
1½ teaspoon salt
fresh pepper (to taste)

Combine tomatoes, pepper, garlic, chives, parsley, basil, olive oil, and lemon juice in chopping bowl and mix throughly. Add consommé and water. Add onion, cucumber, and salt and pepper (vegetables will float on top). Chill. Before serving add a glop of *sour cream* to each bowl and mix thoroughly with soup.

Swedish Fruit Soup

one 11-ounce package dried mixed fruit or apricots and apples
1 cup golden seedless raisins
3 pieces stick cinnamon
4 whole cloves
1 orange, sliced
1 large tin unsweetened pineapple juice
sugar to taste (¼ cup or less)
2 tablespoons quick-cooking tapioca

Combine fruit, raisins, cinnamon, cloves, in 4 cups water and simmer approximately 20 minutes or until fruit is tender. Add remaining ingredients. Simmer an additional 15 minutes. Chill and serve cold. Serves 8 to 10 people.
   Important: Keep stirring while soup is over heat.

Sheila Amsden
Winnipeg, Manitoba

Borscht

8 medium beets
4 medium potatoes
1 large carrot
2 medium onions
2 quarts vegetable stock, beef stock, or water
2 bay leaves
freshly ground pepper
½ small head of cabbage, shredded
2 tablespoons sugar or more (to taste)
juice of one lemon
4 eggs
sour cream
hard-boiled egg slices or cottage cheese

Wash vegetables; slice (don't peel). Slice and peel onions. Add vegetables except cabbage to a 5 or 6-quart pot with stock, bay leaf, and pepper. Salt to taste. Simmer 'til tender (approx. ½ hour). Add cabbage and simmer until cabbage is tender. Add sugar and lemon. Blend 4 eggs and add 2-3 cups broth gradually to blender. Return mixture to soup pot. Chill and garnish with sour cream or cottage cheese and egg slices. Serves 5 to 6 persons.

Marsha Baumel
London, Ontario

Cold Curried Avocado Soup

3 tablespoons butter
1-2 tablespoons curry powder
4 large avocados — one suitable for garnish
7½ cups chicken stock (not consommé)
salt to taste
¼ teaspoon pepper
three 6-ounce cartons or one 16-ounce carton plain yogurt (without gelatin)
lemon juice

Heat butter in large saucepan. Add curry powder; cook gently, stirring constantly, over low heat for about 3 minutes. Peel three avocados; cut in chunks suitable for blender. Add gradually to blender with 1 cup of chicken stock to aid in blending. Add butter. Heat mixture to boiling; cool. Add yogurt and chill. Before serving, garnish with remaining avocado after dipping the slices in lemon juice to prevent darkening.

Raymonde Bowan
Senneville, Quebec

Crême Vichyssoise

6 leeks or 1½ cups minced onion
3 cups sliced, peeled white potatoes
3 cups boiling water
1 teaspoon salt
4 chicken bouillon cubes

3 tablespoons butter or margarine
1 cup cream (heavy or light)
1 cup milk
¼ teaspoon pepper
¼ teaspoon curry powder (optional)

Trim roots off leeks; wash well; slice white part into fine pieces; wash again. Cook leeks, potatoes, water, and salt 40 minutes in covered pan. Press through sieve without draining. Combine mixture with bouillon and remaining ingredients in double boiler. Heat until cubes are dissolved. Cool soup and refrigerate (may be made the day before). Before serving, garnish with chopped chives, mint, or dill. Serves 4 to 6. Goes well with cold lobster or Atlantic salmon.

Anne Nadeau
St. Godefroi, Quebec

Team Canada

I

I don't know how the rest of you feel about today's hockey game and the games that have led up to it, but there have been *women* in my life — a long time ago, mind you, but in my life — with whom I've had less complicated and less involving relationships than I have now with Team Canada. Apprehension, dismay, pity, horror, pride, elation, shame, doubt, disgust, love, hate, birth, death, infinity . . . I've felt them all, and other emotions too, as the Canadians have lost, won, and tied on their road to today's game. This morning, as the game approaches, I'm mostly just hoping. I want them to win as much as I ever wanted any team to win anything, and it will be as impossible to tear me away from a television set today as it will be for the Russians to get Ron Ellis — oh, go *get* 'em, Ron — away from their magnificent winger, Valery Kharlamov.

What does all this say about me, or about one typical Canadian's reaction to this whole series? *I* don't know, for heaven's sake, but I do know I'm enjoying this sporting *event* as I do not remember enjoying very many protracted sporting events in my lifetime — it's Fischer-Spassky with *Canadians* in it! — and I only wish it could go on forever.

What really interests me, though, are the vagaries of my own emotions, for where sports are concerned I am not a particularly fickle fellow. That's me you hear cheering, however faintly, when the Toronto Argonauts of 1972, one of the greatest comedy acts since Frick and

Frack, make two consecutive first downs without a fumble. But with Team Canada . . . well, you may have heard me react on the air already.

Take game one, September 2 in Montreal, when the Soviets cleaned our clocks. With a lot of other people, my first reaction was to join in what at least one newspaper called a day of mourning in Canada, mourning for the myth that hockey was our game and ours alone. But at the same time, there was a kind of secret glee, a glee I didn't even recognize immediately, that the fatty-pants of the National Hockey League, who have been squeezing so many dimes for the past generation or so that their thumbprints now show tails and their index fingers heads, had finally got their come-uppance. And got it, furthermore, from a team with worn skates and helmets, whose players carry their own equipment. Even more than that, the bullies of the NHL had been outplayed in a way that a lot of us who used to play hockey thought *we* used to play hockey — which is hogwash, I happen to think, but makes nice contemplation — stickhandling, passing and sheer cleverness defeating brawn and big bellies. So *there*, all you guys who think you can get along without Bobby Hull, and who this year are going to have teams from Long Island and Atlanta skating into the same record books as Eddie Shore and Max Bentley and Howie Morenz and Lionel Conacher.

Except, if that was how we all really felt, what was that great wave of exultation that swept the country after the win in Toronto? Heaven knows — or *I* know, since I was lucky enough to be there — that we didn't beat them (notice it's "we" after a win) by finesse. We beat them with Wayne Cashman and Tony Esposito and the Mahovlich brothers, and Phil Esposito,

obviously out of shape, playing his wearying guts out to stay on top of or near those flying white sweaters.

The next two games, played as they were in the shadow of Munich, just didn't have that much impact. I guess by the time the Canadian part of the series had wound up, we all figured we'd been lucky to catch them once on the rebound from a win that had surprised even the Soviets in Montreal; that they were clearly the better team and that even when our guys got a goal or two ahead there was something inexorable about those unsmiling Russians, those names we are all learning so well but which yet have no real personalities to go with them — Kharlamov, Zimin, Lebedev, Petrov, Mikhailov, Yakushev — that there was something inexorable about them coming back and sticking it to you, and the trip to Russia was only a charade.

In the interim, of course, came Sweden. I said then and repeat now, that I was ashamed of Team Canada's conduct in Sweden. I can understand it, I suppose, as I think about it and think about the NHL players I know. The Europeans may not be as brutal as Canadian hockey players, but they are quite as capable of being dirty. There is something, in fact, almost endearingly naïve about the NHL's morality of violence. Like, you're not supposed to hurt anyone. Ankles you can slash, headbones you can beat on, and shoulders and elbows you can hurl to your heart's content, but spearing — that is, lifting the point of your stick blade and ramming it into someone's belly — can get you kicked out of the club. So when the Canadians met, as they apparently did meet, spearing and butt-ending — deliberate attempts to maim — from a team like the Three Crowns of Sweden, they retaliated with genuine, but open, anger. I can understand this, as I say, but I can't forgive it. When in Stockholm, I always say, do as sensible people do, and do not have your own ambassador calling you criminals.

Well, that was the low point in my love affair with Team Canada. I have absolutely no understanding of why I felt this way, or how I changed from a feeling of revulsion to one of total sympathy, but by the time they'd pulled into that three-nothing lead in the first Moscow game, they had me so far on their side that Eddie Johnson almost had to move over on the bench to make room for me. I guess a lot of it was the hockey itself. Sure, the Canadians were the cruder of the two teams, but if the extra ice surface, that extra width and the extra space behind the nets that we'd all been reading so much about, if it had any effect on the game at all, it was to equalize the two teams. Our guys actually looked better on the big, strange rink than they had on the smaller, familiar ones. The

real skaters, Henderson, Cournoyer, Gil Perrault — all those players seemed to have more options as they crossed the enemy blue line than to pass, shoot, or dump, and they were using those options. To me, and I may be a hopeless romantic here, it looked a little like the hockey I played as a kid, with far more stick-handling, far more passing, far faster, more wide-ranging play. I had simply been unable to buy the thesis that the NHL is now more reliant on bodily intimidation than it was in the days of Red Horner and Black Jack Sewart, and it did seem to me that I was now seeing, from Moscow, all those winter Saturday afternoons on the frozen ponds and rivers of Canada — the kind of hockey that, no matter how much the Soviets regiment our game and drill little automatic drop-passers, they will never be able to take away from us . . . not from me, anyway.

The hockey is, simply, superb, surely the best any of us has seen for years, if not ever. And no matter how we may deny it, the fact that the Canadians, as of this morning, still have a very real chance of winning it makes it all that much more exciting. Can they do it? Well, I sure as hell hope so. I guess what I *should* wish is for a win today and a tie on Thursday, so the whole series ends in a tie. But dammit, I don't. I like these guys too much. Come on, Phil. Come on, Bobby, and Paul and J.P. and Brad and Gary and Whitey and, most of all, come on you, Ken Dryden. Come on, *Canada*. All of us need a boost.

September 26, 1972

II

My first remarks this morning are to you, who were listening yesterday and who did not put your hands on the radio when I asked you to or did not turn on the headlights of your car. Those of us who did our part — and only we will ever know how important it was — those of us who did our part had to wait, because of you, until nineteen minutes and twenty-six seconds of the third period before our incantations took effect. I hope in future when this country calls upon you, you will respond as required. For those of us who did our part, of course, yesterday afternoon's hockey game was a very satisfying event; in fact, I wonder if I've ever seen Canadians quite as self-satisfied as they look and sound this morning. "From Russia with Glory," says the *Globe and Mail*, the same paper that, less than a month ago, after the Russians had beat

Team Canada in Montreal, said, in only slightly smaller type, "Canada Mourns Hockey Myth."

I can't get too upset about all this, you know. If there's any country anywhere that can afford a little self-satisfaction, surely we're it, and we might as well indulge ourselves – at least until the game against the Czechs tomorrow.

Yes, we won . . . or Team Canada won. We won the series. But we won it by a margin that couldn't have been narrower if we'd been trying to write a razor-blade commercial. And the Russians won too, you know; the Russians won a lot. We won on game points; they won total goals, 32-31. We won on dramatic finishes; they won on penalty minutes – thirty-one minors, two majors and one game misconduct. And please don't give me that stuff about biased referees. They were calling European rules and we were supposed to be playing by those rules. We won on colour; they won on sportsmanship.

I don't know if I have ever been as proud of another Canadian in my life as I have been through this whole series of Phil Esposito, a hockey player whose superstardom, in spite of the apparently infinite number of goals he scores, has always been questionable until this series. He did, after all, have Bobby Orr setting up those goals; he didn't appear to check much; he was what the kids call a goal suck . . . and so on. But not now. He must have played half that game yesterday, and he just never quit. He rallied that team by himself, he never stopped skating or checking or driving his teammates. He was, simply . . . well, I'm out of adjectives. I'd just like to salute him.

But let's think of some other names, and even on this day of national jubilation I see no reason not to mention them. Vic Hadfield, who took his puck and went home from Russia a few days ago because it looked as if coachie wouldn't let him play as much as he wanted to. Wayne Cashman, who gave a steady exhibition of everything that's wrong with Canadian professional hockey every time they let him on the ice. Alan Eagleson, the guy who wants all the credit for getting this series started, and who makes an ass of himself every time a television camera gets near him, and made a particular ass of himself yesterday right in the middle of the game. Way to go, Al.

I'm not trying to throw cold water here, you understand. If you've been listening at all this week you know there are few more passionate fans in all of Canada than I am . . . way to go, Paul Henderson. But somehow, yesterday, that passion was satisfied by Yvan Cournoyer's *tying* goal. That was enough. Team Canada had come back from behind 5-3, and now this superb series between two superb hockey teams – perhaps the greatest exhibition of the

world's greatest game ever staged – could end with a very appropriate draw. Much as I enjoyed Henderson's goal – and I leapt as high from my chair as anyone – it wasn't as *necessary* as the one he'd got before. Do you know what I mean here at all? Of course, if the Russians had scored with thirty-four seconds left, my heart would simply have broken, but the Russians didn't score; Paul Henderson scored, and we won the series, and that's fine.

Well, in a sense, we're all winners . . . all, of course, except the poor little rich men who still have to spend this winter trying to peddle games between the Atlanta Flames and the Minnesota North Stars to people who have seen the major leagues. Hockey has been given new life; Canada has been given a nice boost to its ego, and Phil Esposito, I hope, has been given a car.

September 27, 1972

Love Story

It is 5:45 A.M. A beautiful, late August Saskatchewan morning. A glance out the window. No one moves. No thing moves. A sleep-in day. Only birds sing a welcome to the bright-borning sun in the pristine prairie sky.

Wide awake, you are excited. The world is newing again, and the sun walks its reverse image up your bedroom wall, slowly.

Beside you is a warm woman. No girl. She is forty years old. Also: kindly, familiar and the mother of your seven children. In sleep, still trim and virginal after nineteen years of marriage.

Out loud, hoarsely, you hear yourself say, "Teen-age marriages are bound to fail! B.S.!" It is a snort. A comment. But a smiling one.

Somewhere from beneath a gentle blanket of sleep she hears you, stirs, and in stirring, arouses you. Lord! there are things you want to say to her . . . *things* you want to *do* with her! "Wake her," you tell yourself," . . . but gently."

Brown slavic eyes open slowly. Easily. They look at you and smile. Crinkly webbed and dawn-soft eyes only a generation from Budapest. How many generations from Atilla?

No words. Only a slow, natural melding of friends. And later, a cigarette and a cup of coffee, a question, asked playfully . . . "What do you think of Women's Lib?"

"You wake me up at quarter to six to ask me what I think of Women's Lib?"

"I guess that wasn't the real reason."

An outburst. Both of you collapse in laughter on the morning bed.

"Shhh . . . you'll wake the kids."

That in itself is cause for more giggling. Baritone-whisky-male, and silky-soft alto-female. Both of you know the kids would sleep through Armageddon.

V.E. Brooks
Regina, Saskatchewan

The Great Canadian Novel #'s 7 & 8

It begins in a small, western Canadian town. Our hero is growing up and having an average Canadian small-town childhood (for an average Canadian childhood, it is amazing how few people have had it). He works his way through college (University of Toronto). He gets a job as a salesman for a large American-based firm (IBM). He travels throughout Canada selling.

At the beginning he is a great company yes-man but through his experiences his identity — political, social and emotional — develops. He reaches a point where he can no longer be a lacky for American imperialism. He gets a job in a new, developing frontier town. Here he meets the woman, she is a teacher, who will be the love of his life. After a time (approximately three years) he goes back south. He accepts an offer to work in an advertising firm in Montreal. (Scenes of clever and witty satire dealing with Canada's favourite problem — English-French relations.)

During this time he meets some real FLQ-type people. Later when they are trapped in a house with a hostage, they ask that he be made their mediator. He gets much media exposure ("L'Anglais who understands the French" — Toronto *Star*). This obviously leads to an offer to run for Parliament. (Everything leads to that it seems.) He meets the girl again. She is going to the Maritimes to help organize the fishermen. Through her he is offered a similar job. Politics with fame and fortune or social commitment and love? He goes to a movie instead.

Laizer Kaminsky
Montreal, Quebec

Sometimes a Great Nation, or Pardon Me, Is This Seat Taken?

Author's note: This novel is written on several levels. Superficially, it is a thrilling love story which will ensure bestseller status. But that is not all. Every chapter, every page is filled with Canada's being — the burning issues of strikes, federalism, provincialism, bilingualism, differences in education, fashion and food between East, West and Center. Gestures become significant for students of Canada, mouthings become part of the fabric of the tale. (N.B. Various subtle methods are used to avoid libel actions.)

Justinius Beauregard, son of a Canadian prime minister, meets Miss Gloria Benefit, granddaughter of a western Canadian premier, when both are stranded by a strike in Toronto. True to Canadian tradition there is more talk than action in this novel. There are long discussions, sweetened by the knowledge that this is a love story. They talk of what Justin has learned at his aged father's knee regarding politics and the role of federalism. The girl is a little confused. She is, of course, attracted by the dashing youth with the charisma and receding hairline. However, as she heard the world described in Beautiful British Columbia by her grand-daddy, words like social credit, free enterprise and above all, provincial power, must be included.

Thus a dramatic day is spent at the airport, listening to reports of the strike. The two young protagonists alternately fall in love as naturally as the rain falls over B.C. and become enraged at each other's political dissertations. Wearied at last, and hungry, they decide to explore Toronto, hand in hand.

At last! They have found a subject on which they can agree – "Let's Hate Toronto!" Justin misses the old-world charm of La Poudrière, the elegant Francophone (ugh!) cabarets and restaurants, and Gloria misses her mountains at the end of every street and hates the "oldness" of Toronto.

In agreement and harmony at long last, they are able to spend a joyous and sensual night in a hotel, cut short only by a call from the airlines in the early morning of the following day. . . .

A poignant story – East meets West – loves and parts. They will never forget – but they could never go back. . . .

Mrs. Inge Bachrich
Vancouver, British Columbia

Absenteeism

A couple of weeks ago, my wife and I – the Sherlock Holmes and Dr. Watson of our neighbourhood – discerned a remarkable pattern of absenteeism from school between our two youngest sons. Every Tuesday morning, we noticed in retrospect, one of them (they were taking turns) had a stomach ache. Amazingly, these ailments cleared up by lunch time, and the ill one was able to go to school that afternoon. Holmes – my wife – was the one who solved this mystery. On Tuesday mornings, she noticed, one of the eight thousand television channels that are available to us since we got cable in our house, carries these fantastic monster movies. I wouldn't mind watching them myself, to tell you the truth. Still, one of the rules we try to enforce around our house involves levelling with other people, and the little guys seemed not to be doing that.

The odd Tuesday morning of missed school isn't going to hurt anyone, certainly. In fact, I'd imagine there are lots of monster movies that could teach you more than *anything* you could learn in a classroom. But it still doesn't seem to me a very good thing to . . . well, dodge the truth. Anyway, the two little guys who live at our house are going to school on Tuesday mornings now and all of us think it's kind of funny the way they tried not to.

It's also kind of funny, I suppose, that a number of school teachers, who live in the same part of the country as my kids and I and

Sherlock, have been taking action this week against their employers, the school boards, by calling in sick. To take just one example, there's one school in the Toronto area where, yesterday, fifty-eight of the 105 teachers didn't show up for work because of "illness." Whether they spent the day watching monster movies or not, I don't know. I do know quite certainly that they weren't sick, or not all fifty-eight of them, anyway. They are in the midst of negotiations with their employers – and, if this matters at all, I happen to think that their demands are nearly all justified – but they are not, or at least not all of those who are saying so, *sick*. What bothers me about what they're doing is how I'm going to be able to explain it to my two youngest sons next Tuesday morning. If the teacher can phone in to say he's got a stomach ache when he hasn't, why can't they? What's the *real* difference between watching horror movies and not being satisfied with your job?

There's a serious side to this too, I suppose. We pretend, all of us noble pursuers of the golden aims of education, that our schools aren't babysitting services. And for a lot of parents and a lot of children, of course, they aren't. But for a lot of others, whether we like it or not, they are. There are a great many working mothers, or single parents, who simply couldn't cope with things if their kids didn't have a place to go when they're not home. And if we were going to be perfectly straight about the whole thing, we'd also admit that there are a lot of children for whom school never has been and never will be anything other than some place to go between nine and three-thirty. And when, without notice, that service is simply cut off – because some teachers are "sick" – a lot of things go wrong.

is for urinal,
Winnipeg's pride,
In sub-zero weather
they'll bring it inside.

Sheila Cookson
West Vancouver, British Columbia

A lot of kids who show up at school will go home to empty or locked houses.

All of this is not meant to go against the fine liberal or whatever-it-is tradition of giving teachers the right to strike. If that's the only way they can bring about serious negotiation of their demands, fine, let them strike. But let them strike like anyone else. Or at the very least, let them have the guts to tell their students that the next day they're not going to come to work, and tell them why. Let them level with the people they're dealing with. Either that, I'd suggest, or could one of the teachers who's sick today please call my home and explain to my two youngest sons how come they can't watch *Godzilla Meets Frankenstein's Uncle* next Tuesday morning?

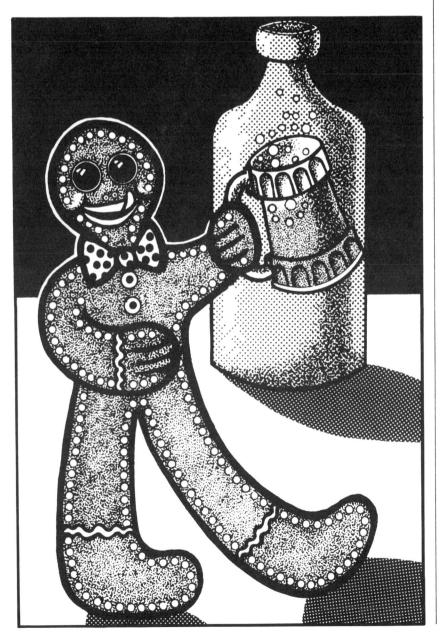

Some Fun Recipes

Ginger Beer

This recipe is rather experimental; therefore, be sure to read and consider the helpful hints following the recipe.

materials:
glass, plastic or crockery container holding at least 2 gallons, with an open top
bottles
bottle capper and caps, or corks
2 ounces ginger root or 3-5 ounces ground ginger
1 teaspoon cream of tartar
1 pound sugar, white or brown
1 teaspoon baker's yeast
1 lemon or lime
1 gallon boiling water

method:
Boil water. Bruise or chop ginger root.
Mix ginger, sugar, and cream of tartar in container.
Squeeze lemon/lime, add juice to mixture; grate peel of lemon/lime and add to mixture.
Add boiling water.
Let mixture cool to lukewarm (about 70 degrees F.); then add yeast and stir.
Let mixture sit in container in a warm, draught-free place while yeast works, stirring daily. After 2 days, ginger and lemon/lime may be strained off. After a total settling period of 7 to 10 days, or when the yeast has almost entirely stopped fermenting, strain or siphon the mixture and bottle.
Make sure cap is attached tightly.
Let bottles sit about 3 days in a cool place, away from people (in case bottles explode).
Serve very cold.

helpful hints:
If you don't strain the ginger and lemon/lime after 2 days, the beer will have a hotter, more "gingery" flavour.
Cream of tartar is a leavening agent, and one of our listeners suggests ¼ to ½ a teaspoon for a less fizzy beer.
Ground ginger is not as good as fresh. If you use it, remember that you don't need as much of it as fresh ginger; also remember that it cannot be strained, and consequently settles to the bottom of the bottles unless you siphon very carefully from the large container.
Fresh ginger can be bruised or crushed with a rolling pin.
The type of water used affects the taste of the beer. Fresh spring water is probably best

but tap water is quite acceptable.

If you use corks, be sure to tie them down or they'll pop. Corks are not as good as bottle caps because they let in more air.

Don't use the white pith of lemon/lime – it gives the beer a bitter taste.

Don't use returnable bottles or bottles with screw caps; they aren't strong enough and may explode.

If you want a more alcoholic beer, add 1 teaspoon sugar per bottle as you bottle the beer.

You can save a "mother" for starting your next batch, as with sourdough bread or vinegar. When you siphon liquid into bottles, keep hose off bottom. Stir this, then pour into a glass container, cap loosely, and refrigerate. Use this for your yeast in the next batch.

Don't use brewer's yeast from a health-food store. It's "dead." Brewer's yeast probably isn't very good in any case because it ferments too strongly for ginger beer.

One of our listeners uses ½ envelope or ⅔ tablespoon of baker's yeast in her recipe.

If the beer turns out bitter, mix with a cheap sparkling wine to make a good punch.

Honey would probably be better than sugar, but more expensive.

Ann Greer, with hints from Sal Herrick, Phil Laflame, Peter Powning, Gavin Guppy and Freda Hanmer

Tommy Thompson's Raspberry Liqueur

Use a clean 25- or 26-ounce bottle with a screw top.

Fill the bottle with at least one pint of *unwashed, uncrushed* raspberries. (Berries should be fully ripe.)

Add one cup of granulated sugar (or sugar to taste if you prefer it sweeter or tarter).

Fill the bottle with drinking alcohol (or vodka) from your liquor store.

Cap the bottle and shake it once a day until all the sugar dissolves (usually takes 4–5 days).

Wait at least two months and then decant the liqueur.

Holiday Punch

3 cups of orange-pineapple juice
3 cups of Rosy Red Canned Juice
1 large bottle each of: Canada Dry Wink
    Collins mix
    club soda
    ginger ale
1 26-ounce bottle of Myer's Planters Punch Rum
1 lemon
1 lime

Place all liquids in a large bowl with ice. Thinly slice the lemons and limes and float on top.

Carole with an E:

1 ounce of Canadian Rye Whisky
¼ ounce (or a dash – to taste) of Southern Comfort
4 to 5 ounces of orange juice
1 dash of Grenadine

Shake with ice and serve with *crushed* ice in a tall glass and sip with a straw.

Carole Collins

**Strawberries in Champagne
(4 to 6 servings)**

Stem a quart of large strawberries.
Do not wash; rinse with white wine (so the berries won't get watery).
Sprinkle with brandy or cognac.
Chill.
Before serving, sprinkle with sugar.
At the table, pour champagne over the berries and serve at once.

Sherried Grapefruit

Cut grapefruit in half and section.
Pour in just enough sherry to be level with tops of sections.
Sugar to taste and serve chilled. Or, cover each sherried grapefruit half with 2 tablespoons brown sugar and dot with ½ teaspoon butter.
Place under broiler until lightly browned; serve hot.

Danish Style Paté

Grind together: 1 pound fresh lean pork
1 pound pork liver
on the finest blade of your meat grinder. If you want it fine, grind it more than once.
add:
salt and pepper to taste
¼ teaspoon powdered thyme
2-3 tablespoons very finely chopped parsley
2 eggs, beaten well
2 ounces brandy
and mix well

Line bottom of paté tin or loaf pan with strips of bacon.
Put meat mixture on to the bacon, cover with more strips of bacon.
Pour 2 ounces dry sherry over the bacon.
Cover the tin tightly with foil.
Bake in 350 degree oven for 2 hours.
If you want the top browned remove the foil after 1½ hours.

Peter Cochrane

Crème Brûlée Québécoise

⅔ cup molasses
2 cups milk
3 tablespoons cornstarch
1 teaspoon almond flavouring
whipped cream

Heat molasses until it has a faint odour of burnt sugar and is slightly caramelized (about 275 degrees F.)
Meanwhile prepare a blanc-mange: gradually blend milk into cornstarch in a saucepan. Cook over medium heat, stirring constantly, until mixture thickens. Cover and simmer gently, 5 minutes more.
Gradually add caramelized molasses to milk mixture; heat and stir until blanc-mange becomes smooth. Add almond flavouring. Strain, if desired. Pour into serving dishes. Garnish with whipped cream.

Jocelyne Gauvin

Peter Gzowski's Ten Rules for Playing Golf If You've Never Played Golf Before

Rule One

Unless you know of a totally vacant golf course this summer, don't play at all until you've gone to a driving range for half an hour or so at least once and preferably several times. If there are no driving ranges around where you live, borrow a club or two and several old balls and bat them around a field or a meadow. Hitting a golf ball is a very pleasant thing to do, but it is not a natural act, and it is one you should at least learn the elements of before you clutter up a course.

Rule Two

Take lessons before you play if you can, for the reasons outlined in rule one. Get some good habits before you get bad ones. If you can't afford or can't find a pro, get a simple book. If you can't find one of those, remember at least these simple but very important principles of swinging a golf club. Keep your left arm straight—this is assuming you swing right-handed—and your right elbow down. Swing *through* the ball, instead of hitting *at* it. Try to get some rhythm into your swing, moving your weight back on to your right leg as you bring the club back and, turning your hips, shift it to the left leg as you swing.

Rule Three

The most common fault of all novice golfers is lifting the head before you hit the ball. Do not commit this fault. Keep your head down and your eyes on the ball, from the moment you begin your backswing until the ball is in the air.

Rule Four

When you do get to a course, don't get all duded up with too many clubs or too much fancy equipment. Rent, or borrow, a driver, a three wood, irons numbered three, five, seven and nine (the higher the number, the more the club will loft the ball) and a putter. Buy a new ball or two to make you feel good but, if you're brand new, you're probably going to lose a ball or two every round, so stick a few old ones in your bag before you go. Don't worry about spiked golf shoes. They're important to George Knudson, but all you need is something comfortable, with soft soles.

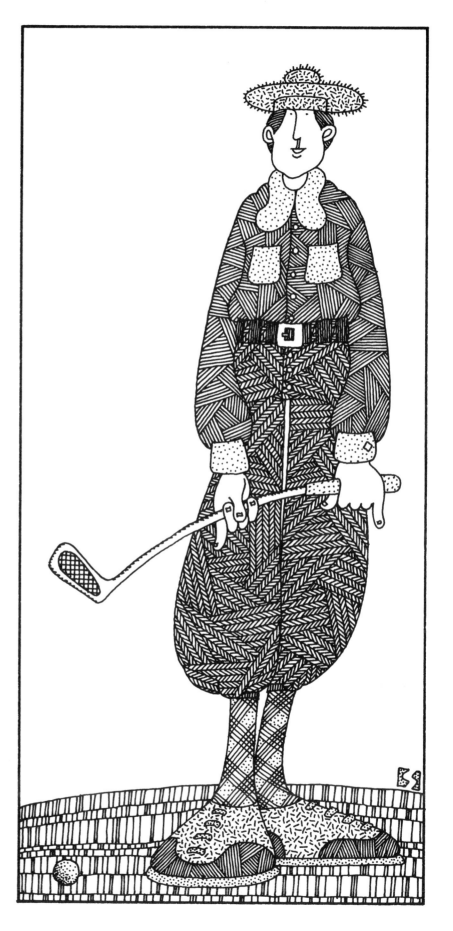

Rule Five

Golf is a game of etiquette. You can spoil other people's pleasure by, for instance, talking when they're hitting, moving when they're putting, failing to help them look for lost balls, failing to replace the divet you've just ground out of the fairway, or, as a novice, dickering your way up a fairway when better players are waiting behind you. Learn at least these principles and abide by them.

Rule Six

If, as you probably will be, you're playing with someone who is much better than you are, don't try to emulate him. If your partner hits one 280 yards off the first tee, don't try to outdrive him . . . that's a few years away yet. Just keep your ball in play, in the middle of the fairway. If he hits a five iron to the green, don't use the same club. Use your three wood.

Far more novices beat themselves by having what golfers call too little club – don't worry about these terms, they'll come to you – than having too much. Don't worry about your score either. One of the pleasures of golf is that you're really competing, as a novice at least, against yourself. If you shoot 193 on your first day, then a good 180 the second is a victory.

Rule Seven

Forget that last hole. Golf is a very mental game, and if you're upset because you put three in a row out of bounds on the sixth hole, you'll probably hit two more out of bounds on the seventh. Give yourself a few putts, too . . . which means conceding to yourself a putt within, say, three feet of the hole. Putting is an art, and it will come to you with time. It is the most subtle part of the game – drive for show, putt for dough, as golfers say – but it can be frustrating too, and if missed putts bother you, don't let them.

Rule Eight

Whatever you heard earlier about conceding yourself short putts, do not cheat. Golf is a game of honour. If you ground your club in a sandtrap, for instance – meaning dig it into the sand behind the ball as you're addressing it – there's a penalty. Add it to your score. If you don't, you won't remember to do it later, when scores will begin to count to you. Besides which, if you do take the penalty, you won't ground your club the next time you play, and there's one stroke saved right there. Remember, as a beginner, it's your own earlier rounds you're trying to beat. Not the person walking beside you.

Rule Nine

By now, you'll be getting all kinds of advice from other golfers. Bend your left knee more. On your grip, try to keep the V formed by the thumb and forefinger of your left hand pointed at your right shoulder; take the clubhead back more slowly, and on and on unto the nineteenth hole. Accept most of this advice. Some of it may help, and it will at least make the person who gives it to you feel good. Keep experimenting until you find a swing, based on good solid fundamentals – keep that head *down*, I said – that suits your age, condition, suppleness, strength and ambition.

Rule Ten

Enjoy yourself. I gave up golf myself several years ago, because I realized that, without the time to practise the way I used to when I was a hot young teenage prospect, I would never break 80 again. Then, this spring, I went out and played a round just for the hell of it. It was marvellous. I even cracked out a couple of good drives. You will too, maybe even on the first day you play. It's a feeling not to be missed.

Vic Dardick.
Box 321 High Level, Alta.
Oct 26 - 72

Dear Peter.

I want to thank you for prasing my letter and reading it on the air. I am sorry to say I did'nt hear it but my Father and several athers have. I was welding in the Locall welding shop when my Father tor in thare shaking my hand and congradulating me he was as happy as a kid at Christ Mass. I must admit I was supprised to say the least. I shure would like to have heard how you got around all them spelling misstakes and everrything I thinck you should be Congratulated on being abeul to read it. I got som letters from people across Canada and they wont me to write more. Tell me Peter do you thinck you could batel your way thaew a nother letter

I won't be abule to write to you about oure wild stalion eny more. Last winter was a tuff one with four (4) feet of snow and steady cold wether of 30 to 47 below for 2 months

His old mair did'nt make it but this spring we saw him and his 2 year old son come out of the bush into our hay field and we wer verry happy that the old boy had an hair to his thron for he surly was a King a thrill just to watch him run with his long main and tail flying in the wind holding his head high defying enyone to catch him. His colt was a carbon coppy of him and it was beutiful

Well like everry whare in this world thare has to be a mean hartles person who can not stand beutyfy beuty or can not see it only that this wild thing might cost him money and it might tramp doun some of his presus crop so he had to shoot this noble animal and his Colt,

Thare are tears in my eyes as I write this not that other weld howes havent been shot in this cuntry but he was one of the verry last. Because he was to clever to be snared or traped he had to be shot Never again will you or I see sutch a thing of beuty a linck from the past when thowsands of sutch noble animals romed this erth wild and free.

3

Can you tell me why Peter Why?
Maybe I am to emotionl to think ther things out clealy But that old horse was seen hear 18 years ago. Years befor most of these homestedero arived. Was it the horses falt that we cleard the land and planted rich crops whare he used to run free?

So sorry I have sutch a sad letter to write.

Yours truly
Vic Dardick

P.S.
I wonder if it is possable for you to send me a recording of you reading that first letter. I will gladdy pay anything for it

Jane Kennedy

Before we leave this morning, I'd like you to meet a truly remarkable person. Her name is Jane Kennedy and she is forty-six years old; she is a nurse, and a deeply, even radically committed, Roman Catholic. If there is a line Jane draws between what she believes and the way she lives, it is difficult to find.

Jane is an American, and until 1969, she had taught nursing at three major universities and was working and teaching in Chicago. She had been deeply moved by the street actions in that city the year before, and by the Vietnam war. In late 1969 she was involved in a complex anti-war demonstration — the details aren't important here except to say that she has already served fourteen months in jail for a part of the action, and for all I know she was not directly involved in the other. Not long ago, I taped several hours of conversation with Jane, and I propose to play some excerpts from my talks with this gentle, kind, good woman because I think it is impossible to know her without thinking a bit about the way you look at yourself, about who you are, or, if you are like me at all, to wonder about the difference in your own life between what you say and what you do.

PG: How did you become an activist?

JK: I really had to decide whether my life was talk or action. Back in 1965, I had a friend who was infinitely more involved in the political scene in Chicago and the issues than I was, although I could talk as well as he about them. One day he said to me, "Jane, you talk like a good liberal, but what are you going to do?" The words weren't profound but they reached me inside and that's when I knew I'd either have to become what I call an unprivate person in relation to social issues, or I would just have to recognize myself as a phoney. But it wasn't just was I a phoney or wasn't I; it wasn't that superficial. It was what do I really care about, what's my responsibility in life and what does it mean to live a life? It's just so clear to me; you are what you do. For instance, if your business is talking, then it's very important what you talk about, with whom you talk, what you say and how you say it; that's behaviour in your occupational role. Behaviour for me is what kind of nurse I am, certainly what kind of woman I am, and how I can act out of love for fellow human beings. Maybe I have such a commitment to my fellow human beings in the aggregate because I am not married and have no children. I wouldn't say it's an either/or proposition; but some of us can only love in the aggregate and perhaps my capacity to love is broader than a family kind of thing.

PG: What do you think triggered other activists in the last few years? What gave "the movement" its momentum?

JK: I think that something different has happened, at least in the States, since the middle of the sixties. There's a difference in kind in the questions people must ask now. You have to ask, what's the world like for those on the bottom of the pile, what's it like for the contemporary leper, although, I suppose, over time, who is leper changes.

I remember during the 1968 Democratic convention in Chicago, when I was on the streets with the medical committee, I came across a whole group of young people absolutely bombed out on drugs, not just a little spaced out, but apparently utterly destroyed mentally. Hardly anyone would go close to them and when they talked about the police beating them, nobody would believe them. If they said they had a funny feeling in their head it was always translated into drug symptoms; nobody would believe that they might have been clobbered on the head with a stick and have some actual physical injury. I got very involved in getting one of them into a hospital because of his head injuries. His gang came to visit him there, all of them dressed beautifully, that is to say, outlandishly. The whole hospital would stop and stare at them, some half bombed, as they marched through the corridors. During his entire stay this boy was never taken seriously and his friends, though not actually put out of the hospital, knew they were not welcome.

Well, I had to ask why these young children were treated this way. Don't they have a right to dress any way they wish? Why look upon them as though they don't belong to the human race? Why, most especially, not believe them? Why say it's all from taking dugs? They needed medical care for things like hepatitis and the other real problems of being on drugs; they needed people to be available to them if they wanted to get off drugs, and yet no one ever was. They were lepers. And of course, in the States, another question we have to ask all the time has to do with Black people, who were slaves for so long and many of whom are still treated like slaves. They're also lepers.

I think you know the questions to ask. But it seems to me there's a limit to what a single individual can accomplish in attempting, for instance, to provide health care for the drug lepers. So I suppose I began to realize that my responsibility was to ask other people to look for themselves, to ask them if they too couldn't see the inadequacies of our society. It seemed important to turn to others and say, Hey, this just won't do, this isn't human; look what we're doing to one another. I don't do it because I believe I'm a great social analyst; I don't pretend to be that. I do it out of a conviction about who my brothers are: you are, so is the Black man and woman, so are the guys and gals on drugs and so are my fellow prisoners. I'm an ancestor of God; you're an ancestor of God; all human beings are ancestors of God and it's that deity we share together. That's the beauty of humanity and it's out of that theological conviction that I ask questions and get answers and then act.

PG: Then, in a sense, that conviction put you in prison?

JK: I was in prison for conspiracy to destroy Dow Chemical company property, scrambling information on magnetic tapes stored in their tape library in Michigan. Later, at a parole-board hearing, they asked if I'd do that again, and I said it would depend on the whole tone and atmosphere of this society when I got out and until then I wouldn't know; I was taking the question seriously. I didn't think that was such a big deal; I was telling the truth. As it turned out, they gave me an eighteen-month flop; the appeal was denied. Nor would I have an opportunity to make another appeal — this is medieval — for eighteen months. I wrote to the parole-board chairman and asked him why my parole had been denied, pointing out that my fellow conspirators, as we're called, were allowed out after serving nine months. The gentleman wrote back and said, we thought it over very carefully and decided that you are a menace to society; we can't let you go because you couldn't tell us you wouldn't do it again. Well, I got very angry because I'd told them the absolute truth.

It all has to do with change, how society changes, how you get it to change and how you can help people to think what it means to kill Vietnamese and to kill Australians and to kill guys from the United States and maybe Canada. What I did was direct, non-violent action, which has great symbolic value. It's very possible that I will commit a non-violent act again. Now, whether or not the parole board would interpret that as social or anti-social behaviour, I really don't know. It's a funny country that would put us in jail for scrambling information on magnetic tapes and call that destruction of property, while it would do nothing to stop human carnage. It's an incredibly sick society that has that kind of value system. So who knows what I might do again?

PG: Would you tell me about being in prison?

JK: As you go through the process of orientation in prison you really don't believe you've turned into a number, that you're no longer a person. But it comes to you very quickly that other people in the prison believe that. I had been there about twenty-four hours when they called some of us to the clinic for vaginal smears and blood tests. The nurse lined us up, programmed us into the examining room, then tossed us out very quickly, but it seemed as though she had an insult for each one of us. With some of the women, those in for prostitution, she would talk about their actual physical dirt; she told them they needed to get a Brillo brush to scrub themselves in the most intimate places. She asked me what I was doing there and when I told her, I got a "You should be ashamed of yourself, you don't belong here" kind of comment. I was whipped out of the room rather quickly. But every one of us came out of that examination having been chastised in some way, having been talked to like children, and bad children at that. It was incredible to watch.

I watched these women, listened to their comments and watched their reactions, because it's very important to learn how to react in prison. Most of them wore very blank faces, so you knew that, whatever they felt, they weren't going to share it with you. But you also knew that meant you shouldn't share anything either. Somehow, that would involve penalties, and I suppose that was prophetic of how you're supposed to behave in prison. You're not supposed to react as a human being; you're supposed to absorb it all, except what's said to you by prison personnel, and not ever respond with any kind of human feeling. Oh, I get so angry when I talk about this! You don't really understand what the totality of prison is all about for maybe three months or so, and then you begin to understand the true awfulness of prison.

Health care was a particular bugaboo of mine; many women in prison today have drug-related problems, so hepatitis is a real problem. I remember that two gals who had hepatitis were put in the clinic, which has very primitive facilities, where they stayed until they were very jaundiced and had very high fevers. Finally, when they were very, very sick, they were transferred to a city hospital. But in the meantime they knew how sick they were, knew they were not being given adequate care and were absolutely terrified about whether the prison was going to let them die.

That's a very real question for all prisoners because you know they don't care about you; you know that you've been converted into a number so that they don't have to respond to you as a human being. That's the terrible evil about prison. I can say that I had never been what you would call an oppressed person until I became a prisoner. I never had the faintest idea what oppression meant, but that was all taken care of in prison. The prisoners are a truly oppressed group in our society; I don't say it's the only one, but it is indeed oppressed. As an oppressed group we generate so very much anger and what do you do with anger? Ordinarily, you would go to the person who caused it and try to get it straightened out, but you can't do that in prison. We're not allowed to speak like that; if you raise your voice you may very well get yourself put in solitary.

PG: You were put in solitary for doing exactly that, weren't you?

JK: I tried to change conditions in the dental lab where I was first put to work for a sadistic dentist. Things became very difficult for all of us working there and we decided we simply could not go on in that way; we could no longer work with this dentist and would have to tell the superintendent that. So we met with the nurse who was our supervisor, and then we wrote a letter to the superintendent, saying, we wish to talk to you immediately about an impending problem that has quite bad ramifications in the dental lab. That was on Friday. The following Tuesday, the supervisor came into the lab at 9:30 and said, "Everybody to the punishment cottage" – apparently, although they didn't tell us so, because we had written the letter to the superintendent. He thought we were threatening him. I said I wouldn't go; I would not voluntarily walk to the punishment cottage when I hadn't done anything. They called five male guards and we had a long talk. Finally I went limp on them, and when they picked me up, one of the nice guards said, "Please don't do this to us, please don't do this to us; just walk down there and talk to the person when you get there." I thought, oh well, it's true, I can't do this to these guys; they don't have anything to do with it, they're only the guards. So all six of us walked down together and they took me before the deputy superintendent.

He had two letters before him. One was the letter we had sent to the superintendent, in which I said I understood he had been discouraging priests from visiting me and that he mustn't dare do that again. He asked why I hadn't signed my name to that letter and I said, "Which letter are you talking about?" to which he said, "You two-bit revolutionary, to the hole." I replied, "You mean the dungeon," because we have a dungeon. He said, "No, back there." I said okay and thought, I've got to act rapidly now, went out of the room and sat down. I wasn't going to walk there; I was so determined not to walk to a punishment I didn't deserve. So they got the guards who just took me under the arms and dragged me along about fifty feet and put me in one of those little cells.

The superintendent apparently got a lot of flack about that. People wrote to him about the question of brutality and he had to be responsive to the press on that. He even sent a man down to talk to me about whether or not there was brutality and so forth. That was one thing I did. It's an example of how prisons treat you like a number and not a human being. Unfortunately, a lot of prisoners have had all that nonsense all their lives. But it seems to me that society is a lot healthier when its members refuse to be turned into unfunctioning non-human beings. I think it's not within our human dignity to allow ourselves to be oppressed like that. I am very proud when people decide they are going to act in a non-violent way and say so to that kind of nonsense.

PG: Doesn't that "nonsense" turn all that anger you were talking about into hate?

JK: I can't hate anyone now. I can understand and I can say change, you must change, you must change what you're doing, which is what I did with the superintendent at the prison. I can't hate anyone responsible for the system, because for me, to say that you and your system are responsible is an absolute cop-out. It's my system and I am responsible, perhaps not as responsible as the head of an organization or the president of a country or the members of Congress, but certainly very responsible for that system, that ugly system. It's part of why I have to work; that's my system that I must change, change radically. I can't say, I'm good but all the rest of it and those guys out there are lousy – I can't say that because we are all equally responsible for what we live with. I am as responsible for the war in Vietnam as any president of the United States. It's my war, they're my dead; anyone who is napalmed is napalmed just as much through my inability to change things as by the airplane pilot who drops the bombs. It's a question of whether or not I take responsibility, and I do.

Why would heads of government, legislators, even heads of corporations, change things, change policies, except for the demands of a mass of people? How can you get the mass of people to demand change, to take responsibility for their lives, to act as a group unless we all say to one another, look at what we're doing – we must change. There are corporate responsibilities, and here I mean corporate in the sense of national, although I don't approve of nationalism – I think that's awful – but I think there is corporate national responsibility of the people. For me to say I believe anything less just wouldn't be true, and I believe just as absolutely that each of us has within him the capacity to live a slightly better life than he is now. I know that we can do better, I just know it.

But it's for each man to see it for himself; it's not enough to sit down and feel guilty and suffer all that anguish. We don't have to make everything perfect, it's a cop-out to say, I can't really make it the way it should be so I won't bother. We can, I know we can.

PG: What does religion mean to you?

JK: That's a funny word these days. I get my ideas of brotherhood from religion, but not from going to church, not from participating in a ritual or inspiring dogma, not from saying five hundred novenas and all that phoney stuff, but from living my concept of brotherhood. I know that life, in part, is living our own heaven or our own hell, and I know that if Christ said anything he said love one another as I love you, and that's kind of special. It's a question of living your love and living your dignity and, I suppose, it's also sort of a risk-taking. Do I like to live a safe life, always doing the safe thing, always doing the socially acceptable thing, or do I open myself up to some new ideas every once in a while? Do I try new ways, do I really listen to somebody, not with my mind all tense to guard against their ideas, but open and risky? That's what religion means to me. It's not a bunch of Hail Mary's or Our Father's.

I'll tell you a story about religion in the prisons. We were expected to stand before each meal and say either an Our Father or the Catholic, Bless us, oh Lord, for these thy gifts. You must understand that prison food is very poor and sort of an unappetizing gray, and one day — the women were feeling their oats — someone said, "We can't say Bless us, oh Lord, for these thy gifts, because this food isn't a gift from the Lord; the Lord wouldn't be seen dead with food like this." So it was decided that we wouldn't say prayers before meals unless it was, Lord, have mercy on us.

Usually the matron in charge at meals just sort of stood there, sometimes making us repeat the usual prayer if it sounded too ragged, but the night we recited Lord, have mercy, the matron said, "Wait just a minute; nobody sit down until you've said a proper prayer." So we just stood there for at least a minute and a half of silence, which is a long time, until she said, "All right, ladies, I have until eleven o'clock tonight to hear your prayer and you'll stand there that long or until you say the prayer." Finally, one woman mumbled, "Bless us, oh Lord, for these thy gifts which we are about to receive, Amen," and sat down. The rest of us started to sit down too but the matron made us stand again until, one by one, we gave in. Finally, four people recited the prayer in unison and she let everyone sit down. We finished a very lumpy meal. Now that's a sham; it's a sham to force people to say prayers like that. If you don't leave prison an atheist, I just don't think you will ever be an atheist.

One of the problems with religion as I see it, is that we are living with concepts, some of which belong to centuries past and others belonging to today's world, so we have that awful clash of the two. Today's heaven is not something you buy with good ideas. My concept of heaven is being able to say yes, to affirm life; that's heaven. Hell is not something we go to after death because we have been bad or evil or ugly or selfish or all of those things many times over. Hell is living with power and wanting power and wielding power over other men and saying no to a spiritual affirmation of life. Hell is sending men into war; hell is making sure that some people get a rotten education so they can't get a job. Heaven and hell are not for the future, they're for the present. Two or three centuries ago, life was pretty rugged and religion promised people a better world, but the better world was later, always in the future. One of the things that the new culture brings us is the insistence that we live now. When you translate that into Man and God and their relationship, you have to talk about heaven and hell in the present tense. What lives after we die are our actions. That's partially why action is so very important. I don't mean acting in order to run away; I mean acting in order to affirm, taking action that affirms the present. It's saying something special about the present: it says yes, the present is to be known, is to be felt. I guess what I'm saying is that the concepts of religion are there because they made sense to the men of that day. We have had this awful lag with religious concepts — religion has the validity of the past. Religious concepts have validity only if they relate to today's world. If I'm going to take my life seriously I must affirm the present; I must affirm my own humanity.

Harry Bruce on a Sure Sign of Summer

He's thirteen now and getting a trace of a moustache and, hey, he says, why don't we go out to the park and throw the old ball around? It was snowing the other day and the leaves of the trees are still closed but he's got the black infielder's glove, the one I bought him back in Ontario six years ago, and he's popping the ball in and out of the pocket, and it is as obvious as though God Himself had made the announcement that springtime has taken over the world.

I say, okay, but I get the good glove.

No way, he says, you get the cheesy one.

I never get the black one. It's a Cooper. It has tough, brown, leather lacing. Thousands of smacking catches, and dozens of tender applications of the animal grease we used to know as "dubbin," have given his glove a worn and super-pliant pocket. You can't read the words in the pocket anymore but, along the little finger, you can just make out "Professional Model." It's a Pee Wee Reese among gloves, but it's his; and I have to settle for the little Eaton's Truline, made in Japan.

Actually, it's not bad, I bought it only last summer for our youngest kid's fifth birthday. At least, that's why I *said* I was buying it. He doesn't get to use it too much. It has only two flaws; it's too small for me, and it's bright blue with white trim.

We arrive at the park. It's on a hill and, behind the thirteen-year-old, the moving blue of the Northwest Arm glitters and dances. I can feel a cold ocean breeze but the sun is strong on my face, and his first throw is high and hard, and I have to jump and make a backhand stab to snag it. Ouch! That's a tough way to catch a ball, with a little blue, Japanese glove with an undeveloped pocket.

I withdraw my steaming and winter-softened hand from the glove and examine it. He's laughing. I unleash my fluid, snakelike side-arm — Ewell Blackwell style — and, trying to put a real hop on the ball, I let him have it. Letter high, on the outside. He plucks it out of the air with the old black Cooper. He is supremely nonchalant. *He doesn't even move his feet.*

After a while his control improves and we settle into a kind of rhythm. Thwack! Pock! Thwack! Pock! Over to you. And back to you. Thwack! We don't say much but if you have never played catch with someone — alone in an empty field as the sun slides down through a long afternoon towards the promise of all the hotter days to come — there may be something you do not know about wordless communication.

He's got a good arm on him, and he doesn't seem even to know that, sometimes, there's a little hook on the ball as it spins and takes a grip on the springtime air about ten feet ahead of me. He doesn't know, until I tell him, that there's more *weight* in the ball, as it hits my glove, than there was even last October. When he was still twelve.

He doesn't know that, if he wants to, if he keeps on throwing, it is inevitable that he will get stronger and better; and that, in the long run, no matter what I want, I will get weaker and worse. Still, the sting in my hand feels very good, as good as it felt a quarter of a century ago, and I know he's feeling good, and that summer is back in our blood. A baseball can tell you things like that.

is for vicious,
the Canadian weather,
Driving many a man
to the end of his tether.

Lynn Abrahamson,
Carl and Peter Buehler,
Howard Karslake
Saskatoon, Saskatchewan

Andrew Allan on British Columbia

It's a hundred and eighty years since that doughty fur-trader, Alexander Mackenzie, reached the Pacific Ocean overland from Canada. In 1793, the cluster of settlements far in the East, which were all that Mackenzie meant when he said "Canada," were a lifetime away from the Pacific. Those mountains and great trees on the eastern side of Marco Polo's ocean were another world altogether.

I rather think they still are.

Speaking personally, I know I always experience a distinct "land change" when I go to British Columbia. In the days when we all went by train, the "land change" felt even stronger, because it had had time to sink in. We'd been through the Lake Superior country and the Lake Winnipeg country and that great sea of the prairies. And we had nudged our way through range beyond range of the surging Rockies — Mountains of the Moon, we thought — until we came to learn, later, that the moon simply cannot compete.

As you came down the Fraser, you began to smell the burning slag, and you knew you had come to the Pacific. The air was different and the light was different. It was, as I said, another world altogether.

Nowadays, when you come in by plane, although you haven't had time for the "land change" to sink in, your surprise is even greater. Because you haven't been able to prepare, you're going to need time for your system to accommodate itself. There is a feeling of space around you — and, perhaps, a less frantic air about people you meet. "Making a living" isn't enough. "Living" is the thing.

The first time I came to the lower mainland of B.C. and to Captain Vancouver's island, I didn't come overland from Canada at all. I came by sea from the South Pacific. I was six years old. Our little family had been brought from Australia — by New Zealand and Fiji and Hawaii — in a spanking new liner called *Niagara*. Twenty-nine years later, when (to my surprise and delight) I was back in Vancouver living and working, I saw the *Niagara* again . . . no longer spanking new, but drab in war paint. She was loading Canadian soldiers for Hong Kong.

What our little family had done was to reverse old Mackenzie — but with a modern convenience he never even dreamed about. We came overland from the Pacific to the fur-trader's Canada by rail. That was the railway that so many people had said never would be built — but without which the Dominion never would have stretched from sea to sea.

Because of those mountains, perhaps, and because of something "heady" in the air, British Columbia will always have an attitude distinctly its own. Years ago somebody wrote a book about B.C., and it was called (if my memory holds) *A Million Miles from Ottawa*. Having worked on that coast myself, I can tell you those astronomical miles can be a benefit. You have to do things on your own, and in your own way — and that's good.

Even with air transport and quick communications, the mountains are a good protection. The "land change" still occurs.

Back in the days when sleight-of-hand financing and Paul Bunyan labour were getting that railway built, they had a phrase about British Columbia. They called it "The West beyond the West."

It still is, you know.

Playgirl

March 15, 1974

Peter:

Just a further thought on your conversation in Thunder Bay concerning *Playgirl* magazine and the possible effects of nude studs on the women and menfolk.

I can't believe that four times this morning I actually heard you ask three guys, "What does it do to your head" to see photos of naked men?

I mean, come on, Peter! This is 1974! And *Playgirl* and *Playboy* and *Venus* and *Gallery* are *not* some amazing social change or stunning reflection of our time. They're crumby buck magazines with four-colour pictures of fantasy figures: reclining ladies tickling themselves with feather dusters and goose-pimpled guys tippy-toeing in icy mountain streams.

Perhaps the only thing worthy of amazement is that it's taken twenty years to get down to the pubic hair. A striptease that went on for two decades! But to pretend amazement at the photos? They're only people! And pictures! In a buck magazine! To take home and look at if you feel like it!

What kind of quivering neurotic would feel threatened by his wife gazing at a four-colour center-fold? What kind of jellybean mentality lives in fear some center-fold stud will make his own plumbing pale in comparison? What kind of dingbat cares what his neighbourhood newsdealer thinks of his sexuality if he buys a copy of *Playgirl*?

Shades of Victoriana! Buying *Playgirl* will grow hair on your palms! My wife is in the kitchen with the vibrator while the tuna casserole burns! Impotence! Sexual dysfunction! A useless, burned-out hulk at age thirty-three! No one will take me to bed because I don't smell of four-colour offset ink!

Come on.

Much more interesting, in my view, would have been a discussion of the social rather than the sexual implications of the flesh magazines. Rather than an opening-up of social attitudes (censorship, freedom of the press), isn't it a constriction? Rather than going out, as in days of yore, and getting my own first-hand glimpses of what naked buttocks look like, I withdraw to my home, dollar magazine in hand, and take — third-hand — some New York editor's two-dimensional version. It's easier. It's cheaper.

Don't the increasing number of photo layouts involving twosomes and synthetic sex acts say something about voyeurism and withdrawal? It isn't a question of self-image or measuring yourself against *Playgirl's* fantasy-figure. As in second-hand sports on television and the growth of spectatorship in all forms, it says *something* about a growing inclination not to risk yourself in social or personal relationships.

It's Orwell, Peter, where life becomes artifice.

Most important, the new nude magazines are in the same class as under-the-counter sex novels or love pulps for ladies. The need they fill is for people who by choice or circumstances do *not* have the real thing. It's *singles* who buy *Playboy* and *Playgirl* — as the business-minded publishers know only too well.

That the nudies have such phenomenal mass-market circulations says something not about our sexuality, but about our withdrawal, our loneliness, our existential outlook. It's a reflection of how alienated and unfulfilled many of us are in an age when communication is supposedly readily available and sexuality is finally free, free, free.

In short, rather than a sniggering shock or shame, the mass *readership*, rather than the magazines themselves, should prompt a certain sadness.

Love and intimacy and sex do not come in four-colour fold-outs. And nobody ever charged me a buck.

Gary Dunford
Combermere, Ontario

Remembrance

The leaves are gone now, and the nip of frost is in the air. In Ottawa, the veterans and the war widows and assorted citizens will be gathering around the Cenotaph for the annual ritual of Remembrance Day. The day always manages to be cruelly cold, with a wind that freezes the trumpeter's fingers and blows the crowd into huddled groups like remnants of a defeated army.

Will Miss Wingard be there again, I wonder? She would be seventy-five now, and perhaps she cannot make it, but to me she *is* Remembrance Day, a victim of the war as surely as any wounded veteran.

When I knew her, she taught English at Commerce High. World War II was on, and we were caught up in its excitement. Now and then a boy skipped a class and turned up a few days later in uniform, immeasurably more grown up, and bragging how he had fooled the recruiting officers about his age.

Miss Wingard told us, when November came, about her war. They were at Queen's University in Kingston, she and her blonde girlfriend who was so very beautiful, and their fiancés, who were both completing medical training. World War I came along, and it was going to be the war that would end war, and the young men marched off to save lives and the girls stayed on to finish their courses. In a year,

or maybe two, the boys would be back, and they would all be married and start rearranging the world with their beautiful idealism.

This is what the world lost, she said, so gently, with just a little catch in her voice, when the two young doctors died in the mud of France. The beautiful blonde girl went into a convent and had her hair all cut off, and Miss Wingard turned all her great courage to teaching English to an endless stream of other people's children. Her memories were faded dance programs and yellowing photographs, and a wide copper bracelet that she never removed.

When you compute the cost of war, she said, remember the young doctors. They might have found that cure for cancer. But add the blonde girl, with her fine brain and loving heart, and the brilliant handsome children who were never born.

And I looked at the frail sad face, surprised to find that our generation hadn't just discovered loyalty or bravery or heartbreak, and mentally I added to the casualties – "and Miss Wingard, too."

She made her vigil each November as she intoned: "They shall not grow old, as we that are left grow old." Did she contrast the ageing face she saw in the mirror with that baby-faced lieutenant in the uniform of 1917?

Please, God, when she joins him – could she be twenty again?

Marion L. Herbert
Ottawa, Ontario

I Resign
I Resign
I Resign
I Resign

I, the proverbial housewife, do hereby unequivocally resign from spiders.

Mean hairy monsters that drop uninvited on to my lap when I am resting on the back porch.

Tiny, almost invisible ones that hurry and scurry into corners and hide when I am wielding the wall mop to clear them away, only to reappear (not so invisible now) when I am entertaining guests.

Bald white ghostly ones that nest in shroud-like balls and festoon the front door and pillars with fine clinging mesh that is worse than

running the gauntlet of a barbed-wire fence.

I have always felt strongly about these scary creepy-crawlies and last year I wrote one of Peter's "bad verses," to persuade myself that they really had a brighter side. Now, after another year of squeamishly cleaning attic and porch, I say:

> To heck with all philosophies
> Beautifying webs that bind us,
> To heck with frosted fairy lace
> I still resign from spiders.

> Pat Gudyin
> Niagara Falls, Ontario

I hereby resign from CBC television salutes to the Northwest Territories.

One such salute recently credited the Northwest Territories with temperatures of "ninety-nine below and twenty feet of snow." A phone call to the CBC arctic weather reporters could have confirmed the fact that temperatures rarely fall below minus sixty degrees and that many parts of southern Ontario receive more snow than the NWT. Closer research would also have disclosed that the song that was in question is about Alaska.

For their next salute, possibly the CBC could consider some material by someone from the NWT. Until that time, I'll watch American salutes to Canada.

> David C. Drane
> Yellowknife, Northwest Territories

I hereby, forthwith and immediately, resign from being tall.

I resign from ducking through low doorways (as a future architect I hope to be able to correct that one).

I resign from *never, ever*, having enough leg-room in cars, trains, boats, planes, theatres, restaurants, classrooms, stadia and sundry other auditoria.

I resign from furniture that is never big enough to contain my six-foot-six, 190-pound frame.

I resign from buying *all* of my shirts, sweaters, jackets, suits, coats, shoes, sneakers, sandals, boots, socks, gloves, ties and any and all items of clothing or accessory worn on the feet or above the waist, from mail-order houses in some far-off place, who never seem to get the colours right and who are always a year out of date with the style of the day.

I resign from hearing idiotic comments, ranging from the ridiculous, "How's the weather up there?" to, "My, how you've grown!" (grown what?), to the insipid, "Why, you've grown another foot!" (Omigod! Where?)

I resign from having thirty-six-inch sleeves, thirty-six inch inseams, and extra-long body and size nineteen shoes (one size larger than Wilt Chamberlain's).

I resign from the never-ending search for that mythical six-foot plus, willowy blonde, whom I can look in the eye without first kneeling.

And finally, my back and the top of my head resign from a world built to accommodate the five-foot ten-inch "norm."

> Yours, with resignation
>
> John Ross
> Halifax, Nova Scotia

It is with boundless relief that I am writing you my belated letter of resignation – from third-down snaps.

Quite frankly, it's a matter of self-respect. No one – not even a center – should be asked to contort himself publicly with head between legs, and then spiral a football exactly thirteen and one-half yards to a punter, all the while knowing that some Herculean defensive tackle is going to knock him helmet-over-hip-pads into the backfield.

Now, it's not that I'm not a team player. I am. Everyone knows that I always let Cassata and Keeling use my towel. And it's certainly not that things haven't improved since Angelo Mosca retired this year. They have. Angie always took a special delight in terrorizing centers.

It's just that I'm now twenty-two years old, and I'd sort of like to see twenty-three. So in the future, my posture on third-down snaps will be unbending. A center's job is thankless enough on first and second down, without dreading what's going to happen on the third.

Because the simple fact of a center's life is that even if he performs amazing feats – what will get photographed? *His cleats!*

> Yours in sport
> Bob McKeown, Center
> Ottawa Rough Riders

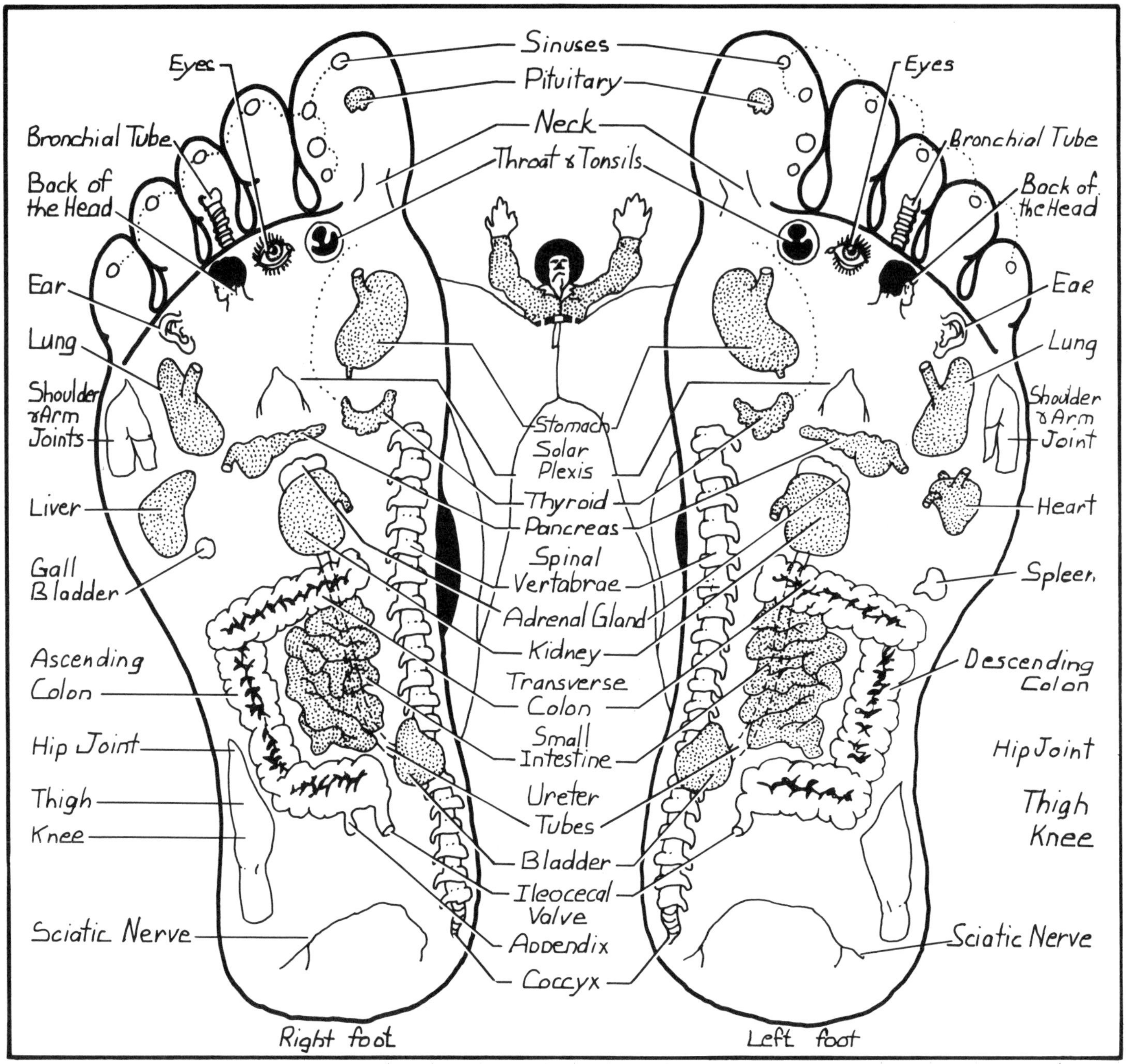
Sinuses
Pituitary
Neck
Throat & Tonsils
Eyes
Bronchial Tube
Back of the Head
Ear
Lung
Shoulder & Arm Joints
Liver
Gall Bladder
Ascending Colon
Hip Joint
Thigh
Knee
Sciatic Nerve
Stomach
Solar Plexis
Thyroid
Pancreas
Spinal Vertabrae
Adrenal Gland
Kidney
Transverse Colon
Small Intestine
Ureter Tubes
Bladder
Ileocecal Valve
Appendix
Coccyx
Eyes
Bronchial Tube
Back of the Head
Ear
Lung
Shoulder & Arm Joint
Heart
Spleen
Descending Colon
Hip Joint
Thigh
Knee
Sciatic Nerve
Right foot
Left foot

January 12, 1974

Dear Mr. Gzowski:

I have been wondering if anyone else in the Dominion of Canada tuned in to "This Country" a couple of weeks before Christmas, as I did, at the precise moment to hear something like:

> **Young female voice**: . . . and his donk was so sore I had to stop.
> **Danny Finkleman**: You're not hurting me.
> **YFV**: But you don't have prostate trouble.
> **DF**: Why do you have to press so hard?

Well, I tell you . . . I was galvanized.

Of course, you've guessed – she was massaging *his feet, for God's sake*!

I thought it was the massage-parlour girl back. Oh, I thought a whole lot of things in about two minutes.

Later, Danny asked her if she'd ever worked on any as big as his, and she allowed that they were pretty big. Danny said "size fourteen." Of course, by that time I knew we were talking about his feet, but if it had come any earlier, I just don't know.

Roberta Wharton
Barrie, Ontario

The Trip North

Angèle Arsenault is a tiny Acadian folksinger and songwriter who comes from Prince Edward Island but now lives in Montreal. One of the silliest, but I imagine one of the most heartfelt, songs she ever wrote has a chorus that goes like this:

> There was an Irish muk,
> And a Scottish muk,
> A Polish muk,
> And a whole bunch of crazy muks
> Who crossed the Arctic Circle.

To begin with the first line, there were really three Irish muks. They were Denis Ryan, Dermot O'Reilly and Fergus O'Byrne, who together make up the group known as Ryan's Fancy. Denis and Dermot and Fergie are three loopy Irishmen who met at Memorial University and now make their homes and their music and do most of their drinking in St. John's, Newfoundland. They, along with Angèle, and Edmonton songwriter Bob Ruzicka, were the musicians we took to the Mackenzie Delta area in the spring of 1974 to put on shows from Aklavik and Tuktoyaktuk.

Of all the places we took "This Country" to in three years, the western Arctic was, for me, the most exhilarating. Aklavik and Tuk are the two smallest communities from which the CBC has ever done full network programming. But, for those of us who went there, the trip was more than a triumph of technology. It was the discovery of . . . I find myself here in the same difficulties I encountered on the radio, trying to communicate the sense of the land. There are simply not enough ways to say magnificent. Brutal in its environment, delicate in its balance. Rich in game, yet with its land in the process of being raped by the southern oil and gas interests. I know how quickly and easily a southerner can become a romantic about the North – the Toronto Eskimo syndrome – and I know that in our brief excursion much of the harsh reality was hidden from us. Only a week or so after we left Aklavik one of the teenagers we'd got to know a little shot and killed a gentle priest who had been in the North since the 1930s, and more shootings followed. As I write, the incident has not yet been explained. Its cause could have been anything from booze to the simple maddening frustration of not being able to move around the land, which cannot be done at Aklavik during break-up. Or its roots could lie in the immeasurable pressures being put on a people who, in the last twenty years, have been

yanked through centuries of what we have decided is progress. It was an ugly event and one we outsiders may never understand, and I mention it now only to emphasize that I do not pretend to understand the North. But I know what I saw there and the people I met, and I know it is not necessary to spend a lifetime with a beautiful woman to know she is beautiful, and so it is with the North.

I'd better explain "muk." A bunch of us travelled one sunlit night up the river from Aklavik, up the Peel River, which is part of the doily-like pattern of the Mackenzie Delta, to the muskrat camp of a glorious old man named Archie Headpoint. He has a longer name in

Innuit, but the people of the North call him Archie Headpoint. The man who drove Denis Ryan and me there was his son-in-law, a soft-spoken Scot named Don McWatt. What he drove us on was a dog sled. A *dog sled*! When I was a kid delivering papers along the winter streets of Galt, Ontario, I used to drive a chimerical dog team. "Mush," I'd say, and "gee" and "haw." Don didn't say any of those things to his malamutes. He said "okay" to make them go, and it was more the tone of his voice than the syllables he used that guided them after that. The same with me. After he'd got them going for a while, Don let me drive, to fulfill, after thirty years, my childhood fantasy. I was pretty good at it too. Ask Don. And after a time we got to Archie Headpoint's camp.

While Denis and I were riding with Don, Angèle and Nancy Button, one of our producers, were travelling on another sled driven by one of Archie's granddaughters. The women's team beat the men's team — which was not altogether

the fault of my driving — so that by the time we got there the tea-drinking and the storytelling had already begun. After tying down our dogs — notice the "our" — we went inside Archie's log cabin to join in. Around midnight, we began to exchange songs. Archie is in his seventies, and can remember back to the time in his native Alaska when he was about to die of starvation from a simple and mysterious loss of appetite; his father sang him the powerful "hungry song" and he began to eat again. He sang us some songs in Innuit. And then Angèle, her eyes alive by the firelight, sang Archie a song in Acadian French, as a gift — which was the way we were feeling — and Archie asked where she came from and then he sang us another Eskimo song. Then Denis sang a song for Archie in Gaelic. I don't know about the others there, but I couldn't help thinking about the Irishman and the Acadian and the old man from Alaska and the young producer who'd grown up in Illinois and the middle-aged guy with a Polish name from the Toronto establish-

ment, and wondering if there was any other place in the world where an evening like this could occur.

Archie asked Denis where he came from.

"I've come to the North from Newfoundland," Denis said, "but I was born in Ireland."

"Oh, an Irish muk," said Archie.

And Denis threw back his great shaggy head and laughed his great shaggy laugh.

"Muk," it turns out, means in the dialect of Archie's native land, approximately, "person."

In Gaelic it means approximately "pig."

Well the fun began on the northern flight,
With everybody singing and feeling all right,
With Denis fiddling and Fergus dancing,
And pretty soon the whole plane prancing.

True. The spirit that was to pervade our whole northern swing began to take shape during our flight to Inuvik. After organizing travel arrangements that rivalled the invasion of Normandy in their complexity — as just one example, those of us coming from Toronto had been on the last plane that took off before a strike shut down the airport — we had all met in Edmonton, and on the plane north we began to loosen up and shake our southern tensions. There were jokes and there was music, and if you look closely at the picture of Ryan and me, you'll discover that each of us thought he was holding hands with one of the stewardesses. In fact, we're holding hands with each other.

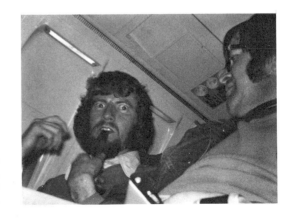

The first town we hit was Inuvik,
Which means "Place of Man" in Innuit.
We couldn't get over the nice warm weather,
And the sun shining bright till nearly midnight.

We couldn't get over how southern much of Inuvik looked either. Inuvik is the town the government decided to build in the 1950s because Aklavik, the traditional fur-trading and missionary center, was too closely surrounded by the delta mud to build summer airstrips or to expand much beyond its population of seven hundred or so. As a result, Inuvik is very much a government town; the words to the Aklavik school song call Inuvik "toytown." It also has: rows and rows of identical houses: enough cars to give it one of the highest traffic-fatality rates in the world; a beer parlor the people call "the zoo"; an A & W; a pool hall and a pizza parlour. I was kind of glad when we got on the bus that drove us along the river ice — the local joke is that next year the government is going to pave the road — some seventy miles to Aklavik.

Aklavik is the town that wouldn't die. In spite of the government's decision of the 1950s, and such inducements as subsidized rent, very few people have really left Aklavik. It is their home.

Well the soccer game left some of us lame,
But we were happy just the same.

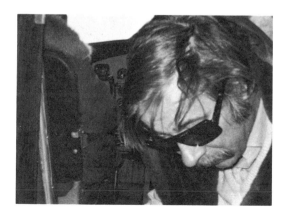

For the concert the whole place was packed,
And Mary Kindy was skinning the rats.

Ah yes, the soccer game. One of the most popular sports in Aklavik is indoor soccer. Because we had at least three Irishmen, one hockey coach (me), one reformed Scot (Alex Frame), two strong technicians (Ron Grant and Ray Sora, the Japanese muk), two guys not ashamed to wear shorts in the Toronto summer (Herb Johnson and Bob Rhodes), Nancy and Bob, who had made all the arrangements for the trip, had issued a challenge to the town team. So on Sunday afternoon we showed up at the school gym for a friendly little scamper around in our stocking feet. Some scamper, some feet. Our first impression of the town team was that they'd been chosen by the size of their shoulders and the fierceness of their faces. For a warm-up they were practising the soccer equivalent of slap-shots from one end of the gym to the other, and the goalie was diving to get any part of his

anatomy at all in front of them. For *our* warm-up we tried to talk them into taking their running shoes off, since we didn't have any with us, and that would make it equal. No way. In less than twenty minutes they had us whupped. Something like 4–0. Dermot wrenched his knee in a collision, and that night had to be treated by one of the two town nurses. Fergie got a blister on his foot that grew so large Dr. Herbert Schwarz (a former Montreal private practitioner and art collector who now lives in an old Hudson's Bay post in Tuktoyaktuk and writes poetry) had to treat it for blood poisoning. And the trouble is, the game was fun.

So was the concert. People came from all over to hear our musicians sing and to dance jigs to Denis's fiddle. Its high — or perhaps low — light was a muskrat-skinning contest among three women, won, as Angèle's song says, by Mrs. Mary Kindy who skinned two rats in one minute, forty-five seconds. Speed in skinning rats is important; insects attack if you're slow.

John

John, the chairman of
   the hamlet council,
in heavy working clothes
picking mail and parcels
from the Northwards aeroplane
then rushing
to meet the VIPs —
queens, ministers, bankers,
oilmen, and government officials —
curious
and visiting
this, Canada's last frontier
on the Arctic Sea.

He struggles to make a living
in his ramshackle garage
with piled up red drums
   of gasoline
facing the small lake,
which the swans and wild
   ducks visit.
Frequently called to appear
on the radio or TV,
soft spoken and shy,
he tells the South
of this land
so fragile
and innocent of avarice and evil.

He goes whaling
with Vince, his brother,
only to return
for the lengthy council meetings,
to deal with an avalanche of
   applications
for seismic work, drilling and
   explorations,
land use regulations,
government directives,
and pressures from the South
which he and his council try
   to understand
then deftly play for time
to save this land
for the Innuit.

Dr. Herbert T. Schwarz
Tuktoyaktuk, Northwest Territories

One of the women worked so fast that the bloody carcass fell off the table we were using on the stage and landed on the face of one of the kids who'd crowded around to watch; what the child did, without taking his gaze off the contest, was reach up and wipe the blood off his face and then lick his fingers.

I skinned a muskrat too.

We flew higher north to the Arctic Ocean.
To Tuktoyaktuk our destination.
The women's fur parkas were a dazzling sight.
And the boats were frozen in the ice.

Tuk is whaling country. For generations the people have been able to harvest as many whales as they have needed for oil and blubber and muktuk for themselves. When the people had filled their needs, about one whale per family per year, they stopped killing. One of the men I talked to was Vince Steen who, because the native people do not like to be singled out

for their expertise — a good hunter has always been "lucky" — would not like to be described as the outstanding whaler in Tuktoyaktuk, so I won't so describe him. Vince and one other man go out in his forty-foot boat and shoot and harpoon the sixteen-foot whales. He often gets them for other people. He told me about the time he'd taken all he needed and he just drove around in his boat and played with the remainder of the pack. He could hear them talking to each other.

When the seismic exploration started near Tuk a few years ago the whales began to desert the area. One year Vince got one whale for the entire community. Muktuk, which is the stuff just under the skin of the whale, and which the old people allow to rot before eating, like cheese, was selling for five dollars a pound. The next year, the hamlet council, of which Vince's

brother John is the chairman, fought a long and tough round of negotiations with the oil companies and the government and now, finally, there is a moratorium on seismic exploration during the whaling season.

I'd like to tell you about John Steen. He is as soft-spoken as Don McWatt, and under that there is as much strength as I have ever seen in any man. He has lived, worked, trapped, hunted and travelled over thousands of miles of his land. In Tuk, he is an airline agent, taxi-owner, truck-driver, and sort of amateur garage-man. When the queen arrived in Tuk during the most recent royal tour, John greeted her at the plane, in his capacity as hamlet chairman, and then went around to the other side to look after the royal baggage. The hamlet council of which he's chairman was the first of its kind in the North — a move towards self-government.

When a couple of roughnecks off one of the oil rigs near Tuk came into town one night, got a little drunk and drove a snowmobile over one man's whaling boat, it was up to John to call the oil company for which they worked and ask for compensation. A man's livelihood had been taken away, and John thought it was part of his job as the man's elected representative to try to help him out. The oil company paid and then, apparently, deducted the cost of the boat from the roughnecks' wages. The next time John Steen was in Edmonton, he happened to be staying in the same hotel as a bunch of oilmen. One night two men jumped him in a hallway,

shoved him into an elevator and beat the hell out of him. They did not, I can assure you, beat the determination.

I think that everybody on this trip,
Has fallen in love with the people of the Arctic.
So don't you be surprised, my friends,
If you see us all come back again.

Much of the trip has faded now into a complex montage of memories. Of reindeer stew and inside jokes. Of walking across the river from Aklavik one evening with Alex Frame and some native people, to the tiny community on the other side that is now a ghost town, of exploring the ghost houses and finding in one a freshly killed caribou, and then of walking back across the evening stillness, so quiet that the loudest noise was the squeak of our footwear on the snow. "Stop," Alex said. "What's that sound?" We listened. From behind us came a soft chirping. We waited. Nellie Cournoyea, who had lived as a child in one of the now-vacant houses we had prowled through, looked at Alex. Now, I knew, we would see the true northerner's wise comprehension of the land. Nellie said: "Birds."

In Tuktoyaktuk, a young athlete, demonstrating some of the northern games, kicked into the air and hit a piece of seal-skin suspended eight feet, two inches above the floor and then landed on the foot he'd kicked it with and kept his balance. In Aklavik we saw Don McWatt break up a fight between two of his dogs by hitting one of them with a log that I thought might have killed a horse, and then the next day we went with him to a quiet Anglican baptism for his newest daughter, and saw the loving expression in his eyes. In Tuk, the gentle Dr. Schwarz refused to accept three small bottles of wine as payment for the "parkie" he had lent Bob Rhodes for over three weeks; instead he made Bob a further gift of an old skinning tool that may pre-date the century. And in Inuvik, Nellie Cournoyea, who is now the manager of the CBC station there, fed all of us a feast that included muskrat, muskox, caribou, both raw (frozen — and delicious) and stewed, Arctic hare, Arctic owl and Arctic char and . . . I think I have forgotten something.

But I have not forgotten the trip, nor Angèle Arsenault's promise, on behalf of us all, to return.

is for Whiteoak,
a family of note,
When they heard the reviews
they got back on the boat.

Sharon Baldwin
Regina, Saskatchewan

THE BARGE SONG

(It's On The First Barge)

Words and Music by
BOB RUZICKA

long johns, bon bons_ and pre-fab-ri-cat-ed stairs. And a hun-dred and four-teen i-

den-ti-cal D. P. dou-ble U rock-in' chairs. It's got base-ball bats, Sun-day hats,_

hob-nail boots, bus-'ness suits, And so much booze_ if they want- ed to_ they could

put Queen Mar-y in-side the zoo._ It's got De-troit cars, han-dle bars_ and an

en-gine a-board a plane. Col-or-ing books_ and pic-ture hooks_ and a toy e-lec-tric

train. There's no wid-er match_ too small, there's no ar-ti-cle_ too large, They

talk as if_ that whole_ damn world was com-in' up-on_ that barge._ You see the

There's just one_ more thing_ that they're bring-in', friends, that makes our_

_ pub-lic health nurse shiv-er. The crew's bring-in' up_ all the

so-cial di-seas-es that they picked up in_ Hay Riv-er._

How to Play the Harmonica

Pop into your neighbourhood music store. Buy a Marine Band Harmonica made by M. Hohner of Germany in the key of C. Any key is all right but C is nice for this instrument and easy to check with the piano, and to play with, as nearly everybody can play piano in C.

O.K. Got your Marine Band? The holes are numbered 1 through 10.

Never mind that horn blower with his tongue business just yet. Place your two index fingers across the holes, but leave #4 hole open. Blow, and you have your low C of your scale; now, draw in on the same hole and you have your D. You're doing great! Now move your fingers to block off everything but the #5 hole. Blow, then draw for E and F. Now the same with the #6 hole, blow and draw for G and A. O.K. Here comes the switch! On #7, first draw in and then blow out and you've got it made with your B and good ol' C.

There, you've just played the ascending scale of C. Now do all that in reverse and you're a harmonica player – almost!

After doing that a few times, try it without the index fingers blocking anything off. See if you can play something that sounds a bit like the scale with the main notes predominating even though you'll probably have two or three other reeds working in on each blow and draw.

Now that you have that working, try and block off the unwanted notes with your tongue until you get the single required note. Having mastered that, you can try releasing your tongue and placing it back on again which will make a chord effect so that you can become your own accompanist. The vibrato can be very pleasing by making a sort of sound chamber with your hands around the instrument and opening and closing your hands.

By making this air/sound chamber as tight as possible, pursing your lips, instead of using your tongue, you can single out a note and create what we used to call (as kids) a dirty note, for blues effects like the sexy sound of a hot muted trumpet in "Sugar Blues."

We wish you good luck!

Bob Eastman

Letters of Resignation

Well, I resign too. I resign from judging contests. As far as I'm concerned, everyone whose letter of resignation I have read on the air so far, as well as a few more you'll read here, can go fly a kite, because they all ought to be winners — as, I'm afraid, should a whole lot of others — so to them, runners-up all, goes our own runners-up award, a kite: a war kite, a butterfly kite, a fish kite, whatever will seem most appropriate to the writer of the letter, and you can do what you will with them. Margaret Steel of Calgary, for instance, who resigned from peanut butter, because, as she said:

> It is those last bits glued to the insides of the jar that prompt me to resign from peanut butter. They defy soaking, scrubbing, scraping and scratching, remaining fixed unmovingly, smugly, defiantly, while my fist sticks in the jar from wrist to fingertips after my endeavours to clean it.

Margaret will get a butterfly kite to set her free. While Doug Bremner of Mississauga, who resigned from his lawn and whose lawn, in return, resigned from him, will get a war kite. And so on. The most common things people wanted to resign from were chores . . . and I guess the most frequently mentioned set of chores concerned the household. Sheila Diakiw of Vancouver, who has won prizes in contests before, wrote, for example, this open letter to six great kids:

> Mrs. Keen, tracer of lost purses, pens, pencils, textbooks, notebooks, basketballs and Bick Bananas; hereby tenders her resignation.
> I have made my last frantic loop around the house, eyes scanning, body crouching to peer beneath furniture in desperate quest of a size twelve running shoe.
> I have viewed "Hee Haw" for the last time, upside down between my knees while groping about on elbows and knees in hot pursuit of a contact lens gone missing.
> Don't think it hasn't been a ball, but from this moment on, what you lose, dear pussycats, you are just going to have to find! Love, Momma.

After household chores, I think, came animal husbandry. We got letters of resignation from gerbils (from Mrs. J.R. Smith of Ottawa), and cattle (from Josephine Hlady of Pincher Creek), from dogs (from Mary Spencer of Ottawa) and from spiders (from Pat Gudyin of Niagara Falls). But I think the animal resigned from the most was pigs: This is from someone who signs herself only "Judy," of Laird, Saskatchewan, but who gave a box number to which we'll send a fish kite:

> I resign from feeding the pigs. I'm tired of carrying buckets of scraps and water all the way down there through weeds three feet high. The water slops into my gum boots and the dog has eaten half the scraps before I get there. I've fed those two pigs since they were three-day-old orphans and I resign. They push and shove and the food ends up all over their backs instead of in the trough. I've fed those pigs through rain, sleet and/or snow; in sickness and in health, and I resign. I also resign from feeding the cats, the dog and the baby and Mike. If we still had those stupid chickens, I would resign from feeding them, too. Up the Revolution!

In all, I cannot get over the variety of things people found to resign from, and to do so with style, grace, feeling and genuine wit. You'll remember, I hope, John Ross, the young architect from Moncton, New Brunswick, who resigned from being tall. Well, others, and I

This A.M. will find me cross-legged, on my gold corduroy love seat, reading a slutty, pornographic novel, its only literary merit being that I can tolerate reading page after page. It will not edify my intellect. It will teach me nothing erudite.

I refuse to be a super-professional wife and mother; or feel guilty that I am not a person capable of cheerily seeing my children off to school (at 8:30 A.M.), the kitchen spic and span. I should then no doubt romp happily off to a nine-to-five job, only to return home to prepare a meal, carefully researched and shopped for — prepared to delight a gourmet. This night I will not feel guilty for not attending a community meeting on public transit, or for not being the model of sensuality and multitudinous orgasms. I resign from feeling guilty that my neurons are rusting and that I am unalterably selfish.

Take this "Ms" as I am, all ye about me. And all ye who have helped to create this independent, selfish Ms, stop telling me what I should be doing all day long. I resign from you and I refuse to feel guilty.

Carolyn Ruddy
London, Ontario

P.S. And tomorrow don't let me back into your achievement-oriented, intellectual society, should I come back pleading.

I can't resign from worldly things
Like politics, or diamond rings.
I'm not a jogger energetic,
Nor a businessman, frenetic.
I am just a simple Mum,
And I resign from Dimplebum!

Rose Beer
Caledon East, Ontario

I am resigning from riding my bicycle! According to popular belief, I am supposed to venture forth on these wheels for the benefit of quick transportation, fresh air, sight-seeing, exercise, tone-up, and a mod, inexpensive way to travel.

According to Doyle, I am to mount from the left (not unlike a horse, which I cannot do), release the stick from ground contact and proceed down the pavement hunchback, only to have pebbles spewed at me, bugs and dirt fill the cavities of my eyes, mouth and hair, exhaust fumes fill my lungs and a wet black stripe decorate my backbone.

If I reach my destination, I dismount, lifting my knotted muscle-bound leg over the saddle, and tether this metal monster with chain – only to return to partial remains!

Yes, I am resigning from bicycling. I will walk. I have to – my wheels are missing!

Elsa Rainey
Calgary, Alberta

Dear Sir:
After ten years of service, it is with great regret that I must inform you that due to a combination of wear and tear, and unavoidable aging, I must relinquish a number of my regular duties. After giving it lengthy consideration, including the possibility of simplification and/or modification of some jobs, the responsibilities listed below must be curtailed. In order to aid you and make this changeover as smooth as possible, I am listing some of the agencies and firms that can be called upon to assume the various responsibilities. I must admit the price will be considerably higher than my wages, but then no doubt the job will be done in a more professional manner.

Landscaping & gardening: Tom's Landscape Service 424-3026
Car service and wash jobs: Esso (tall, dark fellow is very obliging) 488-4285
Painting & decorating: J. Mason & Sons Ltd. 429-4988
Removal of dog droppings: Dominion Disposal Services 454-6084

won't mention all their names, resigned from rainy afternoons, from wearing shoes, from all containers that say "press here to open," from alcohol and allergies, migraine headaches and gambling on the races – but "see you in Vegas" wrote Doreen Lynch of Calgary – and from doing or reading anything at all of socially redeeming value, as did Carolyn Ruddy. People resigned from parenthood, from camping, from trying to be younger than they were, from diets, taxes, bosses, optimism, pessimism and even from resignation itself. A dentist from Winnipeg, who wishes to remain anonymous, wrote:

I'm a member of the union and I like the idea that they promote. Every time the matter of strike or work comes up I always vote for strike. That's the sensible thing to do, at least it gives me time off to rest and relax. I like my undisturbed weekends at the beach; and a plague on my wife when she asks me to mow the lawn or carry out the garbage on a Saturday when I should be enjoying myself by the lake. I resign from the plague of work.

From Seton Portage, British Columbia, Sheila Davidson wrote this, with copies to her Guardian Angel and the Office of the Regulator of the Calendar:

To the Arranger of the Universe
Dear Sir or Madam,

After much thought, and with some regret, I must ask you to accept my temporary resignation from the human race during the month of February 1974.

After our forty-nine-year association I feel it is only fair that I give you my reasons for taking this serious step.

As you know, my birthday falls on the third day of February and I was born in 1924. On the morning of my thirtieth birthday I noted a small cloud hovering overhead for one day. On my fortieth birthday the cloud appeared again; it was darker in colour, and lasted for approximately one week. An extrapolation by our computer has indicated that this forthcoming fiftieth birthday may darken this entire area for as long as a month.

I realize the importance in the scheme of things of the Department of Middle Age which you have allowed me to join, and feeling as I do that I cannot give my whole strength to my work while covered by a cloud, I thought it as well to give you the opportunity of dispensing with my services during the time I have indicated.

I hope that you will endorse my request, first for this temporary withdrawal,

and then for a resumption of my duties as of March 1st, 1974. Should you feel you must dispense with my services altogether, I must, of course, bow to your superior judgement.

Other people resigned from carrots, from having a library card, from bicycles, tidiness, ambition, families, cameras, typewriters, and one woman, from trying to figure out what high school was trying to teach her son. Two priests wrote fancifully – thank heavens, for each of them sounded like the kind of priest I would like to have – about resigning from the priesthood, because, as Father Hieromonk Vasily of the Russian Orthodox Greek Catholic Church of Canada in Ottawa said:

Dear Archbishop:
Having laboured in the vineyard for many a year and never having once succumbed to the grape boycotts, I hereby submit my resignation from the priesthood.

When I was young, they said I lacked experience; now that youthfulness has left me, they complain I am too old.

When I condemn falsehood and uphold the truth, they say I am too cranky; when my sermons fail to please everybody, I am hurting the church.

If I ask for a raise in salary, I am too mercenary; if I decline stipends from the poor, I am too practical.

The congregation you so lovingly gave me to nurture demands and indeed fully expects me to have:

the oratory of a John Diefenbaker
the crowd-drawing capacity of a Billy Graham
the business acumen of a Gordon Sinclair
the compassion of the Salvation Army and the patience of Job plus the wisdom of Solomon.

Alas, dear bishop, these virtues I have not and were I to remain in this pastorate, let alone the priesthood, I should require:

the strength of an ox
the tenacity of a bulldog
the daring of a lion
the wisdom of an owl
the harmlessness of a dove
the industry of a beaver
the gentleness of a sheep
the versatility of a chameleon
the vision of an eagle
the hide of a rhinoceros
the perspective of a giraffe

the disposition of an angel
the endurance of a camel
the bounce of a kangaroo
and the stomach of a horse!
Although I lack the faithfulness of a prophet, the tenderness of a shepherd, the fervency of an evangelist and the devotion of a mother, I have tried my best; none the less, I cannot and will not remain another day. In God's name wisen up and change that damn seminary course of studies!

Signed, a sour priest

Shirley Tennant of Fort Smith in the Northwest Territories said she resigned from her laundry, while David C. Drane of Yellowknife resigned from watching any more television salutes to the North. One of my favourite letters of resignation came from Caryl Parsons of Roxboro, Quebec, who has quit, she says, being anything but Caryl Parsons of Roxboro, Quebec. Here is another letter I liked a lot. It's from Joyce Tingley, of Sackville, New Brunswick:

To Whom It May Concern:
I hereby happily resign from being criticized!
Criticized for sewing a dress in an afternoon but taking two weeks to sew a button on hubby's shirt.
Criticized for wanting to sleep when hubby wants to play Chase around the Bedroom.
Criticized for letting the potatoes burn while reading an article on how to cook nutritious meals.
Criticized for turning up the furnace while opening the front and back doors in order to air out the house.
Criticized for having the TV and radio on at the same time I'm playing the piano.
Criticized for letting a dirty pan soak full of water until the surface of the water turns green.
Criticized because I put things that I mean to take upstairs, on the bottom steps and then keep walking over them until it gets to the point that no one can make it up to a clear step.
Criticized for saving leftovers but never getting around to using them.
Criticized for refusing to play chess again after having lost fifteen games — straight!
Criticized for preferring to read a book instead of doing housework.
Criticized for getting letters and bills ready to mail, but always forgetting to put on the stamps.

Criticized for taking movies with the cover still on the lens.
Criticized for throwing out the lens cover for the movie camera.
I definitely resign from all this criticism, and pity help anyone who criticizes me for doing so!

A man who lives in Clifford, Ontario, resigned from spelling, in a letter that exemplified why. His last name is Wood and I would tell you his first name, except I can't read it; I think he should resign from handwriting, too. People quit taking their kids to hockey, they quit adulthood, motherhood, and daughterhood. One man his putter. One woman her husband's moustache. Others quit shaving their legs, watching legs, watching TV, staying thin, staying fat, washing dishes, listening to the radio or to other people's children. As I've said so often before, I don't think people enter contests to win things, and the winners don't really matter. They — you, I hope — enter to say something about themselves and to have fun. We learn from them, and maybe you do too. Out of this contest, however, our famous panel of independent, wise, warm, fair-minded, honest and impartial judges, which consists entirely of me, has chosen one over-all winner. Her name is Mary Elizabeth Voegelin. She lives in Port Stanley, Ontario, and I'm going to send her the biggest kite I can find, for this:

To four of my five children:
I hereby tender my resignation as an active mother. I'd like to resign from cooking separate dinners for the early scout meeting, the late band practice and the odd-hour baseball games.
No more sitting in the passenger seat, white knuckled, as the licensed driver, while you practise for your driver's test or serving as box mover while you learn to parallel park in the driveway.
I'm going to give up worrying about your being late and I'm going to sleep in when you have to be up early. No more ironing shirts, mending pants or mopping your muddy boot tracks.
I definitely reject any more dancing or swimming lessons or twenty-four-hour hikes. And I'm not going to bail you out when you miss your ride or run out of gas.
You're going to have to make your own dental appointments and find someone else to sit with you in the Emergency room while you wait for the X-rays. You'll set your own alarm clocks and make your own breakfast in the morning.
I'm not going to complain about the length of your hair or tell you when to clean

Floor cleaning, wall washing: Calgary Janitor Services 422-2962 Contact and pursuit of street cleaners, dogs, city inspectors, truck drivers (for free dirt loads and other small favours) — I can only suggest the city emergency number Dial — 100 Snow removal — You might try your son, though he is considered "inexperienced help." Carpet and rug shampoo: Servicemaster Homecare Ltd. 466-4133

I might add that until recently I rather enjoyed these chores, but with advancing age, the pleasure lessens and the effort required seems to increase. I have given serious thought to resigning in order to make room for a younger person, but realize that I might have difficulty finding a new position at my age. Consequently, I have proposed this new arrangement, hoping that our ten-year association will influence you to look kindly upon my efforts.

Taking into consideration the slight cut in salary just prior to last Christmas, I feel that the responsibilities that remain are sufficient for me to continue at the same salary. I trust you will forgive the errors and omissions committed over the years which must have caused you a certain amount of inconvenience, and I trust that this new arrangement will meet with your approval.

Your loving wife
Kay
(Kathleen McDowell)
Calgary, Alberta

I resign from being anyone else but me. I resign from pretending I'm just like anyone else. I'm not. I have crazy drawings all over my walls. I spend my days not as a civic-minded do-gooder, but down in my basement, drawing, painting and sculpting.
I resign from worrying that my neighbours think that I am unneighbourly. Probably I am, not because I don't enjoy other people — I do — but because I enjoy my work too and I think it's more important to me at this time and place.
I resign from worrying about making conversation about the

weather, garden and children. If only someone would like to have a conversation about taking their children to art museums and enjoying art as a family, or about the place reserved in this life for enjoying what we see around us. . . .

Everyone sees the flowers in the garden, but they don't see the shadows cast upon my lawn; they can't imagine what the flower must look like to an ant; they don't see the bark of the tree in relation to parched, dry, cracked earth. I do, and I resign from worrying that my thoughts can't be spoken because others will think them odd. My family accepts me and they don't yet seem to be terribly embarrassed by me, so I resign from being embarrassed by me.

I resign from being too concerned about what others think. I resign from being dishonest about myself. I resign from being anyone else but me.

Caryl Parsons
Roxboro, Quebec

your fingernails. I won't tell you who to go out with or when to come home.

You're probably more puzzled by all this than shocked because you know I haven't done these things for quite a while. You've all been away from home for varying but substantial enough lengths of time for me to know that you've outgrown the need for an active mother and are capable people on your own. I'm sort of in the same position as the stamp-licker watching a postage meter being brought in the door — I want to resign from the job before it disappears completely.

What about your little sister? She's already sixteen going on thirty-five and in a better position than the rest of you since I learned my trade at your expense. I don't react as strongly or become upset as easily with her. Last month I even enjoyed the scenery while she drove to her driver's test and then walked to the store later because she was out with the car and her new licence. She'll be subject to the rules of the house, but that's a fair exchange for the amenities she enjoys beneath its roof. You'd be the last ones to want her to have less supervision than you did.

When this resignation becomes effec-

tive I shall enjoy your visits more. We'll sit together and listen to each other. I'll revel in your plans and successes and sympathize with your problems, but I won't live with them every day. I'll love and admire you for your very individual selves, and because you are each talented and accomplished in your own fields, I'll ask your opinions and use your advice. You'll still call me by the same name, but I want you to think of me as myself rather than the stereotype that "Mom" implies.

What am I going to do when I'm promoted upstairs, as they say in corporate circles? I've had an interesting offer. It involves some travel, a bit of secretarial work, a little accounting, a lot of reading, some cooking and sewing and a great deal of walking by the sea, handholding, laughing and talking. It won't be full-time until seagull #5 has spread her wings but your father says that if I start working on it now, by that time I'll be qualified to return to the job I started twenty-seven years ago.

It's called Wife.

I love you all.
Mom

Winning a prize from the CBC

Dear Peter:

I've been anxiously awaiting my butterfly kite plans. Today was the big day. Today my kite plans arrived!

I knew it was the kite plans because no one sends me big brown envelopes, just no one. The mailman comes early to my house and I'm often there to meet him. Today I was late, so I gingerly pulled the big brown envelope from the green mailbox, along with two other notes of interest. The first implored me to purchase chunky soup. As I understand from the note they sent me, I can eat it with a fork. They do, however, suggest I use a spoon; I mean only a nut, or my friend Bill, would eat soup with a fork. It would be a little sloppy unless you really chilled it first, and if it's anything like gazpacho, I'm definitely not interested. The second extolled the virtue and convenience of a gas-company credit card. The letter came with my name typed at the top and on the second last line from the bottom. The body of the missive was a lithographed form

letter typed on a manual typewriter with dirty keys and old ribbon. The manual's uneven key pressure helped conjure images of a job hand done by a blithe young thing eager to be of service to the motoring public. To say the least, I was suitably impressed.

Up the stairs I rushed, almost stepping on Soot in my haste. Soot is a black cat who lives with us; being an inquisitive little fellow, he was on his way down to investigate the commotion.

I disentangled myself from my feline companion, grabbed the bannister and hauled myself to a vertical position. Up the stairs, no time to waste, round the corner, and into the kitchen.

It was an awful thin envelope, but, as you know, good things come in thin packages, or was that small packages? Never mind. On with the job at hand. *Open* that envelope!

But to my shock — my amazement — my distress! I checked again. It couldn't be. But the evidence was there. It had happened. I mean, you wouldn't think it, would you? I checked again. Same result.

There it was, my big brown envelope, coming to me first class all the way from Torona! It had the blue and white CBC Radio-Canada sticker on the front. My name and address was correct, and there for all to see, in large bold type, was my postal code. I didn't think it cost fourteen cents to send just an envelope from Torona, but it does.

Crestfallen, dejected, but not without hope, a little boy's instinct to fly kites on windy days lives on. So please send me another butterfly kite envelope, and would you please include my butterfly kite plans? Kites, like ideas and emotions, should soar. On a morning as fresh and clean as today, nothing should restrain flight. John L. Seagull lives on!

Jim Preston

P.S. If you haven't got any more kite plans, could you please send two more envelopes and approximately six inches of scotch tape.

My Kite

I've waited and waited
For five weeks on end.
I'm starting to wonder
Will you ever send
Me my kite? Remember –
The kite that I won
On your recent contest
You son of a gun.

Where did it go to
That priceless old kite?
Suppose someone stole it
In the dead of the night?
Wherever it went to
I'll be glad when it's here
For patience is not one
Of my virtues, I fear.

So clean all the corners
Search each nook and cranny,
You won't find my kite
Till you get up off your fanny.
Empty each closet, rummage
	the place,
Send me my kite! Put a
	smile on my face!

My neighbours have polished
	their windows until
They can see without trouble
The top of the hill
Where I, with my finery
Flapping will be,
Flying my kite
From the slow CBC.

But soon it will be
Snowing and blowing.
Folks will be freezing,
But I'll be warm knowing
My kite is a'coming
Though God knows just when.
Will it ever get here?
Must I write again?

Yet I'll keep on waiting
I'll try to be patient,
I'll wait years and years
Until I am ancient.
But if in the meantime
You find it, will you
Please send my kite
To box One Four Two Two!

Joyce Lerette Tingley
Sackville, New Brunswick

is for films,
where clothing is scanty,
My uncle will take me,
but never my auntie.

John C. Sutherland
Charlottetown, Prince Edward Island

December 10, 1973

Dear Joyce,

Your kite will be coming: I wish it was
	mine,
But we're seeking a special This Country
	design.
It would have been easy if they'd been
	on sale

But as kite people say . . . thereby hangs
	a tale.
So be patient, be happy and keep yourself
	sunny,
Remember, we're spending the taxpayer's
	money.

Best wishes
Peter

Karen's Diary

Just four weeks to go!

I've snapped out of the depression I'd been in – I'm not at all worried about the actual delivery or tired of being pregnant or anything. Life just seems really beautiful right now. All the trees changing colour and long walks in the fresh air. . . . I come home with rosy cheeks and then I can look at myself in the mirror and say I really do look beautiful. Last week I felt just so ugly, with a wall-to-wall face and so fat. I guess I have these ups and downs now much more so than at the beginning.

I go to the doctor every week now. I have so many more questions for him now than I did earlier on. I find I need to know just what will happen to me once I get to the hospital. Even the littlest things worry me.

I spent all day outside getting some air and raking leaves, slowly. . . . It was terrific.

I've bought two nursing bras. They're about the most old-fashioned, plain cotton things you've ever seen, and they seem awfully complicated, with all kinds of hooks and straps everywhere. Weird-looking things, but probably super when I'm nursing.

I predicted that the baby will arrive in the middle of our first real snowstorm or in the middle of rush-hour traffic, and I either won't be able to get to the hospital in time or I'll have to go in a police car. I'm sure it won't happen but it's exciting to think about.

I've borrowed a little suitcase, written names and phone numbers into a little book and got myself a hospital outfit. It was impossible to tell how it's going to fit after I've gotten rid of this enormous front. . . . But I guess I'm all set now.

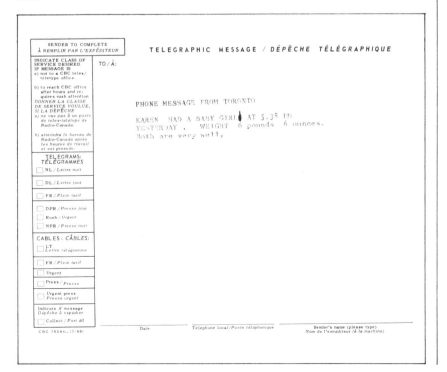

5 | The Pleasures of Guns

I want you to know, if you care, that I am a man of peace, opposed to war, violence, corporal punishment and the slaughter of songbirds. The letters I have read on this program that have either directly or by implication denounced guns, or even hunting, I am in sympathy with. I do not like blood, pain or loud noises. On the subject of guns and shooting I can out-woolly-mind any knee-jerk liberal in the land, but this morning, a clear and brisk one in the part of the country where I was, I had an almost overwhelming urge to shoot something at something. Not to beat around the bush, I wanted to have a BB gun again, and a tin can or a row of bottles or – best of all – one of those green insulators that carry power lines along country roads.

Specifically, I wanted a Daisy pump-action fifty-shot repeater – I never did like Red Ryder – with a lever under the stock that was stiff enough to test my muscle but easy enough that I could pump it myself, without sticking the end of the barrel into the dirt, because that, if you remember, used to clog up the nozzle or whatever the business end of a Daisy pump-action fifty-shot repeater is called, and you couldn't fire again. And I guess I wanted to be near a creek again, so I could float one of those bottles downstream and, risking soakers, ping away at it until I could see it, my victim, sink.

Is all this weird desire, and it is a real one, a result of my super knee-jerk liberal mind becoming suddenly twisted overnight? I doubt it. I had a pleasant evening last night, a bad movie and a good dinner with good friends, a restful sleep, an early breakfast and, all and all, I'm feeling pretty good today. But it's spring, dammit. I'm already looking forward to doing tomorrow's program from out-of-doors in Niagara Falls, and I take my urge to shoot something to be as natural to an urban, presumably civilized North American person of the 1970s as the similar urge I felt last week to go and fly a butterfly kite.

Please put down that pencil. I know BB guns are bad things . . . for all I know they're illegal in some municipalities now, although they seem to be in every catalogue you look at still. I know they're dangerous. But so is climbing trees and so is setting off firecrackers and so is riding a motorcycle and so, I suppose, under certain conditions for certain people, is sex. What's more, at least half, or maybe even all of those things are illegal in some places too. But I also know this: of all the people I have ever met who are opposed to war toys, and I guess BB guns are a kind of war toy, I have never yet met one who did not play war games when he or she was a kid. I do not think that shooting BB guns at road signs develops a killer instinct any more than I think that the taste of ginger ale will turn you into an alcoholic. I don't like shooting *things*, mind you, living things, and I know I could never be a hunter. I shot a groundhog once, when I was about thirteen, and then I went and picked it up, and that was enough for me. I have been grateful ever since that other people kill the animals whose flesh I eat. But I would like, just once more, to squint down the carbon-gray barrel of a pump-action fifty-shot Daisy repeater BB gun,

lining up in the little V at the end of the sights, the point where the two lines on railway-crossing road signs meet, and squeeze the trigger and hear that satisfying ping.

Destroy public property? You *bet*. Show me a part of the country where the road signs are ungunholed and I'll show you part of the country where the people are missing out on one of life's fine small pleasures. And just before you deny your kid the BB gun he wants this spring, especially if he's saved up the money himself, will you absolutely guarantee me that you never shot a tin can yourself?

Divorce and Remarriage

Helen Hutchinson, who's been mentioned before in this book – although perhaps not as much as she should have been – was an integral part of the program during its formative months. Gradually, her interests shifted to television, and eventually she left us. Before she did that, though, she contributed some pretty memorable moments. Two of them stand out in my mind. One was her review of a book about the death of a young girl from drugs. I have not tried to recreate that here, because one of its most gripping qualities was the emotion in Helen's voice; it was not simply what she said about drugs but how she said it. The reason: her own daughter had just come through a very bad experience in the drug world and Helen knew exactly what she was talking about. I did want, though, to share another interview with you. Here again, Helen is talking about something she has been through: divorce and remarriage. She talks about it with someone else who has had similar experiences, the Canadian actor Hugh Webster, and, yes, he is the husband of Elizabeth Webster, whom you met earlier.

HH: Do you find it difficult to talk about your divorce?

HW: Well, I can talk about it all right but I'm not quite sure if I can get into the depths of it because now I can sit back, be objective and assess a lot of things that happened, but without the emotional involvement. I'm not sure how valuable that is to anyone else having problems in their own marriage. Sure, I've been through the lot; I've gone down as far as I could possibly go in that kind of a man/woman relationship. But if I were put back into the same situation again, even after what I think I've learned, I might very well do the same things all over again. I just don't know.

HH: Has being divorced affected your attitudes towards your current marriage in that you don't have to hide behind a facade any more, you don't have to hide the cracks in your marriage from other people?

HW: Not having to live behind that mask any more, not having to project the kind of marriage you thought you wanted and the idea that this is what you had, when it wasn't what you had at all, is a freeing experience, though it takes time to feel that freedom. After the split, a terrible rupture which I think is the important thing, there's a kind of spurious freedom. I didn't have to fight any more, I didn't have to protect myself any more, I didn't have to make excuses any more. Then I went through a period where I was completely aimless; if it hadn't been for my work, requiring me to go on tour, to be on stage every night, places I had to be and things I had to do and audiences I had to please, I don't know what would have happened. There was just that terrible aimlessness. I never sensed a real freedom until I remarried. And my second marriage has made me realize something else. My first marriage was one of those awful, mutually destructive relationships. It was a "Who's Afraid of Virginia Woolf" thing, two people destroying each other and themselves. Being free of that for a long, long time, I found that I almost lost the dynamic of my life. I hadn't realized that all those years of being on edge like that had given me some kind of impetus to live at a pace that I now realize wasn't my real pace at all. I guess that my divorce, and my remarriage, forced me to learn quite a lot about myself.

HH: I know what you mean when you say you were forced to learn about yourself. I had to come to grips with my first marriage and found it was all wrong; it was a myth. I looked at it for a long time and boy, is that a painful thing to do because what it really means is looking at yourself. You ask what the heck did I do and why and how did it go so askew but eventually you come face to face with that ghastly creature called yourself. I realized I'd done everything for the wrong reason; I'd tried to live up to a myth that was created for me in high school and university. I'd let the residue of my Catholic upbringing tell me I wasn't supposed to be divorced, that whatever the cost I had to hold this thing together. I was trying to live by the standards of ladies' magazines and TV commercials. It was a completely false life. I was trying to be the good woman and was also playing the role of the good woman wronged which is a dirty, rotten game because that's the tyranny of the weak. When everyone said, poor Helen, I sat down and started thinking about myself as poor Helen; it wasn't until later that I realized poor Helen was doing a lot of manipulating. I found it very hard, but in retrospect, crucial, to substitute a more truthful image of myself in my own mind.

HW: I found that out very dramatically. I was talking to a friend about lying to yourself, attempting to live up to an image you've been projecting for yourself, and he told me about an experience he had with his wife when their marriage had gone right to the edge. They were having an argument about something silly, taking out the garbage. She said, why don't you take out the garbage, at which point he said, because I'm a bastard. Just that suddenly he realized that he wasn't the knight in shining armour he had imagined himself to be, but was an honest-to-God bastard. Then he was able to begin living like a human being, to look at himself, to see his own faults, and to see what he was doing wrong. I've always remembered that story and every now and then I say to myself, why am I doing this . . . because I'm a bastard . . . well, stop being one.

HH: Did you try to blame the other guy for what happened?

HW: The business of pinning the blame on the other person after it's over is just a pointless exercise and nearly as pointless during a break-up. But it doesn't do any good to accept all the blame yourself either because if you do, and we've both done it, you simply smooth over cracks that shortly show up all over again. You can't hold it together by yourself. You have to go at it with more introspection than just total willingness to accept all the blame. While nobody wants all the ties that are formed in a marriage, nobody wants their marriage to fall apart, no matter how rotten it's become. Nobody wants to go through a divorce and all that mess. But if you do find yourself in that situation, it becomes a very deep experience, an experience where depth can't be avoided. So you dig deep into yourself and as you say, it's horrifying what you can find there.

But that digging is a real advantage in approaching a second marriage. You face it with fewer romantic illusions of what's ahead than you could the first. And by the time I remarried, I was older; I've never known how much difference that made or how much of that maturity was found in my divorce. Legally I was old enough to get married the first time, but mentally and emotionally I was far, far too young. With my second marriage, there's just as much passionate involvement but now I can be intelligent about it. I guess I'm freer to be myself and free enough to be able to let Elizabeth be herself, something I could never do before. In my first marriage I was a worm of self-contained resentment but now I find I just don't have room in myself to hold on to the kinds of resentments I'd always bottled up before. And I know that if I found my marriage floundering now, I'd be free enough to get help from outside; I could honestly admit I was in trouble.

HH: After my divorce, I was given custody of the children; you weren't. How much difference did that make?

HW: That's probably the thing that drove me down deepest, a black, black period of my life, adjusting to not having the children any more, even though I would have them occasionally. It seems silly now, but I remember taking their Christmas presents to them when they were small. I went to the house on Christmas night,

217

gave them their presents, then said good-bye and walked away. Suddenly, with everybody heading for parties and all the rest, I found myself walking back streets until I wound up at an all-night restaurant. In moments like that, it's just as if there's nothing left. And you tell yourself, even now, that if it hadn't been for the divorce maybe they would have been different, maybe they wouldn't have had some of the problems that they've had. And because I had the children only at intervals, it seemed as though they often arrived at a moment of crisis in their lives. Then it was hard slogging to reassert the relationship. The relationship never really works the same way again. It's one of the heartbreaks that follows anyone who's been divorced; there's no way to avoid it.

HH: Do you think it's better for children to live in a second home, with or without a step-parent, than in a rotten, angry home?

HW: A lot of my friends told me it would be at the time I was weeping my eyes out over the loss of the kids. They kept telling me it's better for the kids to be free of all the anger, but at the same time. . . . I was raised in an angry home and vowed that it was never going to be like that in my own home, that my marriage was going to be roses and all the rest of it; but I fell into every trap my parents fell into. I didn't listen to the signals. After my first marriage was all over, I said that's it; I'm obviously no good at this sort of thing so I'd better stay out of it and lead a bachelor's existence for the rest of my life. The only part of it I wanted to have anything to do with was the kids; that was real. All I can say after that is that I fell in love again.

HH: Weren't you scared?

HW: No. Is anybody afraid when they fall in love? Besides, after a divorce, after you've had the lash, you've been through a fundamental experience that shook you to the bottom. After that you can't approach that kind of a relationship with the same naïveté you faced your first marriage with. I guess that's one of the reasons why you read second marriages are often more successful than first ones. You learn to respect yourself first, which is the most important thing, and through that you learn to respect the other person so that you've got two individuals standing up straight instead of two people leaning on each other. And you know what happens when people lean; eventually they fall over.

Pickle Recipes

Fruit Chili Sauce

25 ripe tomatoes
5 peaches (pitted)
5 pears (cored)
5 apples (cored)
5 onions
1 sweet red pepper (diced)
1 sweet green pepper (diced)
½ cup of pickling spices
1½ tablespoon salt
3 cups granulated sugar
1½ pints of cider vinegar

Peel all fruits, tomatoes and onions.

Cut tomatoes and chop the fruit rather finely. Mix well.

Add the other ingredients, having the spices tied in a cheesecloth bag.

Cook for 1½ to 2 hours or until thick, stirring occasionally. Do not allow the mixture to stick.
Yield: 6 to 8 pints

Margaret O'Neill
Windsor, Ontario

Bread & Butter Pickles

8 cups of unpeeled cucumbers (sliced)
6 medium-sized onions (sliced)
¼ cup of pickling salt
4 cups of ice cubes (1 tray)
2½ cups of cider vinegar
2½ cups of white sugar
¾ teaspoon turmeric
¼ teaspoon of celery seed
1 tablespoon of mustard seed

Combine the cucumbers, onions and pickling salt in a bowl, add ice cubes and mix well. The best method for mixing these is to do it by hand. Cover with a plate to weigh it down and allow it to stand at room temperature for 3 hours. Drain.

In a large kettle, mix the other ingredients and add the well-drained cucumber mixture.

Cook over a low to moderate heat, bringing the mixture just to the boiling point. Stir frequently.

Remove from heat, hot pack and seal.
Yield: 9 cups

Marilyn Parsons
Burlington, Ontario

Quick Pickled Mushrooms

2 cans of whole mushrooms
1 small onion, sliced
⅔ cup of mild vinegar
½ cup of water
5 peppercorns
½ bay leaf
1 teaspoon of salt
1 teaspoon of sugar (approx.)
1 tablespoon of cooking oil

Drain the juice from the canned mushrooms, and arrange the onions and mushrooms in alternate layers in a sealer.

Combine the remaining ingredients except the cooking oil and simmer for 10 minutes. Strain and cool.

When the juice is cooled, pour over the mushrooms and top with the cooking oil.

Cover and keep in the refrigerator for 12 hours before using.

This recipe is ideal for cocktail and antipasto trays.

Gloria Marcynuk
Toronto, Ontario

Nana's Relish

8 medium-sized onions
10 large cucumbers
3 sweet red peppers
3 sweet green peppers
salt to taste
2 tablespoons of mustard seed
2 tablespoons of celery seed
3 pints of white vinegar
5 cups of granulated sugar
1 cup of flour
¼ cup of powdered mustard
1 tablespoon of turmeric (more if desired)

Chop all the vegetables and place in a pot; salt to taste. Cover and let stand overnight.

Drain, add celery and mustard seed, vinegar and sugar. Boil for 20 minutes.

Make a paste of the flour, mustard and turmeric. Add this to the vegetables and thicken to the desired thickness.

Hot pack and seal the sterilized jars.

This is recommended as an all-purpose relish and will keep for an unlimited amount of time.

Connie Drybrugh
Winnipeg, Manitoba

Dill Pickles

garlic (1 sliced clove per quart)
dill (1 sprig per jar)
4 cups of vinegar
8 cups of water
1 cup of salt
3 quarts of cucumbers

Wash your cucumbers and place them in sterilized jars. (If they are large, cut them in strips.)

Combine all the other ingredients except garlic and dill, bring to a boil and pour in the jars.

Hot seal your jars and store for at least one month.

Betty Woodside
Fredericton, New Brunswick

Please accept this as my letter of resignation from Mondays, wash day, and the tedious and never-ending job of doing the laundry.

I resign – from picking up dirty clothes.

– from sorting articles into a white pile, coloured pile, hand wash, gentle wash, normal wash, bleachables, non-bleachables, and somehow still managing to get a red sock in with the white pile and ending up with a pink wash.

– from unwinding invisible thread from bra straps, socks, shirt buttons or any other article it sees fit to wind itself around.

– from running up the stairs to answer the phone, only to find the party has hung up.

– from emptying pockets only to find upon opening the washer door that I missed a kleenex in someone's pocket.

– from trying to find that miracle detergent that is going to lessen my laundry-day load and get my whites white, reds red, blues blue, yellows yellow, without contributing to pollution.

– from ironing and folding clothes, only to find them under the bed the next day.
From this I resign and dream of the day when I can dress my family in disposable clothes. But until then, maybe I'll try doing my laundry on a Wednesday!

Shirley Tennant
Fort Smith, Northwest Territories

I hereby resign from being talked into getting any more pets.

Some time ago, in a weak moment, I succumbed to the urgings of my children and bought them a mated pair of gerbils. We called the gerbils Honey and Benny. The day after we got them, I was glancing nervously into the cage, just in time to see Honey giving birth – now we had nine gerbils. Benny was immediately banished to the empty bird cage to sulk, and eventually the babies had to be segregated by sex into different cages. This made an awful lot of cage cleaning to be done mainly by guess who?

During these weeks, it was extremely difficult to get a bath at our house because there were always gerbils in the bathtub, in shifts, getting their exercise.

After a while the babies went to their new homes, Honey and Benny were reunited, and we went through the whole procedure again and again until they died of old age.

No sir, emphatically, I resign. And besides, a dog and two guinea pigs are quite enough.

Mrs. J.R. Smith
Ottawa, Ontario

Plum Chutney

2 pounds of plums (stoned)
1 pound of green or red tomatoes
4 onions (chopped)
1 tablespoon of salt
½ cup of seedless raisins
2 tablespoons of curry powder
⅛ tablespoon of cayenne pepper
2 tablespoons of ground ginger
1½ cups of cider vinegar
2 cups of brown sugar

*If you use red tomatoes, they should be peeled; if green, they should be very finely chopped.

Cut all the vegetables and fruit and place in a large kettle. Bring to the boil, reduce heat and simmer for one hour (or until it reaches the desired consistency).

It can now be hot packed and sealed.

This chutney is recommended for use with cold cuts.

Helen Terrett
Toronto, Ontario

Paul Hiebert's Christmas Message

This is the time of the year when the older people look back upon the Christmas days of their childhood. And one thing they remember with a nostalgic sadness is the songs they used to sing at Sunday-school Christmas parties and the old carols which today have been supplanted to a great extent by such songs as "Rudolph, the Red-Nosed Reindeer." On the whole, poetry, whether it is Christmas poetry or not, today seems to be concerned with the unpleasant aspects of life. Even the poets of Saskatchewan, the School of Seven and a Half, what's left of them, tend to treat Christmas without any great joy. I am thinking for example of Baalam Bedfellows' "God How I Hate Christmas." It is one of his Boom, Boom poems, in which he turns with loathing from Christmas decorations because so much of it contains stuffed birds, and as we know, he hated birds. Or take again Wraitha Dovecote when she writes about the lost joys of the Christmas season, and she is in sad reflective mood; she is evidently in the habit of cleaning up the mess after the Christmas celebrations are over:

When we are gone, who then will gather up,
The angels, coloured lights that now adorn,
The festive tree? Who'll fill the festive cup
When we are gorn?
[Notice the forced rhyme here in the best literary tradition]

And who will gather tinsel from the floor,
And save it for another year, if we
Are gathered too, and neither are no more,
Not you – not me.

Though Christmas spirit shines throughout the way
Or so 'tis said, within our daily walk,
Much good 'twill do us if we're dead,
Nor here to talk.

The moral reads that things of our delight,
Boodle, and booze, and broads go soon enough,
With Christmas angels and the coloured lights –
But boy, it's tough!

The trouble with so much modern poetry today is that it tends, like the poem I just read, to be depressing. Moreover, in its form it departs from the lilt and meter and the rhyme of the poetry we learned in our childhood many years ago. It was possible to memorize poetry in those days and to carry some of its music into our lives. I suppose it is because so much of what the poets wrote about in those days has gone out of date. Who of us today is stirred by Rudyard Kipling's poems of the British Empire, when it no longer exists? Or, to take another case, who of us in this age of surfboards and powerboats can properly respond to a poem such as John Masefield's "Sea Fever"? You remember how it used to go:

> I must go down to the sea again,
> The lonely sea and the sky,
> And all I ask is a tall ship
> And a star to steer her by.

Today we are likely to say about the boat,

> I must check the gasoline again,
> And ask if the oil is high,
> And all I ask, will the darn thing start,
> And whether it's tight and dry.

I ask myself, who can catch the spirit of the mining camps and of the wild and lonely Yukon that Robert W. Service wrote about over sixty years ago, when today the mines have been worked and the Yukon itself is full of American tourists?

And what about William Henry Drummond when he wrote about the *habitant* of Quebec in a broken French-Canadian accent? What about Little Baptiste and the storm on Lac St. Pierre when today we feel that Little Baptiste is probably a separatist, and Lac St. Pierre, for all we know, is now part of the St. Lawrence Seaway?

Now it occurs to me that if we could take some of the poems of the old masters and bring them up to date, to make them, as it were, topical again, they might recover some of their old appeal. And what could be more topical at this time of the year than a poem about Christmas? I ask myself, how would such popular poets as Kipling or Masefield or Service write about Christmas if they were writing today?

I certainly don't think that Kipling could ever quite escape his imperialism. He certainly could not escape his admiration for the British soldier who made the Empire great, the Tommy Atkins, as he called him, who never gave up despite overwhelming difficulties. In this case the difficulty would be, since this is a Christmas poem, the difficulty of bringing back to England a Christmas tree from some of the outposts of Empire, or, as Kipling would have called them, "our far-flung battle line." He would no doubt call the poem, "Tree of Empire," and it would go like this:

Tree of Empire

> Bring home the tree of empire
> Where never sun has set,
> And lug it home for Christmas
> Through Burma and Tibet,

I hereby resign from gambling on horse races.

Yes, gone are the evenings of rushing off to get the racing forms, studying into the wee hours of the morning, listening to the weather report and hoping for a dry track. Most degrading of all, the almost impossible task of trying to extract enough money from hubby for a few daily doubles, the odd exactor and several irresistible quinella tickets which would make my day.

No. No more worries about whether or not "Step Aside Clyde" would actually step aside in order to assist some 50-1 longshot with sore legs and equine fever to shoot through on the rail at the finish line. Or whether "Fallen Britches," the only speed at five furlongs, would knock his head on the starting gate and finish at the rear!

I refuse to come home hungry, miserable, tired, guilt-ridden and broke, with a face longer than anything I had bet on that day, trying to convince my husband that I would do better on a wet day and a muddy track.

Yes – I resign from horse-racing for once and all – you can bet on it!

Doreen Lynch
Calgary, Alberta

P.S. See you in Vegas.

Swing up the Nile through Egypt,
Across Somaliland,
Then somewhere east of Suez
And on to Samarkand –
Go get it, Tommy Atkins,
And home for Christmas Day,
There still are trees in old Rangoon
And some in Mandalay –
So 'op it, Private Atkins,
That lesser breeds may know
That where the flag of England flies
The Christmas tree can grow.

The Christmas tree of England,
Just get it where you can,
Remember, Private Atkins,
You're a first-class fighting man –
So grab a tree in Bangkok,
Or India's coral strand,
And drag it up to Singapore,
And back to Samarkand,
And work it past Gibraltar,
And home to Camden Town –
Bring home the tree of Empire
Where never sun goes down.

So it's, "Thank you, Mr. Atkins,"
For bringing home the tree,
Across the hot and heathen lands
Of Hindi and Chinee –
Bringing home the Christmas tree,
Bringing home the pine –
Bloody British soldier
In a thin red line –
And it's, "Thank you, Mr. Atkins,"
For the little brown brother,
As an extra gift for England,
And the Great White Mother.

How many of us remember Henry W. Longfellow's poem, "Excelsior"? It used to be in the school readers when I was a child, and although we liked the poem we used to wonder what excelsior meant. The teachers we had were unable to tell us. But it sounded fine. Today we know what excelsior means – it is fine wood shavings in which glass and china are packed, and as such it lends itself particularly to a Christmas poem. I understand that the modern excelsior is not only shredded wood but also includes paper and even plastic. This makes it all the more appropriate. "Excelsior," as a modern poem about Christmas, would go something like this:

It's Christmas Day, and falling fast
Wherever Christmas gift has passed,
There lies in whisp, and gob, and wad,
And deeply in the carpet trod –
Excelsior.

Knee deep, like snow upon the pass

It lies with cardboard, broken glass,
And bits of ribbon, tissue, crêpe,
Pine needles, ornaments, and tape –
Excelsior.

"Oh stay," they cry, "beneath the tree,
Is still a package meant for thee,"
But every box for maid or lad
When opened up can only add –
Excelsior.

Tomorrow, when the room is still,
I'll take old-fashioned pail called "swill"
And mop and dust, and clean enough
To rid the place of all that stuff –
Excelsior!

There is no great use in going on with this. The original "Excelsior" of Longfellow's had sixteen verses. It would be too long for a Christmas poem today. But it shows the possibilities. All we have to do is to take the old masters and bring them up to date. If we do we may once again restore poetry to the high place in our culture which it once held.

I like to think of Robert W. Service writing a Christmas poem about the Yukon which does not, for a change, deal with the riotousness and the rough-and-tumble with which he generally describes the scenes of the gold rush days. In this poem, which I have called "The Ballad of Christmas Day," I have put the emphasis upon the kindly spirit of Christmas which has descended upon a group of the Christmas celebrants at Soapy's, one of their cultural clubs. It tells about a girl from the south who, far from home on this Christmas day, sings some of the songs of her childhood. In doing so she moves the hearts of the miners, some of them, in fact, to tears, and she also moves the heart of her teammate in the dance hall, The Lady Known as Lou. In the true spirit of Christmas, Lou not only rises to a deeper understanding and sympathy for her fellow men, but her heart goes out to those creatures of the wild who do not have a Christmas celebration. In her quiet way she takes Dan McGrew out to see the dogs and the sleighs and wanders off towards his cabin at the foot of the Chilcoot. There she meets her friends of the wild who, knowing it was Christmas, were expecting her:

It was Christmas Eve up at Soapy's
And the boys were hitting the gin
And out in the snow it was eighty below
And the cold was creeping in –
But playing the guitar in front of the bar
Was the lady who was known as Lynn.

Now Lynn was a girl from Texas,
Who had left her home and mate
Before she got old, for the lure of gold

222

On the trail of the ninety-eight,
But anyhow, she was tired of cows,
And beginning to put on weight.

So she sang of home and mother
And of dear old Christmas days,
'Till the boys shed tears in their gin and
beers
And swore to mend their ways,
And the lady named Lou, led Dan McGrew,
To look at the dogs and the sleighs.

But out at the foot of the Chilcoot
Awaiting their Christmas share,
And in on Lou's deal, for a Christmas meal
Were three timber wolves and a bear,
And they cried when they saw the luck of
the draw,
"What an answer to our Christmas prayer!"

So they ate McGrew for Christmas
And they sang in praise anew
To the god of the North who had brought
him forth
And especially the lady named Lou,
That the one good meal in their Christmas
deal
Should be dangerous Dan McGrew.

And back in the bar at Soapy's
Where the boys were still hitting the brew,
When she came along, they all joined in
song,
And sang in praise of Lou,
The big-hearted child, with a heart for the
wild,
Who at the same time got rid of McGrew.

One of the Christmas poems I like very much,
since it reflects so much of my own experience,
is "Tree Fever" by John Masefield, who wrote
that very beautiful "Sea Fever." Masefield was
a fine poet but, like all men who are asked to
put up and decorate the tree at Christmas, he
was glad when it was all over. In "Tree Fever"
he expresses it very poetically:

I must decorate the damn tree again, the too
tall tree and high
And all I ask is a step-ladder, and no one
around, or nigh,
And all I ask is to be left alone, and no one's
constant yacking,
And no sighs, or smothered cries, when the
ornaments are cracking.

I must string up the lights again, and find the
ones that are out,
The used ones, and the fused ones, and the
ones put away in doubt,
And all I ask is no advice, or be told that
the tree is wilting,
Or the dear little angels are upside-down, or
the whole damn tree is tilting.

I must decorate the tree again — it's part of
the Christmas life,
And all I ask is no one's help, and least of
all the wife's —
And all I ask is no wise cracks from some
laughing fellow rover —
Just a long rest, and a long drink, when the
job is over.

is for
the lonely Yukon,
There even a husky
keeps his toque on.

Mary Sutherland
Belleville, Ontario

I wish to resign from all responsibilities connected with my two-hundred-pound, sloppy, spoiled-rotten, expensive, beautiful St. Bernard.

I shall no longer keep two vacuum cleaners plugged in for immediate hair-shed removal. (Dog's hair, that is.)

I'll no longer hear him when he smashes open the toilet (cover and seat) to help himself to a drink — therefore, I shan't wash up his drool when he finishes emptying the bowl.

And never again shall I be almost involved in an accident because his huge head was stuck out one window and his tail was flagging the breeze (or something) out the other, as he stood denting the roof of my small car, oblivious to the fact that he was completely blocking my view!

Never again shall I cajole my husband into taking "my" dog for a four A.M. walk "the morning after" some kind soul gave him an unaccustomed "treat" — and got his bowels in an uproar. (The dog's bowels, that is.)

No longer shall I worry about my little guy stepping on broken glass as he heels obediently beside me. I'll not worry that people made that smashed-bottle mess on the sidewalk — and instead of saying, "No! Not there!" — and making him hang on for another few minutes — I'll just let him go.

I wish to resign! But how can I? I, we, love that damned dog! Disqualified — right?

Mary Spencer
Ottawa, Ontario

I have no doubt that if William Henry Drummond were writing today he would still catch some of that simple trust in the miraculous which he observed in the *habitant* of Quebec when he was writing about seventy years ago. Perhaps today, Quebec having changed, he might detect some political overtones. Little Baptiste, for example, being in this poem in the special care of one of the saints, particularly St. Laurent, might aspire some day after he was born to the premiership, or at least to take part in political life. Certainly the miraculous appearance of a Christmas tree at the height of the storm on Lac St. Pierre bodes well for the yet-to-be-born child. I should imagine it would run something like this:

Storm on Lac St. Pierre

One time we live on Lac St. Pierre,
My wife — dats Jeanne-Marie —
She say, "Go take de boat and keeds,
And bring home Christmas tree."

She say, "Wid little boy Baptiste
I stay and make some soup,
Wid peas and ham, but you take keeds —
Come back soon. Allez oop!"

I say, "Ma femme, you dont tink good,
You look-see over dere,
De great big wave come rollin in —
Dere's storm on Lac St. Pierre!"

But Jeanne she say, "Don' be afraid,
I pray to St. Laurent,
You don' get wet — he keep you safe,
Go 'head, let storm come on!"

Now de wind she blaw like 'urricane,
By and by she blaw some more,
And den, by Gar, I cry, "Whats dis
Tree arpents from de shore?"

I cry, "Whats dis? Two arpents now,
Whats dis, whats dis I see?"
And all dem sixteen keeds cry out,
"By Gar, she's Christmas Tree!"

And sure enough, dats what she is,
She's miracle, you bet,
She come from storm on Lac St. Pierre,
We even don' get wet.

And Jeanne, she say, "Dat's ver' good sign,
For leetle boy, Baptiste,
An' when he's born maybe he be,
Premier of Creditiste."

May 24, 1973
Dear Mr. Gzowski:
Since that original interview with Professor Paul Hiebert you have been doing bits and pieces from Sarah Binks, Sweet Songstress of Saskatchewan.

Professor Hiebert was my second-year chemistry professor at the University of Manitoba. It was the beginning of the huge post-war classes and our vast numbers were assigned to one of the largest theatres. He was a good chemist, but every so often either chemistry or the sight of all those students palled, and he would try out a bit of Sarah on us. He had a gentle voice so we nearly knocked each other down to get a seat in the first two rows. You never knew which day was going to be Sarah Binks Day, so the turnout was one hundred percent — just in case. This little gray and brown gnome would come in quietly at the beginning of the lecture period, look over the top of his glasses, and a hush would fall while we waited to see if it was to be chemistry or Sarah. What a disappointment when he began on quantitative reactions! His chemistry never suffered from Sarah, though. The laboratories were spread down both sides of a long corridor. Naturally, the unsupervised side turned to experiments not listed in the curriculum. It was absolutely uncanny the way he could turn up behind the beaker quintet right after it had tuned up and was beginning its first recital piece.

Yours very truly

Constance E. Dwyer
Coquitlam, British Columbia

224

Urjo Kareda's Boxing Day Lament

I'm afraid I have to say that Boxing Day is my candidate for the most loathsome day of the year, the day when we're all of us Scrooged. First of all, let's make very, very clear just *why* we're all feeling so unequivocally lousy today. Let's not, for once, blame the overpriced, overcooked turkey, or tuneless Christmas carols, or tiresome relatives, or Dickens, or wretched gifts or, heaven protect us, any "sadness" that the holiday season may soon be over. (Let's huzzah for that one.)

And let's not, *please*, pretend that we're going to resort to all those familiar, phoney-helpful and useless solutions to the Boxing Day blues. For instance, let's *not* pretend that we're going to look through the cookbooks for One Hundred Scintillating Things To Do with Leftover Turkey; let's *not* jog briskly about the neighbourhood to work off that Christmas dinner; let's *not* spend the day ironing out all the wrapping paper so that it'll be neat and tidy for next year; let's *not* run downtown to participate in some wretched unmissable Boxing Day sale; let's *not* sit around the fireplace trying to re-kindle the nostalgia of that nice Christmas feeling; and, for your own sake, let's not pretend that it all never happened.

No, courage, courage. Let's face the specific and precise facts about why we are feeling so grisly, and let's speculate whether anything at all, at this late date, might be salvaged.

If you're at all like me, then on Boxing Day, you just cannot believe that you've done it all again—that you've spent so much money buying so many things for so many people, getting in return so many things that you wanted so little; that you stocked up on the old happy bottles to get you all the way through the holidays and then drank them all in six hours, just to get through the first holiday; that you did such idiotic things as (1) sending cards, (2) receiving cards, or (3) keeping this year's cards for next year's list; that you devoured a Christmas dinner that has now developed into the size and consistency of a smallish Volkswagen in your stomach; or that you pretended, somehow, that this Christmas would be different and that you'd learned from all the ghosts of Christmas past. That's the killer: those who forget Boxing Day are doomed to re-live Christmas.

My advice is to fight the constructive with the destructive. Are you ready? March right into the kitchen, grab a sharp object, and stab your turkey—or whatever is left of it. You'll be amazed how therapeutic that will be. Or pick the very worst gift you received and stuff it right into the turkey and boot them both out the door; you'll be glad to be rid of both of them. Group activity? Get the family out for a nice game of turkey soccer. Energy crisis? Make a bonfire, starting with your tree (you won't be getting much more fun out of it: did you ever?) and then your mistletoe (and if you're still relying on the Druids to get kissed, you may be beyond help), and finally, all the wreaths; throw the culinary carcass on top of them all, and let them roar, until everything is reduced to a manageable pile of spruce and turkey cinders. Bury the whole mess in your garden, muttering darkly to your neighbours about Aunt Ida, who's sung her last Noël.

All such behaviour is, of course, wanton, yes, and sadistic, cruel, childish, petty and malicious, but your spirits, I think, will find themselves soaring. And when your friends are cheerlessly nibbling their way through their thirtieth consecutive serving of turkey croquettes, you can smile inwardly and think of that poor, bruised, badly abused fowl, gone forever from the regurgitation treadmill.

Boxing Day Re-construction shouldn't end with Turkey Annihilation, of course. I think you're going to have to come to terms with eggnog as well. Isn't that a disgusting word? Eggnog. Like "turkey" or "plum pudding," it sounds just like it tastes. But it's the holiday drink, isn't it? But all *that* means is that it is so revolting that nobody could bear to drink it all year round.

Use Boxing Day, then, to begin your campaign to ban this frivolous potion. Swear at once that you've nogged your last egg. After all, you've let yourself get trapped again, lugging home the cartons or God help you, mixing your own; swilling it around; grating nutmeg on top; lacing it with brandy to make it seem better; and then pouring good stuff on to bad just to kill the taste.

Spend today in Eggnog Shock Therapy. Give yourself the scare of thinking what would happen if this *eggnog* thing really took over—if your wife announced next year that she was going to stuff the turkey with eggnog, trim the tree with eggnog, deck the halls with eggnog and wrap the presents in eggnog. Imagine eggnog, not Santa, sliding down the chimney. A few moments of rich fantasy may save you for life. If you're not sure you'll remember, write down what you feel like now, and keep it on file for next year.

Another way to pass time is to try to figure out just exactly how much this Christmas cost you. Leave out nothing—not the tip to the garbageman and paperboy for their crummy

I would like to resign from that daily chore of milking the cow.

No longer do I want to make my way to the barn through the knee-deep snows of January, the soggy rains of June, the howling winds of November, nor the blistering heat of July.

No longer do I want to search the far ends of the pasture for that beast who insists on grazing there *just* at milking time.

Gleefully I resign from ever having to sit beside old Daisy again, to balance myself on a wobbly three-legged stool, to protect myself and the milk bucket from fidgeting hoofs and swishing tail, to contend with the frustrations of a cow who will not let down her milk, to be careful not to aggravate that barbed-wire scratch on the right-front quarter and to put up with that look of utter contempt as she finally realizes that I am in control of the situation.

Goodbye, dear Daisy, I'm off to the supermarket for fifty pounds of powdered skim.

Regretfully
Josephine Hlady
Pincher Creek, Alberta

service; not the money for Scotch tape or Alka-Seltzer; not the extra electricity for the gaudy lights which gave you a headache. Your findings will either send you into such shock that you'll turn sober and alert all day (which makes it a good day to go to the office and write crabby memos to people who didn't turn up), or into such despair that you may become comatose, not to wake, hopefully, until Groundhog Day.

A slight variant is to figure out how much money you *made* on Christmas. This involves the slightly unpleasant but entertaining chore of calling the people who gave you presents, to ask, subtly but pointedly, where *did* they get that unusual gift, *did* they keep the receipt, and *do* they think the store would be open today? Suggest you cannot wait. If you are blessed, this will offend your friends sufficiently to keep them from buying you anything next year, which of course leaves you liberated too. Next year's tally is bound to be better.

There are a few quick and simple personality transformations you could make to your whole lifestyle. For instance, you could give yourself a book on snake-breeding and announce that by next year, you'll be raising your own little Christmas gifts. You can count on those holidays being cancelled. Or you could declare yourself a saint-in-progress, proposing to start a life of selflessness by giving away the possessions of those nearest and dearest to you. They'll think twice about having you around next year. Or you might, like the British, declare yourself a European, which would allow you to have your big bash on Christmas Eve. That would mean that Christmas Day itself would be the morning after and by Boxing Day, when all about you are losing their heads and blaming it on Yule, you can be on the road to recovery, one step ahead.

But probably the thing that will have you feeling the dumbest today is the high lunacy of Christmas cards. By now, you're probably surrounded, like Custer with those Indians, by wall-to-wall kitsch. People you never talk to send you cards, people you talk to every day send you cards, people you don't even *know* send you cards.

As far as I've been able to discover, Christmas cards have absolutely no recycling value. Who serves Christmas-card croquettes? They are a drastic nuisance, reducing sensible people to a state of paralysis. Remember, earlier this month, how you actually spent a minute from a rapidly diminishing lifespan deciding whether to send Cousin Bernice a card when you know that if you saw her on the street, you'd jump under a bus? Remember how confused you became in the store trying to decide just which schlocky arrangement of candles and pine branches would bear your honour this year? Remember your cynicism about the cards that arrived on Christmas Eve in *sealed* envelopes, with that *extra* penny postage, from the folks who panicked about you at the last minute? Can you honestly stand the inhumanity to which the Hallmark Company has reduced you and your friends?

Plan ahead now for next year, or do it this year if you still can. Here's the trick. When the cards arrive, don't even open them; just mark them "Return to Sender" and throw them into the mailbox. You'll have done your bit. You'll have received and sent (even if you did receive and send the same card). You'll have your revenge, too, on the post office. The ecological aspects, of course, are momentous. If everybody participates, we'll have a Christmas when nobody receives cards, but there will be ten zillion cards always in transit. A final touch: you might scrawl, on the envelope, in your most festive hand: THE SAME TO YOU. FELLA.

Happy survival.

Smelling the Flowers

One of the rules I try to apply around our house – I'm not always successful, but I try to apply it – is never to begin sentences directed towards relatives younger than myself with the words, "Why, when *I* was your age . . ." I'm sure you know what I mean, either as a sender or receiver of such messages. I lived on four cents a week, went to work for fourteen hours a day, delivered three thousand newspapers, memorized *Oedipus Rex* . . . and so on. The truth is, of course, that I *did* all those things, whereas my parents did *not* live on two cents a week, go to work for twenty hours a day or memorize all the books of the Old Testament. But still I know how annoying it is to listen to, and I try not to talk like that.

I am voicing these thoughts this morning, though, because of a bunch of phone calls I had to make last night. They happened to involve hockey, although hockey is not what I'm talking about. Another guy about my age and I manage a hockey team of fifteen-year-olds – and a damn good team it is, too, if you care – and because there is a shortage of ice time around our city this year we sometimes have to scramble to find a place and a time for them to practise. This week I found two hours on Sunday afternoon, and last night we were calling the kids to let

Let it be known to all and sundry that I do hereby relinquish for now and all time the title of Chief Someone, and attendant duties of said title so fatuously cast upon me by you all. Some are born to greatness, whereas others have greatness thrust upon them. Therefore, effective immediately, I thrust back upon you the responsibilities of the Someone of this household. Now, when the dirty dishes are stacked in the sink, the garbage overflows its container, the dust swirls crazily with every draft, and the family chants in unison, "Oh, leave it, Someone will clean it up in the morning," the Someone shall not be I.

Sincerely
Mother
(Judith Krawchuk)
Winnipeg, Manitoba

them know about it. Each of us, separately, noticed that there was a certain amount of grumbling about "my only day off . . . ," or "but I want to see the football game on TV." That sort of thing. I don't want to make too much out of this, because I still think it's possible for people like me to take hockey more seriously than the kids we are trying to provide it for, and one of the reasons I am in organized hockey this year is because I want to change that. Furthermore, I am reasonably certain that all of our players, plus a couple who are still trying to make our team, will show up on Sunday and will work very hard when they do. But I am still wondering, the morning after that casual and friendly series of phone calls, if I will ever see a clearer set of sign posts marking the way in which at least one aspect of our world is heading. And that aspect is its attitude towards work.

I say this partly because the man with whom I shared that experience last night began talking to me about it. He is a little older than I am, and he does very well at a profession that keeps him on call seven days a week. He has worked very hard and very well for more than half of his life, and now he has a big car and a swimming pool and a great desire that creeps into a lot of conversations to get the hell away from all those things. He wants out, as so many of us want out. To be totally corny, he wants to smell the flowers. And so do I. And so, I bet, do you. Whether he or I – or *you* – will ever have the (a) nerve, (b) opportunity, or even (c) the financial resources to get out is, I think, beside

the point. That's an individual decision. But what is to the point, I would suggest, is that one of the reasons some of us want out is that it is becoming more and more evident that fewer and fewer of our children want in. My parents were ambitious for me, as their parents had been ambitious for them. And I am ambitious. But I am also ambitious for my children, and I am slowly beginning to realize that I am probably more so for them than they are for themselves. There were points in my life, I'm sure, when this would have bothered me a great deal. The old "I've sacrificed myself, etc." line, and I am not totally certain that it doesn't bother me now. I mean when *I* was their age – but no. Emotionally, it's a tough thing to get your head around. But reflected upon in tranquility, it's hard not to accept the argument that they're right and I'm wrong.

I am not one of those who believe that the young will necessarily save the world. I will no more accept the idea of a new and totally wise generation that is coming along behind us than I will agree that every old man has achieved wisdom. I know too many stupid, arrogant and unbending people of every age to go along with either of those propositions. But I cannot help but sense that among the people who are my children's age, there is an increasing number of people who know what real values are, and that before this century is over, a lot more flowers are going to be smelled. I know I want to smell some more myself.

Have a pleasant day. I'm Peter Gzowski.

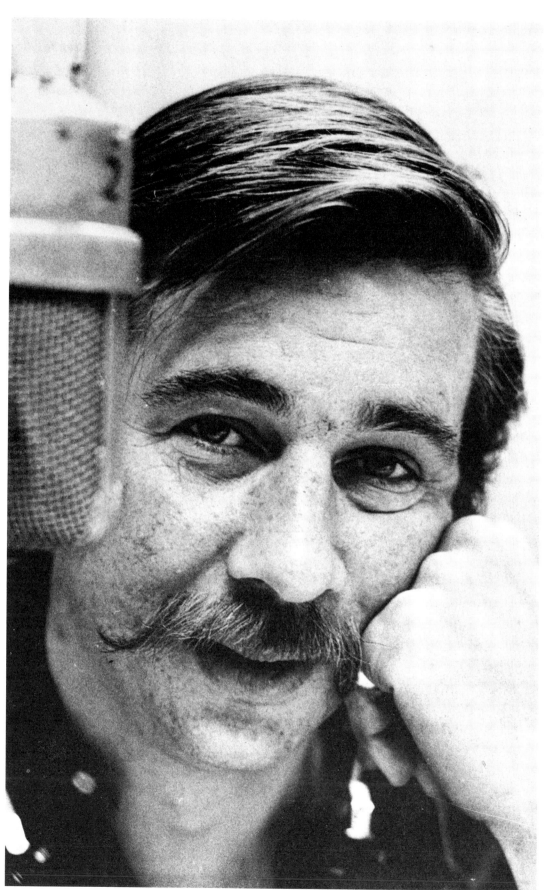

is for zebra,
not Canadian, you say?
There's a place by that name
down Ontario way.

Mary Craig
Winnipeg, Manitoba

Picture credits

Photographs by Graham Bezant:
Pages 31, 45, 96, 153, 174, 229.

Illustration by Ed Franklin
Page 10.

Illustrations by Emma Hesse:
*Pages 18, 36, 40, 103, 128, 141,
144, 171, 182/183, 184, 197, 209,
220, 226.*

Photographs by John Meacham:
Pages 118/119, 120/121, 122/123.

Photographs by Denis Ryan:
Pages 201, 202/203, 204/205.

Illustrations by David Shaw:
*Pages 4/5, 6/7, 26, 32, 58, 65,
97, 112/113, 125, 129, 132, 150/151,
155, 175, 177, 179, 185, 186, 199,
208, 218, 223, 227, 228.*

Illustrations by Rene Zamic:
*Pages 1, 8/9, 35, 48, 62, 78, 82/83,
104, 123, 124, 130, 159, 168/169,
200, 215, 221, 232.*

This book was designed and
produced by David Shaw.

First edition, 1974.